WORLD® AIR POWER

J O U R N A L

Aerospace Publishing Ltd
AIRtime Publishing Inc.

Published quarterly by
Aerospace Publishing Ltd
179 Dalling Road
London W6 0ES
UK

Copyright © Aerospace Publishing Ltd

Cutaway drawings copyright
© Mike Badrocke/Aviagraphica

ISSN 0959-7050

Aerospace ISBN 1 874023 60 3
                (softback)
                1 874023 61 1
                (hardback)
Airtime ISBN   1-880588-07-2
                (hardback)

Published under licence in USA and
Canada by AIRtime Publishing Inc.,
10 Bay Street, Westport,
CT 06880, USA

Editorial Offices:
WORLD AIR POWER JOURNAL
Aerospace Publishing Ltd
3A Brackenbury Road
London W6 0BE   UK

Publisher: Stan Morse
Managing Editor: David Donald
Editor: Jon Lake
Associate Editor: Robert Hewson
Sub Editor: Karen Leverington
Editorial Assistant: Tim Senior

Origination and printing by
   Imago Publishing Ltd
Printed in Singapore

Europe Correspondent:
   Paul Jackson
Washington Correspondent:
   Robert F. Dorr
USA West Coast Correspondent:
   René J. Francillon
Asia Correspondent:
   Pushpindar Singh
Canada Correspondent:
   Jeff Rankin-Lowe

The editors of WORLD AIR
POWER JOURNAL welcome
photographs for possible publication,
but cannot accept any responsibility for
loss or damage to unsolicited material.

The publishers gratefully acknowledge
the assistance given by the following
people:

Rinaldo Piaggio SpA for their help
with the Avanti and P.166 briefings.

Joe W. Stout of Lockheed Fort Worth
for his assistance in compiling the
Lockheed F-16 Variant Briefing.

Robert L. Burns for his inestimable
contribution to the NASA Air Power
Analysis.

The following for their information,
sightings, enthusiasm and
encouragement while producing the
Red Stars over Germany feature:
Martin Baumann, Rob de Bie, Dave
Bowers, Hendrik J. van Broekhuizen,
Marc Brouyere, Lesley K.E. Delsing,
Tieme Festner, Lutz Freundt, Marcus
Fülber, H.A. Gravemaker, Werner
Greppmeier, Martin Herbert, Fred van
Horrik, Jan Jørgensen, Gert Kromhout,
Frank Laurenssen, Chris Lofting, Hugo
Mambour, Hans Nijhuis, Kieron
Pilbeam, Anno van Rijn, Frank
Rozendaal, Martin Scharenborg, Emil
Sloot, Eric Stijger, Jeffrey van
Summeren, Gert Tricht, Berry Vissers,
Peter van Weenen, René van Woezik
and the editors of AIM, ACE and Full
Stop.

World Air Power Journal is a
registered trademark in the
United States of America of
AIRtime Publishing Inc.

World Air Power Journal is
published quarterly and is
available by subscription and
from many fine book and hobby
stores.

SUBSCRIPTION AND BACK
NUMBERS:

UK and World (except USA and
Canada) write to:
Aerospace Publishing Ltd
FREEPOST
PO Box 2822
London
W6 0BR
UK

(No stamp required if posted in
the UK)

USA and Canada, write to:
AIRtime Publishing Inc.
Subscription Dept
10 Bay Street
Westport
CT 06880, USA
(203) 266-3580
Toll-free order number in USA:
1 800 359-3003

Prevailing subscription rates are
as follows:
Softbound edition for 1 year:
      $58.00
Softbound edition for 2 years:
      $108.00
Softbound back numbers
(subject to availability) are
$19.00 each. All rates are for
delivery within mainland USA,
Alaska and Hawaii. Canadian
and overseas prices available
upon request. American Express,
Discover Card, MasterCard and
Visa accepted. When ordering
please include your card
number, expiration date and
signature.

Publisher, North America:
   Mel Williams
Subscription Director:
   Linda DeAngelis
Retail Sales Director:
   Jill Brooks
Charter Member Services
Manager:
   Janie Munroe

WORLD AIR POWER

JOURNAL

CONTENTS

Military Aviation Review

International

Sentry upgrade

Boeing at Seattle installed new avionics in NATO E-3A LX-N90442 during the autumn and the aircraft was due to take to the air again early in 1995. The 'Block 1' upgrade includes new colour displays, Have Quick secure speech radios and full-standard (Link 16) JTIDS communications. The remaining 17 E-3As in the Geilenkirchen-based fleet will be modified by DASA at Manching.

Western Europe

BELGIUM:

Two-crew Hercules

A modern 'glass' cockpit was installed by SABENA's engineering department in a Belgian Lockheed C-130H Hercules during the autumn, converting it for operation by two crew. Known as Integrated Vehicle Mission Management System, the upgrade will be incorporated in all 12 FAB/BLu Hercules before the end of 1997.

At the same time, Belgium and the Netherlands agreed to pool their Hercules fleets, giving the RNethAF call on Belgium's aircraft to augment its own two (the second of which was delivered on 9 October). In reciprocation, BAF F-16 Fighting Falcons will be allowed to refuel from RNethAF KDC-10 tankers when they become operational in 1995.

FRANCE:

Three decades of deterrence

France celebrated 30 years as a strategic nuclear power when survivors of the original deterrent force, plus some later additions, were gathered at Mont-de-Marsan on 20 October. It was at that base in south-west France that Escadron de Bombardement 1/91 'Gascogne' of the Forces Aériennes Stratégiques (FAS) was declared operational on 1 October 1964, equipped with Dassault Mirage IVAs and AN11 atomic bombs, supported by Boeing C-135F tankers. Within two years, nine squadrons with 36 armed aircraft were on stand-by, remaining thus until the fleet was run-down from 1975.

Today, the surviving 18 Mirages have been upgraded with new avionics to IVP standard; their weapons have progressed (via AN21 and AN22) to the ASMP stand-off missile; and the 11 remaining tankers are C-135FRs, re-engined with CFM56s. ASMP also equips the three squadrons of Dassault Mirage 2000Ns which were transferred to the FAS from Tactical Command on 1 September 1991. The 45 Mirage 2000Ns of EC 1/4 'Dauphin', 2/4 'Lafayette' (both at Luxeuil) and 3/4 'Limousin' at Istres will be increased to 60 when the Mirage IVP is withdrawn from bombing in 1996. After EB 2/91 'Bretagne' disbands at Cazaux with the end of the bombing role, EB 1/91 will be retained until 2002 for recce duties.

The C-135s will continue well beyond then, all of them now concentrated at Istres with ERV 1/93 'Aunis' and ERV 3/93 'Landes' (the OCU), but actually 'owned' by the technical support unit, Escadron de Soutien Technique Spécialisé 15/93. The three additional KC-135Rs loaned by France were returned to the USAF and were all undergoing maintenance at Pemco Aeroplex, Birmingham, AL, in June 1994. However, two were re-acquired on a temporary basis during the autumn while France sought outright purchase of five more. This second batch would be of stored KC-135As upgraded before delivery with CFM56 turbofans. Following 736 '93-CH', the second C-135FR fitted with Cobham Mk 32B refuelling pods is 474 '93-CE'.

Lesser-known elements of the manned strategic force are Escadron d'Avions 1/59 'Bigorre' at Evreux with four Transall C.160H ASTARTE communications relay aircraft used for signalling to patrolling submarines. In the training role, CITac 339 at Luxeuil has been part of the FAS since July 1992, equipped with Falcon 20s, Jaguars and loaned Alpha Jets. The air force's strategic element is completed by 18 silo-based S3 missiles controlled by Escadron de Tir 1/200 at Apt.

Multi-purpose squadron expands

Escadron de Transport Léger 1/62 'Vercors' at Creil gained its third aircraft type on 1 September when three DHC-6 Twin Otters were transferred from ET 65 at Villacoublay. Established on 1 August 1993, ETL 1/62 gained the first of its six CASA-built Airtech CN.235M-100s on 28 September that year, although three Aérospatiale AS 555N Fennecs had been received from 31 August to provide communications for the tri-service operational HQ at Creil. The CN.235s are tasked with light transport and parachuting – as are the Twin Otters, except that the main purpose of these latter white-painted aircraft is to support the UN Multinational Force at el Gorah in Sinai, where one is always based. Two more CN.235s have been funded by the sale to Spain of five secondhand Mirage F1s, and these transports will be delivered in 1995 to ETOM 82 at Papeete, in the Pacific, to replace three Sud Caravelles.

FY 1995 defence budget

Funds were reserved late in 1994 for 28 aircraft to be purchased for the French armed forces in the 1995 defence budget, not including 14 upgrades of existing equipment. Five more Dassault Rafale Ms lead the naval section, increasing the total to eight (plus two for the air force in previous years). Four more Aérospatiale AS 565 Panthers are to be ordered for the navy, as are the first two Grumman E-2C Hawkeyes and four refurbished Dassault Super Etendards. In the course of 1995, the Marine Nationale will take delivery of three Dassault Atlantique 2s, two Panthers and 12 modified Super Etendards funded earlier.

The Armée de l'Air has a particularly thin year ahead, its sole new funding being for three of the five extra Boeing C-135FRs it needs to boost the tanker fleet and 10 upgrades of Dassault Mirage 2000C to 2000C-5. Acceptances will comprise three Mirage 2000Bs, 10 Mirage F1CT conversions from F1C, 12 Mirage 2000Ds, 11 upgraded Transall C.160Rs, three TBM700s and 30 Tucanos.

Army helicopters ordered are six single-engined Aérospatiale AS 550 Fennecs, three AS 555 Fennecs, four more AS 532U2 Cougars and a HORIZON battlefield surveillance system based on the Cougar. No aircraft from previous funding will be delivered this year.

Tucanos awaited:

As 1994 drew to a close, it became apparent that quantity deliveries of the

This year's Tornado meet was hosted by JBG 33 at Büchel. German aircraft dominated the impressive line-up of aircraft.

Left: France's newest transport squadron is ETL 1/62 'Vercors', equipped with CN.235s and Fennecs and DHC-6 Twin Otters.

To celebrate 30 years of operational flying, France's Forces Aériennes Stratégiques painted up Mirage IVP No. 31.

Jagdbombergeschwader 35 celebrated its 35th anniversary and disbandment in fine style by painting this F-4F. The unit was established as Jagdgeschwader 73 at Oldenburg in 1959, flying Canadair Sabres. Later that year it moved to Ahlhorn, and to the present base of Pferdsfeld in 1960. It began operating G91Rs in 1964, and redesignated as LKG 42 at that time. In 1975 it became JBG 35 and the proud operator of the F-4F. The unit came full circle on 1 October 1994 when redesignated JG 73 in preparation for a move to Laage in 1996 to join a squadron of MiG-29s.

48 EMBRAER EMB-312F Tucanos required to replace Magisters at the Ecole de l'Air at Salon de Provence were long overdue. The aircraft, to be numbered 456-503, were intended to join the two pre-series machines which have undergone a year of trials with the CEAM at Mont-de-Marsan: 438 '330-DJ' and 439 '330-DM'. Of these, No. 438 was delivered to Salon on 6 July, escorted by two Magisters, to correspond to the original timetable, but the follow-up of two deliveries per month failed to materialise. To compensate for lost time, 30 aircraft are due in 1995, as noted above, the last of the 48 to follow in June 1996.

Squadron news

An additional squadron to be expanded from two to three flights has been EC 2/7 'Argonne', the Jaguar OCU at St Dizier. To the original two *escadrille* badges of SPA 31 (a Spartan archer) and SPA 48 (the head of a cockerel) has been added SPA 154 (a black and white crane, with neck lowered, looking to the rear). Like some flights recently added to existing squadrons, SPA 154 has no recent history, having last disbanded in March 1919.

Similar changes are expected in some of the other Jaguar units. At Toul, HQ 11 Wing (EC 11) headquarters and EC 1/11 'Roussillon' both disbanded on 24 June, leaving EC 2/11 'Vosges' and EC 3/11 'Corse' as autonomous squadrons, possibly to be expanded from 15 to 20 aircraft each.

The Reims-based EC 3/33 'Lorraine' (EC 3/30 until 1 July) was built up to 20 Dassault Mirage F1B/F1Cs following the disbandment of its companion, EC 1/30 'Valois' on 27 June. The base also houses newly-arrived Mirage F1CRs of ER 1/33 and 2/33 and is parent to the Mirage F1C squadron detached to Djibouti. The last-mentioned, 'Vexin', changed its designation from EC 4/30 to EC 4/33 on 1 June.

EC 1/2 'Cigognes' (Storks) at Dijon painted Mirage 2000C No. 37 with prominent decorations on 9 September to celebrate 100,000 hours of flying with the type since the first was delivered in July 1984. No. 37's underside marking of three storks in different attitudes was to mark the simultaneous award of a third flight to the squadron: SPA 12 (joining SPA 3 and SPA 103). Resuscitation of SPA 12 was not entirely welcomed by the Storks, as its World War I badge was a somewhat uninspiring pennant. The situation was saved by creating an entirely new stork badge (which is the uppermost of the three on the squadron badge) for SPA 12. Aircraft of EC 1/2 now wear differing combinations of the three stork badges on opposite sides of their fins, No. 37 having SPA 12 to starboard and SPA 3 to port.

GERMANY:

Tornados improved

The Luftwaffe has ordered 55 reconnaissance pods for the ex-naval Panavia Tornados of AG 51. Additionally, both Germany and Italy have been seeking a laser-designator pod for their Tornado ECRs, the latter having recently decided on a Thomson-CSF PDLCT. Germany will make a decision in April 1995 between PDLCT, the UK's TIALD or Israeli-designed Litening.

MiGs move base

Germany's Mikoyan MiG-29 'Fulcrum' wing began moving from Preschen to its new permanent base on 1 October when the first aircraft of 2 Staffel/Jagdgeschwader 73 transferred to Laage. At the same time, JG 35 at Pferdsfeld (Sobernheim) was redesignated 1/JG 73, although it will not begin moving its McDonnell Douglas F-4E Phantoms to Laage until 1 October 1996. JG 73's Phantoms will be the only Luftwaffe F-4Es not to receive the ICE upgrade.

Naval disbandments

Having earlier lost its Mil Mi-14 'Haze' ASW helicopters, the Marinefliegergruppe at Parow stood-down on 30 September with the withdrawal of the last five Mi-8 'Hips'. Formal disbandment took place on 31 December. Earlier in September, the final Dornier Do 28D Skyservant was withdrawn from 2/MFG 5 at Kiel/Holtenau (although 1 Staffel continues to operate the Westland Sea King).

Airfields close

Closing the book on Canadian military involvement in Europe, the former fighter base at Lahr was handed over to the German authorities in August to become a civil airport and reserve NATO airfield. Nearby Söllingen was shut down in the previous January.

ITALY:

Air force reduction plans

Reductions in staff from 72,000 to 60,000 and closure of four of its 24 bases were foreshadowed in a late 1994 report as the Italian air force prepared for the 21st century and braced itself for a 20 per cent cut in funding. Administratively, the AMI is to scrap its three regional commands and place operational aircraft directly under a new Air Forces Command (Comando Forze Aeree).

At lower levels, the present structure of wings and squadrons will be tidied up so that most stormi have two component gruppi. Squadron strength will be fixed at 15 on establishment, of which 10 are to be fully serviceable for immediate operations. Currently, fighter squadrons have 18 aircraft, compared with only 12 in fighter-bomber units. When complete, a decade hence, the new structure will give Italy six squadrons and an OCU of Eurofighter 2000s; four squadrons of strike/attack Tornados; six squadrons and an OCU of AMXs; and four transport squadrons.

Eurofighter deliveries will begin in 2000 with 12-14 two-seat aircraft to establish an OCU. In 2005, the AMI will begin receiving 50 new transport aircraft – FLA is being considered – to replace its G222s and Hercules, despite which it is hoped to obtain four more C-130s to rectify immediate shortcomings. In the shorter term, the AMI needs more Avantis as a follow-on to the present communications fleet of 35 SIAI-Marchetti S208s, 17 Piaggio P166s and 20 Piaggio PD808s. Six Avantis are in service, although it is highly unlikely that the target of 38 will be achieved.

In the training role, delivery is to begin of 56 AMX-Ts and there are plans to obtain 20 more Aermacchi MB.339FDs ('fully digital' avionics) for pilot training. A requirement for 10 electronic warfare versions of AMX-T will be met by conversion. Likewise, the Panavia Tornado ECR programme for 16 aircraft is a conversion exercise, although the whole Tornado force is being updated by 2002 with avionics and weapon improvements including provision for a Thomson-CSF PDLCT laser-designation pod.

In advance of the ECR programme, the designated operating unit, 155 Squadron at Piacenza, has been dedicated to defence suppression since 1 April 1994, having received AGM-88 HARM anti-radar missiles last December. The 24 ex-RAF Tornado F.Mk 3s (and their 96 Sky Flash missiles) which the AMI is to lease from the RAF will be returned when Eurofighter is operational.

Assisting the Tornado interceptors will be four squadrons and an OCU of Lockheed Starfighters modified for greater air defence potential with equipment including radio and navigation aids from the AMX. Building on the existing F-104S-ASA update only recently completed, the aim is to have two squadrons and the training unit operational in three years' time. The modified aircraft will be 90 F-101S-ASAMs and 18 TF-104GMs. However, if there are any more delays with Eurofighter, Italy will shelve the

To honour the retirement of the type from Luftwaffe service, JBG 32 gave a special paint scheme to this 323 Staffel HFB 320ECM Hansa.

Retiring from AMI service was the F-104G, of which this was the last example. The aircraft served with 4° Stormo at Grosseto, which acts as the Italian Starfighter OCU.

ASAM and go for purchase of an interim fighter.

Not mentioned in forward planning is the requirement for four AEW aircraft. At present, there is no funding allowance for the programme, although the AMI is continuing with an evaluation of the Saab 340AEW, Lockheed P-3AEW&C, Lockheed C-130AEW and IAI Phalcon (707).

'Gina' retirement

Italy's last Aeritalia G91Ys were due to have been withdrawn from 101° Gruppo of 8° Stormo at Cervia before the end of November 1994. The twin-engined and considerably modified G91Y version of 'Gina' first flew in December 1966 and entered service at Cervia in January 1971. Just one other squadron, the 13th of 32 Wing at Brindisi, operated the type until disbanded in November 1992. Only 67 were built.

Replacement of the G91Y by AMX has been slower than planned. Official sources revealed in the autumn that only 77 have been delivered to the AMI by Aermacchi and Alenia, confirming suspicions that the aircraft has been effectively out of production since December 1992. The 77 comprise five prototypes and 72 series machines, but exclude two trainers flown in 1990. Italian requirements

Spain has bolstered its Mirage F1 force with 11 F1EDA and two F1DDA aircraft purchased from the Qatari air force, and three F1Cs and two F1Bs from the Armée de l'Air. This F1DDA is seen at Valencia-Manises wearing the codes of Ala 11, whose Escuadron 111 operates the Mirage.

have been cut to 136 aircraft, most of which after No. 72 are expected to be two-seaters.

NORWAY:

Updated F-5s

Delivery was completed in July of seven Northrop F-5As and eight F-5Bs which have been fitted by Sierra Technologies in the USA with F-16-type avionics to act as lead-in trainers for the Lockheed Fighting Falcon. All serve with Skvadron 336 at Rygge. The update, known as Tiger-PAWS (Program for Avionics and Weapon System improvements) includes the same HUD and throttle as the F-16, plus a digital databus, ring-laser gyro INS and repositioned instruments. Optional equipment includes a new jamming pod developed in Norway and known as Samovar (SAM Obstruction in Velocity, Angle and Range). Although packaged in an AN/ALQ-176 outer shell, Samovar uses off-the-shelf equipment integrated locally. As the next stage in RNoAF upgrades, Bristol Aerospace of Canada has been contracted to provide 10 new wing sets (with five more on option).

Combat training in UK

An agreement signed on 5 September between BAe and the RNoAF provides for the latter to use the privately-operated North Sea ACMI Range, becoming its 12th customer since the facility became fully operational in 1990. In common with other users, aircraft are expected to reside at RAF Waddington while making use of the

range. Additionally, the NSAR (otherwise known as 'Showground') has recently expanded its debrief facilities and terminals are now available at Waddington, Coningsby, Lakenheath, Leeuwarden, Twenthe and Volkel.

SPAIN:

More Mirages

Delivery of 13 surplus Qatari Dassault Mirage F1s to Spain began on 23 August with five F1EDA variants to Valencia/Manises, an additional F1EDA and an F1DDA following from Dassault (where they had been on overhaul) on 1 September. The aircraft now equip 111 Squadron of 11 Wing and wear serials/codes beginning with C.14-74 '11-01'. Since the Mirage IIIE was withdrawn in October 1992, 11 Wing has been using Mirage F1s borrowed from 14 Wing at Albacete and was due to return most of these on 31 December. The remaining six F1EDAs will not be delivered until 1997, after Qatar has received its Mirage 2000-5s.

Spain's inventory was also boosted by deliveries from France. A single F1B was delivered in November, to be followed by four early-version F1Cs at the rate of one per month by March 1995. All five were taken from storage at the Chateaudun maintenance unit.

Ex-USN Hornets considered

In spite of the extra Mirages, Spain continued its search for additional combat aircraft during the autumn, having concluded that it will otherwise suffer a fighter gap early next century because of delays in the Eurofighter 2000 programme. While a USAF offer of 50 surplus F-16A/B Fighting Falcons remains open, the US Navy has countered with about 30 F/A-18As. These would appear to have the advantage, in that Spain already operates the Hornet.

SWEDEN:

Sk 60 upgrade begins

During 1994, Saab began installing a pair of Williams Rolls-Royce FJ44 turbofans in an Sk 60 trainer which will act as the production prototype for upgrading of the entire fleet. FJ44s were ordered in 1993 to replace General Electric J85s and the first conversion should fly by June 1995. Delivery of nine more aircraft is due in 1996 and an additional 105 by the end of 1998.

TURKEY:

Seasprite buy

Proposals were announced in the autumn for the sale to Turkey of 12 Kaman SH-2F Seasprite naval helicopters. The Seasprites are surplus to USN requirements and are to be based aboard four 'Knox'-class Frigates which Turkey is leasing from the USA. An additional two SH-2Fs will be cannibalised for spares. According to one source, the helicopters will be rebuilt by Kaman to SH-2G standard.

Phantom upgrade

Some surprise has been generated by Turkey's late 1994 decision to award Israel's IAI the contract to upgrade 50 McDonnell Douglas F-4E Phantoms. The IAI offer (subject to financial arrangements being agreed) is based on the Phantom 2000 programme in Israel and involves the Norden Systems/ UTC multi-mode radar supplied by the USA.

UNITED KINGDOM:

Transport competition intensifies

The FLA-versus-Hercules II competition was one of the main talking points at the Farnborough air show in September, with BAe and Lockheed strongly promoting their rival aircraft. The former brought a full-size replica to the show to reinforce the additional credibility afforded by the immediately-preceding announcement of a partnership between EuroFLA and Airbus Industrie. The EuroFLA-Airbus link gives FLA a prospective manufacturer and the new company could also be used to promote military versions of the Airbus airliners.

BAe spent mid-1994 lobbying hard for the RAF to be forced by the UK government to become launch customer for the FLA within the next year. Dire consequences, such as Britain being replaced by Germany as the designer and builder of Airbus wings, were being forecast unless plans are abandoned for an early order for up to 30 C-130Js. The government was swayed by BAe's arguments and placed the replacement Hercules on 'hold' until the consequences for UK industry could be examined in detail. Lockheed's strongpoint is the jobs already

created in the UK by C-130J sub-contracting, while BAe promises higher technology work – but not until next century. FLA is due to fly in 2000 and enter service two years later.

Despite the pressure for an RAF order, FLA is perceived as a Franco-German project, but neither country is firmly behind it. Germany has questioned whether the recent switch from turbofans to turboprops (8,600-shp/6450-kW M138s which now have to be designed and tested) will meet its requirements, and France admits that if the aircraft is too costly it will not be built. Furthermore, a McDonnell Douglas official stated at Farnborough that Germany and France are in regular contact with regard to the C-17 Globemaster. The RAF is also being appraised of the aircraft's progress and Douglas says it could buy up to 20 to replace the second half of the Hercules fleet and VC10 tankers.

As 1994 drew to a close, political reports suggested that the UK government was about to compromise on the question of C-130J or FLA. It appeared that the RAF would be allowed to proceed with its preferred solution of a first-batch purchase of around 25 C-130Js but, in order to placate BAe, the UK would become a full member of EuroFLA. With large sums of taxpayers' money then being invested in FLA, second-batch purchase of any other aircraft early in the next century would be out of the question.

In a related move, the MoD offered five Hercules (four C.Mk 1s and a tanker C.Mk 1K) for sale between April 1995 and April 1996. The aircraft form the operational reserve at RAF Lyneham and their premature disposal has caused some concern in view of the rapidly declining serviceability of the remainder of the fleet and increasing overseas commitments for peacekeeping and humanitarian operations.

German presence to decline

Further shrinkage of the RAF presence in Germany was announced in the autumn when it was revealed that No. 2 Group (formerly RAF Germany) will disband on 30 March 1996. Remaining RAF aircraft on the continent are likely to be subordinated to No. 1 Group at Benson. They currently comprise four squadrons of Panavia Tornados, two of BAe Harriers and a helicopter unit, but there are reports that most or all with be withdrawn to the UK by the turn of the century.

As an illustration of the constraints placed upon RAF aircraft in Germany, Harriers of Nos 3 and IV Squadrons detached to Bentwaters for Exercise Hazel Flute in September and again to Coltishall for a fortnight beginning 7 November. Hazel Flute was the practice of operations from a dispersed site, hitherto regularly undertaken in the German countryside. On the second occasion, the aircraft were to practise flying with night vision goggles and

FLIR because a 1,000-ft (305-m) height restriction in Germany makes such training unrealistic.

Lynx get 360° radar

The Royal Navy has placed an order with GEC-Marconi for the upgrading of the Seaspray radar on Westland Lynx HAS.Mk 8 ASW/ASV helicopters from Mk 1 to Mk 3000 standard. Most significantly, this increases search coverage from 180° to 360°, thereby making full use of the under-fuselage radome installed when Lynx are modified from Mk 3 to Mk 8. (The original nose position is required for the Sea Owl thermal imaging equipment.) Associated changes of processing equipment provide for full integration of radar data on the colour Central Tactical System.

The first Lynx HAS.Mk 8 delivered to the FAA is XZ732, now in service with the Lynx Operational Evaluation Unit within 815 Squadron at Portland. Two more will be received for a year of trials before the type enters service.

Last Mk 1 Chinooks enter rebuild

Boeing's Ridley plant in the USA is now working on the last of 32 RAF Chinooks which are being upgraded from HC.Mk 1 to HC.Mk 2 standard and expects redelivery to take place in July-August 1995. The two helicopters are ZA683 (No. 31) and ZA670 (No. 32), which were loaded aboard the Atlantic Conveyor for shipping to America on 17 July. Of passing interest is the fact that ZA670 was the RAF's first Chinook, flown 23 March 1980. It had been intended to include a damaged Chinook as the 33rd conversion, but its repair at Fleetlands was abandoned and it is now used for battle damage repair training at St Athan.

Jaguars gain TIALD

RAF plans to equip some SEPECAT Jaguars with the GEC-Ferranti TIALD (Thermal Imaging Airborne Laser Designation) pod were revealed in more detail late in 1994. In parallel with the recent purchase of Paveway III bomb guidance units, nine pods (like those used by Tornados) will be purchased and shared between 12 upgraded Jaguars, which are also to gain a GEC-Marconi A4 wide-angle head-up display, global positioning system, digital databus, multi-purpose colour display (for TIALD and moving map imagery, replacing the original projected map display), video recorder for TIALD imagery and HOTAS control column including operating switches for TIALD. Such changes have been made necessary by the increased pilot workload, Jaguar's single-seat cockpit and its lack of TV screens, as are standard fit in the rear cockpit of Tornados. First deliveries were expected at Coltishall in February 1995, the programme to be complete by the end of the year.

Above: RAF Tornado F.Mk 3s have begun to carry GR.Mk 1-style outer wing pylons. This allows the carriage of extra defences.

Below: No. 101 Sqn's VC10 fleet is being repainted from the previous hemp scheme into this light grey with low-visibility cheat line.

Following the initial conversion at DRA Boscombe Down, remaining Jaguars are being upgraded at RAF St Athan.

CASOM competition

The competition to supply RAF Tornados, Harriers and Eurofighter 2000s with a Conventionally Armed Stand-Off Missile (CASOM) gained in momentum at the Farnborough air show in September with the unveiling of three contenders. Submitted to meet Staff Requirement (Air) 1236, for which a formal request for proposals was expected before the end of 1994, these included the GEC-Marconi/BAe Pegasus, McDonnell Douglas/Hunting Grand Slam winged development of Harpoon and Rockwell AGM-130. Other submissions are expected in the form of Aérospatiale Asura derivative of the supersonic ASMP, Hughes Air Hawk, Kentron MUPSOW from South Africa, MATRA APACHE single-warhead, Rockwell AGM-130 version, Rafael Popeye 2 version and Texas Instruments JSOW. In-service date is planned to be 2000/2001.

801 converts to Sea Harrier 2

Immediately following its return from Bosnian patrol duties in August, the Fleet Air Arm's 801 Squadron disposed of its fleet of BAe Sea Harrier FRS.Mk 1s in preparation for converting to the F/A.Mk 2 variant at Yeovilton. First arrival was XZ455 '001', which was received from 899 Squadron on 5 October along with ZA716. Although four SHOEU/899 Squadron F/A.Mk 2s were previously deployed to the Adriatic for duties over Bosnia (joining

800 Squadron's Mk 1s on 24 August 1994), 801 is the first specific seagoing squadron to operate the Mk 2 Sea Harrier. Following an air combat training detachment to Waddington (for the North Sea ACMI) in November, it was scheduled to achieve full strength by January 1995, in time to deploy aboard HMS *Ark Royal* for a six-month tour off Bosnia.

The first Harrier T.Mk 8 conversion for the FAA, ZB605, made its maiden flight at Dunsfold on 27 July after a two-year rebuild. Conversion of an additional four aircraft was to begin in January 1995 for eventual delivery to 899 Squadron at Yeovilton. All five are to be produced from late-built Harrier trainers, of which ZB604 and '605 are the survivors of three T.Mk 4Ns delivered to the Navy in 1983. The remaining three (ZB600, '602 and '603) are ex-RAF T.Mk 4s. The new Mk 8 is compatible with the Sea Harrier F/A.Mk 2, except that it has no radar.

Bell tolls for Scout

As expected, the Army Air Corps acquired three Bell 212s to replace the Westland Scouts of 'C' Flight at Seria, Brunei, from October. The unit, which was formerly a component of 660 Squadron at Hong Kong, became 7 Flight in October, but its Bells are only leased from Bristow Helicopters.

Cyprus Wessex change

No. 84 Squadron at Akrotiri converted from Westland Wessex HC.Mk 5Cs to grey-painted Wessex HC.Mk 2s in November. On current plans, the unit is to make a further change to Sea

Turkey's main transport organisation is 12 Ana Hava Us, based at Erkilet and Etimesgut. At the latter base 224 Filo flies a variety of staff transport types, including two Cessna 650 Citation VIIs.

Kings in 1999. Other RAF Wessex being made redundant by recent changes will be stored at Fleetlands, where a new hangar is being built.

ECM Canberras retire

The bulbous-nosed BAC Canberra T.Mk 17 was withdrawn from service on 31 October with disbandment of No. 360 Squadron at Wyton. As the RAF's youngest squadron, the unit was allocated an entirely new number when it formed in 1966 to reflect the fact that 25 per cent of its personnel (and every fourth commanding officer) would be from the Royal Navy. No.

360's task was to give experience in combating offensive jamming to radar operators on land, sea and in the air, for which it was assigned 16 of the 24 Canberra B.Mk 2s which had been upgraded by BAC at Preston to Mk 17s. By October 1994, that total had fallen to seven, plus two T.Mk 4 trainers and a pair of PR.Mk 7s used as targets for ground radar calibration. The Mk 4s and 7s have been transferred to No. 39 (1 PRU) Squadron at Marham for continued service. No. 360's final operational flight was flown on 21 October against the radar station at Staxton Wold using T.Mk 17 WD955 – the RAF's oldest working jet aircraft, delivered on 12 December 1951 as the 27th production Canberra and now earmarked for preservation with some 8,000 flying hours to its credit. No. 360's role has been taken-over by Dassault Falcon 20s operated by Cobham Ltd (formerly FR Aviation).

Eastern Europe

CHECHNYA:

Air attacks intensify

Attacks by unmarked, but almost certainly Russian aircraft on the breakaway Caucasian state of Chechnya intensified during September and October. Officially, the aircraft are operated by opponents of the self-styled president of Chechnya, although

it is well known that rebel groups have Russian backing since Moscow refused in July to recognise the Cherchen state.

Russian helicopters allegedly made night arms delivery flights into the country early in August and on 2 September helicopters from Mozdok made four attacks on Cherchen settlements. Mil Mi-8 'Hips' attacked again on 27 September, but on the same day a Mi-

24 'Hind' with Russian crew was shot down. In several more attacks during early October, two airfields (including Kalinovskaya) were targeted by Russian/rebel helicopters. The small Cherchen air force appears to have gained some Aero L-39 Albatros armed trainers to add to its L-29 Delfins and Antonov An-2 'Colts' but one of the last-mentioned was shot down on 21 September, although its crew escaped. A Chechen 'fighter' unsuccessfully attempted to intercept helicopters which raided the regional capital of Gorozny on 2 October.

CZECH REPUBLIC:

Western engine for L-159

Aero Vodochody announced that its new L-159 trainer/light attack aircraft will be powered by the AlliedSignal F124 6,300-lb st (28.02-kN) turbofan. The Czech air force is expected to order 60 L-159s. Prototype first flight is scheduled for April 1996, with IOC following in 1998.

HUNGARY:

MiG-21 retired

Formal retirement of the Mikoyan MiG-21 from Hungarian service was celebrated by a flypast at Kecskemet on 29 July, although a few of the type were scheduled to remain in service until the end of 1994, when replacement by 28 MiG-29 'Fulcrums' was due for completion. The grounding and storage (at Papa) order appears to affect MiG-21bis 'Fishbed Ns' as well as the older MiG-21MF 'Fishbed Js', even though the former were due to receive Western IFF to prolong their operational usefulness.

ROMANIA:

Air force woes

The derelict state of the Romanian air force became public knowledge on October when the Mikoyan MiG-21 fleet was grounded after a series of fatal accidents. In all, 11 Aviatiei Militare

aircraft of several types were lost during 1994, including an Antonov An-24 'Coke', MiG-23 'Floggers', a MiG-29 'Fulcrum' and two helicopters. It may be significant that almost half the Romanian combat force of 300 aircraft is over 20 years old and that the air force has only 12 per cent of the funds required to conduct proper maintenance. Pilot experience is another important contributory factor to the poor safety record, as fighter crews fly only 15-20 hours per year – about one-tenth of their counterparts in NATO.

RUSSIA:

The 'Bear' goes home

After 49 years of occupation, the last of 546,000 Russian troops officially left Germany on 31 August following a march-past reviewed by President Yeltsin. With their resettlement costs paid by Germany, the departing forces have taken home 12,400 tanks and armoured vehicles, but left behind 950 sq miles (2460 km²) of land previously used for barracks, airfields and exercise areas. These have been stripped of all conceivably useful components, including door handles and electric cable. Final aircraft departure was an Antonov An-22 'Cock' which took off from Sperenberg in the small hours of 6 September.

With less ceremony, Russian forces also left the Baltic States on 31 August, having invaded and occupied Latvia, Lithuania and Estonia in 1940. By agreement, 210 specialists remain to dismantle the Paldiski nuclear base in Estonia and 600 are stationed at the Skrunda early-warning station under a five-year agreement. Lithuania's final occupying troops departed in 1993. Estonia's last Russian aircraft was an unidentified transport which left Amari on 29 August, while Latvia's was a Tupolev Tu-134 'Crusty' out of Riga/Skulte two days later.

Official ceremonies in Berlin on 8 September marked the withdrawal of British, French and US troops, although all three countries continue to base forces in what was West Germany.

As a pointer to possible air operations which might follow, the first Russian-US army exercise, Peacekeeper 94, took place in Totskoye between 2 and 10 September. About 250 troops from each country participated in a practice of a hypothetical UN peacekeeping operation. Meanwhile, the Hungarian and British troops were involved in Exercise Hungarian Venture between 1 and 25 September although, again, no aircraft were

A new Tornado variant to fly is the TIARA (Tornado Integrated Avionics Research Aircraft), based on an F.Mk 2 airframe. The aircraft is seen here at DRA Farnborough, preparing for its 18 October first flight, which was also the last RAE/DRA sortie launched from this historic airfield. The aircraft landed at Boscombe Down, where it will be used for advanced avionics trials.

involved. In a larger demonstration of harmony under Partnership for Peace, six NATO and seven former Warsaw Pact nations began five days of exercises in Poland on 12 September with the codename Co-operative Bridge 94. Air participation was restricted to army helicopters operating in the medical role, including Polish PZL W-3 Sokols and US Army Sikorsky UH-60A Black Hawks of 159th Medical Co from Wiesbaden, Germany.

FORMER YUGOSLAVIA:

NATO air strikes

Two RAF SEPECAT Jaguars and a USAF Fairchild A-10A were called into action on 22 September when a Bosnian Serb T55 tank inside the Sarajevo heavy weapons exclusion zone fired rockets at a French APC, injuring one soldier. The retaliatory attack involved the Jaguars each dropping one 1,000-lb (454-kg) bomb and the Thunderbolt strafing the – by now unoccupied – tank with cannon fire. This was the fourth such operation against the Bosnian Serbs who, in reply, threatened to shoot down relief aircraft flying into Sarajevo. The airport was closed two days later.

NATO aircraft were unable to prevent a violation of the 'No-Fly Zone' on 9 November when a SOKO Orao fired 'a rocket' at an ammunition factory in Muslim-held Bihac in Bosnia, causing at least nine civilian casualties. The same aircraft, or perhaps an accompanying machine, also launched a second missile at Zeljava airfield, immediately north-west of Bihac. The raid originated in Krajina, the Serb-held area of Croatia, and an unsubstantiated claim was later made that an aircraft was shot down by Bosnian forces during its return flight. As November progressed, the Serbian assault upon Bihac intensified.

Earlier, on 6 November, an outbreak of shelling around Sarajevo was calmed after pairs of F-15 Eagles and F/A-18 Hornets flew low over both sides' emplacements. On an unspecified date in October, a shoulder-launched SAM was fired at a French

This Czech air force Mi-17 'Hip-H' is on the strength of the 11 VRP at Line. The helicopter is used in the emergency medical evacuation role.

Wearing a new camouflage scheme amended with purple and light green patches, this Su-22M-4K serves with Poland's 6th PLM-B at Pila. The aircraft carries bombs under the fuselage racks and O-25 pods for the single S-25OFM rocket on the outer wing pylons.

reconnaissance Dassault Mirage F1CR over Bosnia. An alert wingman raised the alarm and the pilot was able to release flares which decoyed the missile.

In order to gain relief from UN sanctions, the republic of Serbia (in other words, Yugoslavia in its now greatly reduced form) officially cut ties with the Serbians fighting to take control of Bosnia-Herzegovina and others occupying part of Croatia renamed as Krajina. An immediate effect was the opening to international traffic of Belgrade-Surcin airport on 5 October. First to be reinstated was the JAT service to Moscow.

NATO force changes

Four BAe Sea Harrier F/A.Mk 2s of the SHOEU/899 Squadron were deployed to HMS *Invincible* on 24 August to join Mk 1s of 800 Squadron. The carrier and its air group were then on their way to the Adriatic for patrols of Bosnia and became operational on 29 August, giving the Mk 2 its first taste of action. Two Sea Harriers were fired on by SAMs near the Bihac pocket in north-western Bosnia on 8 September, for which Serbian troops were blamed. Neither was hit.

Lockheed F-16Cs of the 555th FS/31st FW at Aviano returned to Deny Flight operations over Bosnia armed with the Martin-Marietta LANTIRN system. LANTIRN is a night navigation and target-designating system carried in two pods attached beneath the forward fuselage, allowing the aircraft to find targets and self-designate for laser-guided bombs. The system is currently used by McDonnell Douglas F-15E Eagles of the 492nd FS/48th FW, which have been detached to Aviano from Lakenheath since 14 February 1994. The only other night-capable unit is VMFA-(AW)-224, which has eight McDonnell Douglas F/A-18D Hornets at Aviano as successors to the F/A-18As of VMFA-251.

Belgium, Denmark and Norway were asked by the RNethAF to pro-

vide aircraft and pilots to assist the Deny Flight F-16 detachment at Villafranca, as its operational readiness is being threatened by the protracted presence in the Balkans. Dutch F-16s fly some 10,000 hours per year in Deny Flight operations, all of which has to come from its allocation of 29,000 F-16 hours. Tightly-controlled patrols of Bosnia have minimal training value. 315 Squadron of the RNethAF took over on 1 October from '623' Squadron at Villafranca. The unit derived its number from the addition of Nos 311 and 312, the Volkel-based

squadrons which pooled their aircraft for rotations to Italy.

Four Dutch Daimler-Benz BO 105s of 299 Squadron were withdrawn on 27 September. Their operations had been curtailed by the refusal of Bosnian Serbs to permit operations from the proposed base at Srebrenica and the helicopters had flown only 240 sorties since becoming operational on 18 March. With the USAF element of Deny Flight, the US-based A-10As returned home in September, to be replaced at Aviano by the 81st FS/52nd FW.

Middle East

BAHRAIN:

Naval air arm

First confirmation that Bahrain's small navy had established its own air arm was received in August when a Daimler-Benz BO 105CBS-MSS was delivered from Germany. The MSS version is equipped for maritime surveillance and SAR with provisions including Bendix 360° search radar in an under-nose radome and cockpit lighting compatible with night vision goggles.

ISRAEL:

Ex-USAF F-16s

Following acceptance of the first six on 1 August, deliveries continued to the IDF/AF during the autumn of 50 early-model (Block 10) Lockheed F-16A/B Fighting Falcons taken from storage at Davis-Monthan or donated by units of the ANG and AFRes. It has not been revealed how many F-16B trainers are included in the 50, although it is understood that this will be higher then the usual proportion as some will be used to replace McDonnell Douglas A-4 Skyhawks in the operational training role.

After local overhaul and modification, it is intended that the ex-USAF F-16s should be assigned to the 4th F-16 Wing at 28th Air Base, Nevatim, re-equipping 104 Squadron (ex-104 Reserve Squadron with IAI Kfir C2s) and two former McDonnell Douglas A-4N Skyhawk squadrons, 115 and 116. The A-4Ns will be passed on to other Reserve squadrons, allowing their last A-4Es to be withdrawn.

These plans may be changed as the result of unexpected funding cuts

which have placed the future of Nevatim under threat, despite it being the newest major IDF/AF base, opened in October 1983. If the financial reductions go ahead, the station will be retained for non-operational duties, perhaps involving relocation of the Technical School from Haifa Airport (21st Air Base). A new home will therefore have to be found for the three reformed F-16A/B squadrons, as well as the Kfir wing due to be established at Nevatim in 1995 when 143 Reserve and 251 Squadrons were scheduled to arrive from Ovda to join the resident 132 Reserve Squadron. (The last Nevatim-based A-4N Skyhawk squadron, No. 141 Reserve, is to transfer to Hatzerim in 1995.)

The outlook is similarly bleak for Sde Dov and Hatzor, both of which are threatened with flight restrictions because of nearby large civilian settlements.

Black Hawks arrive

After their arrival aboard four Lockheed C-5 Galaxies on 16-17 August, 10 Sikorsky UH-60A Black Hawks were officially taken into service with the IDF/AF at Palmachim on 30 August. Former US Army aircraft, they have been given the local name of Yanshuf (Eagle Owl), although Na'mer (Tiger) was first mooted when the purchase of new UH-60s was considered in 1983. Operating squadron is No. 124 'Flying Swords', which is in the process of passing some of its Bell 212s to augment those of No. 123 at Hatzerim. No. 124 formed a 'Yanshuf Flight' in April 1994 and began crew training on the Black Hawk in the USA the following month.

Above: In Warsaw Pact days Hungary trained its pilots in the Soviet Union or Czechoslovakia. That is no longer feasible, so a training element has been procured. These 20 L-39ZOs were bought from Germany for advanced training.

Right: An unusual summer visitor to Rotterdam was the Admiral Kharlamov, an 'Udaloy'-class destroyer. The ship's hangars contained two Ka-27PL 'Helix-A' anti-submarine helicopters.

Lightplane requirement renewed

Having been forced by funding cuts to delay replacement of its Cessna U206 liaison aircraft from 1991 (when Beech A36 Bonanzas were to have been bought), the IDF/AF is to try again. The selected new type is the SOCATA TB20 Trinidad which is to be assigned to 100 Squadron at Sde Dov (the present U206 operator) and several base flights. In IDF/AF service the Trinidad will be known as Pashosh (Lark).

SAUDI ARABIA:

More aircraft from UK

An additional Saudi Arabian order under the Al Yamamah II programme was announced on 8 September when it was revealed that 20 BAe Hawk Mk 65s and 16 Pilatus/BAe PC-9s are being acquired. These follow the second batch of 48 Tornado IDSs ordered at the 1993 Paris air show, but there is still no movement on the RSAF requirement for up to 60 combat-capable Hawk 100/200s. The PC-9s are likely to be modified to RSAF requirements by BAe at Brough, where the first batch of 30 was prepared in 1986-88. Hawks have served the RSAF since the first of 30 were delivered in October 1987.

UNITED ARAB EMIRATES:

New F-15/F-16 variants offered

A proposal for a considerably modified F-16 Fighting Falcon was presented to the UAE in October as Lockheed's bid to secure an order for up to 80 long-range interdictors. In competition with the McDonnell Douglas F-15E Eagle and Sukhoi Su-30MK/Su-35 'Flanker', the F-16U is a two-seat, stretched-fuselage, delta-winged aircraft with even greater payload/range capability than the F-16ES unsuccess-

fully offered to Israel in 1993. As part of the development programme for other possible F-16ES customers, a single-seat aircraft (F-16C 83-1120) was flown for the first time on 5 November with two dummy conformal tanks on the upper fuselage. No less than 24 ft (7.3 m) in length, and 2 ft (0.6 m) square at their greatest cross-section, the tanks would hold an extra 3,200 lb (1451 kg) of fuel.

Also offered by the US, the F-15U Plus is an F-15E variant optimised for the UAE requirement. Characteristics include a thicker, clipped-delta wing with 50° leading-edge sweep and holding 5,700 lb (2585 kg) of additional fuel.

A further contender for the potential UAE order is the Eurofighter 2000. Because this will not be ready in time to meet the requirement, the UAE is being offered the lease of up to 19 RAF Tornado IDSs. These would be refurbished to GR.Mk 4 standard before delivery and perhaps even flown by seconded British officers. However, the RAF appears willing to release only 12 Tornados.

YEMEN:

Air force rebuilds

Following the defeat of southern-based rebel forces in July, further information emerged on the source of air equipment rushed to the South in an attempt to avert their downfall. Moldavia is known to have delivered four MiG-29 'Fulcrums', including the two which were captured, but did not claim to have supplied the MiG-21 'Fishbeds' and Su-22 'Fitters' reported by some sources but conspicuous by their absence when the fighting ended. Uzbekistan is given as the prospective supplier of Su-22M-3s and Mil Mi-8 'Hip-Cs' to the rebel forces, although these appear not to have arrived.

Clearly harbouring no hard feelings against the rebels' arms suppliers, the official Yemeni ambassador in Moscow subsequently met with the Moldavian defence minister and announced on 27 October an agreement to purchase 30 more MiG-29s, the first batch of 10 to be delivered in mid-1995.

Southern Asia

INDIA:

New Russian arms order

Russia and India were reported on 30 October to have agreed on another batch of aircraft for the IAF, comprising 35 MiG-33 (MiG-29M) 'Fulcrums' and between 20 and 30 Sukhoi Su-30 'Flankers'. The latter, the two-seat air superiority version, would be the first 'Flankers' in IAF service. Less welcome news for Russia is that the IAF has had second thoughts on the MAPO MiG-21-93 upgrading programme and has turned to Israel for assistance in upgrading its MiG-21bis 'Fishbed N' fighters.

PAKISTAN:

K-8 trainer plans

Hand-over took place to Pakistan on 21 September of the first of six NAM/PAC K-8 Karakorum 8 jet trainers jointly developed by Pakistan and China and built in the latter country by Nanchang Aircraft. The September delivery date was specified in the official contract, signed in Rawalpindi on 9 April 1994, but the aircraft were not due to fly to Pakistan until late November. PAF requirements are understood to cover 60 more K-8s, although plans for local production have been shelved, "for financial and infrastructure reasons." Unconfirmed reports suggest 16 have been ordered by export customers, of

which Bangladesh and Sri Lanka are the two identified thus far. The first production batch comprises 15 aircraft, including Pakistan's six, although nothing is known of Chinese orders, if any.

In Pakistan, the K-8s are undergoing six months of evaluation by the Air Academy at Risalpur. If this is successful, further orders will be placed. The eventual configuration of the aircraft is uncertain, as moves are being made to replace the Garrett TFE731 turbofan with a Ukrainian-built Progress DV-2 because of concerns that a US technology-transfer embargo enforced on China between 1992 and 1993 might be re-imposed. Specific PAF modifications incorporated in the first six K-8s include an improved environmental system, anti-skid brakes and Imperial unit measurements on the CRT-presented flight instruments.

Lynx delivered

Naval aviation received the first two of three Westland Lynx ASW/ASV helicopters on 18 August when the former Royal Navy HAS.Mk 3s were loaded aboard a supply ship at Plymouth following an overhaul at RNAY Fleetlands. The third is to follow during 1995 and an option is held on a further three.

This Gulfstream IV operates as the presidential transport for Botswana. It flies with 12 Squadron (Z12).

Far East

CHINA:

New fighter reported

Israeli know-how salvaged from the cancelled IAI Lavi programme is reported to be incorporated in a jointly-designed fighter under construction for a first flight early in 1996. Neither country has confirmed the report, which suggests that the prototype is being assembled in Israel, although production aircraft will come from a Chinese factory. China will also supply the engine. It may be presumed that the aircraft is required to replace the Shenyang J-8 II interceptor, development of which was abruptly halted by a US embargo on technology transfer after the Tienanmen Square massacre. A regiment of Sukhoi Su-27 'Flankers' has been delivered to fill the most pressing air defence gap, but the high cost of these aircraft makes an indigenous substitute essential.

JAPAN:

Peacekeepers deploy

Having resolved to play a more prominent part in world events, Japan broke a self-imposed taboo on 2 October when two JASDF Lockheed C-130H Hercules landed at Goma, Zaïre. The aircraft carried the first Japanese military units to deploy overseas under their own command since the end of World War II. The purpose was peaceful and approved by the UN, as the ground troops and air force personnel (eventually totalling 290 and 180, respectively) were dispatched to administer humanitarian aid to Rwandan refugees.

'Stealth' fighter revealed

The popular media immediately attached the epithet 'Zero' to the FI-X programme when the Japan Defence Agency (JDA) revealed in October its broad plans for a next-generation interceptor. A successor to the locally-produced McDonnell Douglas F-15J Eagle, FI-X would have a trapezoidal wing and slightly inward-canted twin fins. Two engines, drawing air from an intake below the fuselage, are intended to have two-dimensional thrust vectoring nozzles. Japan plans to use 'stealth' technology on FI-X, which will have a span of approximately 30 ft (9.15 m) and a length of 44 ft (13.40 m), plus fly-by-light controls, conformal radar and an IR seeker/tracker.

The target date of 2008 has been set for first flight of an FI-X demonstrator. However, no contractor has yet been appointed and the sole firm step to date is the award of funding in FY

A8-132 is the first of 21 RAAF F/RF-111Cs to undergo the Avionics Upgrade programme (AUP) at Rockwell. It flew again for the first time in late 1994.

Rarely seen transports are the Alenia G222Ls operated by Libya. This variant is powered by the Rolls-Royce Tyne.

1995 for development work by the JDA on a suitable engine in the 11,200-lb st (50.0-kN) class. If the project is approved, Mitsubishi is likely to gain the airframe contract, assisted by Fuji and Kawasaki, while engine work will go to IHI.

Combat helicopter unveiled

Photographs released in September of a mock-up were the first evidence that the JGSDF is pursuing development of a new combat helicopter to replace the Kawasaki/McDonnell Douglas (Hughes) OH-6. Japan acquired 107 OH-6Js and 182 later OH-6Ds, of which 37 and 148, respectively, remain in service. Designated OH-X Kontanga Kansoku (New Small Observation) and to be built by Kawasaki, the new helicopter is of typical gunship configuration with tandem armoured cockpits, flat transparencies and stub wings, giving a total of four weapons pylons. A roof-mounted sight will incorporate a IR sensor, colour TV camera and laser range-finder. OH-X is to be powered by a pair of 800-shp (660-kW) Mitsubishi XTSI-1 turboshafts and will fly in 1996. Six prototypes will be followed by the first production aircraft in 2000, the total requirement being for up to 200.

SOUTH KOREA:

Trainer requirement postponed

Daewoo's KTX-1 turboprop trainer was given a chance of selection as a Cessna T-37 replacement by the RoKAF in 1997 after plans were abandoned in 1994 to buy Pilatus PC-9s or Shorts Tucanos. While the latter was an outside chance in view of terminated production, Korea had gone to considerable lengths to define the operational fit of the required 20 PC-9s. The three-year delay in choosing a new trainer will allow Daewoo to address technical and performance problems afflicting the KTX-1 but also gives the RoKAF time to digest the results of the JPATS competition.

Australasia

AUSTRALIA:

Orion update awarded

E-Systems, a US company, was awarded the $750 million contract to update all 19 remaining RAAF Lockheed P-3C/W Orions. Project Air 5276 will include ASQ-504 MAD, new radar, upgraded acoustic processing equipment, better navigation and communications aids and a structural refurbishment. Two (rather than the previously reported three) low-houred P-3Bs are to be obtained as trainers as part of the programme as TAP-3Bs.

Trainer requirement accelerated

Problems with extending the lives of CAC/Aermacchi MB.326Hs as far as the planned target date of 2005 resulted in the early issue of a replacement requirement. Potential contractors were given until 25 November to register interest in tendering for Project Air 5367 and expect a decision to be made before the end of 1996. The RAAF requires between 36 and 47 lead-in trainers for its McDonnell Douglas F/A-18 Hornets and General Dynamics F-111Cs, with service entry in 1999, at the latest. Contenders include the BAe Hawk, McDonnell Douglas T-45, Aermacchi MB.339 and Dassault/Daimler-Benz Alpha Jet.

NEW ZEALAND:

Plans for 21st century

A comprehensive review of equipment and commitments for the RNZAF, published late in 1994, envisages few changes to the equipment inventory until early in the next century and reliance upon improvement programmes to keep existing aircraft operational. The recently updated McDonnell Douglas A-4K Skyhawks are to be retired between 2007 and 2010 and enhanced in the short term by self-protection measures against laser-, radar- and IR-guided threats. Aircraft will be modified to receive a jammer and laser-designator and later gain a GPS-based navigation system and new anti-ship missiles. Lockheed P-3K Orions will have their service lives stretched to 2015 by two programmes: Project Kestrel for structural upgrades and Project Sirius for avionics improvements probably to include a new acoustic processor, MAD, EW equipment, datalink (Link 11) and navigation equipment (including GPS).

The sole firm aircraft requirement before the turn of the century is for six secondhand Bell UH-1 Iroquois to join the existing fleet. All will have their engines, airframes and (to a limited extent) avionics upgraded for a further 20 years of service. A slight possibility exists that replacements will be found for the two Boeing 727s

because they breach new noise-abatement regulations, although the cheapest solution would be to fit hush-kits. The nine BAe Andovers appear set to serve until 2005/2006 and are about to begin a flight-deck modernisation programme. Five Lockheed C-130H Hercules are to undergo corrosion rectification which will keep them going until 2004/2005, when the C-130J may be purchased. Even the Navy's Westland Wasps will be persuaded to last until 2000/2001, when a new shipboard helicopter is to enter service.

Africa

ALGERIA:

Major Mil order

An announcement on 25 September disclosed that a large batch of 47 Mil Mi-8 'Hip' helicopters was shortly to be delivered to the Algerian armed forces. Built for the Russian civilian market, the Mi-8s became surplus when the intended purchaser was unable to make payment. They have now been converted for 'combat' use, presumably with provision for armament.

Central America

MEXICO:

Schweizer spyplanes

Delivery took place in July of at least one Schweizer SA 2-37A powered sailplane (serial OES-2252) to an undisclosed Mexican air force unit. Under the designation RG-8A, the SA 2-37 has been used by US government agencies for silent surveillance of drug-running operations, and it may be assumed that the FAM aircraft will be assigned the same mission. At least nine of the type have been built, including a company demonstrator and testbed (N9237A), three for the US Army (85-0047, -048 and 86-0404, of which two survivors went to the Coast Guard in 1990 as 8101 and 8102) and three for another US government department in 1990 (N7508U, '08W and '08Y).

Some or all of the three are in use with the CIA as communications relay aircraft for Gnat 750 reconnaissance RPVs, one of them operating in conjunction with surveillance of Bosnia early in 1994. The two in service with the US Coast Guard have been converted to twin-engined SA 2-38 configuration in 1994-95.

Navy buys Russian

Some surprise was generated in October when the Mexican navy's air arm announced that it has bought eight Mil Mi-8 'Hips' from Russia via the arms export agency, Rosvooruzheniye. The intended role has not been disclosed, but is likely to be general-purpose transport and support.

South America

ARGENTINA:

More US aircraft expected

Having broken the 10-year moratorium on arms supplies imposed after the 1982 Falklands War, the USA was considering further deliveries to Argentina during the latter part of 1994. The Aviación Naval is looking at redundant USN Sikorsky SH-3 Sea Kings and pursuing its purchase of

three Lockheed P-3B Orions, while the Ejercito (army) is anticipating the arrival of its 14th and 15th Grumman OV-1 Mohawks and received six more surplus UH-1H Iroquois in August, increasing its ex-US Army total to 18. To two former USAF C-130Bs previously delivered, a further three were added in mid-1994, with possibly two more being due to follow in October. A nominally civil sale from Sikorsky concerned a VVIP S-70A delivered to the Presidential Squadron on 4 September, serialled H-01 (the former identity of a Sikorsky S-61R, which has been moved down the pecking order to H-02). Argentine connections with France have also been maintained, resulting in a naval order for four Aérospatiale AS 555 Fennecs to be delivered in March 1995.

North America

CANADA:

Fighter cuts planned

A recommended cut of 25 per cent in funds allocated to fighter operations was one of the main items included in a defence policy document presented to the Canadian Parliament in the autumn. Yet to be formally implemented, the reduction would eliminate one of the four operational McDonnell Douglas CF-18 Hornet squadrons in the Canadian Forces, leaving it with only one committed to immediate overseas intervention. The training squadron No. 410 would also remain, having a current total of 20 aircraft.

Previous cuts have already reduced the Hornet force. Out of 125 in the inventory, only about 72 are in operational squadrons and the ratio of pilots to aircraft has declined to 1.28:1, compared with the former 1.5:1. Furthermore, CF-18 pilots now fly an average of 210 hours per year, or 30 fewer than the NATO-stipulated minimum. Doubts also hang over the future of the 36 (cut from 46) CF-5s which Bristol Aerospace is upgrading as lead-in trainers to the Hornet. The sole recent good news for Air Command is that the proposed sale of an Airbus A310/CC-150 Polaris has been cancelled and all five of the type will be retained.

UNITED STATES

Operation Vigilant Warrior

The United States government responded quickly to the potential threat posed by the regime of Saddam Hussein at the beginning of October when tens of thousands of his elite

The intertwined national flags on the nose indicate this aircraft as one of the Mirage 5BA MIRSIP aircraft sold by Belgium to Chile, which has christened the aircraft Elkan. A training unit has been established in Belgium to facilitate the transfer of the aircraft.

CHILE:

New Chilean Mirages

The first Mirage 5M Elkan (Guardian) was rolled out at SABCA's plant in Belgium on 11 October. Serialled 711, the aircraft was one of 15 single-seat former Belgian Mirage 5BAs upgraded in the MIRSIP programme. Chile has also bought five Mirage 5BD trainers which are being modified, as well as four 5BRs and another 5BD.

The Mirage 5M Elkan features small canards, structural improvements, HOTAS, new cockpit displays, a zero-zero ejection seat and new VHF/UHF equipment, IFF, weapons-delivery and navigation aids. Full designations are M5MA for single-seat aircraft and M5MD for the trainers.

Republican Guard were moved close to the Kuwaiti border. Under Operation Vigilant Warrior, some 100,000 ground troops were airlifted to the Middle East, while prepositioned weapons and equipment in the region were2 made ready. A sizeable contingent of US Air Force aircraft was already stationed in Saudi Arabia under Operation Southern Watch. Several US naval warships were moved to within striking position, while a variety of aircraft types were dispatched from the USA to the Middle East to add to the deterrent. Most of the aircraft were drawn from Air Combat Command units stationed in the USA. Other forces were placed on standby at their home bases to move eastward should the need arise. In the event, the Iraqis responded to the United Nations' demand to move the forces and reduce the potential threat. With so many US and coalition forces gathered together in the region, their respective governments agreed to hold a series of joint exercises to maintain proficiency.

Approximately two dozen squadrons were ordered to be ready to move some or all of their aircraft, although less than half of these actually deployed. A statement issued initially suggested the response involved approximately 200 aircraft, including combat types composed of 42 OA/A-10s, 42 F-15Cs, 66 F-16Cs, 12 F-117A, and six B-52Hs. However, it would appear these figures differed from the number of aircraft which actually relocated to the Middle East.

Six F-16Cs of the 20th FW from Shaw AFB, SC, arrived at Dhahran AB, Saudi Arabia to replace a similar number of F-4Gs of the 561st FS, 57th Wing which left the following day. This was a preplanned exchange, as the crisis had yet to manifest itself. The six Falcons were drawn from the 78th and 79th FS and were fitted with the Texas Instruments AN/ASQ-213 HARM targeting system for the defence suppression role. Of the six F-4Gs, only four successfully returned to the USA, with the two stragglers being overtaken by events and remaining in Europe. They were joined by an additional 10 which landed at Lakenheath on 12 October. Thick fog in the UK delayed their departure to the Middle East until 17 October, when 10 finally completed their journey, by which time the threat had diminished. Saddam Hussein's compliance with the UN edict enabled the US to begin the gradual withdrawal, with the 10 F-4Gs departing on 16 November.

The 74th FS, 23rd Wing at Pope AFB, NC, dispatched 15 F-16C and an F-16D to Dhahran on 12/13 October, with a stopover at Spangdahlem AB, Germany. The squadron was to have participated in a Red Flag exercise at the time but was withdrawn at the last minute. A pair of 347th Wing F-16Cs from Moody AFB, GA accompanied the deployment. A dozen 20th FW F-16Cs followed next day, although they were delayed in Europe until 17 October due to their inflight refuelling being affected by fog at Mildenhall.

Other units known to have been involved in Vigilant Warrior included the 1st FW at Langley AFB, VA, whose F-15Cs were among the first aircraft to deploy. Twenty-seven Eagles were earmarked initially with some aircraft flying to Dhahran on 9/10 October. Additional F-16Cs from various units were to have flown to the Gulf during the third week of October, although most appear to have remained on standby at their home stations. These included 36 from the 347th Wing at Moody AFB and 18 from the 388th FW at Hill AFB, UT. Eighteen aircraft from the latter unit were already at Dhahran AB as part of Southern Watch, having taken up residency during mid-September.

A number of OA/A-10As were deployed, consisting of the 75th FS, 23rd Wing from Pope AFB whose entire complement of 24 was allocated to the operation. In addition, 18 Thunderbolts of the 55th FS, 20th FW at Shaw AFB and 24 from the 355th Wing at Davis-Monthan AFB, AZ were placed on standby, with an unspecified number from the latter unit deploying to the Gulf. The USAF subsequently announced its intention to base 24 A-10s at Ahmed al-Jaber AB, Kuwait City from late October as an ongoing commitment to further deter the Iraqis. It is likely the aircraft and crews will be rotated for three-month periods of duty, with the 75th FS initiating the sequence.

The 27th FW at Cannon AFB, NM had 12 EF-111As and 18 F-111Fs on standby in the USA. The 4th Wing at Seymour Johnson AFB, NC was similarly tasked, with 36 F-15Es remaining at readiness. Twelve F-117As from the 49th FW at Holloman AFB, NM were among the combat types identified for deployment initially, although it is unknown if these actually completed relocation to the Middle East.

Strategic bombers were included in the composition of the operation, with six B-52Hs from the 5th BW at Minot AFB, ND being deployed to the region, while nine B-1Bs of the 28th BW at Ellsworth AF, SD remained committed at their home station.

Reconnaissance assets have been an ongoing part of Southern Watch, with RC-135s stationed at Riyadh/Military City Airport and U-2Rs operating from Taif. A small number of additional RC-135s were flown from Offutt AFB to increase coverage of Iraqi communications, together with four 9th RW U-2Rs which were flown from Beale AFB, CA to Taif, arriving in Saudi Arabia on 11/12 October. A dozen RF-4Cs of the 192nd Reconnaissance Squadron at Reno, NV was prepared for service in the Gulf, but were not needed. Three EC-130s from the 355th Wing at

Davis-Monthan AFB were dispatched to the region, possibly the EC-130E Airborne Battlefield Command and Control Center (ABCCC) version. The number of E-3 Sentries was to have been increased from six to 10, although it seems quite likely the quantity remain unchanged.

The 23rd Wing was extensively committed, as the unit sent 14 C-130Es to the region in addition to their A-10s and F-16s. The 23rd Wing has the primary mission of close support of ground troops. Air Mobility Command airlifters and chartered civilian carriers were employed to ferry personnel and equipment to the region, with C-5s and C-14s performing the bulk of the transportation requirements. Air National Guard and Air Force Reserve personnel performed a sizeable number of the AMC airlift missions. A pair of C-17As from the 437th AW at Charleston AFB, SC performed non-stop sorties to the Gulf, ferrying equipment for the US Army's 7th Transportation Group.

The majority of air assets assigned to Operation Southern Watch have operated from the giant Dhahran AB on the eastern side of Saudi Arabia, although the U-2Rs have been stationed at Taif. Despite the Royal Saudi air force E-3 Sentries moving from

Operational testing of the C-17A Globemaster III continues at a rapid pace, including deployment missions to the Kuwait theatre. Here an aircraft demonstrates the capabilities of the IR decoy flare system. The second operational squadron is going to be the 14th Airlift Squadron.

Riyadh/Military City Airport to Al Kharj, the USAF E-3s have continued to fly from the former facility. Many of the US aircraft dispatched as part of Vigilant Warrior were flown to Dhahran, as well as Al Kharj and King Khalid Military City Airport in Saudi Arabia. The Gulf States provided facilities including Sheikh Isa in Bahrain, and Doha in Qatar which housed tanker aircraft.

The removal of the Iraqi troops from the Kuwaiti border enabled the Pentagon to abandon plans to deploy additional aircraft to the Middle East. However, this was on the understanding that Iraq would maintain troop numbers south of the 32nd Parallel at the same level as before the crisis. The Pentagon also stated that any Iraqi violation would result in swift action by the US. Initially, the US force structure would be maintained at 165 combat aircraft, 84 support planes and 34,000 troops pending a review to enable more units to return home.

Further to the Briefing in **World Air Power Journal,** *Volume 20,* **Lockheed Aeronautical Systems Company** *has modified a* **USCS P-3 AEW&C** *with a new 360° radome under the forward fuselage housing an active aperture antenna, part of the* **CEC (Co-operative Engagement Capability)** *equipment. The aircraft is undergoing trials in concert with* **US Navy** *ships to study the CEC concept, whereby aircraft are used to greatly extend the over-the-horizon detection capability of shipboard sensors, while also acting as a link between surface and air assets.*

Operation Uphold Democracy

The full-scale assault by 18,000 troops to oust the military junta of General Raoul Cedras in Haiti was averted when a last-minute agreement was brokered by former US President Jimmy Carter. A US Joint Task Force was airborne in 61 C-130s and C-141s when General Cedras agreed to stand down with effect from 15 October and permit exiled President Jean-Bertrand

Military Aviation Review

The QF-4E is now in use as an aerial target with the 475th Weapons Evaluation Group at Tyndall AFB. On a similar topic, the US Navy expended its last QF-86 drone in late 1994.

Aristide to assume power the following day. The aircraft contained elements of the 82nd Airborne Division who were to have been the first troops to land on Haitian soil as the spearhead for the remainder of the force.

On 19 September 2,000 US troops, most of whom were from the 10th Mountain Division (Light) at Fort Drum, NY were airlifted ashore from ships of Joint Task Force 190 located off the Haitian coast. US Army UH-60s ferried the troops to Haiti while AH-1 Cobras flew protective air cover. The helicopters operated from the aircraft-carrier USS *Eisenhower* (CVN-69). This was the first occasion in which the Adaptive Joint Force Package concept, involving the integration of various services, had been employed operationally. In excess of 50 US Army helicopters were embarked on the US Navy aircraft-carrier for the operation.

US Air Force aircraft played a supporting role, with the majority forward-deployed to the naval station at Roosevelt Roads, PR. E-3 Sentries of the 552nd ACW from Tinker AFB, OK monitored the skies above Haiti as well as the air space around Cuba. Twenty-four F-15Cs of the 33rd FW from Eglin AFB, FL were stationed at Roosevelt Roads along with nine KC-135s as a precautionary measure to perform combat air patrol if needed. In the event, the Eagles were not required

when the invasion was cancelled and they returned home after only four days. Other USAF types included three EC-130Es of the 42nd ACCS, 355th Wing from Davis-Monthan AFB, AZ which performed airborne battlefield management. AC-130H Spectre gunships were on hand to provide firepower if necessary, while RC-135 Rivet Joint aircraft monitored communications.

The initial complement of 2,000 US Army forces was boosted to 15,000 within a week to ensure the country remained stable during the transition back to democracy.

USAF unit news

Air Combat Command extended its number of composite wings when the 347th FW was redesignated as the 347th Wing on 1 July 1994. The two existing F-16C/D squadrons (68th and 69th FS) were joined by the 52nd Airlift Squadron operating the C-130E. The wing will add the 70th FS flying the OA/A-10A during the early part of fiscal year 1995.

At Hickam AFB, HI the Air National Guard has received a small number of brand new C-130Hs. A new unit has been formed to operate these aircraft, probably designated the 204th Airlift Squadron.

At Misawa AB, Japan the 432nd Fighter Wing inactivated when it was replaced by the 35th FW on 3 October 1994. The 16th SOS, 16th SOW at Hurlburt Field, FL received its first two AC-130Us during July. An addi-

tional eight were awaiting conversion and delivery outside the Rockwell and Lockheed facilities at Palmdale, CA during October 1994. Special Operations Command had intended to transfer its AC-130Hs to the Reserves following delivery of the AC-130U into operational service. However, the Command is now anxious to retain the AC-130H for the time being, which will result in the 711th SOS at Duke Field, FL soldiering on with its ancient AC-130As.

Air Force Materiel Command has established numbered air base wings to control activities at their air force bases. The new ABWs have been activated even though most of the facilities house a major flying wing, and reversed the one wing/one base concept. The new units are as follows:

66th ABW	Hanscom AFB, MA
72nd ABW	Tinker AFB, OK
75th ABW	Hill AFB, UT
76th ABW	Kelly AFB, TX
77th ABW	McClellan AFB, CA
78th ABW	Robins AFB, GA
88th ABW	Wright-Patterson AFB, OH
95th ABW	Edwards AFB, CA
96th ABW	Eglin AFB, FL

Air Mobility wings formed

Air Mobility Command (AMC) formed its two long-awaited air mobility wings during the early autumn. The 60th Airlift Wing at Travis AFB, CA changed to AMW status on 30 September, having gained the 9th ARS from March AFB, CA on 1 September. The unit had received 10 KC-10As from the 4th Wing at Seymour Johnson AFB, NC by the end of October, with others due to follow during 1995. The wing will receive a second Extender squadron when the 6th ARS transfers from March AFB during 1995. The 60th AMW already had two squadrons operating the C-5A/B Galaxy and an additional two flying the C-141B. The StarLifter will gradually be withdrawn from service over the next few years, with some being retired while others will join the Reserves.

To enable operations at March AFB to continue during the transition period, the 722nd ARW was formed

when the 22nd ARW was transferred to McConnell AFB, KS, earlier this year. The 6th ARS has remained at March AFB operating the KC-10A, while the 9th ARS has moved to Travis but without personnel or equipment. However, the aircraft of the 9th ARS have remained at March AFB for the time being, with the 709th ARS being formed to allow operations to continue.

At McGuire AFB, NJ the 438th Airlift Wing was inactivated on 30 September, with the 305th AMW being formed next day. The new wing has already begun to receive its initial complement of KC-10As from the 458th Operations Group, 380th ARW at Barksdale AFB, LA. The latter unit was responsible for the 32nd and 2nd ARS, and it is quite likely these be transferred without change.

The Air Force announced that AMC was to receive all 19 Air Combat Command KC-10As flown by the 4th Wing, thereby becoming the operator of the entire fleet of 59 Extenders. However, this plan has subsequently changed with an unspecified number, possibly six, due to join the 22nd ARS, 366th Wg at Mountain Home AFB, ID replacing a similar number of KC-135Rs.

Apart from the creation of the AMWs, the Command has almost completed the establishment of its tanker hubs. The object of the reorganisation was to relocate the KC-135 fleet from 11 bases to six, with the aircraft all located at wing headquarters instead of having some stationed elsewhere on a tenancy basis. At the beginning of 1994, AMC was composed of five KC-135 wings and one independent operations group responsible for 20 air refuelling squadrons.

As stated earlier, the 22nd ARW moved from March AFB to McConnell AFB in January 1994. Subsequently, KC-135s have ceased operations at Barksdale, Beale, Dyess, Ellsworth, Griffiss and Loring AFB. In addition, the 93rd ARS at Castle AFB, which has performed the training of KC-135 aircrew, moved to Altus AFB during late 1994/early 1995. The squadron was transferred to Air Education and Training Command (AETC) in July 1994, and is due to be redesignated as the 55th ARS imminently.

At Robins AFB, the 912th ARS was redesignated as the 712th ARS earlier in 1994, and relinquished control of the two Altus-based squadrons which joined AETC. The 22nd ARW added the 344th and 349th ARS to become a three-squadron unit during 1994. The 319th ARW has likewise expanded with the addition of the 906th, 911th and 912th ARS being added. At Malmstrom AFB, the 43rd ARW has been reduced from seven squadrons at five bases to just one, with the 91st ARS remaining assigned to the 43rd ARW. Finally, the 380th ARW has halved it five squadrons, with the remaining two scheduled to inactivate once the 305th AMW at McGuire AFB becomes fully operational as the East Coast air mobility gateway. The 92nd BW at Fairchild AFB became an

Departing the Rockwell factory at Palmdale is an AC-130U gunship, displaying the new 25-mm rotary cannon in the forward fuselage. This has replaced the twin 20-mm guns of previous versions.

92nd BW at Fairchild AFB became an air refuelling wing in July 1994, with its two tanker squadrons being joined by the 96th, 97th and 98th ARS. The activations, inactivations and moves have resulted in the KC-135 unit structure of AMC being as follows:

15th Air Force

22nd ARW McConnell AFB, KS
344th ARS	KC-135R
349th ARS	KC-135R, KC-135T
384th ARS	KC-135R

43rd ARW Malmstrom AFB, MT
91st ARS	KC-135R

92nd ARW Fairchild AFB, WA
43rd ARS	KC-135R, KC-135T
92nd ARS	KC-135R
96th ARS	KC-135R
97th ARS	KC-135R
98th ARS	KC-135R

21st Air Force

19th ARW Robins AFB, GA
99th ARS	KC-135R
712th ARS	KC-135R

380th ARW Plattsburgh AFB, NY
310th ARS	KC-135R, KC-135T

319th ARW Grand Forks AFB, ND
905th ARS	KC-135R
906th ARS	KC-135R
911th ARS	KC-135R
912th ARS	KC-135R

F/A-18E/F progress

McDonnell Douglas opened the F/A-18E/F Hornet assembly line in St Louis on 23 September 1994 when the first two nose landing gear drag braces for the new strike aircraft were moved into position. First flight of the advanced Hornet, on which the US Navy has essentially staked the future of carrier aviation, is scheduled for December 1995. Production of the F/A-18E/F actually began earlier, in May 1994, when Northrop Grumman began assembling centre/aft fuselages in Hawthorne, California.

The F/A-18E/F programme encompasses seven flight test aircraft and three static test airframes, and is expected to lead to the first aircraft becoming operational in 2001. The US Navy's formal requirement is for 1,000 F/A-18E/Fs to be delivered between 2001 and 2015.

C-17 deliveries

The 437th Airlift Wing at Charleston AFB, SC received its 10th C-17A on 29 September when 93-0599 was delivered from the McDonnell Douglas plant at Long Beach. Two additional aircraft were due to be delivered to the wing before the end of 1994, bringing the 17th Airlift Squadron up to its full complement of 12. One of these will be the fifth C-17A, 89-1190, which was engaged on development work with the 412th Test Wing at Edwards AFB, CA. The aircraft has spent several months at Tulsa, OK having test equipment removed, while at the same time being upgraded to full operational standard. The other C-17A due for delivery should be 93-0600, which performed its first flight on 4

On display at Tyndall AFB during 'William Tell 94' was this Mikoyan MiG-23ML 'Flogger-G'. The aircraft sports a non-standard radome believed to have been raided from an F-106.

November 1994.

McDonnell Douglas has leased a hangar at Tulsa since January 1994 to perform modification work on the C-17. Among the improvements being carried out by the manufacturer have been a retrofit to the fuel system as well as necessary work to the wing and fuselage. Four aircraft had been completed by September with two more due for modification by the end of 1994. In addition, three Globemaster IIIs had a defensive suite fitted to counter heat-seeking air-to-air missiles.

The development fleet of five C-17As operated by the 417th Test Squadron at Edwards AFB, CA had completed more than 3,900 flight hours by the autumn, with test work due to be largely finalised by December 1994. The completion of test duties was scheduled to coincide with the 17th AS at Charleston becoming operational with their 12th airframe.

Iceland Defence Force shake-up

Having defended the strategically important Iceland region since November 1953, the 57th Fighter Squadron is to deactivate as part of a major streamlining of US Air Force assets in Iceland in the light of the considerably reduced threat in the North Atlantic.

For many years the 57th was a Fighter Interceptor Squadron operating as part of the overall NORAD structure, since October 1979 as part of the Air Forces Iceland organisation. In 1992 the squadron was integrated into Air Combat Command and the parent unit became the 35th Wing. On 3 October 1994 this number was transferred to the 432nd FW at Misawa, Japan, and the Iceland unit renumbered as the 85th Wing, the subordinate aircraft-operating units being the 57th FS and the 56th Rescue Squadron.

Drawdown for the 57th Fighter Squadron began in late October 1994, when the first pair of F-15Cs left for Tyndall AFB and reassignment. The squadron is due to deactivate on 1 March 1995, to be replaced by rotational deployments of F-15Cs from other units in four-jet packages. These deployments were scheduled to begin in January, and would be on a 90/120-day rotation. At the same time as the

Seen at Van Nuys Airport, this F-117A wears the badge of the 7th Fighter Squadron, the F-117 type conversion unit at Holloman AFB, NM. Previously known as the 'Bunyaps', the 7th FS has retained its original badge of a mythical fanged creature, but has renamed as the 'Screamin' Demons', wearing the new name on a fin-stripe.

57th FS deactivates, the 85th Maintenance Squadron will also disband, to be replaced by the 85th Operations Support Squadron to provide maintenance for the rotational Eagles.

Unaffected is the 56th RQS and its HH-60Gs, which will remain to provide SAR coverage for Iceland and the surrounding seas with HC-130 tanker support provided by other units. As the final part of the streamlining, the 85th Wing will downgrade to Group level on 1 July 1995.

USAFE news

The former US Air Force base at RAF Bentwaters was employed briefly for Exercise Hazel Flute during the latter half of September with RAF Harriers from 2 Group deploying for a bare base operation. The Ministry of Defence stressed that the exercise would in no way affect the plan to sell the site. The latest information available suggests that a consortium of British Aerospace and Shell UK Ltd are interested in obtaining the base to operate visiting aircraft for a second range to be established in the North

Sea. Existing Shell platforms would be used to site the necessary Air Combat Manoeuvring Instrumentation (ACMI) sensor masts.

While operational as a USAFE facility, Bentwaters was connected by land line to the current ACMI range, so it should not be too difficult to extend the capability to the second area. At this stage it is not clear if the possible usage of Bentwaters would have an effect on the ACMI visitors to Waddington, which regularly include RAF and other NATO arms. Lakenheath also has a direct link to the range, and plays host to USAFE fighters together with those of the Norwegian and German air forces. Apart from Lakenheath and Waddington, debrief facilities are located at RAF Coningsby, as well as the three major Dutch fighter bases of Leeuwarden, Twenthe and Volkel.

Work is progressing well with the construction of Special Operations Command facilities at Mildenhall to house the three squadrons currently stationed at Alconbury. The MC-

Originally procured by the USAF, the BAe C-29A flight check aircraft is now operated by the FAA in civil registrations. However, the fleet is maintained and flown by USAF crews, and the operation is essentially still in the military domain.

130Hs of the 7th SOS and the HC-130N/Ps of the 67th SOS are scheduled to transfer to Mildenhall during the forthcoming winter months, with the MH-53Js of 21st SOS due to be the last squadron to arrive. Helicopter crews from the 21st familiarise themselves with their future new station by performing 'touch and goes' on regular occasions. Special Forces C-130 Hercules often practice take-off and landing on the taxiways at Alconbury, although this will not be possible at Mildenhall due to the location of parking aprons adjacent to taxiways.

Once the Special Forces squadrons have relocated to Mildenhall, Alconbury will begin the process of running down its flight operations before officially closing on 1 April 1995. The future of U-2 operations at Alconbury has yet to be decided, although this will need to be relocated prior to the closure date. The base has indicated that the choice is between Fairford and Decimomannu, Sardinia.

A number of C-5, C-130 and C-141 visitors to Fairford during the first half of October 1994 airlifted B-52 ground equipment back to the USA, indicating that bomber deployments will no longer be taking place.

A recent disclosure by the Department of Defense stated that the US is seeking to close another major fighter station in Europe. There are currently three in USAFE: Aviano AB, Italy with the 31st FW operating two squadrons of F-16C/Ds along with temporary residents supporting Operation Deny Flight; RAF Lakenheath, UK whose 48th FW is equipped with

the F-15C/D and the F-15E; and Spangdahlem AB, Germany with the 52nd FW flying the OA/A-10A, F-15C/D and F-16C/D. In addition, Ramstein AB, Germany has facilities to house and operate fighter aircraft. The ongoing civil war in the Balkan region has seen a huge increase in the number of sorties launched from Aviano. The choice is therefore between Lakenheath and Spangdahlem.

The air defence role of the Spangdahlem-based 53rd FS within USAFE could be performed by the 493rd FS at Lakenheath, backed up by squadrons from the USA if necessary. The A-10s of the 81st FS at Spangdahlem could move to Aviano, which would seem a logical step as part of the squadron is regularly deployed for Deny Flight duties. Various options would be available for the F-16C/Ds of the 22nd and 23rd FS, including transferring one or both to Lakenheath, or one to Lakenheath and the other to Aviano, or even withdrawing both back to the USA. The latter option would help USAFE attain its eventual goal of 2.3 flying wings equivalent.

Air Force Reserve reorganises

The Air Force Reserve (AFRes) undertook a major reorganisation to realign its structure, enabling all units responsible to Air Combat Command (ACC) or Air Mobility Command (AMC) to be grouped together within the three numbered Air Forces. In the event of mobilisation, units under the 4th and 22nd Air Forces would be assigned to AMC, while ACC would gain those of the 10th Air Force. The changes became effective on 1 October. Prior to the reorganisation the majority of combat types were assigned to the 10th Air Force, while the theatre airlift squadrons operating the

C-130 were divided between the other two. Since 1 October the combat units have been joined by the C-130 airlift squadrons within the 10th Air Force. The 4th Air Force has responsibility for tanker and intercontinental airlift assets located on the western side of the USA and part of the Midwest, while the 22nd Air Force has authority over East Coast units.

One of the most significant features of the reorganisation was the upgrading to Wing status for all the groups with AFRes. Squadrons stationed at the same base as the wing headquarters have traditionally reported directly, whereas those units located away from the parent wing were administered by a group. Instead of 21 wings and 17 groups responsible for 58 squadrons, the revised structure features 38 wings controlling 60 squadrons.

Another milestone was the abandonment of the Associate status for airlift, air refuelling and aeromedical airlift squadrons whose crews augmented their front-line colleagues operating active-duty aircraft. Five Associate wings were involved in the programme. The change of designation will not see any reduction in the number of sorties flown in part or fully manned by Air Force Reserve personnel.

AFRes formed a new unit at McConnell AFB, KS with the establishment of the 931st Air Refueling Wing on 1 January 1995. Two squadrons will be assigned, with the 18th ARS activating on 1 October 1995, followed one year later by the 44th ARS, both flying the KC-135R. Personnel of the 77th ARS at Seymour Johnson AFB, NC currently perform their duties aboard active-duty KC-10As, although the transfer of the Extenders to the AMWs at Travis and McGuire will see the squadron receive its own KC-135Rs during 1995. The 89th Fighter Squadron at Wright-Patterson AFB traded in its F-16A/Bs during 1994 and transitioned to the C-141B, becoming the 8th AS. The squadron operates alongside the 356th AS and both have been assigned to the 445th AW, which reformed at Wright-Patterson AFB on 1 October 1994.

Naval Air Training Command

During the last few years, Naval Air Training Command (NATC) has undergone a major overhaul of its structure with the introduction of new aircraft types. The reorganisation was necessary to enable the Command to

Updating the Tomcat operators feature in the last volume, VF-102 'Diamondbacks' now operates the F-14B, having transitioned to the F110-powered aircraft in late 1994.

be effective within the changing requirements of the Navy in the 1990s, and to operate within the restraints of a limited budget. A recent edition of Naval Aviation News presented some interesting details, and we acknowledge due credit to this journal.

The introduction of the T-45A into service during 1993 permitted the Navy to reduce costs, as the Goshawk is much less expensive to operate than the older and more maintenance-intensive T-2 and TA-4 airframes. Initial Goshawk deliveries were to Training Wing 2 at NAS Kingsville, TX with VT-21 and VT-22 being assigned 50 T-45s by 30 September 1994. The milestone in delivery schedule had enabled the two squadrons to transfer their TA-4s and T-2Cs elsewhere. The third squadron of TW-2, VT-23, moved to NAS Meridian, MS with its T-2Cs during the second half of 1994.

Due to the protracted approval of the T-45 programme and the funding being spread over a longer period, the Navy has a programmed production buy of only one aircraft per month. This will require NATC to keep the T-2 Buckeye in service longer than originally planned. Accordingly, the Chief of Naval Air Training has devised a plan to consolidate at one base all T-2/TA-4 operations dedicated to training strike pilots. The plan will see the Skyhawk remain in service until October 1997, while the Buckeye will soldier on until 2003, when there will be sufficient T-45s in the inventory to perform all strike training.

The first aviation class to use the T-45 Training System received its wings upon graduation from VT-21 in a ceremony at NAS Kingsville on 5 October 1994. The training began in January 1994 for the nine students involved.

Carrier qualification (CQ) has been a major part of the aircrew training programme. For many years USS *Lexington* was employed exclusively for the training role with TA-4s and T-22s deploying aboard daily to familiarise students with traps and catapult launches. However, the ship was retired from duty and is now a museum exhibit in Corpus Christi Bay, TX. USS *Forrestal* was transferred to NATC as a replacement, although the vessel was only in service for a short period, as budget cuts forced retirement and decommissioning in September 1993. To enable students to continue CQ training, NATC aircraft regularly deploy aboard Fleet aircraft-carriers where they operate alongside front-line squadrons. Despite initial reservations in certain quarters, the new system appears to be working well.

The Navy, along with the Air Force, will introduce a new primary trainer aircraft towards the end of the decade under a programme known as Joint Primary Aircraft Training System (JPATS). Although destined for use by both services, the source selection will take place at Wright-Patterson AFB, OH between July 1994 and February 1995. Seven manufacturers are contending the programme, with the

VMAQ-1 is one of four Marine squadrons operating the EA-6B. The unit is based, with the others, at MCAS Cherry Point.

selection due to be finalised during the spring of 1995.

In the meantime, the Navy and Air Force have begun to integrate procedures with the exchange of instructors to spearhead joint flight training. The first primary training squadrons selected for the programme are VT-3 at NAS Whiting Field, FL and the 35th Flying Training Squadron at Reese AFB, TX. Courses have begun at both stations, with Air Force students learning to fly the T-34, while naval trainees are being taught to fly the T-37. The programme will gain momentum at a steady rate, eventually building up to a level whereby 100 students from each service will be assigned to the two squadrons. Further plans include multi-engine tuition of all USAF C-130 pilots by VT-31 at NAS Corpus Christi, TX on the T-44A, while the 52nd FTS at Reese AFB will ultimately train Navy personnel destined for the E-6 Mercury. The first C-130 course began in July 1994 with Air Force pilots fresh from completion of their primary flight training on the T-37B. Students are assigned to NAS Corpus Christi for the advanced multi-engine flight syllabus in the T-44A before being awarded their Air Force wings.

Joint USN naval flight officer/ USAF navigator training commenced during October 1994 with all Air Force student F-111 and F-15E weapons systems operators receiving their training with TW-6 at NAS Pensacola, FL. October also saw the Naval Air Training Unit combining with the 562nd Flying Training Squadron at Randolph AFB, TX to form the first true joint training squadron. The unit will perform advanced training for maritime naval flight officers.

Naval Air Training Command is currently divided into five Training Wings, together with the NATU at Randolph AFB. Training Wing 1 at NAS Meridian performs intermediate jet training within VT-19 and VT-23 with 85 T-2Cs assigned, while advanced jet training is carried out by VT-7 with 76 TA-4Js. Training Wing 2 at NAS Kingsville has 50 T-45As assigned to VT-21 and VT-22 to provide intermediate and advanced jet training. Training Wing 4 at NAS Corpus Christi has VT-27 and VT-28 with 71 T-34Cs for primary flying duties, while VT-31 has 57 T-44s conducting advanced maritime training. Training Wing 5 at NAS Whiting

Liberally festooned with radomes and pods, this civil-registered Gulfstream II serves with Air Force Materiel Command's Electronic Systems Center at Hanscom AFB, MA, operated by the 66th Air Base Wing. The precise nature of its tasks is unknown, but trials of C³I systems is the most likely. Similar equipment has also been carried on a civil-registered Falcon 20, also flown from Hanscom.

Field is the largest unit, responsible for VT-2, VT-3 and VT-6 flying 148 T-34Cs teaching primary flight, while those destined to transition to helicopters receive their tuition from HT-8 and HT-18 with 120 TH-57B/Cs. Finally, Training Wing 6 at NAS Pensacola is divided into two squadrons providing naval flight officers with primary flight tuition by VT-10 with 35 T-34Cs, and advanced flying with VT-86 with 10 T-2Cs and 17 T-39Ns. Crews destined for either the E-2 or C-2 are trained by VT-4 with 10 T-2Cs. Pensacola also houses the Naval Aviation Schools Command.

Apart from utilising the home station, NATC units routinely fly to auxiliary landing airfields in the locality. In the case of TW-5, the home station is in effect split into two, with the fixed-wing T-34Cs flying from Whiting's North Field and the rotary-wing elements being located at South Field. The five squadrons perform more than 400 sorties daily, accumulating in excess of 800 flight hours. To accommodate the training requirements effectively, TW-5 aircraft disperse to 13 auxiliary airfields, enabling students to practise landing and take-off procedures in comparatively uncongested air space.

Looking to the future, the arrival of JPATS will be a significant move towards commonality of aircraft types. This may well lead, eventually, to specific roles being allocated to one service exclusively rather than the present system whereby the Air Force, Navy and Marine Corps duplicate one another. However, this is unlikely to occur until the next decade at the earliest.

Re-engined U-2

Lockheed turned over the first three U-2S (re-engined U-2R) reconnaissance platforms to the US Air Force at Palmdale, CA, in October 1994. The rebuilt U-2S replaces the 17,000-lb

(75.65-kN) thrust Pratt & Whitney J75-P-13B turbojet engine with the 25,000-lb (111.25-kN) thrust General Electric F118-GE-101 turbofan, the latter being based on the powerplant of the Northrop Grumman B-2 Spirit.

The already long-legged U-2S will now have a much-improved thrust-to-weight ratio, better fuel economy and the capability to fly missions lasting as long as 20 hours, although pilot fatigue remains a major factor. The US Air Force now has authority to re-engine, and in some examples improve the sensors of, 33 U-2Rs and three two-seat U-2RT trainers, all flown by the 9th Reconnaissance Wing at Beale AFB, CA. A further U-2R damaged some years ago is to be rebuilt to flying condition as a U-2RT. Some aircraft will be upgraded with Senior Year electro-optical sensors.

757 testbed for F-22

Boeing is modifying a 757 transport to serve as a flying test bed for the Lockheed/Boeing F-22 advanced tactical fighter. First flight for the 757 in its new configuration is slated for 1998, after the start of EMD (Engineering and Manufacturing Development) flight operations with single-seat F-22A and F-22B development prototypes.

Modifications to the 757 will mate the F-22 forward fuselage to the forward pressure bulkhead of the transport, while a representative 'sensor wing' will be attached to a small fairing above the cabin just aft of the flight deck, giving rise to the nickname 'Catfish'. The 28-ft (8.66-m) wing will contain electronic warfare, communications, navigation and identification sensors. The grafting of the F-22 nose section increases the 757's overall length by 9 ft (2.78 m). Internal modifications include structural support for the new nose and wing, as well as new electrical power, liquid cooling and instrumentation systems.

BRIEFING

Renaissance twin

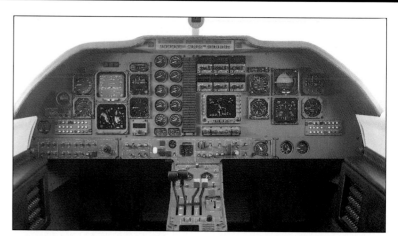

The mock-up of the cockpit shows the ease with which one pilot could operate the aircraft, with all main instruments being located at his station or along the centre.

Led by the example of Burt Rutan, aircraft designers began to throw off the shackles of conventional aircraft construction in the 1970s. Advanced aerodynamics and new construction techniques, including the use of composites, allowed them to design far more efficient shapes, including those with canard foreplanes and rear-set wings. Among the front-runners in this new area of aircraft design was Rinaldo Piaggio S.p.A., a Genova-based company which had been building aircraft since 1915.

Work began on a new twin-engined aircraft which, it was hoped, would gain siginificant orders in the executive field, and for military staff transport/liaison work. Initial work established the configuration of the aircraft, which was subsequently refined over the next four years to the point that, in 1983, wind-tunnel and computer-prediction results were so encouraging that an official go-ahead was announced.

Quite unlike any other aircraft in terms of its configuration, the futuristic Avanti held high promise on account of its very advanced aerodynamics. The main wing section allows extended natural laminar (with much-reduced drag) flow back across some 50 per cent of the chord. Previously this form of drag reduction had only been applied to sailplanes, and had not been thought practical for powered aircraft. Positioning the engines behind the wing does not disturb the airflow as it strikes the leading edge, thereby allowing the full laminar flow effect across the entire span. Using the outside-in tech-

The first three P.180s for the AMI display the type's futuristic lines. In late 1994 the service was the only military customer for the Avanti, with orders standing at nine. Sales from other Italian agencies are likely.

nique of construction, whereby the skin is formed first to which are attached the inner structures, makes for a very smooth wing skin, further increasing laminarity. In planform the wing has very high aspect ratio, with low induced drag characteristics and excellent range performance.

Numerous benefits are gained from the overall configuration. By adding a fixed (laminar-flow section) foreplane, the main wing can be set way back on the fuselage. This in turn means it can be mid-set on the fuselage, reducing wing/fuselage interference drag, without impeding the cabin area, which is all located forward of the wing carry-through structure. Additionally, the foreplanes offload the tailplane, allowing it to be set at very low incidence (and therefore less drag). The pusher engines are well behind the cabin, with a corresponding beneficial effect on internal noise. Furthermore, the aft-mounted engines improve directional and longitudinal stability, and the Piaggio-developed five-bladed propellers are counter-rotating to ease lateral and directional trimming, and to allow the trim surfaces to be neutral with the wing (and therefore less draggy) in normal flight.

Control is effected by ailerons on the outer wing, a conventional rudder and elevators on the standard T-tail. Flaps are fitted to both the foreplane and the main wing, the latter being area-increasing Fowler flaps, with characteristic guide fairings. Delta fins on the lower rear fuselage aid stability, notably at high angles of attack when they provide a pitch-down force to avoid entering a deep stall. The engine nacelles, much of the vertical fin and portions of the rear fuselage are made from a CFRP composite, totalling about 20 per cent of the airframe. The remain-

der is aluminium.

The fuselage itself is one of the cleanest aerodynamically of any aircraft. Eliminating the conventional flight deck step while retaining excellent visibility is a major factor, as is the close-tolerance exterior surface smoothness. The engine nacelles are area-ruled to improve high-speed performance.

Nearly 5,000 hours in the tunnel went into the final design of the Avanti, and the result is an aerodynamic masterpiece.

On the power of its two PT6A-66 turboprops, the Avanti offers impressive performance to beat its turboprop-powered rivals easily, and to challenge executive jets, proving on average 30 per cent more fuel-efficient than the nearest props and 50 per cent better than a jet. Maximum altitude is 41,000 ft (12500 m) and the maximum speed is 395 kts (454 mph; 731 km/h), while normal range with IFR reserves is 1,400 nm (1,611 miles; 2592 km).

Internally the cabin can accommodate nine passengers in considerable comfort, and in cross-section out-dimensions all its rivals, with a height of 5 ft 9 in (1.75 m) and width of 6 ft (1.83 m). On the flight deck the pilot has a two-screen (ADI and HSI) Collins EFIS display, while the co-pilot has a

standard attitude indicator and an electronic HSI for navigation data. Between the two pilots is a multi-function display which can present data from the Collins WXR-840 colour weather radar (which can also be overlaid on the HSI displays), expanded navigation information or checklists. The cockpit is arranged so that it is certificated for single-pilot operations.

Handling is exemplary, especially in the low-speed regime. The aircraft is very manoeuvrable, and the standard Avanti demonstration even includes a tailslide, a manoeuvre usually reserved for specialist aerobatic machines and Russian fighters. Normal landing and take-off runs are about 2,860 ft (870 m), allowing the Avanti to use many airfields denied to its competitors, while on a single engine it can climb at a healthy 756 ft (230 m) per minute.

Two prototype Avantis were built, the first of which (I-PJAV) first flew on 23 September 1986. The second (I-PJAR) followed on 14 May 1987, and initial Italian certification was granted on 7 March 1990. On 30 May that year the first full production machine flew at Genova. The forward fuselage is manufactured by Piaggio Aviation Inc. at Wichita and shipped, along with composite

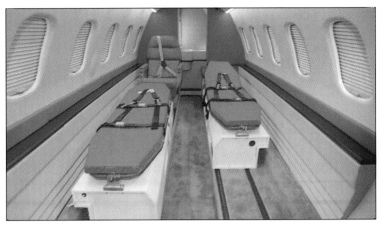

One of the AMI interior layouts is the combi, with two seats forward and a pallet behind for cargo carriage. Track mounts run the length of the cabin for rapid reconfiguration.

In the air ambulance role the Avanti can accommodate two stretchers and a medical attendant. In the rear of the cabin in all layouts is a toilet/galley area.

structures made by Edo and Sikorsky, to Genova for mating with Italian-built wings and rear fuselage for final assembly.

At first sales were slow, largely due to customer inertia, but confidence in the futuristic design appears to be growing. By 1994 over 20 had been sold, and in early 1994 Piaggio was holding talks with Northrop Grumman to work out a deal for US distribution. The 1994 price is approximately $4.8 million with full equipment, and production established at 10 aircraft per year.

Intended primarily for the business market, the excellent performance, economy and capacious cabin makes the Avanti ideal for a number of military applications. Numerous internal configurations are available, these including five-seat VIP staff transport with galley and toilet facilities in the rear of the cabin, eight-seat high-density staff transport, cargo carriage of up to 1,737 lb (788 kg), cargo/passenger 'combi' with two seats and 1,314 lb (596 kg) and air ambulance with two seated passengers, two stretchers and medical equipment. The Avanti also offers an attractive proposition for multi-engine and navigation training.

Special mission options include the P.180APH for aerial survey, offering high-altitude cruise performance and low gust response. Two options are available: APH-A with two Zeiss or Leica downward-facing cameras in the floor of the cabin, and APH-B, with one camera and one Daedalus multi-spectral scanner. Both options have

a navigation telescope, GPS, onboard computers and a single operator station. A P.180RM two-operator flight aids inspection aircraft is offered with either Alenia or Aerodata flight inspection equipment, as are two maritime patrol options. Both of these feature extra fuel, optical camera system and LLLTV (low light-level TV), but the P.180GDF 'A' is a low-altitude version intended for the customs role with a choice of Ericsson or Motorola SLARs in two slender cylindrical fairings under the forward fuselage, while the 'B' is a high-altitude patroller with a digital linescan sensor. The Bendix RDR 1400C forward-looking radar is fitted in the nose, with a communications aerial being mounted in the tailcone.

The first, and so far only, military customer for the Avanti is the

Italian air force, which now has six in service with a further three on order. The initial three (MM 62159/60/61) were delivered in November 1993, followed by MM 62162/63 in March 1994 and MM 62164 in June. The aircraft perform general transport tasks, and were supplied with the kits for VIP, high-density, combi, cargo

and air ambulance work. Floor tracks allow the rapid conversion of the interior configuration from one mission to another. Service trials were conducted by the Reparto Sperimentale en Volo at Pratica di Mare. The AMI would eventually like 38 Avantis, but this seems highly unlikely to be achieved. **David Donald**

Right and above right: This Avanti is seen while being operated by the Reparto Sperimentale en Volo, the Italian air force's trials unit based at Pratica di Mare. The type's revolutionary layout provides outstanding economy and handling, with surprising agility for this class of aircraft.

Piaggio P.166

Italy's utility gull-wing

Undertaking its maiden flight on 26 November 1957, the quirky Piaggio P.166 is still in limited production today, albeit vastly improved since the first models and now optimised for the maritime surveillance and policing roles.

Design of the P.166 stemmed from experience with the P.136-L amphibian (also marketed as the Tracker Royal Gull), which first flew in 1948 and was used by the Italian air force for coastal patrol. It featured two pusher engines mounted on a cranked wing, thereby keeping the engines and propellers clear of the water. This configuration proved successful for waterborne operations, but also showed many aerodynamic benefits. Retaining the wing and engines (340-hp/253.6-kW Lycoming GSO-480) of the P.136-L, the P.166 was developed by a team led by Prof. Giovanni Casilaghi and Alberto Farabioschi with a new landplane fuselage with retractable tricycle undercarriage, the main units being semi-enclosed in bays under the wingroots.

Many were sold on the civilian market, and the P.166M military variant, introduced in March 1961, found favour with the Aeronautica Militare Italiana, which purchased 51. Originally intended for field

support of the G91 force, the P.166Ms mostly served on multi-engined training tasks and with liaison flights. Survivors fly with 653ª Squadriglia Collegamenti, 53º Stormo at Cameri (three), 423ª Squadriglia, Centro Militare Volo a Vela at Roma-Guidonia (four) and 303º Gruppo Volo Autonomo at Guidonia (eight). Two were fitted with aerial survey equipment. Under the designation P.166S Albatross, 20 were sold to the South African Air Force for coastal patrol and transport work in October 1968. Operated by No. 27 Sqn from D F Malan Airport, the P.166s were nicknamed 'Converters' (for, it was said, turning fuel into noise!) in SAAF service and were retired in the late 1980s.

Civilian developments included the P.166B Portofino, which appeared in March 1962 and which was re-engined with the 380-hp (283.5-kW) Lycoming IGSO-540, and the P.166C in October 1964 with an extra cabin behind the wing spar and a new main undercarriage housed in sponsons. In May 1975 the first P.166-BL2 appeared, this aircraft being similar to the Portofino but with revised systems, higher take-off weight and increased fuel.

In 1976 Piaggio introduced two

South Africa used the P.166S version, tailored for maritime patrol with No. 27 Squadron.

models. The P.166-DL2 was based on the BL2 but featured a revised fuselage to cater for special mission requirements, including new cabin windows in a large double cargo door. The optional wingtip tanks were included as standard. Following hot on the DL2's heels was the P.166-DL3, which was similar apart from the installation of Avco Lycoming LTP 101-600 turbo-props, each rated at 587 shp (438 kW). This first flew on 3 July 1976, and is still the current production model, albeit now with LTP 101-700 engines of 600-shp (447.5-kW) rating.

From the outset the P.166-DL3 was intended for a wide range of special missions. The aircraft was certificated for paradropping up to 10 troops and light cargo carriage, while kits available include those

for fire-fighting, aerial photogrammetry, coastal patrol, environmental control, geophysical survey and even armed counter-insurgency and rescue. Internally the aircraft has a raised flight deck for the two pilots, with a large cabin, with enough height to stand, forward of the wing. A bulkhead separates this from the rear cabin, which is principally used to house mission equipment, although it can be accessed in flight through a door in the bulkhead.

The AMI purchased six aircraft (MM 25153/8) for service with

The first military purchaser for the turboprop-powered P.166-DL3 was the AMI, buying six for survey work to augment earlier P.166Ms.

This internal view shows the cabin of a P.166-DL3APH, as used by the AMI for aerial survey. The hatch in the floor is for a vertical camera.

303ª Gruppo Volo Autonomo in the survey role, each equipped with a vertical Zeiss camera in the cabin. Four P.166-DL3s (MM 60210/3 – CC-213/6) were supplied to Somalia, but these ended up in unairworthy condition on the Mogadishu dump during the civil war.

Recent sales have been of the P.166-DL3SEM (Sorveglianza Ecologica e Marittima) variant, a surveillance platform. This is equipped with a comprehensive navigation/communications suite, including HF/SSB comms, ANI-7000 LORAN-C, TACAN, Doppler and radio/radar altimeters. Standard mission equipment includes a Fiar/Bendix RDR 1500B 360° radar in a radome under the nose, which provides search and weather modes and is interfaced with the aircraft's navigation system. A CRT display is provided in both the pilot's and system operator's station.

For maritime search the aircraft carries a Daedalus AA 3500 digital scanner which can work in either UV or IR. This sensor is useful for pollution control, and provides a TV image on a cabin display. Data can be recorded digitally. Alternatively, a Daedalus AADS 1268 thematic mapper can be fitted, with a 12-channel (visible and IR) spectrometer. Under the port wing is a FLIR 2000 turret, which can present a display at either the system operator's station or on the pilot's radar screen. The FLIR has 360° coverage in azimuth and is stabilised. A wide-angle (28° x 15°) view is complemented by a 5.6X zoom function with 5° x 2.68° view.

Further reconnaissance equipment consists of two Vinten Mod. 618 cameras with 70-mm lens. One is mounted in the aircraft side

The Capitanerie has a fleet of 12 P.166s for monitoring shipping and pollution around Italy's coastline.

to give coverage from 20° to 60° below the horizon, while the other, mounted vertically, provides 60° to 100° coverage. The cameras are remotely controlled from the operator station. For search duties the starboard wing mounts an Optical Radiation Corp. Locator II searchlight of 10000-lumen power and a range of around 2,000 ft (610 m). With a beam spread of 4°, the searchlight is operated by the co-pilot using a joystick, and can traverse through +/- 90° in azimuth and +30°/-90° in elevation. Typical mission profiles include five hours on coastal patrol at 3,000 ft (914 m) altitude, and 3½ hours on a night patrol at 1,000 ft (305 m) after a one-hour transit leg and similar return leg.

Two Italian quasi-military organisations have procured the P.166-DL3SEM for surveillance work. The Capitanerie di Porto (Italian merchant/marine ministry) bought 12 SEMs (MM 25159/70 – 8-01/12) for sea surveillance and pollution control, the batch being completed in 1990. These are distributed in groups of four to 1º Nucleo Aereo Capitanerie at Catania-Fontanarossa (where they serve alongside AB 412s), 2º Nucleo at Luni-Sarzana and 3º Nucleo at Pescara. The Guardia di Finanza (customs patrol) has 12 (MM 25171/82 – GF-01/12) in the process of delivery to operate alongside a fleet of Nardi-Hughes NH500s, Agusta A 109s and AB 412s. The sea-search P.166s are specifically for patrolling Italy's Exclusive Economic Zone which extends to 200 nm (230 miles; 370 km) from shore. **David Donald**

The Guardia di Finanza operates the P.166-DL3SEM on patrol duties in connection with customs work. Note the searchlight and FLIR under the wings.

BRIEFING

366th Wing 'Gunfighters'
Mountain Home update

The 366th Wing at Mountain Home AFB, ID, was the subject of a photo-feature in *World Air Power Journal*, Volume 16, and since that time there have been significant changes to the structure and capabilities of the wing. These have largely come about due to the adoption of two new types of aircraft. The KC-135R (22nd Air Refueling Squadron), F-15C (389th Fighter Squadron) and F-15E (391st Fighter Squadron) remain unchanged, but the bomber and F-16 components have adopted new equipment.

Until early 1994 the 34th Bomb Squadron flew B-52Gs as part of the 366th Wing, flying the aircraft from Castle AFB, CA, rather than at the wing's main base. On 31 March 1994 the squadron transferred to Ellsworth AFB, SD, where it began to operate the Rockwell B-1B, seven now being on strength for adding strategic muscle to the composite force's mix. The B-1Bs are based at Ellsworth alongside those of the 28th Bomb Wing simply to ease maintenance. As with the B-52G before it, the B-1B is optimised for the conventional mission, although at present this consists solely of free fall weaponry. In the future such

The 34th Bomb Squadron was the last operational user of the B-52G, but traded these in early 1994 for seven B-1Bs. The 366th Wing may gain KC-10s in place of its KC-135R tankers as these offer far greater rapid deployment capacity.

A pair of F-15Cs from the 390th Fighter Squadron 'Wild Boars' simultaneously releases flares during a training mission. The 390th FS is equipped with latest-standard MSIP F-15s, complete with JTIDS. This communications system allows the jam-resistant real-time transfer of aerial battlefield data between aircraft (including E-3 Sentries), displaying this information on a colour cockpit display.

guided weapons as JDAM, JSOW and TSSAM will be available, but the stand-off PGM capability provided by the B-52/AGM-142 Have Nap combination is temporarily unavailable.

Previously flying Block 25 aircraft from the very first production batch of F-16C/Ds, the 389th Fighter Squadron has now adopted the latest Block 52D aircraft. Powered by the Pratt & Whitney F100-PW-129 IPE (improved performance engine), the Block 52D can be fitted with the ASQ-213 HTS pod (featured in *World Air Power Journal*, Volume 18) to give a lethal SEAD (suppression of enemy air defences) capability when carrying AGM-88 HARM. This new-found role is undertaken alongside the previous air-to-ground roles of CAS/BAI and general daytime bombing/missile attack.

Established as a composite wing in 1992, the 366th is the only Air Force unit which can be directly tasked by national command authorities, bypassing the usual chain of command to expedite its deployment. It is expected to deploy at a moment's notice, fight unsupplied for a week, and for a further 20 days once a supply bridge is in place. In March 1993 around 30 aircraft were deployed as a composite force to Nellis AFB

The new-look 'Gunfighters': a 22nd ARS KC-135R refuels a 34th BS B-1B, flanked by pairs of F-16Cs, F-15Cs and F-15Es from, respectively, the 389th FS, 390th FS and 391st FS. The F-15Es carry four GBU-10 laser-guided 2,000-lb class bombs each. Since the B-52Gs were retired, the Mountain Home Wing has also lost its Northrop T-38s.

for a Green Flag exercise, followed by a deployment to the ANG training location at Volk Field, WI, to test the establishment of combat operations at an austere location. After a visit to Alaska, the 366th undertook its first full overseas deployment in November 1993 when it sent 24 aircraft to Central Command's Bright Star exercise. This not only involved a major deployment exercise, but also composite force training with other services, including the Egyptian air force.

To speed deployment, the 366th takes its own control, communications and intelligence assets. If required, the 366th is ready to undertake a single surgical strike, or can be rapidly deployed as a 'gorilla' force to undertake first strikes and hold the line until other air power units can arrive.

Four pre-planned packages have been crafted from 366th resources, to provide a measured response in most scenarios, although packages can be tailored to individual situations. Package A, known as the 'SWAT Team', is intended primarily for limited operations in areas where air supremacy is assured and comprises eight F-16s, six F-15Es and six KC-135Rs. Package B is similar except that it adds six F-15Cs to cater for potential air threats, while Package C increases the firepower to eight F-15Cs, eight F-15Es and 12 F-16Cs. Finally there is Package D, which comprises all of the wing's PAA (primary authorised aircraft), consisting of 18 F-16Cs, 12 F-15Cs, 12 F-15Es, six KC-135Rs and seven B-1Bs. In most scenarios the 366th would draw on small numbers of specialist support aircraft from other units, notably command and control support from the 552nd ACW (E-3) and 355th Wing (EC-130E), additional lethal SEAD from the Idaho ANG or 57th Wing (F-4G) and non-lethal SEAD from the 355th Wing (EC-130H) and 27th FW (EF-111A).

Radar-hunting 'Viper': the 389th Fighter Squadron employs the latest Block 52D variant of the F-16C, seen here in lethal SEAD configuration with two AGM-88 HARM missiles and the ASQ-213 pod under the starboard side of the engine intake. Wingtip missiles are AIM-9M rather than AIM-120 AMRAAMs. Like other Block 50/52D aircraft, those of the 389th are not solely employed in the defence suppression role, being fully compatible with a wide range of air-to-ground stores for close air support and general attack duties.

EH Industries
EH101

A sophisticated ASW platform and capable battlefield transport, the EH101 was born in the days when there were obvious enemies to fight and significant orders to be chased. While the Royal Navy and, hopefully, the Italian navy will proceed with their planned acquisitions, anything else the future holds for the EH101 is, at best, uncertain.

By 1986, the US estimate of the number of Soviet submarines at sea stood at an alarming 375. Sixty-four of these vessels were ballistic missile submarines – the remainder were mostly attack boats, the 'hunter killers'. While these submarines and their crews were seen, in public at least, as inferiors, Soviet boats were often faster and deeper-diving than their Western counterparts, and there were far more of them. Facing this threat from the 'Evil Empire' were the NATO navies, not least those of the western European members. In time of war the 'return of forces to Germany' would have come chiefly from the United States, and

the US Navy, with its unique carrier battle groups, would also have undertaken any major sea-going combat operations . As a result, the European navies were all strongly biased towards anti-submarine and anti-air duties for convoy or capital ship protection.

The Royal Navy was a key element of this 'future war' and since the mid-1970s the backbone of the British ASW fleet had been the 'Broadsword'-class (Type 22) frigates. The 14 ships of this class were built in three batches, but in 1987 they were joined by the first of 16 'Duke'-class (Type 23) frigates. Laid down in 1985, HMS *Norfolk* was commissioned in 1990

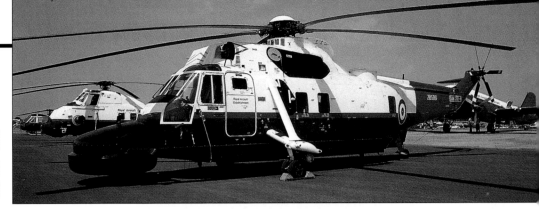

Left: Launched in May 1991, HMS Iron Duke was the Royal Navy's fourth Type 23 frigate and integral to the service's EH101/Merlin HAS.Mk 1 sea-going trials.

as the first Type 23, a class intended to operate in a high-threat (North Atlantic) environment against a multitude of Soviet surface vessels, submarines and aircraft. The Royal Navy could also call on its Type 42 destroyers which embark a Lynx HAS.Mk 3 in a limited ASW role. The larger ships also rely on the Lynx, although in the case of the Batch 2 and 3 Type 22s the more capable Sea King HAS.Mk 6 provided the RN's principal airborne ASW asset.

The Westland Sea King entered Royal Navy service, in its basic HAS.Mk 1 form, during 1969. Although this version was similar to the Sikorsky-built SH-3 (but with Rolls-Royce Gnome turboshafts and UK-developed onboard systems), Westland developed the Sea King over the years into a progressively more capable aircraft. The current HAS.Mk 6, which entered service in 1989, combined previous improvements (such as the Sea Searcher radar in a larger dorsal radome) with composite main rotor blades, uprated transmission, AQS-902G-DS sonar digital processing/display system and Orange Reaper ESM. Despite these advances, the Sea King remained a helicopter with its roots in the 1950s, and if the Royal Navy were to exploit its new ASW vessels to the full, a new shipboard helicopter was a priority.

Westland's 'Sea King Replacement'

Planning for this new aircraft began as far back as 1977 when the UK Ministry of Defence issued a Naval Staff Requirement – SR(N)6646 for a 'Sea King Replacement' (SKR). Westland was seen as the prime airframe contractor for the project but, from the beginning, it was hoped the project would be a pan-European collaborative one. To this end, the Defence Ministers of Britain, France, Italy and Germany agreed, in July 1978, that there was a (European) community interest in co-developing several new military helicopters, one of which would be an anti-submarine aircraft. A steering committee was set up to work out the details and oversee those projects already underway. Under an existing MoD feasibility study, Westland had began drawing up plans for the WG.34, as a dedicated SKR, in early 1978. Later that year a deal was signed with Italy's Agusta providing for joint design and manufacture. The UK and Italian firms were already connected through a Memorandum of Understanding (MoU) signed between Westland, Agusta, MBB and Aérospatiale in 1975. The subsequent MoD project definition study addressed the specific requirements of the British and Italian navies (the latter, the Marina Militare Italiana – MMI – operated Agusta-built SH-3Ds) and by late 1978 this study had reached four broad conclusions.

I. The new aircraft should be capable of operating at great range from base (or parent ship), and independently.

II. This autonomy of operation would be achieved through using sonobuoys instead of

Right: Prior to its October 1987 maiden flight PP1 found itself stuck firmly in the mud at Yeovil, having slipped off the tarmac during towing in the early hours of the morning. Some anxious moments followed as staff strained to rescue and recheck their new fledgling.

Above and right: As part of the Blue Kestrel radar development, 10 sets were built. Two were flight tested, one on the RAE's Sea King Mk 4X (ZB506) and one on Westland's dedicated EH101 testbed Sea King HAS.Mk 2 (XZ570), which flew 424 hours of EH101 avionics research (including radar, ESM sonics and sonobuoys).

traditional dipping sonar (sonobuoys were eventually introduced on the Royal Navy's Sea Kings, but only as an 'interim' measure).

III. An automated data processing system would be needed to exploit the capability of its acoustic sensors (radar, magnetic anomaly detector – MAD – etc.).

IV. To carry this weight of sensors, avionics and weapons and still achieve a useful endurance, the new helicopter would require a larger payload (and thus operating weight) than the Sea King HAS.Mk 2 then in service.

Potential solutions to these issues came in the form of Westland's WG.34. This new design was, at first, intended to be slightly smaller than

Right: Before the EH101 there was the 'Iron Bird'. Installed at Agusta's Cascina Costa plant, this ground test vehicle first undertook dynamics and vibration testing followed by avionics electromagnetic trials. A fully instrumented fatigue test airframe was constructed at Yeovil where Westland also used a Drop Test Vehicle to simulate deck landings for undercarriage qualification.

the Sea King, with a fuselage length of 56 ft 9 in (17.34 m) as opposed to 57 ft 2 in (17.42 m). This belied the fact that the WG.34's intended MTOW was 24,000 lb (10886 kg), some 3,500 lb (1587 kg) more than the Sea King. A crew of three, comprising single pilot, observer and systems operator, was accommodated, while the advanced airframe featured retractable gear and an internal weapons bay. Central to the WG.34's anti-submarine mission was its avionics fit, and the following items were all specified for inclusion: a development of the AQS-901 acoustic processor then being fitted to the Nimrod MR.Mk 2, a development of the Lynx's Seaspray radar and its ESM equipment,

EH Industries EH 101

secure voice communications, a JTIDS datalink, a US-supplied ASQ-81 towed MAD and a digital tactical data handling system to enable the small crew to manage all the sensors at their disposal. The WG.34 was to be twin-engined (although this was later increased to three), with powerplants in the 1,500-1,800-shp (1117-1341-kW) range, such as the Turboméca Makila, Rolls-Royce Gem (derivative), Allison PLT-27 or the General Electric T700. Westland was not slow in placing contracts with other suppliers for onboard systems. Marconi Avionics (then part of GEC-Marconi Electronics) undertook to supply the acoustic processor, based on its experience with the AQS-901, as delivered to the RAF and RAAF. Smiths Industries, in collaboration with Louis Newmark, was selected to carry out studies for a four-axis, fail-safe automatic stabiliser and autopilot for the WG.34's automatic flight control system. A development of Ferranti's Argus M700 was chosen as the WG.34's prime onboard computer system. While the WG.34 was being driven as a military project, it was acknowledged that the design had commercial potential and that a civil version could be developed in the future.

In September 1979 the UK MoD awarded a $5 million contract to General Electric for the supply of nine 1,600-shp (1192-kW) T700-GE-700 turboshafts for use in Westland's WG.34 ground rigs and three engine flight dynamics test vehicles, the WG.34As. It was pointed out that the T700s were for trials purposes only and were not necessarily the chosen production powerplants. Rolls-Royce was then developing the 2,500-shp (1865-kW) RTM321 engine, in conjunction with Turboméca, specifically for such a helicopter.

Founding European Helicopters

During the Paris air show of 1979, Westland Helicopters and Construzioni Agusta announced the establishment of a joint company, with equal shares for each partner, to proceed with a Sea King Replacement for their respective navies. This closer integration with Italian requirements (which placed greater emphasis on shore-based operations) saw the design become less closely associated with Westland and, as a result, in June 1980, a new company was founded to undertake the project. European Helicopter Industries Limited, with its head offices in London, formally undertook to develop the helicopter, now renamed the EH101, beyond its original design brief. In addition to the naval version, plans for a military utility version (with rear loading ramp) and a 30-seat civilian version became an integral part of the programme.

As an aside, Agusta had been responsible for the 1964 Agusta A 101G helicopter which bore a surprising resemblance to the EH101 of 20 years later. It, too, was a three-engined design, with Bristol Siddeley H.1200 Gnome engines driving a five-bladed rotor. The pod-and-boom design featured a large cabin with rear-loading ramp and was intended for civil and military use. The A 101G proved to be ahead of its time and underwent only a brief evaluation by the Italian air force's test (RSV) unit.

Back at EH Industries, design of the primary shipboard EH101 was still not fixed as the debate over powerplants, their type and number, continued. Some facts did begin to emerge, such as the slowly increasing empty and maximum

take-off weights that now stood at an estimated 15,046 lb (6824 kg) and 28,660 lb (13000 kg), respectively, although this did provide for an ordnance load 1½ times that of the Sea King. EH Industries announced that the final definition period would not be completed until 1982, with design and manufacturing due to begin by mid-1984 and mid-1985. This path was smoothed by the decision of the British government, on 12 June 1981, to award EH Industries a £20 million contract covering a nine-month development period, and the signing of a second MoU which allowed the UK MoD to act as agent of the Italian government.

Division of labour

With two years of collaboration already under their belts, Westland and Agusta predicted a market for 750 EH101s over the first 15 years. Production would be sub-contracted to the two firms, each establishing their own assembly lines, without duplicating component production. Agusta would eventually be responsible for rear fuselage, tail unit, the main and tail rotor hubs, tail rotor blades, transmission, fixed and rotating controls, hydraulic and electrical systems and AMC. Westland would supply the cockpit, forward fuselage and main cabin, main rotor blades, engine installation, superstructure, undercarriage, fuel system, flotation devices, environmental control system (ECS) and automatic flight control system (AFCS).

At the 1981 Paris show both Westland and Agusta exhibited models of a range of EH101 versions. Quite apart from the ASW aircraft, EH101s were shown in Exocet-armed anti-shipping, military troop and vehicle transport, commercial passenger, cargo, rig-support and VIP versions. Westland would have design leadership for civil versions, with Agusta assuming responsibility for the rear-loading military/utility version.

It was expected that one-third of those built would be for the military but, thus far, the Royal Navy alone had expressed firm interest in the type and even then this was only for 60 EH101s. The Navy was embroiled in an ongoing debate over its future role and the service was being cut back at an alarming rate. The dramatic events in the South Atlantic during 1982 put an end (at least for the time being) to this reduction in forces. Six weeks of combat operations underlined the worth of the Sea King, but did little for their fatigue lives and reaffirmed the need for a replacement.

By November 1982 the EH101 had reached the end of its project definition stage. The UK Defence Minister, John Nott, said the programme showed "very heartening progress." At the same time, a study for a 30-seat commercial version was formally launched by the British and Italian Secretaries of State. Mr Nott went on to say, in the House of Commons, that "the most important feature of the Type 23 (frigate) for ASW will be a specially designed platform for a new helicopter, the Sea King Replacement. This will be heavier than the existing Sea King but it will be very much more agile, enabling it

Initial naval flying was conducted by PP2 aboard the Italian frigate Maestrale. Pilots used to the Sea King appreciated the EH101's increased tail rotor authority which enabled them to land in winds gusting up to 50 kt, from any direction. PP2 went on to conduct increased weight trials.

to operate in safety from small ships in foul weather. It will have much greater load-carrying capability and will carry Stingray torpedoes as well as advanced avionics. In this respect it will have some of the capabilities of the Nimrod, which will make it a formidable ASW platform. It will provide a full capacity in one helicopter both to detect and kill enemy submarines at longer range."

Specifically, the EH101 is required to operate from a 3,500-ton, frigate-sized vessel and to be capable of launch and recovery in sea states 5-6 with the ship on any heading and at any speed. Its offensive systems are integrated through two MIL-STD-1553B databuses and its primary ASW mission equipment includes GEC-Marconi Blue Kestrel radar, GEC-Marconi AQS-903 acoustic processing system and Racal Orange Reaper ESM.

Development airframes

EH101 development and trials would require 10 aircraft, not prototypes as such but pre-production aircraft. 'PP0' would be an Agusta-built 'iron-bird' ground test airframe, followed by nine flying examples. First flight was planned for mid-1986, leading to some 3,300 hours of flight trials and 2,000 hours of 'maturity flying'. The EH101 would be launched with General Electric T700-GE-401/CT7 (for civil versions) turboshafts, with an option to change these at a future date. The entire development cost for the military versions was slated at £450 million.

Early in 1984 the US Department of Defense directed the USN to consider the EH101 for its carrier battle group 'inner zone' ASW screening requirement – the 'CV-helo'. A development of the LAMPS III Sikorsky SH-60B, the SH-60F, had been earmarked for this task but the $18.7 million allocated by the USN in its FY1984 budget for the SH-60F had been frozen after a

Defence Resources Review Board called for the selection process to be opened to competition. The contract for 175 aircraft was eventually awarded, in March 1985, to Sikorsky and the SH-60F Ocean Hawk. Prior to this, in February, the formal contract for EH101 development, and the project's third MoU, was signed in Rome by representatives of the UK government, EHI, Westland and Agusta.

Work continued on Agusta's 'iron bird', or helicopter system bench. With a steel structure replacing most of the fuselage and tailboom, three T700s were mounted along with actual rotor, transmission, electrical, hydraulic, fuel (apart from the tanks) and flight control systems. The rig was instrumented with vibration, stress, pressure and temperature sensors recording 500 parameters.

The 'Westland affair'

By the Paris air show of 1985 a full-scale mock-up of the basic EH101 was on display, when it was announced that the first flight date had slipped towards the end of 1986. Orders for the type then stood at 50 for the MMI and 40 for the Royal Navy. Less welcome to the project was the financial collapse of Westland in February 1986, which caused a bitter debate, and ministerial resignations, over the new ownership of the company. Westland plc shareholders ultimately voted for a consortium comprising United Technologies (owners of Sikorsky) and Italy's Fiat to assume control of the company. The UK MoD had supported a rival European bid for Westland, while the Department for

Trade and Industry favoured the successful bidders. At a cross-party Commons defence committee, called to investigate the so-called 'Westland affair', Mr Norman Lamont (then Minister for Defence Procurement) announced that EH101 development costs had risen alarmingly to a projected £650 million and could rise to £1.5 billion by the time production commenced. He also revealed that ways were being examined to adapt the design to meet the Royal Marines and British Army's new transport helicopter requirement in an attempt to reduce costs.

At the 1986 Farnborough show the EH101 appeared in mock-up form only, as the first flight date slipped again, this time into the first quarter of 1987. By September 1986 PP1 (c/n 50001) was largely complete at Westland's Yeovil factory and the British firm had supplied major sub-assembles to Agusta, at Cascina Costa, Milan, for PP2 (c/n 50002). Engines were delivered from Alfa Romeo, which was responsible for producing the EH101's uprated -T6A stage-3 growth version of the T700 together with GE and FiatAvio. Next to arrive

PP4 was the UK's initial naval trials aircraft, which carried many of the developmental avionics intended for the Merlin. It undertook over-water navigation and AFCS testing before becoming the first EH101 to be fitted with RTM322 turboshafts, in place of the GE T700.

Wessex/Puma replacement. Orders then stood (supposedly) at 50 for the Royal Navy, 38 for the Italian navy (from a specified requirement for 42) and an initial 25 for the RAF. It was also suggested that the RAF decision might require a 10th airworthy development aircraft.

Canada enters the picture

Early in 1987 the Canadian Department of National Defence (DND) issued a request for proposals to answer its New Shipborne Aircraft (NSA) requirement. By 1967 the Canadian Armed Forces had taken delivery of 41 licence-built CHSS-2 (later CH-124A) Sikorsky Sea Kings for ASW duties. Under a Cdn $2 billion programme 50 new ASW helicopters were being sought and EHI lobbied hard for the contract in the face of competition from the Aérospatiale Super Puma. At the very earliest stages of the EH101 project Canada had been invited to participate, but had instead opted to upgrade its ageing Sea Kings. The new RFP specified the inclusion of active ASW equipment (dipping sonar) instead of the passive measures (sonobouys) preferred by the Royal Navy, but the Canadian desire for autonomous hunter/killer capability was central to the EH101's design brief. In the event of an order a sizeable industrial offset deal was also proposed and EH Industries (Canada) was founded to handle the business. The promise of a Canadian order boosted EHI's hopes considerably, and presentations were also being made to the Indian government for an EH101 troop transport at the same time. These marketing efforts were rewarded with the selection by the Canadian government, in August 1987, of 50 (although this later swung from 28 to 45) ASW-configured EH101s as its Sea King replacement.

1987 was crowned on 9 October when PP1, now allocated the RN serial ZF641, made its maiden flight, in the hands of Trevor Egginton

Above: PP4 (ZF644) made several landings on board HMS Ark Royal while in the English Channel. Ark Royal has a standard complement of nine Sea King HAS.Mk 6s and two AEW.Mk 2s.

Left: The Merlin's 'front office' is dominated by the screens of the Thorn EMI pilot's mission display unit, integrated through two MIL-STD-1553B databuses. Commercial variants will use the Canadian Marconi CMA-900 FMS.

at Yeovil were the tail pylon and stabiliser modules from Agusta, followed by the third example of the Italian-developed gearbox (the first two gearboxes remained under test at Cascina Costa). After only nine trial attempts (15-20 was more normal) Westland settled on the definitive bonding method for the five-bladed carbon/glassfibre main rotors. The first completed set was used for rig testing, while the second was fitted to PP1.

The dark-blue painted PP1 was finally presented to the world during a 'roll-out spectacular' at Yeovil on 7 April 1987. It bore none of the radomes and other protuberances associated with the military versions, but one noticeable feature was its paddle-tipped rotor blades. These used Westland's BERP (British Experimental Rotor Project)-derived wide-chord tips with which a modified Lynx set a world helicopter speed record of 216 kt (399 km/h, 248 mph) in August 1986. The EH101 possesses a more modest top speed of 167 kt (308 km/h, 191 mph) but its advanced rotor does allow it to cruise comfortably at 160 kt (295 km/h, 183 mph), appreciably faster than other comparable helicopters. EHI by then had revised the orders total for the EH101, not least after its provisional adoption by the Royal Air Force as a

Like PP2, PP5 (ZF649) adopted a paint scheme more at home with its operational environment. The first full Merlin-standard EH101 for the RN, PP5, is seen here with HMS Norfolk, the Type 23 frigate with which it completed its first batch of sea trials.

EH101 Merlin

1 Fixed horizontal tailplane
2 Rear Orange Reaper electronic support measures (ESM) antennas
3 Tailfin, canted to port
4 Tail navigation light
5 Anti-collision beacon
6 Tail rotor hydraulic actuator
7 Final drive right angle gearbox
8 Four-bladed composite tail rotor

9 Tail rotor drive shaft
10 Bevel drive gearbox
11 Powered hinge tail pylon fold point
12 Self-aligning shaft coupling, pylon folding
13 HF aerial rail
14 Tail rotor transmission shaft
15 Shaft bearings
16 Beam Orange Reaper antennas
17 Crew toilet
18 Engine ground start air connection

19 Light stores carrier
20 Smoke floats or marine markers
21 Sponson flotation bag
22 Starboard main undercarriage, aft-retracting
23 Tie-down point
24 Port navigation light
25 Undercarriage hydraulic retraction jack
26 Pressure refuelling adaptor
27 Sonobuoy stowage rack
28 Rear underfloor fuel tank
29 Engine washing connector
30 Rotary sonobuoy dispensers

31 Winch
32 Dipping sonar housing
33 Sonar cable reel and drive motor
34 Starboard Rolls-Royce-Turboméca RTM322 turboshaft engine
35 Engine oil tank
36 Accessory equipment gearbox

37 APU air intake
38 Auxiliary power unit (APU)
39 Centre engine, offset to port
40 Intake particle separator air duct
41 Rotor head fairing
42 Composite main rotor blades
43 Hinged blade root attachment joints, blades folded for deck stowage
44 Metal-cored composite main rotor hub
45 Elastomeric blade root bearings
46 Drag dampers

47 Swash plate mechanism
48 Rotor head hydraulic actuator (3)
49 Bevel drive power input from centre engine
50 Transmission oil cooler
51 Main rotor gearbox
52 Bevel drive power input from outboard engines
53 Engine fire suppression bottles
54 Engine air intake particle separator
55 Starboard engine air intake
56 Jump seats
57 Emergency exit hatch
58 Marconi Stingray homing torpedoes
59 External stores carrier
60 Sliding cabin door

61 Forward underfloor fuel tanks
62 Mission avionics racks, data processing equipment
63 ASW systems officer and observer's keypads
64 Display consoles with colour CRTs
65 Main gearbox mounting
66 Rotor brake
67 Accessory equipment gearbox
68 Generator
69 Hydraulic equipment modules
70 Cooling air intake
71 Port crew entry door upper segment, open
72 Automatic flight control system actuators
73 Avionics cooling air supply

74 Mission console aft-facing seats
75 Observer's swivelling seat
76 Avionics equipment racks, port and starboard
77 Battery
78 Ground power socket
79 Ventral radome
80 Ferranti Blue Kestrel 360° search radar
81 Forward flotation bag
82 Sliding, jettisonable side window panel
83 Pilot's seat
84 Centre control pedestal
85 Co-pilot's seat
86 Cyclic pitch control levers
87 Overhead engine condition levers

88 Electrically heated windscreen panels
89 Windscreen wipers
90 Instrument panel shroud, electronic flight information system (EFIS)
91 Collective pitch control column

92 Rudder pedals
93 Downward vision window
94 Nosewheel hydraulic steering
95 Nose undercarriage, forward-retracting
96 Pitot head, port and starboard
97 Forward Orange Reaper ESM antennas

and Colin Hague (the chief and deputy-chief test pilots). They were followed by Agusta's PP2 on 26 November, although Agusta arranged a 'public' first flight for VIPs and the press on 14 December. Egginton also flew PP2 on these early occasions, although Agusta's chief test pilot Raff Longobardi occupied the 'command' right-hand seat. Within the first 45 hours, PP1 (fitted with an interim Louis Newmark AFCS) had flown at its maximum all-up (naval) weight, attained 140 kt (258 km/h, 160 mph) and 45° angles of bank, and reached 10,000 ft (3048 m) altitude. In February 1988, 14 CT7-6/6A turboshafts (including two spares) were ordered for the four civil and utility EH101s under construction. CT7s would also be fitted to one of the Italian-built naval airframes, while the other four all received military-spec T700s. The Italian navy next announced that its aircraft would be powered by General Electric's CT7-6As.

Merlin for the Royal Navy

In the spring of 1988 the Royal Navy confirmed that its EH101s would become Merlin HAS.Mk 1s, while the name Griffon was under consideration for the substantially different RAF transport version. Events in Canada moved forward with the allocation, in July 1988, of Cdn $31.25 million for a project definition contract covering the detail of the aircraft's technical performance, life cycle, production costs and the Canadian industrial offsets which (then) amounted to 78 per cent of the total EH101 contract value. The Halifax-based IMP Group was chosen to assemble the Canadian aircraft, and if the CT7 was selected as powerplant it would be assembled by Standard Aero, of Winnipeg.

On 30 September 1988 PP3, the civil prototype registered G-EHIL, took to the air – the first EH101 to be fitted with the Smith Industries SEP20 digital AFCS. When PP3 became involved in weapons carriage trials in 1993 it was allocated the serial ZH647. PP3 also first flew the Westland/Moog-developed Active Control of Structural Response (ACSR) system which reduces airframe vibration by imposing an opposing-wave vibration, thus cancelling the disturbance. PP1, meanwhile, was involved in handling tests and further expanding the EH101's flight envelope (and had been fitted with a rotor head vibration absorber in lieu of ACSR), while PP2 undertook flight dynamics research. In October 1988 PP1 was transported to Genoa and then flown to Cascina Costa where it joined Italy's PP2 for an integrated flight test programme headed by test pilots Derek Marpole and Raff Longobardi. For 18 months the two aircraft flew together in the far more temperate Italian climate, and were later joined by PP6. When this phase of the programme came to an end PP1 returned, over the Alps, to Yeovil.

Ferranti's Blue Kestrel sea-search radar was to be fitted to the Merlin and, in November 1988, the first two B-model development sets were delivered to Westland. One was tested on a ground rig and the other on a Sea King flying testbed (XZ570). An A-model prototype had been flown two years prior to that in an RAE Bedford Sea King (ZB506). Blue Kestrel 5000 is derived from the Seaspray radar fitted to the Navy Lynx. Now built by GEC-Marconi Avionics it is a lightweight, I-band pulse-compression radar utilising a large flat plate antenna and travelling wave tube with 360°

coverage for sea search, anti-ship and anti-submarine detection and over-the-horizon targeting, as well as SAR and navigation functions.

Further flight trials

Out of numerical sequence, the Agusta-built PP6 flew on 26 April 1989, to act as the Italian navy's dedicated trials aircraft. The Westland-built PP4 (ZF644) took to the air on 15 June 1989, and was devoted to overwater navigation trials and AFCS development. PP4 was the initial British naval trials EH101 fitted with a full EFIS cockpit, MIL-STD-1553B databus, radar altimeter and Royal Navy communications equipment. Westland next flew PP5 (ZF649) on 24 October. This was the first full-standard 'Merlin' and became heavily involved in shipboard trials with Type 23 frigates. PP5 integrated the Merlin's mission sensors (such as Blue Kestrel) and the avionics that previously had only been flown on separate aircraft (PP4). Colin Hague referred to PP5's maiden flight as "the first flight of the EH101 as a fighting machine." In September another developmental milestone was reached when GEC Avionics completed the flight trials of the Merlin's AQS-903 acoustic processing system which had begun on 28 July using a Sea King. The fourth, and final, EH101 to fly in 1989 was Agusta's PP7 (reregistered I-HIOI in November 1993) on 18 December. This was the first ramp-equipped aircraft, the Military Utility, without the folding tail and rotors of the naval versions. A mock-up of the rear-loading EH101 had been used earlier that year by British troops on Salisbury Plain.

1990 saw the arrival of PP8 (G-OIOI), Westland's 30-seat Heliliner civil transport version, which first flew on 24 April 1990, following the

Above: PP6 was the dedicated trials aircraft for the Italian navy. Together with the carrier Garibaldi and the helicopter cruiser Andrea Doria it undertook sea trials in the Mediterranean, including bad weather operations, during 1991.

Left: The CH-149 Chimo would have been a more than capable successor to the CH-113 in its vital SAR role. Like Canada's ASW EH101 (the CH-148 Petrel), it fell victim to a political bun fight.

Left: PP7, the Military Utility, was the first EH101 to appear fitted with the rear loading ramp. It is seen here, in flight, with the ramp-equipped Civil Utility – PP9. On a typical mission the Military Utility could carry 30 troops over a 75-mile (120-km) radius of action, at 150 kt (277 km/h, 172 mph) and a height of 1,650 ft (500 m). It could make this round trip twice before refuelling. Trials have seen 30 soldiers deplane in 40 seconds.

lead set by PP3. It became engaged in ADF and DME trials along with navigation, EFIS and civilian-standard AFCS testing. An important development for the British aircraft came in June 1990 when a decision was made in favour of the 2,312-shp (1724-kW) Rolls-Royce/Turboméca RTM 322 turboshaft (built around the core of the RTM321) for production Merlins, while Italy decided to stay with the 1278-shp (1714-kW) General Electric engines. The Merlin/EH101 emerged unscathed from the Options for Change defence review of July 1990 and the UK MoD next sought tenders to become prime contractor for its aircraft. This was not an open and shut case for Westland, as

it teamed with IBM (with its US Navy LAMPS III experience) to act as systems integrator. Bidding against them for the 50-helicopter (plus three years of technical support and avionics integration) contract was a British Aerospace/GEC-Marconi alliance (Merlin Management). A decision was also to be made regarding the addition of a dipping sonar to the Merlin (a strange reversal of policy) with the Plessey Cormorant and Ferranti/Thomson-Sintra Flash in contention. It was to be over a year before these issues were resolved.

By November 1990 the eight pre-production EH101s had chalked up 850 of their intended 4,000 flying hours. The design top speed of 167 kt

had been achieved and the EH101 had been flown sideways and backwards at 50 kt (92 km/h, 57 mph), and 60° angles of bank had been demonstrated. Several problems encountered in flight test had been solved. Early on, a tendency for the aircraft to pitch up when transitioning into, or out of, the hover had been discovered. Caused by the main rotor downwash impinging on the tailrotor, several redesigns were tested on PP2. Moving the tailplane to the opposite side of the rudder was tried and rejected. Fitting an all-moving tailplane and mounting a small tailplane halfway along the rear fuselage, permanently in the downwash, were also dismissed. Instead, a low-set asymmetric surface was mounted to starboard and successfully flown during PP2's sea trials. A lateral airframe shuffle (of approximately twice the rotor frequency) was cured by fitting a large domed fairing – the 'beanie' – above the rotor hub to direct 'dirty' air away from the tail rotor, and by adding aerodynamic fairings over the main rotor blade root ends and tension links, and a so-called 'horse collar' lip over the top structure aft of the engines. A teetering rear rotor hub was designed by Agusta to reduce tail vibration. Finally, PP1 first tested anhedral rotor tips to improve the rotor's thrust efficiency. The new tips, combined with refinements of the spread section and geometry of the notch where the tips meet the blades, removal of the after fin section on the tail and halving the size of the tail fin fairing, reduced the EH101's power demand in the hover by 250 hp (186 kW).

Italy begins sea trials

The first EH101 to go to sea was PP2 (by then fitted with ACSR) which began deck trials in September 1990. Based at the Mediterranean naval station of Luni, PP2 began flying from the 2,500-ton frigate *Maestrale*, which normally embarks a pair of AB 212ASWs. It later was joined by PP6 which flew from the carrier *Guiseppe Garibaldi* and the cruiser *Andrea Doria* (until October 1991), both of which provided ample room for manoeuvre.

The last pre-production EH101, Agusta-built PP9 (I-LIOI), took to the air on 16 January

Structure

The fuselage has been designed in four sections with the front, centre-sections and tailcone common to all versions. The tailboom in the ramp-loading versions is slimmer and dispenses with the tail-folding option. The fuselage structure is mainly of honeycomb aluminium-lithium with bonded composite panels. The main frame (for the cabin) has multiple primary and secondary load paths – a fail-safe, damage tolerant design.

Anti-icing measures

Much effort was expended to overcome the inflight icing problems to which the Sea King was prone. The sideways-facing intakes for the engines are one such specific design feature. The Merlin's engine intakes, along with the main and tail rotors, are also protected by Lucas electrothermal de-icing mats. On the rotors these are bonded to the leading edges of the composite blades and protected by a titanium erosion shield. This system was tested on specially modified versions of the Westland Sea King, Westland 30 and Wessex. An instrumented Wessex ice research vehicle, fitted with a developmental system, undertook 50 trials flights in Canada, and 1,000 static rig tests, in temperatures as low as -30°C (-22°F). Similar tests were also undertaken at the UK's National Gas Turbine Establishment, at Pyestock, on an EH101 aerodynamic model.

Emergency flotation gear

The Merlin relies on four Kevlar-reinforced polythene floats, inflated by bottled helium. The system, developed by BAJ Ltd, features two floats on either side of the nose and two in the undercarriage sponsons.

ASW configuration

The Merlin's forward cabin will be given over to the two operators stations for the GEC-Marconi AQS-903 (export designation AQS-930) acoustic processing system. This handles and displays all inputs from deployed sonobouys and the dipping sonar. It is integrated with the rest of the Merlin's onboard systems via a MIL-STD-155B databus. Commercial EH101s will use an ARINC 429 databus. Two rotary sonobouy dispensers are located at the rear of the cabin. The dipping sonar, a late addition to the Merlin, is fitted in front of the port sonobouy dispenser. Up to four homing torpedoes can be carried on asymmetrical external pylons (two weapons on either side) and other stores carriers are located under the rear of the undercarriage sponsons.

Dipping sonar

Ferranti-Thomson Sonar Systems was selected in 1991 to provide the FLASH (Folding Light Acoustic System for Helicopters) sonar array and STRAP (Sonar Transmitter Receiver and Acoustic Processor) for the Merlin. Initial trials were carried out at the French navy's Lake Chaudanne facility.

Powerplants

By July 1993 PP4 had been fitted with RTM322 turboshafts. The engine layout has the No.1 engine to port, No. 2 on the centreline and No. 3 to starboard. A small intake to starboard feeds the APU.

Undercarriage

A hydraulically retractable tricycle undercarriage with steerable nosewheel has been developed by AP Precision Hydraulics in association with Officine Meccaniche Aeronautiche. Westland has drop-tested the EH101 to a survivable velocity of 35 ft (10.6 m) per second.

EH101 PP5 (Merlin HAS.Mk 1 ZF649)

Merlin systems integration

Westland's partner in the Merlin programme is now Loral ASIC, which acquired the previous contractor, IBM Federal Systems after a $1.5 billion deal, in March 1994.

Orange Reaper

The Merlin is fitted with Racal's Kestrel airborne ESM system, which bears the Royal Navy name Orange Reaper. With 360° azimuth coverage of the C- to J-bands, Orange Reaper displays threat information to the pilot on the standard tactical display, within one second of intercept. The system relies on a 'threat library' of emissions, and SADIE signal processor, to identify signals. A bearing accuracy of 3.5° is claimed through the use of very thin 'eggshell' radomes that permit highly accurate DF beam forming. The Merlin's six Orange Crop antennas are located above the nose, above the sponsons and on the upper rear fuselage.

PP5 was the sixth EH101 to fly, on 24 October 1989. Such was the confidence of the crew in their aircraft that this one-hour flight ended in an unscheduled night instrument landing. ZF649 went on to complete the first Merlin deck landings aboard HMS _Norfolk_ in November 1990. The second phase of sea trials, in March 1993, comprised 69 landings in 40-50 kt (74-80 km/h, 46-57 mph) winds and 20 ft (6.09 m) waves. The first two of seven production Merlins (RN1 and RN2) are scheduled to undertake operational performance acceptance trials in the Bahamas in 1998-1999. RN3 will go to the A&AEE, at RAF Boscombe Down, for service release trials, along with PP4. RN4 to RN7 will form the definitive Merlin trials unit in 1999. Further deliveries will take place in 1996 (three), 1997 (seven), 1998 (11) and 1999 (12).

Rotor head

The EH101 rotor uses both fibre-reinforced and metal components. The system is resistant to hits from a 23-mm shell and will continue running for 45 minutes with no oil in the gearbox.

Torpedo armament

Prime weapon for the Merlin is the Marconi Stingray torpedo, which entered development in 1977. Stingray became operational with the Royal Navy in 1985 as an advanced, lightweight and high-speed ASW weapon with a revolutionary propulsion system. Two contra-rotating water jets, along with four control surfaces, replace conventional propellers. Power is supplied by a magnesium/silver-chloride battery that uses sea water as the electrolyte. As a result, Stingray is inert until it enters the water, but can then 'power up' in only 1.5 seconds. On dropping, the torpedo descends on a parachute, then begins a pre-set (deep-diving) search pattern before acquiring the target with active/sonar sensors, which are reported to be almost impossible to evade. A still-classified 88-lb (40-kg) directed-energy warhead has been developed by Royal Ordnance. Italy's chief air-launched torpedo is the Whitehead Moto Fides-built A244/S, which replaced the US-designed Mk 44. A244/S is a lightweight, electrically powered weapon for use in shallow water, with a high-explosive, shaped-charge warhead. It uses an advanced guidance system, CIACIO-S, which combines active, passive and mixed modes to find its target.

Fuel system

The standard EH101 fuel load is 3222 litres (851 US gal) distributed between three tanks, each feeding a single engine. Emergency cross-feeding is possible, as is fitting a fourth and fifth tank for a maximum fuel capacity of 5370 litres (1417 US gal). A single-point pressure refuelling system allows the aircraft to be completely refuelled (three standard tanks) in less than five minutes

EH Industries EH 101

1991. Both it and PP8 later became involved in 6,000 additional flying hours (beyond the original total of 4,000) for reliability trials and to prove the hoped-for MTBO of 3,000 hours for the type. Royal Navy sea trials began in August 1991 when PP5 began Type 23 interface testing aboard HMS *Norfolk*. These included deck locking (using the Fairey Hydraulics-developed 'harpooning' system), recovery handling, rotor and tail folding and weapons handling. PP5 then went to sea aboard HMS *Iron Duke*, carrying out the first overwater sonobouy releases, and completed this phase of testing by December 1992.

UK and Canadian go-ahead, at last

The Westland/IBM team was finally selected by the MoD as its prime contractor with the signing of the EH101 project's fourth MoU, on 30 September 1991. At last a firm order (amounting to £1.5 billion), for 44 Merlins, was signed on 9 October 1991. The first example would be delivered in 1996, with deliveries completed by 2001. UK and Italian civil certification was now planned for 1993 and this would encompass the increasingly important utility version. This version was to feature, unexpectedly, in the final Canadian EH101 deal, announced by Canada's Defence Minister, Marcel Masse. The number of aircraft in this contract, which was signed on 24 July 1992, was at last fixed at 50. The Cdn $4.4 billion order was divided between the original New Ship Board aircraft requirement and a New Search and Rescue Helicopter (NSH), replacing the 13 remaining land-based CH-113A Labrador search and rescue (SAR) helicopters. Canada agreed to acquire 35 ASW EH101s under the designation CH-148 Petrel, along with 15 SAR-configured transport versions as the CH-149 Chimo (Inuit for 'welcome'), with deliveries beginning in 1998.

On 30 October 1991 a Canadian Hercules crashed at the far northern base of Alert. Although SAR missions were launched from three other bases, rescuers were finally air-dropped from another Hercules, in winds gusting to 50 mph, because no helicopters could reach the crash site in time. In an epic journey a CH-113 took three days to reach the stricken CC-130. Over that time the SAR crew could undertake only 'hot' refuellings as they were too afraid to shut down the Labrador's engines in the Arctic conditions. In April 1992 a CH-113 crashed after an engine failure. These events, among others (a Sea King was lost in April 1994, along with two crew, and a Labrador and Sea King were both forced down with technical problems within days of each other in June 1994),

reinforced the need for a modern SAR helicopter. A CH-149 would be capable of reaching anywhere in Canada below the Arctic circle in 12 hours, or eight with inflight refuelling support. With IFR a CH-149 could have reached Alert in 18 hours.

Agusta would supply 'empty air vehicles' for the CH-148, and Westland those for the CH-149, which would be then be outfitted in Canada. Total offsets for Canadian industry were worth 113 per cent of the contract value, with Canadian firms supplying 10 per cent of the airframe and 83 per cent of the electronics. In addition, Canada would supply 10 per cent of components for future EH101 production. Paramax Systems Canada was responsible for integrating all the Canadian-specific mission equipment, which varied considerably from version to version.

Canada's sea-going NSA

The CH-148 Petrel (NSA) was intended to replace the 32 (now 29) surviving CH-124A Sea Kings. Twenty-three would be based at Shearwater, Nova Scotia, on the east coast and 12 at Comox, British Columbia, on the west. The CH-148 would have a crew of four (two pilots, navigator and sensor operator) and go to sea aboard Canada's 12 new 'Halifax'-class frigates, two 'Annapolis'-class destroyers and the navy's three operational support ships.

The NSA's complex mission system, integrated by Paramax, combined a FLIR, ESM, search radar, IFF, sonar and (24) sonobouys, stores management system and a mission data system using a large, four-MFD Mission System Data Handling console in the main cabin, operated by the SENSO (sensor operator). The screens on the MSDH were colour units, but data could also be displayed on two monochrome screens in the cockpit. The less sophisticated, purely land-based CH-149 (NSH) needed a sea-search radar, weather radar and FLIR integrated through a common display. Furthermore, it demanded a long-range communications fit and homing receivers for emergency beacons. Based on the ramp-equipped utility EH101, it also required a rescue hoist mounted above the port cabin door. A crew of five (two pilots, navigator and two SAR specialists/winchmen) would be carried as standard, in addition to a rescue team of 30, or eight stretchers and 10 sitting casualties. The Italian-built PP6 conducted successful rotor downwash trials to qualify the EH101 for its SAR role. In all, 39 names were considered for the CH-148 (including 'Sylphid', 'Lucifer' and 'Ptarmigan') and 15 for the CH-149 (including 'Descry' and 'Nereus').

The contract for the airframes alone was worth Cdn $2.1 billion (in 1991), with the CH-148 and CH-149 priced at Cdn $44 million and Cdn $33 million (including development costs), respectively. The first Basic Vehicle (BV) EH101 was expected to fly, in Europe, during the first half of 1996, with the first NSA BV due to be delivered to Canada later that year. Delivery of the first NSH was expected in 1998. NSA mission testing would run from 1998 to late 2000, with production deliveries commencing in 1999. Agusta would continue building the 35 NSA airframes until 2001. NSH flight testing was to begin in mid-1998, followed by service deliveries in early 1999. Production would continue until 2000 at Yeovil.

EHI lost a 1993 Dutch order for 17 transport helicopters to the Eurocopter Cougar (which, along with the Sikorsky Blackhawk, was always better placed to win). Despite this, the Utility EH101 is still the type's best sales prospect.

PP5 was warmly adopted by HMS Iron Duke during the time it spent aboard. For the aircraft's second batch of trials in the English Channel and North Atlantic (over four days in March 1993), Colin Hague was the pilot in command.

Even at this early stage, the EH101 decision was a subject of political controversy. The opposition Liberal party, not disputing the EH101's suitability, balked at the programme's substantial cost. In its defence, the Conservative government pointed to Canada's recent involvement in Operation Desert Storm, the ongoing use of CH-124s in support of Canadian troops in Sarajevo and the need to have a modern SAR helicopter to cover the nation's 20 million km² landmass and coastline.

Westland and Agusta continued EH101 flight testing as planned until tragedy struck in Italy, early in 1993. PP2 had been fitted with the first full Active Control of Structural Response (ACSR) system and had completed fatigue life testing on its dynamic components. It commenced noise suppression trials at Cameri air base, where it crashed after entering an uncontrollable roll following a rotor brake failure, on 21 January. All four crew on board were killed and flying was suspended until 24 June.

Canadian controversy

The EH101 was also in trouble in Canada, where it had become a serious election issue. Appalled by the programme's rising cost, Jean Chrétien, the opposition Liberal leader, pledged to cancel the EH101 immediately upon taking power. The Conservatives responded by cutting the order, in September 1993, to 43 aircraft, at an alledged saving of Cdn $1 billion. They also pointed to the enormous price of cancellation, which even the Liberals admitted could cost the country $Cdn 100-300 million in addition to the $Cdn 350-400 million already spent on the programme. In due course, Chrétien was elected and on day one of his term personally announced the death of the EH101 in Canada – effectively tearing up a signed contract. The deputy NSA project manager thus became the head of the NSA termination team and personally assessed the cancellation costs at $Cdn 250 million. The president of Paramax (a former Chief of the Defence Staff) stated that with all the hidden costs factored into the equation it could amount to $Cdn 1 billion. The 1994 Canadian Auditor General's report made no mention of the subject.

Work continues on the Royal Navy's Merlins, with PP4 and PP5 both flying with RTM322 engines. PP4 was the first to be so fitted, making its first flight with the new powerplants as early as 6 June 1993. PP5 is currently involved in trials of the Ferranti-Thomson-designed FLASH dipping sonar and associated AN/AQS 950 acoustic processor. In November 1994 GEC took over Ferranti International's 50 per cent share in the Anglo-French sonar company, with Thomson's agreement, thus buying itself back into the EH101 sonar programme.

Talks have been held between the UK and Saudi governments on a possible Merlin sale in response to Iran's acquisition of Russian-built 'Kilo'-class attack submarines. Other Gulf states are interested in a new ASW helicopter, although the poor performance of the 'Kilo'-class boats in Iran's hands (an expected third example will probably not now be delivered) may lead to a lessening of the percieved threat in the region.

EH101 and the army

The EH101 is faced with a 'lessening of the percieved threat' worldwide as it becomes yet another modern combat aircraft that was conceived in the Cold War only to emerge into a very different political scene. EHI is struggling to have the type adopted by the RAF and is placing increasing emphasis on the type's transport capabilities, as the high-tech ASW scenario has, in the eyes of many, become non-existent. By mid-1994 the RAF's long-standing support helicopter requirement seemed almost certain to be filled by a mix of perhaps (15) Chinooks and (25) EH101s. The proposal to replace elderly Wessex HC.Mk 2s with surplus Army Air Corps Lynxes has also alarmed the RAF. The Lynx is viewed as far too small and aircrew-intensive by the RAF, and so the EH101 is a contender as a Wessex/Puma replacement also. On 1 December 1993 a government statement confirmed that the EH101 was the aircraft of choice as the RAF's next 'tactical transport helicopter', but no timetime or number for acquisition has been confirmed.

The lessening of tension in Europe, in the EH101/Merlin's intended arena at least, has seen the need for its sophisticated ASW skills become much less important. Orders for a military utility version, a task to which it is eminently suited, would most likely be driven by a successful introduction into service with its initial customers. The UK has still only signed for 44, and the Italian buy has been gradually chipped away to a mere 16 with options on eight. Even this was thrown into confusion with the cuts announced in the 1995 Italian defence budget, when L120 billion was withdrawn from the initial tranche of EH101 funding. Further bad news for Agusta came in an even more severe (L190 billion) cut in funds for the Mangusta attack helicopter. The Italian firm was still recovering from the liquidation of its state-owned parent company, EFIM, from which Agusta SpA was transferred to its current owner, Finmeccanica, in January 1993.

The implications that this loss of funding will have for Agusta, Westland (now owned by the UK's GKN, since early 1994, as part of GKN Aerospace and Special Vehicles) and the entire EH101 programme is still unclear, but it places the 'helicopter without a role' even closer to having no customers, either. This situation does no justice to the EH101's technical excellence and obvious ability. **Robert Hewson**

The Royal Navy and Marines (and RAF) have a significant number of Sea Kings fulfilling a variety of roles. While not as old as some of their compatriots worldwide, a modern successor would be warmly welcomed. It remains to be seen to what extent that successor will be the EH101.

Fouga Fanfare

The Armée de l'Air's prime Magister operator is Groupement d'Instruction 312, part of the Ecole de l'Air at Salon-de-Provence. The first of its four component squadrons began Magister operations in May 1956, although the CM.170's days are now numbered with the advent of the EMBRAER EMB-312 Tucanos.

Fouga et Cie had been a builder of only glider and experimental aircraft until the CM.170 Magister first flew in 1952. Nearly 1,000 Magisters were built over the next 19 years, not only in France but also in Germany, Finland and Israel. Forty years on, this classic design is still training French air force and naval aircrew.

Etablissement Fouga et Cie had managed an aircraft factory at its Aire-sur-Adour home (near Toulouse) since 1936. In the post-war years the company dabbled with early jet designs, mating simple engines with the graceful glider/sailplane designs with which the firm had extensive experience. By the early 1950s, the Armée de l'Air had a pressing need for a primary jet trainer to prepare pilots for its (NATO-supplied) F-84E and F-84Fs, and the imminent F-100s. In 1951 Fouga won a contract from the French Air Ministry for three prototype CM.170R Magisters, a slender swallow-tailed two-seat trainer, to fill this requirement, and the first aircraft made its maiden flight on 23 July 1952. An order for 95 Magisters placed in 1954 soon grew to 350 for France alone, and production was undertaken at Toulouse. An extensive evaluation of the type was made by NATO's Military Agency for Standardisation, which recommended that the CM.170 become the standard NATO basic and intermediate trainer.

While these plans were upset somewhat by France's departure from NATO, the Magister entered service in Belgium (to train Dutch pilots also) and Germany, in addition to seven other customers for new-build aircraft around the world, such as Austria, Finland, Cambodia and Lebanon. For the French navy, Fouga developed the CM.175 Magister Marine – with the French service name Zéphyr – which first flew on 31 July 1956. A total of 30 was placed on order by the Aéronavale, along with two prototypes.

In September 1956 Établissement Fouga was absorbed by a conglomeration of Breguet, Dassault, Morane-Saulnier, Sud-Est and Sud-Ouest Aviation, while production and development of the CM.170 continued apace. The new firm, known as Air-Fouga, was then incorporated by Établissments Henry Potez, changing name once more to Potez Air-Fouga in May 1958.

On 28 August 1962 the prototype CM.170 Super Magister with uprated Marboré VI turbojets, instead of the original Marboré IIAs, took to the air at Toulouse-Blagnac. Potez also attempted to further the design under its own name, as the Marboré VI-powered Potez 94 (originally CM.173 Super Magister). This version featured increased fuel capacity, ejection seats, increased armament options and, more noticeably, a reprofiled, pointed nose. The prototype Potez 94 flew on 8 June 1964 but the type never entered production. In April 1967 Potez became part of Sud-Aviation and, when the latter merged with Nord and SEREB to produce Aérospatiale, the Magister came under the aegis of that company for the final years of its production life.

The last CM.170 to be built was a Super Magister delivered to the Brazilian air force in 1971. In total, 929 Magisters were delivered to 11 nations. In the years that followed, Aérospatiale did a slow but steady trade in refurbishing and reselling aircraft, ensuring that the type remains in constant use with several air forces to this day. Aérospatiale also attempted to breath new life into the design with the Fouga 90. This hump-backed trainer retained the basic wing and tail layout of the Magister (although without tip tanks) while adding a stepped cockpit, modern systems and avionics, and Turboméca Astafan IIG turbofans. The sole Fouga 90 made its maiden flight on 20 August 1978, but the aircraft attracted no orders.

Today, the largest Magister operators are, naturally, the Armée de l'Air and Aéronavale, which took delivery of 400 (including 130 Super Magisters) and 32 (CM.175), respectively. Despite the advent of the Alpha Jet and Epsilon trainers, perhaps 70 Magisters remain with the air force alongside 12 hook-equipped navy aircraft.

Above: The Magister's cockpit has not changed at all since the day it was delivered and is supremely unsophisticated – the instrument panel is open at the back, exposing a clutter of wiring for all to see. The large red handle to the left is the canopy locking mechanism

Right: The crew can simply swing their legs over the cockpit sill to get into a CM 170 and once inside a parachute pack contributes to the passenger's comfort in the small wooden seats.

Above: The current Armée de l'Air Magister training syllabus includes some 64 flying hours, after candidates have transitioned from the CAP 10. GI 312 has four component escadrons: 1 EIV 'Defens', 2 EIV 'Montmirail', 3 EIV 'Côte Bleue' and 4 ECS 'Verdon'.

Below: GI 312's southerly home at Base Aérienne (BA) 701 Salon-de-Provence places the unit's aircraft and crews within a few minutes' flying time of the Golfe du Lion and French Mediterranean coast.

Above: All the Escadrons d'Instruction of GI 312 wear the parent unit's badge of a dark blue bird of prey carrying a black dagger to its chicks in their nest. The remaining Armée de l'Air CM.170s are now all Super Magister standard aircraft fitted with two 4.7-kN (1,058-lb) Marboré VI turbojet. As befits an engine of its diminutive power output, the Marboré is a tiny piece of engineering which takes up perhaps 10 per cent of the Magister's mid-set engine intakes.

Left: The instructor in the rear seat of the CM.170 relies on a (surprisingly effective) periscope for the majority of his forward vision, as any occupant of the compact rear cockpit sits on exactly the same level as the front seat and has to cope with heavy canopy framing, too. In the background can be seen an Alpha Jet of the 'Patrouille de France', with which GI 312 shares BA 701.

Right: Based at Hyères, 59 Escadrille undertakes carrier qualification training for the Aéronavale with the CM.175 Zéphyr and Dassault Super Etendard. Primary flying training for all French navy pilots is undertaken by the Armée de l'Air. 59S formed at Hyères in February 1956 as an all-weather fighter pilot training squadron equipped with the F6F Hellcat and So 30P Corse. The Zéphyr was added to the fleet in October 1959, and for a period the unit also operated the Breguet Alizé. With the advent of the Rafale M and the Charles de Gaulle nuclear-powered carrier, replacement of the ageing Zéphyrs is becoming urgent.

Left: The Zéphyr boasts an arrester hook and strengthened Messier landing gear for shipboard operations. The nosewheel gear has been lengthened by 0.15 m (6 in) when compared to that of the CM.170 to cope with the catapults aboard the current Aéronavale carriers, Clemenceau (R98) and Foch (R99). The CM.175 undertook its own deck landing trials and qualification at RAE Bedford in 1956, before going to sea for deck trials aboard HMS Bulwark – Clemenceau was not completed until November 1961 and Foch not until July 1963.

Below: The canopy of the Zéphyr has been modified to incorporate two separate rearward-sliding hoods – the Magister's cockpits are fitted with upward-hinging units. The badge of 59S features a white goose, with yellow beak and feet, landing on a black turtle against a light- and dark-blue background of sky and sea. As the question of a CM.175 replacement looms, possible answers may come in the form of a navalised 'Alpha Jet N' or the T-45 Goshawk.

F-15E
Strike Eagle

Turning the West's best air-to-air fighter into a nocturnal mud-mover was an idea opposed by many, yet today's F-15E is without doubt the most capable strike/attack platform in the world, while having lost little of its air combat prowess. A sophisticated attack system, centred around the ground-mapping capabilities of the APG-70 and the terrain-following and night vision functions of the LANTIRN pods, allows unmatched bombing accuracy with a wide variety of weapons, across a full range of delivery profiles, while the radar confers advanced BVR capability in the air-to-air arena.

Main picture: An F-15E of the 48th Fighter Wing cavorts over the Turkish coast. The asymmetrical weapon load includes all three available air-to-air missiles (AIM-7 Sparrow, AIM-9 Sidewinder and AIM-120 AMRAAM) with two GBU-12 500-lb (227-kg) laser-guided bombs.

fficially, it is now known simply as the F-15E Eagle. Its makers called it the Strike Eagle while, at times during the hard-fought contest which created the aircraft, its detractors dubbed it the 'Strike Pig' or 'Wart-Eagle' on account of its less than graceful looks. Spotters talk of 'Beagles', while pilots of other aircraft refer to 'Mudhens'. Its own crews usually call it simply the 'E' – a non-descriptive epithet which somehow renders the aircraft as something very special. And special it is.

Ugly it may be, but the F-15E is without doubt the most capable and versatile warplane in service today. It may not be as comfortable as an F-111 at low level, but its attack weapon system is without peer in a service aircraft. Whip the bombs off and what remains is basically a standard F-15 Eagle – the West's premier air-to-air fighter with an unmatched track record and an estimated 96-nil kill/loss score. An F-15E pilot described his job succinctly: "We blow things up on the ground, and we shoot things down in the air."

Genesis

"[It shows a] tremendous air-to-ground capability." These prophetic words were uttered by Major General Benjamin N. Bellis, head of the Air Force F-15 SPO (System Project Office) on the event of the first prototype YF-15A Eagle being rolled out at St Louis. First flying on 27 July 1972, the YF-15A was clearly going to be a winner in air-to-air combat, but McDonnell Douglas also extolled its ability to drop bombs with great accuracy without detracting from its primary counter-air mission. During early development work YF-15s carried bombs on multiple ejector racks under the wing and centreline pylons to emphasise the fact, and brochures were printed depicting a variety of delivery profiles, including EO (Electro-Optical)/laser-guided bombs and CCIP deliveries. Early production aircraft were wired for air-to-ground ordnance, but the software was never integrated into the weapon system. Later, production fighters gave up even the wiring, and from 1975 there was no official interest whatsoever in the Eagle's secondary capability. The sign 'Not a pound for air-to-ground' was hung in the F-15 SPO, and no-one dared suggest otherwise apart, that is, from the manufacturer.

While the F-15 SPO at Wright-Patterson AFB, OH, actively discouraged any attempt to turn the F-15 into a fighter-bomber, McDonnell Douglas nevertheless maintained its belief in the aircraft's dual-role potential, and kept working on proposals for such a machine. The goal was to augment and eventually replace the Air Force's fleet of General Dynamics F-111s, which had ended production in 1976, replace the remaining F-4s in service and to augment the F-15 fighter force. The main theatre of operation was seen as Central Europe, where the USAF's two wings of F-111s would have been hard-pressed to meet the long list of demands made of them in time of war.

Left: Much of the F-15E development was undertaken by the company's two-seat demonstrator, 71-0291. Much earlier, the aircraft was used to test the standard F-15's ability to drop bombs, carrying 18 Mk 82 low-drag bombs on three MERs.

Below left: During YF-15 trials this Eglin-based aircraft released an early GBU-10 Paveway I laser-guided weapon. At the time the F-15 had not been tested with any autonomous designation equipment.

Below: A dramatic shot from the mid-1970s shows '291' releasing its impressive bombload. From the outset the F-15 showed great attack potential, but the Air Force insisted on it being strictly an air-to-air fighter when it entered service.

NATO was embarking on a new strategy of FOFA (Follow-On Forces Attack), based on the realisation that an enormous and unaffordable force would be needed to meet the Warsaw Pact's opening assault, but by using smaller numbers of sophisticated weapons on deep interdiction attacks to stop supplies and reinforcements reaching the front, the initial assault would be unsustainable and would grind to a halt after a short advance, by which time battlefield systems could have been deployed from CONUS to decimate the cut-off vanguard of the WarPac advance. The interdiction aircraft would assume even greater importance after the ratification of the INF treaty, which removed theatre nuclear missiles from the FOFA equation.

Although the late-production F-111F was an excellent aircraft in most respects for the FOFA role, there were insufficient numbers to achieve the USAF's goals, and from a political standpoint the whole 'Aardvark' programme was set against a backdrop of a disastrous development saga, inauspicious combat debut and continuing maintenance nightmares with some of the earlier models. Mud sticks, and no amount of pinpoint bombing in appalling weather could shake off the load which 'McNamara's Folly' carried with it.

In 1978 the Air Force ordered the Tactical All-Weather Requirements Study to evaluate the McDonnell Douglas proposal, now known as Strike Eagle, and other options. The initial recommendation was the purchase of further

Right: In Strike Eagle guise, '291' was an awesome aircraft, shown here with a full load of Mk 7 Rockeye CBUs on wing and fuselage pylons. Only one pylon was mounted on each CFT. The Strike Eagle was also known as the Advanced Fighter Capability Demonstrator, hence the 'AFC Demo' badge on the fin.

Below: Essential to the ability of the F-15E to undertake its deep strike mission, the conformal fuel tanks are easily removed when not required, using a standard bomb trolley. This photograph was taken during tank development, when they were still known as FAST Packs. Not surprisingly, the trials aircraft for the initial tests was the long-suffering '291'.

Opposite page: For its initial demonstrations and DRF trials, '291' wore a two-tone tactical camouflage. Here the aircraft is seen carrying an AVQ-26 Pave Tack target acquisition and designation pod under the port CFT pylon, while the centreline pylon accommodates a GPU-5 cannon pod. Unlike production F-15Es, '291' had no cannon fitted, but was tested extensively with up to three of the pods.

F-111Fs, as the aircraft had matured into a reliable weapon system with blistering low-level terrain-following performance and an outstanding ability to deliver weapons with then unmatched precision. After further deliberation (believed by many to be as a result of political rather than operational considerations), the TAWRS group adopted the Strike Eagle as its recommendation for a future strike platform. History later added its own irony during the Gulf War, when the F-111F proved by a considerable margin to be the most destructive and cost-effective warplane fielded by the coalition. In late 1994, with ongoing attempts to 'kill' it coming from many sides of the political forum, both in the Pentagon and on Capitol Hill, the F-111F continues in service as the USAF's prime PGM (precision-guided munition) muscle, and seems likely to be funded through 1999.

In the Vietnam War, some F-111A missions were accomplished with single aircraft, without the need for costly packages of escort fighters, AWACS and electronic warfare support. In the late 1970s, the USAF still wanted this single-aircraft strike mission capability, but the projected threat from enemy fighters with new look-down/shoot-down radars meant that aircraft such as the F-111 would require fighter cover during operations through high-threat airspace. Therefore, any new strike aircraft would not only have to match or better the F-111 in precision bombing and low-level navigation, but also be able to fight its way through enemy fighters if the situation required such action. The programme acquired the name ETF (Enhanced Tactical Fighter), and later Dual Role Fighter (DRF).

Airborne demonstrator

To further its Strike Eagle proposal, McDonnell Douglas teamed with radar supplier Hughes to fund a strike demonstrator. The aircraft chosen was the hard-working second TF-15A prototype 71-0291, which first flew in its new guise on 8 July 1980. Also known as the Advanced Fighter Capability Demonstrator, this aircraft had previously been used to undertake trials with conformal fuel tanks (CFTs). These had been developed in 1974 (first flown on 27 July) for the standard fighter Eagle under the designation FAST Pack (Fuel And Sensor, Tactical). Fitting snugly along the sides of the engine trunks, the FAST packs were 32 ft (9.75 m) long, and added 1,446 US gal (5474 litres) to the internal fuel capacity. Although they could not be jettisoned in flight, they could be removed in as little as 15 minutes.

In addition to the considerable amount of extra fuel, McDonnell Douglas had envisaged FAST Packs to cater for a variety of tasks. Cameras could be fitted in the front of the pack for reconnaissance, or electronic warfare equipment for defence suppression. Alternatively, the 'Strike

F-15E Strike Eagle

Assist' package could mount a FLIR or LLLTV turret for all-weather attack, and a laser designator. Another scheme was to mount rockets in the rear of the pack to assist high-weight take-offs. Weapons could be mounted on the lower corner of the packs, and in the event this was the only feature to be adopted for the production pallets, with F-15Cs carrying two AIM-7 Sparrows from each tank. The FAST Packs carried by the Strike Eagle demonstrator had only one hardpoint mounted midway along their length.

SAR radar

By far the most important component of the Strike Eagle was its new radar, a modified version of the APG-63PSP used in the fighter Eagle. While retaining all of the modes of the APG-63, the new radar also incorporated a synthetic aperture (SAR) high-resolution mapping (HRM) mode. Previously this had been reserved for side-looking reconnaissance radars, such as that fitted to the OV-1D Mohawk. The fighter Eagle's look-down/shoot-down radar already had a ground-mapping mode with a resolution in the order of 50 ft (15 m), but the Strike Eagle's HRM could produce extraordinary god's-eye view images of near photo-like quality, known in the trade as patch maps. As will be explained later, these allowed the early acquisition and designation of targets, and could be used to cue other sensors.

For the Strike Eagle, the principal sensor package was the AVQ-26 Pave Tack pod, later used to devastating effect by the F-111F. Carried under a FAST Pack, the AVQ-26 had a fully articulated turret housing a forward-looking infrared for target acquisition and a boresighted laser designator/rangefinder, allowing the autonomous launch of laser-guided weapons and assisting greatly in the all-weather delivery of free-fall stores. The rear cockpit of the aircraft was 'missionised' with CRT (cathode ray tube) displays for the radar and Pave Tack imagery.

Hughes delivered the prototype SAR radar in late 1980, shortly after 71-0291 had made an impressive showing at the Farnborough air show, where it had been displayed carrying five of the McDonnell Douglas MER 200 supersonic multiple ejector racks and a wide range of weapons includ-

ing AGM-84 Harpoon anti-ship missiles and MATRA Durandal runway-cratering munitions. Through 1981 the aircraft demonstrated and refined the outstanding capabilities of its new technology so, when the USAF officially launched the Dual Role Fighter competition in 1982, McDonnell Douglas and Hughes were far better prepared than the General Dynamics team which faced them.

Of course there were other contenders for the DRF requirement. Panavia's Tornado was an obvious candidate, but it lacked convincing air-to-air capability, and was perceived in the US as being short on range. No matter how good it may or may not have been, it never seriously challenged simply because it was not American. That left the Strike Eagle in a head-to-head confrontation with the General Dynamics F-16XL.

Known by the acronym SCAMP (Supersonic Cruise and Maneuvering Prototype), the cranked-arrow wing F-16XL

was a most promising design, which by virtue of radical aerodynamics had raised the standard F-16's performance, load and range figures through the roof. Prototypes were produced of single- and two-seat versions, which would have had the service designations F-16E and F-16F respectively.

To complement the Strike Eagle demonstrator in the DRF evaluation, McDonnell Douglas used the first F-15C to test new conformal fuel tanks. 71-0291 had only one pylon on each of its tanks, but new tanks were developed which each had two rows of three pylons, giving the aircraft a total of 12. So equipped, 78-0468 flew 91 sorties during early 1983 from Edwards. In order to preserve the range performance of the production aircraft the CFTs were considered a permanent feature, although they are still routinely and easily removed from F-15Es for maintenance. Further evaluation was undertaken using the Nos 27 and 36 F-15Ds, 80-0055 flying 22 weapons separation evaluation sorties at Eglin AFB, while 81-0063 performed 36 operational evaluation sorties from Edwards.

Under the direction of Brigadier General Ronald W. Yates, Deputy for Tactical Systems at Aeronautical Systems Division, the DRF evaluation ran through 1982 and the flying was completed by May 1983. On 24 February 1984, the F-15E was announced the winner of the competition, effectively ending any chance of the F-16XL attaining production, despite its obvious qualities. There were several key factors in the decision, notably the low development and production cost of the F-15E, which virtually existed anyway, and the size of the aircraft, which allowed it to easily accommodate the required systems while still providing room for future growth. Range and performance requirements were met with ease, and the aircraft had its astounding air-to-air capability already proven. Projected attrition rate was expected to be lower than that for the F-16XL.

The prize was an expected order for around 400 aircraft, later formalised at 392 units. While tests continued with the Strike Eagle, mainly concerning the radar, McDonnell Douglas began construction of the first production F-15 DRF, now designated F-15E. Resplendent in the charcoal grey scheme which has adorned all subsequent aircraft, 86-0183 was flown for the first time at St Louis on 11 December. After initial manufacturer's trials the aircraft was shipped to Edwards, where it remains today in a test function.

Delivery to the US Air Force of production aircraft began on 12 April 1988, when the first aircraft arrived at Luke AFB, AZ, for the 405th Tactical Training Wing,

For its first flight, 86-0183 was not fitted with any CFTs, pylons or other accoutrements of an 'E', looking for all the world just like an F-15D. Close examination reveals the stencil 'E001' on the fuselage side.

First service recipient of the F-15E was the Luke-based 461st TFS, which was instrumental in developing many F-15E operational tactics.

which undertook F-15 training for Tactical Air Command. The first squadron to form was the 461st TFS 'Deadly Jesters', later joined by the 550th TFS 'Silver Eagles' from May 1989. Front-line deliveries began to the 4th Tactical Fighter Wing at Seymour Johnson on 29 December 1988.

Airframe and powerplant

While externally similar to the F-15D, the 'E' is considerably redesigned within to cope with the rigours of the air-to-ground mission. Approximately 60 per cent of the structure was redesigned to allow 9*g* manoeuvring with heavy loads, and to handle the maximum take-off weight of 81,000 lb (36741 kg), although parts commonality with the F-15C/D remains high. Fatigue life has been extended to 16,000 hours. Further changes include the adoption of a Lear Astronics digital flight control system in place of the analog system used previously. The system is triply-redundant, with a mechanical back-up, and is tied into the terrain-following radar for full hands-off low-level flight. Likewise, the hydraulic system is triplicated for safety, and the voids between the fuel tanks and engines are filled with fire-retardant foam.

From the outset, the F-15E was designed with a common engine bay able to take either the Pratt & Whitney F100 or the General Electric F110. However, with one exception, the Pratt engine has powered all F-15Es to date. This initially came in the form of the F100-PW-220, rated at 14,670 lb (65.26 kN) dry and 23,830 lb (106.0 kN) with full afterburner. The Dash 220 was itself an improvement of the original F-15 engine (Dash 100), featuring digital engine control, new materials and heat transfer technology to extend life and increase safety.

On 2 May 1990 a 6512th Test Wing F-15E took off for the first time from Edwards AFB under the power of the F100-PW-229, Pratt's Improved Performance Engine. The IPE developed 17,800 lb (79.18 kN) thrust dry, and 29,100 lb (129.45 kN) with afterburner, for the installed weight penalty of just 505 lb (229 kg) per engine. With Dash 229s fitted, the F-15E easily 'supercruised' (flew supersonically without afterburner) during test flights. Another Edwards aircraft, 87-0180, was fitted with General Electric's IPE, the F110-GE-129, offering similar thrust performance to the Pratt & Whitney powerplant, and featuring a similar diameter of 3 ft 10.5 in (1.18 m). The GE engine is slightly shorter (15 ft 2 in/4.62 m as opposed to 15 ft 11 in/4.855 m), but in the event the F100 was retained for service aircraft.

Dash 220s powered the first 134 aircraft, but from August 1991 and aircraft 135 (90-0233) the Dash 229 was fitted, providing considerable extra performance which is much appreciated by the crews when hauling heavy bombloads. Externally there is little to tell the engines apart, but the Dash 229 has a very noticeable bluish tinge to the afterburner flame compared to the orange of the 220, and engages with quite a thump when the pilot guns the throttles. The latter phenomenon comes courtesy of the new DECU (Digital Engine Conrtol Unit), which allows the pilot to move from idle to full afterburner in under four seconds, half the time taken by earlier F100s. The DECU is contained in a modular package that can be easily taken out without removing the engine, although an engine change need only take 20 minutes in a combat scenario. Further improvements in maintainability have brought about a 50 per cent reduction in man-hours, while a novel automatic engine trim control has eliminated the need for fuel-costly trim runs, with a consequent six per cent fuel saving.

A capacity of 2,019 US gal (7643 litres) of fuel is carried internally, housed in structural wing tanks and six Goodyear fuselage tanks, all with internal foam filling. To this volume can be added a further 723 US gal (2737 litres) in each of the CFTs, carried as standard on all but basic

Thundering from Lakenheath's rain-drenched runway, a 492nd FS 'blue-tail' gets airborne for a mission in typically ugly English weather. The bluish tinge to the afterburner plume identifies this aircraft as a late-batch machine, powered by the powerful Dash 229 engine.

From head-on the F-15E appears especially brutish, befitting this aircraft's 'Screamin' Demon' nickname scrawled on the HUD cover. This aspect also serves to illustrate the considerable extra fuel capacity afforded by the CFTs.

flight handling training missions, and three 610-US gal (2309-litre) drop tanks on the two wing pylons and centre-line. Maximum fuel capacity is therefore 5,295 US gal (20044 litres). Naturally the boom receptacle is retained in the port wingroot.

Armament

In the starboard wingroot is the trusty 20-mm M61A1 Vulcan cannon, a six-barrelled rotary weapon with an ammunition drum mounted centrally behind the forward fuel tank holding 512 rounds. Able to lift a hefty 24,000 lb (10886 kg) of external stores, the basic F-15E has three main hardpoints, one under each wing and one on the cen-treline, all of which are plumbed for tanks. These are also able to mount triple or multiple ejector racks, although these are rarely seen as the pylons are usually required for extra fuel or heavy weapons. On either side of the wing pylons are shoulder LAU-114 launch rails for either AIM-9

Sidewinder or AIM-120 AMRAAM air-to-air missiles, with a mix of both being common (AIM-120 on outboard and AIM-9 on inboard). Also attached to the basic airframe are the LANTIRN pods under the engine intakes, and without CFTs the aircraft can also launch AIM-7 Sparrows from fighter F-15-style ejector racks on the fuselage 'cor-ners'.

However, giving the F-15E its considerable weapon load flexibility are the CFTs. Having undergone several recon-figurations during its development, the production F-15E CFT emerged with a continuous rack on the lower posi-tion, and a row of three small stub pylons in the upper position. While the stub pylons can only mount one weapon, usually of the 500-lb (227-kg) class, the lower rack can be reconfigured with various combinations of shackles to mount up to three smaller bombs in a row, two air-to-air missiles or two larger bombs. Combining the CFT posi-tions with the aircraft's fixed positions gives the F-15E

*Few aircraft can match the F-15E for its huge range of weapon options and armament configurations. This pair of Mountain Home 'Tigers' displays a typical loadout, seen often in Desert Storm, of four **GBU-10 Paveway II** LGBs. The more capable **GBU-24 Paveway III** is also available to the F-15E but is rarely seen, and is mainly issued to the F-111F force.*

Owing to the enormous range of weapon options, the clearance work undertaken by the Eglin-based 46th Test Squadron has been far more intensive for the F-15E than most types, and is ongoing. This example, liberally festooned with movie cameras to record the intimate moments of weapon release, carries four inert Mk 84s.

47

some impressive theoretical loads such as 26 Mk 82s, 15 GBU-12s or seven GBU-10s, and many variations of mixed loads. In practise, however, the loads are far more conservative but nevertheless still impressive in an operational scenario.

In an air-to-air configuration, ejector racks are fitted to the lower CFT positions to enable up to four AIM-7s or AIM-120s to be carried which, combined with the wing pylons, gives a maximum of eight AAMs. No more than four AIM-9s or four AIM-7s can be carried, but all eight positions can be occupied by AMRAAM if required. In some cases during the Gulf War, F-15Es were seen carrying AIM-7s from one CFT, with bombs on the other. The standard bombload for general purpose BAI work consists of 12 Mk 82s, or any of a variety of CBUs, carried on the upper and lower CFT stations in four rows of three. Alternatively, four Mk 84s can be carried, front and back, on the lower CFT position, with a further weapon optional under the centreline.

Precision attack

Several precision-guided munitions are currently available to the F-15E. The AGM-65 Maverick TV/IR-guided missile is carried on LAU-88 triple launchers from the wing pylons only, while the 2,000-lb (907-kg) GBU-15 EOGB (Electro-Optically Guided Bomb) is carried only from the wing pylons. The AGM-130 is a rocket-boosted version giving greater stand-off range. For both these weapons the AXQ-14 datalink pod is required, and this is installed on the centreline. The datalink receives TV or IR pictures from the seeker in the nose of the bomb, and displays them on the cockpit CRT screens, allowing the WSO to steer the bomb by reverse datalink.

Laser-guided bombs come in 500-lb (227-kg) or 2,000-lb (907 kg) class, the latter featuring either Paveway II (GBU-10) or Paveway III (GBU-24) seekers. The small GBU-12s can be carried fore and aft in the upper and lower CFT positions for a total of eight, while the GBU-10/24 is usually carried from the lower position or wing pylons only. GBU-24s are restricted from carriage on the rear of the CFT rack. The GBU-28 'Deep Throat' bomb was originally intended for launch by an F-15E, and is likely to be a current option, mounted on the wing pylon. Weaponry of an even more serious nature consists of the B61 tactical nuclear weapon, of which a total of five is theoretcial, although two is more practical, slung under the lower CFT rack. From 1995, AGM-88 HARM will be carried, while the F-15E is a prime candidate to receive the next generation of INS- and GPS-guided PGMs (JDAM, JSOW and TSSAM).

Radar

At the heart of the F-15's weapon system lies the APG-70 I-band radar and LANTIRN system. The radar is based on the F-15C's APG-63, but has significant improvements. Five old LRUs (line-replaceable units) have been replaced by four higher performance units, while two further LRUs have also been enhanced. Increased stability and higher average transmitter power result in greater range, and a new signal processor employing modular parallel processing elements can undertake over 30 million complex operations per second. This makes the processor five times faster than its predecessor, with memory increased tenfold. The planar array antenna is mounted on a three-axis gimbal, and the drive rate has been doubled to 140° per second.

In addition to its phenomenal mapping capabilities, the APG-70 has the full air-to-air modes used in the APG-63. For close-in work under 10 nm (11.5 miles; 18.5 km) the radar has three automatic acquisition modes, triggered by HOTAS controls, comprising boresight mode, 'supersearch' (where the radar locks on to the first target to enter the HUD field of view), and vertical scan. The radar automatically acquires and tracks the target, and generates steering cues in the pilot's HUD. A wide range of PRFs, pulsewidths and processing modes is available to make the APG-70 a most versatile air-to-air radar. However, in the context of the F-15E, it is its ability to produce very detailed patch maps that is the most noteworthy.

The process by which the radar produces such images is highly complex, involving the exploitation of the Doppler effect. Doppler shift from ground returns is a function of the relative velocity of the aircraft and the object reflecting the radar return. All of the points on the ground with a similar Doppler shift are arranged in a horseshoe around the nose of the aircraft: objects directly ahead of the aircraft have a much higher Doppler shift than those nearly abeam the aircraft where the relative velocity is much lower. A radar beam transmitted across a wide angle (at least 10° off the velocity axis) will then intersect these imaginary horseshoes at various points. The SAR radar 'knows' which Doppler shifts correspond to the axis of the beam, and can then interpret the raw radar returns to effectively narrow the beamwidth to a very low figure, thereby vastly improving resolution. Not only does this electronic number-crunching demand a very powerful computer, but it cannot produce imagery in real-time, requiring a few seconds to process the data.

In HRM mode, the aircraft is required to fly at least 10° off the direction to the target to allow the SAR technology to work to the full. Resolution and patch map size are a function of radar range to the target area, as presented in the table below which provides data from the maximum range down to the minimum resolution possible:

Range from target nm (miles; km)	Patch map size nm (miles; km)	Resolution ft (m)
160 (184; 296)	10 x 10 (11.5 x 11.5; 18.5 x 18.5)	127 (38.7)
80 (92; 148)	4.7 x 4.7 (5.4 x 5.4; 8.7 x 8.7)	59 (18)
50 (57.5; 93)	3.3 x 3.3 (3.8 x 3.8; 6.1 x 6.1)	42 (12.8)
20 (23; 37)	1.3 x 1.3 (1.5 x 1.5; 2.4 x 2.4)	17 (5.2)
10 (11.5; 18.5)	0.67 x 0.67 (0.77 x 0.77; 1.24 x 1.24)	8.5 (2.6)

Another limiting factor is the grazing angle, which is the angle subtended by the radar beam as it arrives at, or 'grazes', the horizon. In the case of the APG-70 the minimum is 0.5°, which equates to an altitude of 1,000 ft (305 m) at 20 nm (23 miles; 37 km) range. In order for the patch map to be made, the F-15E has to pop up for a few seconds to allow the radar to work in HRM mode successfully. Other complications arise from the radar's ability to work simultaneously in other modes, causing a 'timesharing' problem at the signal processor. Furthermore, the aircraft's inertial navigation system is required to work at six times its normal speed to furnish the radar with precise positional data during the mapping process.

LANTIRN

Equally important to the F-15E in its ability to perform its mission is the Martin Marietta (Lockheed Martin) LAN-TIRN (Low-Altitude Navigation and Targeting Infra-Red for Night) system. LANTIRN was one of the USAF's most important projects of the 1980s, growing out of an initial

desire to equip day-only F-16 and A-10 attack aircraft for the night mission. Again, the projected high-threat battle on the European Central Front was the spur to development: Pentagon war-gamers forecast huge losses to both enemy fighters and groundfire if the day-only mission was proceeded with. Equipping such aircraft with night systems would render them vulnerable primarily to radar-guided systems, which could be countered more easily through the use of jamming and lethal SEAD. In the event, it was the F-15E which was chosen as the 'launch' vehicle for the LANTIRN system, followed closely by the F-16C/D Block 40. The A-10's obsolescence and shift in mission removed it from the list of LANTIRN candidates.

LANTIRN comes packaged in two pods. Carried under the front of the starboard engine trunk is the AAQ-13 navigation pod, which has two components. The main pod

F-117 and F-111 crews may claim to own the night, but the combination of the APG-70 radar and LANTIRN makes the F-15E the most likely aircraft to find and hit a target in the dark. Such skills are practised regularly.

Carried beneath a 57th Wing F-15E are two BDU-38 training shapes for the deadly B61 'Silver Bullet'. This nuclear free-fall weapon has varying yields from 10 to 500 kT, and a wide range of delivery profiles.

section houses a Texas Instruments Ku-band terrain avoidance/following radar. This sensor has its antenna behind a small bullet-shaped radome, the rest of the main pod section consisting of a central spine to which is attached (from front to rear, starboard) the receiver/exciter, pressurisation unit, radar power supply and radar interface unit, and (front to rear, port) the transmitter and pod control computer. At the rear of the pod is the environmental control unit to maintain even temperatures. Initially the radar could only

supply terrain-avoidance commands on to the pilot's head-up display, but was subsequently integrated into the flight control and autothrottle system to provide full hands-off terrain following down to 200 ft (60 m). Due to its narrow beamwidth and power control, the TFR does little to give away the aircraft's position to hostile passive detectors, and it is difficult to jam.

Situated in a fairing above the TFR pod is a forward-looking infra-red. This is used purely for night/adverse

Testing for the LANTIRN system was undertaken with several aircraft, including the first F-15C, previously used for CFT development work. Here a prototype AAQ-14 targeting pod is carried during an October 1985 test flight, over a year before the first F-15E flew. This half of the system proved to be somewhat troublesome, and was much delayed. Working pods did not reach the operational units until late 1990.

Left: A remarkable view provides a graphic illustration of the relative sizes of the two pods which constitute the LANTIRN system. The AAQ-13 navigation pod is much smaller than the AAQ-14 targeting pod, although it contains two main components (TFR and FLIR). The AAQ-14 has a magnifying FLIR and laser in the nose, housed in a rotating and swivelling mount which can stay boresighted on a target in a nearly hemispherical area beneath the aircraft. The 610-US gal (2309-litre) drop tanks are usually carried on centreline and wing pylons for a maximum of three, and are a regular feature of F-15E operations. The CFTs and 81,000-lb (36740-kg) MTOW allow the aircraft to still carry a hefty bombload even when the mission radius requirements dictate that all three 'bags' must be carried.

Dominating the skies, the well trained and well co-ordinated F-15E crew are potentially the most capable warriors over the battlefield – at their control is the most sophisticated multi-role fighter aircraft in operational service. However, to use the F-15E and its systems to the full requires not only a thorough grounding in the many capabilities of the system, and much experience in using it, but also a close co-ordination between the two cockpits. Most tasks can be performed from either seat, so a perfect understanding between pilot and WSO is required for maximum crew performance.

Mk 84-carrying 3rd Wing F-15Es pull hard on a training mission. Although various PGMs are the weapons of choice for precision attacks, the weapon system can generate HUD steering cues for highly accurate free-fall bombing.

weather flying, and has a fixed field of view which correlates to a 1:1 image on the pilot's HUD. This allows him to fly head-up at night, with those few features that are visible by ambient light augmented by an overlaid FLIR image. A BIT (Built-In Test) module is located behind the FLIR, and a pod power supply behind that. As a whole, the AAQ-13 weighs around 430 lb (195 kg) and measures 12 in

(0.305 m) in diameter and 6 ft 6.2 in (1.98 m) in length.

Altogether heavier at around 540 lb (245 kg), and larger at 15 in (0.381 m) diameter and 8 ft 2.5 in (2.5 m) long, the AAQ-14 targeting pod occupies a similar position under the port engine intake. Surprisingly, the LANTIRN system on the F-16C has the sides reversed, with the AAQ-14 to starboard. Pods are basically interchangeable between the

Right and opposite page: Two views from either end of the refuelling operation. A Rand study into the payload/range characteristics of the F-16C Block 50 and F-15E concluded that inflight refuelling greatly increased the cost-effectiveness of both aircraft. McDonnell Douglas is investigating larger drop tanks, larger CFTs and greater internal fuel capacity for the F-15E. While it may not be possible to raise the take-off weight without structural changes, the maximum inflight weight could possibly be increased to cater for the extra fuel, enabling F-15Es to top off after take-off for much increased range.

The 'missionised' rear cockpit is dominated by the four CRT displays. This is a typical configuration, with the left colour MFD showing navigation data and the right colour MFD the tactical situation display (moving map). The two central monochrome MFDs show radar data (right) and a HUD repeater (left). The latter comprises standard flight data overlaid on a FLIR image from the AAQ-13 navigation pod.

During refuelling the pilot keeps station on the tanker while the WSO checks the boom as it mates with the receptacle in the port wingroot. The dominant feature of the front cockpit is the very large HUD, upon which a 1:1 FLIR image can be presented to give the pilot a 'window in the night'.

two types of aircraft, albeit with minor interface software changes. As its name suggests, the AAQ-14 is the main attack sensor for the F-15E, and is similar in function to the much larger Pave Tack carried by the F-111F.

In the nose of the pod is a fully-articulated turret housing a FLIR and laser. The targeting FLIR has a much narrower field of view than the nav FLIR, and has several magnification settings for zooming in on a target for designation. Boresighted with the FLIR is a laser, which can be used as a rangefinder for accurate dumb weapon release, or fire coded pulses of laser energy to designate for laser-guided weapons. Like other such systems, it has a contrast auto-tracker (working in area or point modes) to remain locked on to a designated point, the turret moving relative to the aircraft to keep the sensor (and laser) firmly aligned with the target. There is also an automatic infra-red Maverick hand-off system which cues and locks on the missile to the pod's designated target. Provision is made for an automatic target recognition function.

Behind the FLIR/laser turret are LRUs housing a pod control computer, missile boresight correlator, laser synchroniser and range computer, central electronics unit and pod power supply. Again at the rear is an environmental control unit with a small airscoop on the starboard side. In addition to the power supplies, the pods interface via MIL-STD-1553 databuses to the flight control and weapon systems. The latter interface allows the APG-70 radar to cue the targeting pod to the target area from considerable distance. Video channels provide data to the cockpit displays.

Production AAQ-13s were first handed over to the USAF on 1 April 1987, and the system integration was performed without fuss. However, the first targeting pod was not delivered until the summer of 1988, and proved rather troublesome, causing a considerable slippage in deliveries. During the Gulf War, there were few combat-coded AAQ-14s to be handed around the 48 F-15Es assembled in-the-atre, and none for the F-16C Block 40s. Consequently many missions were flown with an AAQ-14 aircraft 'buddy-lasing' for other aircraft. Certainly the lack of targeting pods gave the F-111F its chance to monopolise the PGM glory, an opportunity the 'Aardvark' community took with both hands. Post-war deliveries of AAQ-14 speeded up, and with the bugs ironed out the whole LANTIRN package proved to be an outstanding success.

Cockpit

From the point of view of an avionics technician, the F-15E with APG-70 and LANTIRN is a masterpiece, but where this sophistication really counts is in the cockpit. Drawing heavily on experience with the F/A-18 Hornet, which featured the first really 'modern' cockpit based on large CRT displays, McDonnell Douglas endeavoured to match the crew work-stations with the aircraft's state-of-the-art avionics.

In the front cockpit the pilot has a single Sperry 5 x 5-in colour display in the lower centre position, and two Kaiser 6 x 6-in monochrome displays in the upper left and right positions, between which is an UFC (UpFront Controller) for entering nav/comms information, IFF and HUD commands. The colour CRT is often used for an attitude display or moving map, while the monochrome CRTs give attack and navigation data.

Above the cockpit dash is the very large Kaiser ID-2349/A HUD holographic wide field-of-view HUD. This features a single combiner glass allowing the unit to be very light, in turn needing slender support struts and therefore obscuring the pilot's view far less than earlier HUDs. A variety of data can be presented on the HUD, including standard calligraphic flight data, radar symbology and steering cues overlaid on FLIR imagery. The FLIR imagery employs a raster scan to build the image, while the calligraphy is stroke written during the retrace between each scan. Control of much of the display system, particularly for switching between functions in the vital attack phase, is handled by HOTAS switches. The throttle grips mount switches to change between missiles and guns, to designate and undesignate a target, to operate the laser rangefinder, chaff/flare dispenser, IFF interrogator and various radar functions. The stick has a traditional pickle button and gun trigger, but is surmounted by a toggle for changing the aircraft trim, and features a thumb switch for changing the CRT screen displays which doubles as a countermeasures dispenser. Another switch controls the automatic acquisition modes of the radar. Below the CRTs are small standard analog flight instruments to back up the electronic displays, while an armament selection panel is located on the left-hand side.

WSO station

In the rear cockpit, domain of the Weapon Systems Officer, are four large CRT displays, as originally prototyped on the Strike Eagle demonstrator. The two centre units in the F-15E are 6 x 6-in (15.25 x 15.25-cm) monochrome displays, flanked by two 5 x 5-in colour CRTs. As with those in the front, surrounding each display are selector buttons, which call up menus for changing the data to be presented. Two stick controls, with HOTAS buttons, are provided for the WSO to allow control of the weapon system and to move cursors across the screens to designate targets once the basic attack display architecture has been established. The system is so flexible that the WSO can run with whatever displays on whichever screen are the most practical and comfortable, depending on personal preference or situational dictate. New displays can be called up from the stick control.

In addition to the FLIR/radar sensor imagery usually presented on the central monitors, the WSO may elect to have a HUD repeater on one of the colour displays, aircraft status display on the other, or alternatively a simple E-scope image (the so-called 'ski-tip') from the TFR or a simplified threat array. There are 18 basic displays available, including full checklists. The HOTAS concept in the rear cockpit allows the WSO to operate the system much faster than the

traditional knobs-and-buttons approach. A repeat of the UFC is in the back seat, although it is located over to the starboard side. A Bendix/King RP-341-A remote moving map is the main tactical situation display, reading preloaded film strip. It is hoped in the near future to substitute a digital moving map with a complete global store. The moving map can be used to cue the radar system for target search. Like the pilot, the WSO sits on an ACES II zero-zero ejection seat, and has simple duplicated flight controls for the control of the aircraft if the pilot is incapacitated.

"The pilot rows the boat and the WSO shoots the ducks" is a favourite saying of F-15E crews when describ-

Above: Seymour Johnson F-15Es begin their break from the tanker. The 4th Wing was established to provide a rapid-intervention force, controlling three operational squadrons of F-15Es, based in CONUS but ready to deploy to exert considerable muscle on a global basis. Their first test came with Desert Storm.

Few places on the planet provide the kind of exhilarating terrain flying that Alaska has to offer, but there are equally few places with such a hostile climate. F-15Es are the perfect aircraft for this region: long-legged to straddle the vast inhospitable tracts, fully auto-TF capable and equipped with sophisticated navigation systems.

F-15E Strike Eagle

A pair of F-15Es skirt Alaskan mountains at medium altitude. When first delivered to the USAF, the F-15E LANTIRN system was not fully integrated with the flight control system. Therefore pilots had to relay on LANTIRN-generated steering/pull-up commands and the 1:1 nav FLIR image, both displayed in the HUD, for terrain avoidance. While this remains an option, the aircraft is now fully integrated for hands-off terrain-following flight. The pilot has various altitude options, and can select the degree of terrain-following ('hard' or 'soft' ride).

Above right: Steam boils from the wing surface as a 3rd Wing F-15E thunders into wet Alaskan air. The maximum take-off weight of the aircraft is set at 81,000 lb (36740 kg), considerably greater than the 68,000 lb (30844 kg) of the F-15C. Uprated Dash 229 engines in the later aircraft help offset the weight increase.

Opposite page: High over northern Iraq during a Provide Comfort mission, a 48th FW 'Mudhen' demonstrates the ALE-45 chaff/flare dispenser. The aircraft is configured to meet a range of threats, armed with AMRAAM and Sidewinder for air combat, and carrying a pair of GBU-12 LGBs for surface attack.

ing the work-share in the cockpit, although the truth is far more complex. At basic level the job of the pilot is to fly the aircraft while the WSO works the weapon system, but as virtually all of the functions can be performed from either seat, and there is a high workload on the crew, the demarcation line becomes ill-defined. Unless there is air-to-air trade in the immediate vicinity, the pilot usually prefers the WSO to work the radar, although he will take over control of the radar if the situation changes. One of the tasks that is solely the pilot's responsibility is the launch of air-to-air missiles. Either crew member can command patch maps or work the LANTIRN pods, but in most cases this is the WSO's job during the final attack phase. Both crew share the navigation and communication functions.

One of the disadvantages of the F-15E is simply the sheer complexity and flexibility of the system and its displays. While it is considered fairly simple to perform the 'high-end' functions such as commanding a patch map, there are so many variations, many hidden on sub-menus, that it is conceivable to miscue the system or inadvertently neglect a key switch function. The answer lies in continual training, allowing the switchology to become instinctive to the crew. The analogy with computer games is apposite: F-15 WSOs, when asked how they would perform a certain task, may take five minutes to explain the switchology, yet sit them in the rear cockpit and the function will be performed in a second. Another key to an effective crew is how they co-ordinate in extracting the maximum results from the system. This vital empathy between the front and rear seats is only achieved through regular flying and sim time together.

Avionics

Control of the aircraft's many functions is entrusted to an IBM CP-1075C VHSIC (Very High Speed Integrated Circuit) computer, recently upgraded from CP-1075 standard. Basic avionics equipment includes a Teledyne Electronics APX-101 IFF transponder to inform other friendly ground stations and aircraft that the F-15 is not hostile and to transmit range, azimuth and elevation data to air traffic controllers. Conversely, the aircraft has a Hazeltine APX-76 IFF interrogator with Litton reply evaluator to check the 'friendliness' of target aircraft.

At the centre of the navigation system is a Honeywell CN-1655A/ASN ring laser gyro INS (inertial navigation system), which is not only the major navigation data source, but is the primary attitude reference. It is backed up by a Honeywell ASK-6 air data computer and an ASN-108 AHRS (Automatic Heading Reference System). The navigation function of the INS is correlated by a Collins ARN-118 TACAN and ADF, although from 1995 a Rockwell

Collins miniature GPS (Global Positioning System) is expected to be integrated with the INS. Teledyne Avionics angle of attack sensors are used, while landing is accomplished using a Collins ARN-112 ILS receiver and a Dorne and Margolin glideslope localiser antenna. The communications suite includes Magnavox ARC-164 UHF transceivers, and has cryptographic capability.

Defences

Vitally important to the F-15E's ability to operate in a high-threat environment is its electronic defence system, based on that fitted to the late model F-15C. The TEWS (Tactical Electronic Warfare System) is fully integrated into the airframe to reduce drag and free up pylon space, and provides a full warning function with automatic mechanical and electronic countermeasures. The warning function is handled by the Loral ALR-56C RWR (Radar Warning Receiver), which has four spiral antennas mounted in fin-tip fairings and on each wingtip to cover high-band frequencies, while low-band frequencies are covered by a single blade antenna just forward of the nosewheel door, both systems providing omnidirectional warning in azimuth. Covering the E- to J-bands, the superheterodyne receivers and associated processors are capable of sorting and identifying all current and projected threats, assigning priorities, managing jammers and mechanical countermeasures, and generating a visual display and audible warnings. The ALR-56C is an improved model of the original ALR-56A fitted to the early F-15 with an increased range of threats and greater ability to cope in a high-density threat environment. A Magnavox ALQ-128 EW warning set also provides warning data to the aircraft, thought to cover the frequency range beyond the capabilities of the ALR-56.

Based on information from the ALQ-128 and ALR-56C, the TEWS employs either mechanical or electronic countermeasures against the threat. The former are provided by Tracor ALE-45 chaff/flare dispensers under the rear fuselage, while the latter are handled by the Northrop Grumman ALQ-135C, otherwise known as the ICS (Internal Countermeasures Set). The ALQ-135C consists of two

Barrelling down a valley in northern Iraq, an F-15E crew lets the TFR take them on a wild ride through the mountains. Despite the fact that most Desert Storm bombing missions were flown at medium altitude to escape groundfire, the high-speed low-level penetration mission is still regarded as the most likely attack profile for future conflicts, at least until the nature of the air defence threat is ascertained.

jammers, known as Band 1.5 and Band 3, which can cover up to 20 GHz and handle both pulse and CW (Continuous Wave) jamming. The system can react automatically to changes in the hostile signal while jamming. Antennas for the system are located in the extreme rear of the tailboom fairings and in the port fin-tip bullet fairing.

Mission profile

So complex and versatile is the F-15E that there is no such thing as a typical mission, but the job for which the aircraft is optimised is pinpoint attack through hostile airspace at night. Like most modern attack aircraft, the mission route can be pre-planned on a computer in the ops room, and the data transferred to the aircraft's navigation system by cassette. Of course, the UFCs allow the crew to load nav data while on the move, or to alter an existing route. Most of the key systems have a BIT function, which allows the crew to monitor their performance before and during the mission. Checklists are stored in the aircraft and accessed through the CRTs.

Once airborne, the crew performs a quick check of the terrain-following system over safe terrain before trusting the aircraft totally to its capabilities. Ingress is usually made at high level through safe air space, before descending to 200 ft (60 m) AGL in a hands-off TFR mode, the crew monitoring both the terrain using LANTIRN nav pod imagery and navigation waypoints, which can be updated using the radar's mapping mode. A safety feature of the APG-70 is that it will pick up obstructions such as power lines which are often missed by the TFR, and long before they are visible in the FLIR imagery.

Due to the conflicting nature of the mission requirements, the F-15E has a higher than desired wing-loading for low-level TFR flight. With full tanks and bombload the wing loading is around 130 lb/sq ft (635 kg/m^2), giving a very smooth ride, but during the attack phase a wing loading of around 90 lb/sq ft (440 kg/m^2) can be expected, making the aircraft responsive to ground buffet and causing some discomfort to the crew. At a similar point in the mission, a Tornado or F-111 will still have about 120 lb/sq ft (586 kg/m^2) on the wing, dampening the buffet to give a much smoother ride. However, the F-15E pilot faced with aerial opposition can haul out of the ground buffet and fight with excellent manoeuvrability thanks to the low wing loading, and no 'E' crew is willing to sacrifice that ability for a smoother TFR ride.

Using the moving map as primary navigation reference, the F-15E nears the target area, using the APG-70 mainly in the air-to-air mode to watch for enemy fighters. If any

are detected, the crew may elect to continue at low level in the hope of remaining undetected, or to fight through the opposition using Sparrow or AMRAAM to take a long-range shot at the defenders. With drop tanks and bombs it is unlikely that the F-15E crew would want to get involved in a close-range fight, for to meet the enemy on equal terms would require ditching the bombs, thereby defeating the object of the mission.

Pop-up mapping

At some considerable distance from the target area, the F-15E would pop up to medium altitude, and the WSO command a radar patch map based on the moving map display. From about 50 nm (57 miles; 92 km) the resolution is good enough to provide a picture of the area to allow the WSO to isolate the immediate target vicinity. The pilot puts the aircraft back down on the deck, the radar back into air-to-air and the aircraft continues its ingress, checking away from the target with an offset angle of between 10° and 45° to allow the HRM mode to work. This has an added tactical advantage of disguising the aircraft's ultimate destination until shortly before weapon release. At around 10 nm (11.5 miles; 18.5 km) from the target the pilot would pop up again, and the WSO command another patch map of much higher resolution. On this map individual vehicles can be seen, and buildings can be easily identified.

To create these maps, the radar requires a few seconds painting the target to achieve the synthetically large aperture, and once the image has been created it is frozen by the WSO to allow him to designate the precise aim-point. To command such a map the WSO squeezes a trigger on the left-hand stick control, which also immediately cues the targeting pod sensors to the same spot as the radar, providing additional FLIR imagery of the target area to aid aiming.

With the aiming point now locked in to the weapon system, the pilot again descends and turns directly towards the target for the final run-in. Again the radar can be thrown back into air-to-air mode to give a final sweep for air threats without losing the precious targeting data. Delivery profiles vary according to the ordnance carried and tactical situation, from a simple visual delivery using an aiming cue generated in the HUD to autonomous laser bombing. By squeezing a trigger on the right-hand stick control, the targeting pod can be locked on to the aim-point, allowing the laser to be used for accurate rangefinding or for designation. Bombing using offset points instead of a target designation is sometimes employed.

Whichever profile is being employed, the weapon system generates steering cues for the pilot in the HUD. Even in popping up for a loft or dive attack, azimuth steering information is presented as a line on the HUD, sloping to left or right to indicate the desired steering. For a shallow dive attack, the standard profile involves a pull-up to about 2,000 ft (610 m) AGL, half-roll to the inverted, pull-through and then a half-roll to right the aircraft, leaving the aircraft in the desired dive and aiming roughly towards the target. HUD symbology will show the exact position of the target, as designated previously, but if this is slightly out it can be very swiftly refined. Now all the pilot has to do his press the pickle button to assign consent for bomb release to the weapon system, and fly to the HUD symbology. When the illuminated target symbol on the HUD passes through the computer-predicted impact point, the weapons are released automatically. Of course there are other delivery profiles, but the CCIP dive delivery offers the greatest accuracy for dumb weapons.

With weapons released the crew can take immediate evasive manoeuvres and egress at low-level on the TFR, ever watchful for further fighter intervention. During laser attacks the aircraft can begin egress, but must remain within the 'look' parameters of the targeting pod until impact to allow the laser to designate the target. Without tanker support but carrying three drop tanks, the F-15E can take four Mk 84 bombs and defensive missiles on a hi-lo-hi profile to a target some 800 miles (1290 km) away, comparing quite favourably with the 1,000-mile (1610-km) combat radius of an F-111 with similar load.

Desert Storm

Like many other Western weapon systems, the F-15E received its baptism of fire over Iraq and Kuwait in January 1991. At the time of the initial aggression against Kuwait to create Iraq's 19th province, only one squadron (336th TFS/4th TFW) of F-15Es had achieved IOC, and this was rushed to the theatre a week after the first deployments of Operation Desert Shield. Hasty training work saw the 335th TFS also achieve IOC before the end of 1990, and they too were dispatched to the Gulf to create a force of 48 F-15Es by H-hour.

Initially based at Thumrait in Oman, the F-15Es moved forward to the central Saudi base at Al Kharj, which became known as the 'Camel Lot'. The 4th TFW (Provisional) was established to control their activities, and also those of two squadrons of attack-configured F-16 squadrons from the Air National Guard, and a single squadron of fighter Eagles from Bitburg. Like other fighter-bomber units, the 4th TFW(P) reported to the 14th Air Division (Provisional) at CENTAF headquarters in Riyadh.

Above: Rolling into the attack, an F-15E prepares to dump a load of 'pig iron' on to a sea range. The blue bombs are inert Mk 82s, filled with concrete rather than explosive.

Left: At the end of a laser-bombing training mission, a 3rd Wing 'E' settles back on to the Elmendorf runway, the pilot holding the nose high for aerodynamic braking, augmenting the stopping power of the huge dorsal airbrake. The Eagle is highly regarded for its soft landings – by the time the F-15 returns to base most of the fuel has been burned off and ordnance expended, leaving the wing lightly loaded.

Inside the F-15E

Above: An F-15E simulator provides a graphic illustration of the MFD display system. Note the patch map on the right central MFD in the rear.

Above: Providing an interesting comparison with the service F-15E cockpit, this is the 'missionised' rear cockpit of the Strike Eagle demonstrator, with different MFDs and a centrally-positioned UFC.

Above: The F-15E rear cockpit looks simple, but from the two hand controllers and menu buttons surrounding the screens the WSO can draw on a huge wealth of information. The central stick is a duplicated flight control column. Just visible below the right-hand MFD is the 'upfront' controller (UFC).

Below: How to build an F-15E – this diagram shows how the individual components of the aircraft piece together. Titanium is mainly concentrated in the hot areas around the engines, with aluminium construction for most other areas of the airframe. Steel is largely restricted to the undercarriage.

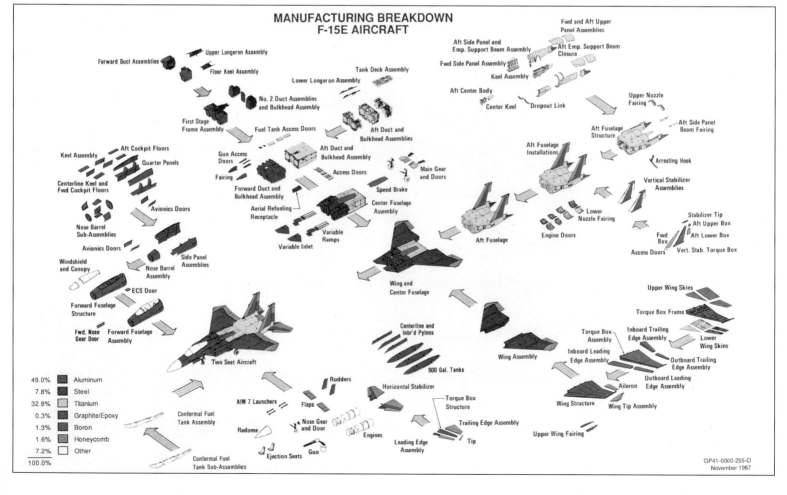

MANUFACTURING BREAKDOWN F-15E AIRCRAFT

Forward Duct Assemblies
Upper Longeron Assembly
Floor Keel Assembly
Lower Longeron Assembly
Tank Deck Assembly
No. 2 Duct Assemblies and Bulkhead Assembly
First Stage Frame Assembly
Fuel Tank Access Doors
Aft Duct and Bulkhead Assemblies
Aft Duct and Bulkhead Assembly
Keel Assembly
Aft Cockpit Floors
Quarter Panels
Gun Access Doors
Access Doors
Main Gear and Doors
Centerline Keel and Fwd Cockpit Floors
Fairing
Speed Brake
Avionics Doors
Forward Duct and Bulkhead Assembly
Center Fuselage Assembly
Nose Barrel Sub-Assemblies
Aerial Refueling Receptacle
Avionics Doors
Variable Ramps
Side Panel Assemblies
Variable Inlet
Windshield and Canopy
Nose Barrel Assembly
ECS Door
Forward Fuselage Structure
Wing and Center Fuselage
Fwd. Nose Gear Door
Forward Fuselage Assembly
Two Seat Aircraft
Centerline and Inbr'd Pylons
Wing Assembly
500 Gal. Tanks
Rudders
Horizontal Stabilizer
AIM 7 Launchers
Flaps
Torque Box Structure
Conformal Fuel Tank Assembly
Nose Gear and Door
Radome
Engines
Trailing Edge Assembly
Leading Edge Assembly
Tip
Conformal Fuel Tank Sub-Assemblies
Ejection Seats
Gun

Fwd and Aft Upper Panel Assemblies
Aft Side Panel and Emp. Support Beam Assembly
Aft Emp. Support Beam Closure
Fwd Side Panel Assembly
Keel Assembly
Aft Center Body
Center Keel
Dropout Link
Upper Nozzle Fairing
Aft Fuselage Structure
Aft Side Panel Beam Fairing
Aft Fuselage Installations
Arresting Hook
Vertical Stabilizer Assemblies
Lower Nozzle Fairing
Aft Fuselage
Engine Doors
Stabilizer Tip
Aft Upper Box
Fwd Box
Aft Lower Box
Access Doors
Vert. Stab. Torque Box
Upper Wing Skins
Torque Box Frame
Torque Box Assembly
Inboard Trailing Edge Assembly
Lower Wing Skins
Inboard Leading Edge Assembly
Outboard Trailing Edge Assembly
Aileron
Outboard Leading Edge Assembly
Wing Structure
Wing Tip Assembly
Upper Wing Fairing

49.0%	Aluminum
7.8%	Steel
32.8%	Titanium
0.3%	Graphite/Epoxy
1.3%	Boron
1.6%	Honeycomb
7.2%	Other
100.0%	

GP41-0000-255-O
November 1987

Radar

The remarkable Hughes APG-70 radar is based on the APG-63 which was fitted to all pre-MSIP fighter Eagles, these later aircraft also featuring the APG-70. In addition to its SAR mode for high-resolution ground mapping, the APG-70 offers a wide range of general mapping and air-to-air modes, operating across a number of frequencies in the I/J-bands. Further flexibility is gained from varying pulsewidths and processing modes. Among the most useful features are the three automatic acquisition modes for short-range air-to-air work, triggered by a switch on the control column, which automatically locks the radar on to a target without the pilot having to designate it. The radar is fully compatible with the AIM-120 AMRAAM missile to give some semi-passive kill capability. In terms of hardware, the APG-70 consists of a three-axis gimballed antenna array driven mechanically at up to 140° per second. Behind this are three racks mounting the associated equipment LRUs. The centre rack mounts the highly-stable transmitter, which has a gridded TWT (travelling-wave tube), while the lower rack has the receiver/exciter. Compared to the unit in the APG-63, this has increased bandwidth, improved ECCM (electronic counter-countermeasures) and greater sensitivity, and gives longer range. Above the transmitter on the upper rack are an analog signal converter, signal processor and radar data processor. This latter unit performs general-purpose calcualtions, and has 1024 k of memory. This is divided between air-to-air modes (220 k), air-to-ground (110 k), BIT (built-in test) function (200 k) and scratchpad memory (64 k). The remaining memory has been provided to cater for any future improvements.

McDonnell Douglas F-15E Eagle
48th Fighter Wing
RAF Lakenheath, England

From nuclear bombs to anti-personnel mines, the F-15E is the most favoured delivery system in most scenarios. The combination of APG-70 and LANTIRN makes the aircraft a formidable ground-pounder, able to deliver unguided weapons with exceptional accuracy, while demonstrating the ability to drop PGMs to the full extent of their capability. In addition, the F-15E can take care of itself in hostile airspace, being provided with a powerful integral defence system, and an air-to-air capability as good as most dedicated fighters. However, this sophistication and flexibility comes at a price roughly half as much again as the latest F-16C although, in some scenarios, the F-15E has been projected to be more cost-effective as it can carry a larger weapon load further.

Surprisingly, the US Air Force has purchased only 209 of these impressive warplanes, and has not announced plans for any future acquisitions, despite vigorous canvassing from the manufacturer and an obvious requirement for more. McDonnell Douglas has proposed a 'big-wing' version with even more impressive range/payload figures, but this aircraft is seen by many observers as being too close in capability to the Lockheed F-22, which the Air Force sees as its most important programme. The argument goes that any further acquisition of F-15Es or derivatives may severely jeopardise the already drastically slashed buy of F-22s.

With a small number engaged in test work, the F-15E force is spread between four main operating units, upon which a heavy burden is placed to provide rapid intervention forces in out-of-area operations. Indeed, the two wings based in the continental United States have the rapid intervention role as their primary tasking. The 366th 'super wing' is a carefully crafted mix of types able to deploy *en masse* with very little notice, while the 4th Wing is dedicated to the F-15E, maintaining three operational squadrons with about 72 aircraft for deployment on a global basis as and when required.

Out on the 'front line', so to speak, are two theatre forces, stationed in Alaska and England, covering the Pacific and Europe respectively. Both can be rapidly reinforced by the CONUS units, which are also the most likely to deploy back to Kuwait should the need arise. From its base near Anchorage, the 3rd Wing is much closer to Pacific Rim hot-spots than any CONUS-based unit, and views Korea as its most likely theatre of operation. In Europe, the two squadrons of the 48th Fighter Wing look across a vastly different continent to that of a decade ago. War on the Central Front now seems impossible, although the F-15Es serve a purpose as a powerful reminder to factions of the Russian political system who may wish to revert to the Cold War stand-off. Today the key zones are in former Yugoslavia and the Middle East, where tensions increase and occasionally boil over into direct action.

From England, the 48th FW deploys aircraft to both theatres as part of multinational peacekeeping forces. Northern Iraq is covered from the Turkish base at Incirlik, F-15Es joining various types of aircraft enforcing a 'No-Fly Zone' north of the 36th parallel. Over Bosnia, the 48th FW aircraft fly from Aviano in Italy. In both theatres, F-15Es carry a mix of air-to-air missiles with air-to-ground stores, the GBU-12 being the favoured munition for its precision aiming ability. When NATO undertook its first-ever major bombing mission, targeted against the Krajina Serb airfield of Udbina, just over the Bosnian border in Croatia, it was no surprise that the 48th Fighter Wing was in the thick of the action. In its F-111F days, the 48th had been called upon to undertake the long-range mission against Tripoli in 1986, and was the most destructive unit during Desert Storm. On the Udbina raid, it formed the core of the strike package, 492nd FS F-15Es using GBU-12s to hit the runway and airfield defences. Two days later Lakenheath F-15Es destroyed a SAM site which threatened NATO aircraft, and which had survived an anti-radar attack made earlier.

The considerable weight of the F-15E rests on single high-pressure Michelin tyres. This aircraft belongs to the 391st FS.

104 Formation lighting strip
105 Engine bleed air primary heat exchangers, port and starboard
106 Port trailing edge fuel tank bay
107 Flap hydraulic jack
108 Port plain flap
109 Aileron hydraulic actuator
110 Port aileron honeycomb core construction
111 Fuel jettison
112 Port formation light
113 Port navigation light
114 Forward ECM transmitting antenna
115 Engine bleed air primary heat exchanger air intake and exhaust ducts
116 GBU-28 'Deep-Throat' laser-guided bomb

The rear end of the F-15E reveals the large bulk of the F100 engines, the complicated convergent/divergent nozzles and the position of the emergency runway arrester hook. The ends of the fin mounting fairings house ECM equipment.

117 GBU-12 laser-guided bombs
118 CFT pylons
119 Port conformal fuel tank (CFT)

120 AXQ-14 datalink pod
121 Mk 84 2,000-lb HE bomb
122 GBU-24 laser-guided bomb
123 Outer wing panel dry bay
124 Port wing integral fuel tankage
125 Multi-spar wing panel structure
126 Port pylon hardpoint
127 Wing stores pylon
128 Missile launch rails
129 AIM-120 AMRAAM
130 AIM-9M Sidewinder air-to-air missile
131 Leading-edge flush HF antenna
132 Stores management system equipment
133 CBU-87 sub-munition dispensers

134 Port LANTIRN targeting pod
135 Centreline external tank
136 AGM-65 Maverick air-to-surface missiles
137 Triple missile carrier/launch rail
138 GBU-15 electro-optical guided glide bomb

Mike Badrocke

Left: *The AAQ-14 has a large window for the FLIR and a smaller aperture for the laser. This unit rotates to protect the windows when not in use.*

Above: *The AAQ-13 consists of a TFR in the lower portion, with dielectric radome, and a nav FLIR peering through the window in the fairing above.*

McDonnell Douglas F-15E Eagle

1 Glass-fibre radome
2 Hughes AN/APG-70 I-band pulse-Doppler radar scanner
3 Radar mounting bulkhead
4 ADF sense antenna
5 Avionics equipment bay, port and starboard
6 UHF antenna
7 Pitot head
8 AGM-130 laser-guided air-to-surface weapon
9 TACAN antenna
10 Formation lighting strip
11 Incidence probe
12 Rudder pedals
13 Instrument panel shroud
14 Pilot's head-up display
15 Frameless windscreen panel
16 B61 tactical nuclear weapon
17 AIM-7F Sparrow air-to-air missile
18 LANTIRN navigation pod, mounted beneath starboard intake
19 FLIR aperture
20 Terrain-following radar
21 Upward-hinging cockpit canopy
22 Pilot's ACES II ejection seat
23 Side console panel
24 Engine throttle levers
25 Boarding steps
26 Extended boarding ladder
27 Forward-retracting nosewheel
28 Landing/taxiing lights
29 Nosewheel leg shock absorber strut
30 Underfloor control runs
31 Flying controls duplicated in rear cockpit
32 Radar hand controller
33 Weapons Systems Officer's ACES II ejection seat
34 Canopy hinge point
35 Cockpit air conditioning pack
36 Port variable capture area 'nodding' air intake
37 Boundary layer spill air louvres
38 Nodding intake hydraulic actuator
39 Variable-area intake ramp doors
40 Intake ramp hydraulic actuator
41 Boom-type flight refuelling receptacle, open
42 Air supply duct to conditioning system
43 Ammunition magazine, 512 rounds
44 Forward fuselage fuel tanks
45 Ammunition feed chute

46 Engine intake ducting
47 Centre fuselage fuel tanks
48 Fuel tank bay access panel
49 Airbrake hydraulic jack
50 Dorsal airbrake honeycomb construction
51 Upper UHF antenna
52 Starboard intake by-pass air spill duct
53 M61A1 Vulcan 20-mm cannon
54 Anti-collision light
55 Starboard wing pylon carrying GBU-10, AIM-7M and AIM-120
56 Pylon mounting hardpoint
57 Starboard wing integral fuel tank, fire suppressant foam filled
58 Leading edge flush HF antenna panels
59 Ventral view showing carriage of 12 Mk 82 500-lb bombs
60 610-US gal external fuel tanks (3)
61 LANTIRN navigation and targeting pods
62 Wing pylon mounted AIM-9M and AIM-120 air-to-air missiles
63 Forward ECM transmitting antenna
64 Starboard navigation light
65 Wingtip formation light
66 Fuel jettison
67 Starboard aileron
68 Starboard plain flap
69 Trailing-edge fuel tank
70 Engine bay cooling intake bleed air louvres
71 Compressor intake
72 Central airframe mounted engine accessory equipment gearbox
73 Machined main fuselage/wing spar attachment bulkheads
74 Pratt & Whitney F100-PW-229 afterburning turbofan engines
75 Engine bleed air cross-ducting
76 Forward engine mounting
77 Main engine mounting 'spectacle' beam
78 Afterburner ducting
79 Rear fuselage/engine bay diffusion-bonded all-titanium structure
80 Tailplane hydraulic actuator
81 Starboard fin
82 Fintip ECM antenna
83 Anti-collision light

84 Starboard rudder
85 Starboard all-moving tailplane
86 Aft ECM transmitting antenna
87 Variable area afterburner nozzle
88 Nozzle actuating linkage
89 Nozzle shroud panels
90 Fueldraulic afterburner nozzle actuators
91 Two-spar fin torsion box structure
92 Boron-fibre fin skin panelling
93 Radar warning antenna
94 Port rear ECM antenna
95 White strobe light
96 Port rudder honeycomb core construction

97 Tailplane pivot mounting
98 Port aft ECM transmitting antenna
99 Port all-moving tailplane
100 Boron-fibre tailplane skin panelling
101 Machined tailplane trunion mounting fitting
102 Leading edge dog-tooth
103 Runway emergency arrester hook, lowered

AMRAAM missile

Developed by Hughes, the AIM-120 is one of three AAMs currently available to the F-15E for air combat, and despite having a range of about 30 miles (50 km) against head-on targets, more than the AIM-7 Sparrow, can be carried on the shoulder launch rails, leaving the lower CFT positions free for offensive stores carriage. The missile is powered by a solid propellant low-smoke motor, controlled by the four movable rear fins, and the warhead is a 48-lb (22-kg) directed fragmentation unit, fused by active radar. The weapon has two basic modes, depending on conditions. Long-range missile shots involve the missile being launched and guiding itself inertially with periodic command guidance updates transmitted from the aircraft's radar. As it nears the target it goes into autonomous mode, using inertial guidance only, and during the terminal phase uses its own active I-band monopulse radar for final guidance. Short-range engagements can be accomplished using the missile's own radar from the launch, and can be undertaken at ranges down to a few hundred yards. AMRAAM also has a 'home-on-jam' capability, guiding itself towards aircraft attempting to protect themselves electronically.

Laser-guided bomb

The Paveway LGB is the main precision-guided munition for the F-15E. There are four options currently available: the 500-lb (227-kg) GBU-12 shown here, of which eight is the normal load, the 2,000-lb (907-kg) GBU-10 and GBU-24, of which four are carried, and the 4,700-lb (2132-kg) GBU-28, usually carried singly with a 'dumb' Mk 84 to counterbalance it. The LGB consists of three sections. The central warhead is either a Mk 82 or Mk 84 conventional high-explosive bomb, or in the GBU-10I or GBU-24A versions it is a BLU-109 penetrating warhead. To the warhead is attached the fin-group, which has pop-out wings to improve glide range, and on the front is the CCG (computer control and guidance) unit, which has the laser seeker head and four control fins. The GBU-10 and 12 employ the Paveway II CCG, while the GBU-24 and 28 have the much better but more expensive Paveway III.

Keith Fretwell

Powerplant
The Pratt & Whitney F100 is a highly reliable turbofan with high thrust-to-weight ratio. It has powered all F-15s and all the early F-16s. Only in the later F-16s has it been challenged by the F110. The F100 is a two-stage axial turbofan, the heart of which is a smokeless annular combustor with 24 airblast nozzles and continuous capacitor discharge ignition. The combustor is supplied with air from a 10-stage compressor upstream, which provides a pressure differential ratio of 32. Power for the axial compressor is provided by low-pressure and high-pressure turbines downstream of the combustor, each with two stages. At the front of the engine is a three-stage fan which blows both air into the engine for combustion and cool air around the side of the engine with a bypass ratio of 0.36. An 11-segment mixed-flow afterburner is fitted, exhausting through a fully-variable convergent/divergent nozzle.

ue box made of
titanium, to
rons made of
wing features
and has a
r-chord
ord ratio falls
the wingtip.
ouglas would
ld they be

LN

l48 W

F-15E Strike Eagle

Camouflage

The overall dark grey has been worn by every F-15E since the type's first roll-out. The colour is thought to provide the best camouflage during the night/adverse weather mission at low level, offering protection from both ground and air attack. A similar colour has subsequently been adopted by the B-1 and B-52.

Undercarriage

All three undercarriage units are made by Cleveland, and feature Bendix wheels with Bendix five-rotor carbon disc brakes. Michelin AIR X tyres are fitted (22 x 7.75-9 on nosewheel, 36 x 11-18 on main wheels), inflated to 305 lb/sq in (21.03 bars) pressure.

Self-defence missiles

For self-protection the F-15E usually carries two AIM-9M Sidewinders (as depicted). The AIM-120 AMRAAM can also be carried on the wing pylons.

Cluster bomb options

This aircraft is depicted configured for a short-range CAS/BAI mission, carrying the standard 12 bombs on the CFT pylons, but also substituting the drop tanks for a further weapon on each wing pylon. In this case the bombs are SUU-30H cluster munition dispensers, which are available with a range of sub-munitions. All are spherical in shape, with small flutes which cause the bomblet to spin-arm once the dispenser has broken apart, releasing the munitions into the air. The CBU-52 is an SUU-30H containing 217 BLU-61 grapefruit-sized bomblets which explode on impact, while the CBU-58 has 650 of the smaller BLU-63. CBU-58A also has incendiary bomblets, while CBU-71 includes 650 BLU-86 mine sub-munitions which explode at random intervals. Other dispensers include the old Mk 7 (247 Mk 118 bomblets) and the SUU-64/65. The latter are used with three main options: CBU-87 has an SUU-65 dispenser with 202 BLU-97 combined effects munitions, CBU-89 has 72 BLU-91 anti-personnel munitions and 22 BLU-92 anti-tank weapons in the SUU-64, while CBU-97 has 10 BLU-108 'Skeet' sensor-fuzed weapons (SFW), again in an SUU-64. The SUU-64/65 spins at a preselected rate prior to splitting to provide optimum bomblet dispersion.

McDonnell Douglas F-15E

Able to undertake a wide variety of missions, the F-15E mirrors the USAF's goal of greater flexibility and effectiveness in a cost-conscious era. Purchasing and operating costs of the F-15E are roughly half as much again as for the F-16C Block 50, but in key scenarios, notably in a wide conflict with many targets a long distance from base, the F-15E scores heavily on cost-effectiveness. Where the F-16C scores is in the smaller conflicts for which the aircraft was envisaged.

Depicted wearing the tiger-stripe colours of the 391st Fighter Squadron 'Bold Tigers', this F-15E is one of 12 primary aircraft assigned to the 366th Wing 'Gunfighters', in addition to bridging the gap in the 366th force structure between the 'lightweight' F-16Cs and heavy bombing capacity of the B-1B, the F-15E can augment the air superiority role if required.

Specification

McDonnell Douglas F-15E

Powerplant: two Pratt & Whitney F100-PW-229 turbofans, each rated at 29,100 lb (129.4 kN) thrust in full afterburner and 17,800 lb (79.18 kN) dry

Wing span: 42 ft 9¾ in (13.05 m)
Length: 63 ft 9 in (19.43 m)
Height: 18 ft 5½ in (5.63 m)
Tailplane span: 28 ft 3 in (8.61 m)
Wheel track: 9 ft 0¾ in (2.75 m)
Wheelbase: 17 ft 9¾ in (5.42 m)

Wing area: 608 sq ft (56.5 m²)
Tailplane area: 111.36 sq ft (10.34 m²)
Fin area: 105.28 sq ft (9.78 m²)
Operating empty weight: 32,000 lb (14515 kg)
Maximum take-off weight: 81,000 lb (36741 kg)
Maximum fuel (external and internal): 34,420 lb (15613 kg)
Maximum weapon load: 24,500 lb (11113 kg)
Maximum speed: Mach 2.5 at altitude
Maximum range: 2,400 nm (2,762 miles; 4445 km)
Maximum combat radius: 685 nm (790 miles; 1270 km)

Aircraft systems

A Garrett APU provides limited ground power and engine starting. The main hydraulic power is provided by a triply-redundant system working at 3,000 lb/sq in (207 bars), driven from the engine by Abex pumps. The electrical system is by Lucas Aerospacer, with Sundstrand drive units, while the air conditioning system is by AiResearach. The original liquid oxygen system has been replaced by a Litton MSOGS (molecular sieve oxygen-generating system).

Control surfaces

The all-moving tailplane and ailerons are driven by National Water Lift hydraulic actuators, while the rudders are driven by Ronson hydraulic units. Simple flaps and a large dorsally-mounted airbrake complete the moveable surfaces.

Lights

The F-15E has navigation lights on the rear of the fins, wingroots and wingtips (the latter in green and red). Low-voltage formation (LVF) 'slime' lights are positioned on the sides of the fore and rear fuselage, and on the wingtips for night formation flying, while landing lights are mounted on the nosewheel strut.

Wings

The wing is based on an exceptionally strong tor[...]
integrally machined skins and ribs in light alloy an[...]
which are attached wingtip sections, flaps and ail[...]
aluminium honeycomb. Set at zero incidence, the[...]
1° of anhedral to destabilise it in the rolling plane[...]
NACA 64A aerofoil section throughout. The quart[...]
sweepback is set at 38° 42', while the thickness-[...]
from 6.6 per cent at the wingroot to 3 per cent at [...]
New 'big' wings being developed by McDonnell t[...]
mate with the existing wing attachment bolts sho[...]
produced.

WARNING

DANGER ARRESTING HOOK

AF 91

Weapons of the F-15E

Above: The AIM-120 AMRAAM is usually carried on the wing pylon launcher rails.

Above: AGM-65 Mavericks can be carried from the wing pylons on LAU-88 triple-round launchers.

Right: Up to eight GBU-12 500-lb (227-kg) Paveway II LGBs can be carried on the CFTs.

Left: For air-to-air work, AIM-7 Sparrows are carried on the lower CFT pylon for a maximum of four. Often one side mounts Sparrows while the other has bombs.

Right: The GBU-15 (and rocket-boosted AGM-130 version) are EO-guided, requiring the AXQ-14 datalink pod to be mounted on the centreline pylon. Two fin groups are available, this being the earlier version. Later weapons have rectangular fins.

Below: Armourers fit 2,000-lb (907-kg) Mk 84s to the lower CFT pylon.

Below: Various cluster bombs are available for carriage primarily from the CFT hardpoints. These are CBU-87 Combined Effect Munitions, based on the SUU-65 Tactical Munitions Dispenser.

Above: This close-up shows the gimballed seeker head and moving control fins of the GBU-10 Paveway II. This LGB has pop-out wings at the back to improve stand-off performance, but not as large as those fitted to the GBU-24.

Right: Known colloquially as the 'Sue', the SUU-20 is the main training bomb carrier. Six BDU-33 'blue bombs' are carried. Although each weighs only 25 lb (11 kg), they simulate the ballistics of a retarded 500-lb (227-kg) Mk 82.

The 336th Fighter Squadron was swift to answer the call of Desert Shield, arriving in the Gulf in early August 1990. However, they did not bring LANTIRN targeting pods with them. When the 335th TFS deployed in late December, they brought a few pods along which were shared with the resident squadron at Al Kharj.

the capability of the radar which allowed the type to become one of the key types in the 'Great Scud Hunt'. Although these medium-range surface-to-surface missiles were of limited tactical value while fitted with conventional warheads, the omnipresent threat of them being armed with chemical warheads made them priority targets, while their political effect, especially when turned against Israel, far outweighed their destructive power. Consequently, the coalition turned many of its assets to combatting the 'Scud' threat.

Most missiles were launched in Iraq's vast and empty western desert, travelling on mobile launchers under cover of darkness and hiding under road bridges or flood culverts during the day. A-10s rooted out many in daylight hours, but it was the F-15E which became their scourge at night, working with the E-8A J-STARS radar platform. As they shared the same SAR technology, the J-STARS and F-15E could 'see' similar images. The E-8s spotted potential 'Scud' launchers, and provided position and target data. Taking patch maps of the area assigned by J-STARS allowed the F-15E crews to see similar images, and to locate the launchers. 'Scud' hunters usually flew in pairs, the lead aircraft sporting one of the rare targeting pods and four GBU-10 LGBs while the wingman carried a mix of CBU-87s and Mk 82 iron bombs. Missions were long and gruelling, hanging around on the tanker waiting for a target. The F-15E was the only aircraft in-theatre capable of accepting a target in mid-air, and finding it. The 335th TFS alone accounted for 48 'Scuds' in this way. The success of the campaign became obvious to F-15E crews: 'Scuds' became extremely scarce as the war progressed. Naturally, there were pre-fragged secondary targets to attack if no missiles were found, to avoid wasting the mission.

Tank plinking

As the war progressed, the F-15E increasingly turned away from strategic targets and joined the anti-bridge and airfield campaign, while also attacking armoured formations. The 335th claimed as many as 45 aircraft on the ground, and 36 bridges. In the run-up to the ground war the F-15E joined F-111Fs on 'tank plinking' operations. This again utilised a two-ship, with the lead aircraft designating tanks for attack by GBU-12 LGBs from both aircraft. Hundreds of armoured vehicles were destroyed in this way. One of the most highlighted actions of the war occurred on 14 February, when a targeting pod-equipped F-15E of the 335th TFS, 89-0487, caught a Hughes 500 helicopter on the ground in central Kuwait. The crew designated the helicopter for attack with an LGB, but the Hughes took off while the bomb was in flight. The WSO continued to designate the helicopter, which was hit in mid-air by the bomb. This remains the F-15E's only air-to-air kill.

At first the aircraft were armed with four Sidewinders and some with Sparrows (the latter reportedly in an attempt to kill 'Scuds' just after launch), but the failure of the Iraqi air force to intervene effectively, and the ease with which F-15C fighter cover dispatched any MiGs which took to the air, allowed the F-15Es to reduce to just two AIM-9s. Thanks to fighter cover and SEAD assets, the principal threat for the duration of the conflict came from undirected yet very intense groundfire, which could be countered by adopting medium-level bombing tactics.

Some 7,700 combat hours were logged by the F-15E crews, each squadron flying around 1,200 missions. The high-time aircraft was 87-0200, with 54 missions logged. Despite the dearth of targeting pods and of training in their use, the F-15E showed itself to be a most capable aircraft with awesome potential once the full system was up and running. Although the basic weapons clearance work had been completed before service entry, during Desert Shield and Desert Storm test units back in the US were expediting work on clearing weapons and systems for the aircraft, and

Heavily committed from the opening assault on the night of 16/17 January, the F-15Es proved to be effective bomb-trucks. As noted previously, there were only a handful of LANTIRN targeting pods available at the time, and the aircraft was restricted mostly to using its radar only for accurate freefall attacks until later in the war, when more AAQ-14s were available. During the initial attacks the F-15Es went in at low level, losing two aircraft on the second and fourth nights to groundfire. The chief targets were communications facilities, airfields and strategic bridges – targets which the APG-70 could find and designate with ease.

F-15E missions fell into three categories: strategic missions into Iraq, missile-hunting in the desert and BAI missions in the KTO (Kuwait Theatre of Operations). It was

Left: Armed with four GBU-10 LGBs, a 335th TFS aircraft waits for a Desert Storm mission. Much use was made of this weapon on 'Scud' hunts, especially when the Iraqis hid the launchers in trenches covered with tarpaulin. Ironically, this camouflage made the position of the launcher much easier to spot, the trenches showing up well on the APG-70 patch maps.

this work continued with vigour after the war, drawing heavily on combat experience. The key item was the full integration of the AAQ-14.

Two years after the start of Desert Storm, the F-15E went into action over Iraq again, but this time as a fully mature warplane. While most Desert Storm aircraft returned home soon after the end of the conflict, a sizeable force, concentrated in the 4404th Composite Wing at Dhahran, remained behind as a powerful reminder to Saddam Hussein, and to police the 'No-Fly Zone' south of the 32nd parallel (Operation Southern Watch). Manned by periodic rotations from Seymour Johnson, the 4th TFW had a detachment as part of this deterrent force. During December 1992 and January 1993, in the dying days of the Bush administration, Saddam had mounted a series of challenges to the UN sanctions, including refusal to allow inspection teams into his weapon factories, penetrations by Iraqi fighters into the 'No-Fly Zone' and movement into the area of SAM sites. On 27 December there was considerable aerial jostling, beginning with a confrontation between F-15Es and Iraqi MiGs and culminating in the destruction of a MiG-25 by a USAF F-16D.

Further provocations in the coming days resulted in the inevitable: at 9.15 pm local time on 13 January, 100 coalition aircraft took off for selected targets in southern Iraq, the package including RAF Tornados, and French Mirage 2000s. Among the attacking force were 10 F-15Es, which followed six F-117s into the target areas. Both aircraft types were hampered by bad weather, but the F-15E demonstrated its superior weapon system by hitting eight of its 10

allotted aim-points, while the F-117 could hit only two of six. US Navy A-6s and F/A-18s which followed in much better weather only achieved seven from 14. From the F-15E's point of view the raid was a major success, but it did not dampen Iraq's attempts to provocate the UN.

Three days after the raid Iraq was still loudly threatening to shoot down coalition aircraft, but on the next day a MiG-29 was blasted by an F-16 over the northern 'No-Fly

Below: Two views show F-15Es resting at Al Kharj. A shortage of drop tanks resulted in many 'Es' going into battle sporting light grey tanks raided from the stocks of fighter Eagle units. During the initial onslaught, F-15Es went in at low level against communications sites, key bridges and fixed 'Scud' launch sites.

Zone'. The US Navy launched a 45-missile TLAM-C (Tomahawk) attack against a nuclear plant, and on 19 January a 69-aircraft package went back into southern Iraq to destroy SAM sites and air defence centres. This attack was made in daylight, and the F-15Es were again in the thick of the action, attacking air defence centres at Najaf, Samawah and Tallil.

Subsequently, the F-15E remained on guard at Dhahran until mid-1994, when the detachment was recalled to Seymour Johnson. However, by this time the aircraft was also

embroiled in another United Nations operation, this time over the beleagured ex-Yugoslav republic of Bosnia-Herzegovina. Operation Deny Flight was originally established to police a 'No-Fly Zone' over Bosnia, but in the middle of 1993 air activity was widened to encompass the provision of air-to-ground support for UN troops in-country.

Following the completion of its transition from the F-111F to the F-15E, the 48th Fighter Wing, based at RAF Lakenheath in England, was tasked with supplying aircraft to the NATO force supporting UN activities on a rotational basis. Flying from Aviano in Italy, the 48th FW detachment provides armed F-15Es to patrol over Bosnia, ready to respond to a UN call for air support. Aircraft such as the F-16, A-10 and Jaguar fly the daytime missions, the F-15Es being tasked with night patrols, working in co-ordination with AC-130 gunships.

By far the majority of missions over Bosnia were routine patrols, the handful of attacks made up until November 1994 being undertaken by F-16s, A-10s and F/A-18s. However, on 21 November, Strike Eagles got into the act. Serbian Oraos operating from the airfield at Udbina, located in the Krajina Serb enclave in Croatia, had earlier made two attacks on Muslim positions near Bihac, in defiance of the NATO 'No-Fly Zone' and close to a UN protected area. A 39-aircraft package, centred around 492nd FS F-15Es operating from Aviano, attacked the airfield, the F-15Es following defence suppression aircraft which had knocked out the airfield's defences. The 'Mudhens' flew at medium level, using LGBs to attack the runway and defensive positions. Several bombs were seen to hit the runway, leaving large craters, while taxiways were also hit. Two days later, USMC F/A-18Ds attacked three Serb SA-2 missile sites with HARMs, but failed to destroy one. F-15Es were called in to ensure the destruction of the site with LGBs. At the time of writing further direct action over Bosnia seemed likely. F-15Es also detach to Incirlik in Turkey for Provide Comfort missions over northern Iraq.

Strike Eagle sales

Originally, the US Air Force planned to procure 392 F-15Es, but this number was subsequently to stand at 200. Eager to keep its Eagle production line at St Louis open to cater for future demand, McDonnell Douglas has made several unsolicited bids to the Pentagon to supply further aircraft, but was only successful in adding a small batch of nine, comprising three Gulf War attrition replacements and six new aircraft with funds generated by the sale of 24 surplus F-15Cs to Saudi Arabia, to bring the current USAF total to 209. In June 1994 McDonnell Douglas proposed cutting production to two aircraft per month to prolong the production, and fixed a price of $50 million per copy.

Where McDonnell Douglas has been successful is the sale of the Strike Eagle to two existing F-15 operators, although not without considerable effort. Firstly, Saudi

Still armed with LGBs and AAMs, Eagles of the 4th TFW (Provisional) survey their handiwork shortly after the end of the war with Iraq, flying over an airfield that bears the familiar traces of LGB attack against the shelters. The 4th TFW(P) controlled the F-15Es of the 336th TFS (top aircraft) and 335th TFS (centre), and also the F-15C air superiority fighters of the 53rd TFS. This unit deployed from the 36th TFW, normally based at Bitburg in Germany. While the F-15E accounted for one helicopter with an LGB, the 53rd TFS shot down one MiG-21, four MiG-23s, one Mirage F1 and two Su-25s during the campaign, followed by two Su-22s and a PC-9 shortly after the ground war had ended. The three Eagle squadrons also shared Al Kharj with two ANG F-16 squadrons.

Below: An important tasking for the 48th FW is support of UN operations in Bosnia. Flying from Aviano, where this 492nd FS pair is seen, F-15Es fly nightly patrols over the province, armed with a mixed load of AAMs and LGBs to provide both 'No-Fly Zone' support and close support cover for UN ground forces. The night mission is entrusted to the 'Mudhen' owing to its sophisticated weapon system, although USMC F/A-18Ds and US Navy A-6Es have also undertaken the nocturnal patrols.

Arabia has ordered 72 examples of the F-15S, a downgraded version of the F-15E, in the face of competition for more Panavia Tornados, which is already in RSAF service and for which an order for 48 is outstanding. The F-15S is a culmination of a succession of projected variants starting with the F-15F, a downgraded single-seat version. In the event the predicted workload proved too high for a single pilot, so the two-seat cockpit was reintroduced. The result was the F-15H, which was then supplanted by the F-15S, also known in-house as the F-15XP (for eXPort).

As for the sale itself, this has not been easy, and once was actually officially called off, although this was seen by many observers to be merely political leverage by the Saudis to force the United States government into supplying an aircraft with a more acceptable level of equipment. The US government approved the initial Saudi request in December 1992, assigning the first funds on 23rd December. The Saudi government signed the deal in May 1993.

Certain modes are eliminated from the APG-70 including, it is believed, the HRM mode. The LANTIRN pods

are replaced by the similar but downgraded Martin Marietta Sharpshooter system, and CFTs will not be supplied, restricting the F-15S in both range and weapons-carrying capacity. Some ECM equipment will also be deleted, but the aircraft will still be capable of launching Maverick and laser-guided bombs, and a wide variety of freefall bombs and cluster bombs will be available. Twenty-four of the aircraft are envisaged for a primary air-to-air role, while 48 will be optimised for air-to-ground. Delivery will begin in 1995, with production running at one aircraft per month.

Selling the F-15H to the Saudis caused a considerable wave of dissent in the powerful pro-Israeli lobby on Capitol Hill, so the aircraft was subsequently offered to the Israelis when they issued a requirement for a long-range 'strategic' fighter-bomber in 1993. Known as the F-15I, the aircraft for the IDF/AF is expected to be virtually identical to the USAF F-15E, with full-spec APG-70, LANTIRN and Dash 229 engines. The TEWS defensive system is deleted, to be replaced by equipment of Israeli origin. The McDonnell Douglas product was selected in November 1993, facing stiff competition from a considerably upgraded version of the F-16 tendered by Lockheed-Fort Worth. The F-16ES featured dramatically increased fuel capacity to meet the range requirements, by virtue of conformal tanks over the wingroots, and features such as integral infrared/laser sensors. Despite being offered at an attractive price, the F-16ES was ousted by the F-15I for much the same reasons as the F-16XL had lost out to the F-15E in the original ETF programme a decade earlier: existing technology with low development risks and speedy delivery, larger airframe for growth potential, commonality with existing in-service F-15A/Cs, and proven air-to-air prowess.

Israel confirmed its order on 27 January 1994, and officially ordered 21 with four options on 12 May 1994. It is due to receive F-15Is from 1997, at the rate of one per month, and at present that is the end of the line for the Eagle. McDonnell Douglas remains sanguine about the aircraft's future, with undaunted optimism in the USAF purchasing further aircraft, despite a series of statements to the

contrary from the Pentagon. In 1994 MDC submitted a proposal covering 36 aircraft at $50 million per copy to cater for projected attrition through the life of the aircraft. Furthermore, the company can seethe chance of an order for around 100 aircraft if the Pentagon decides to replace the F-111, for which a 'big-wing' long-range F-15 version may be developed. In addition to the prospect of further sales to Israel, another nation which may conceivably entertain the type in the future is current F-15 licence-producer Japan, especially if it is forced to withdraw from new-generation fighter programmes currently under way.

Another potential customer is the United Arab Emirates, which requires between 20 and 80 strike fighters. A basic variant of the F-15E may be offered, or a radically improved version with a new, more angular and much bigger wing known by the tentative designation F-15U. Lockheed (with either an F-16C Block 50 or an 'F-16U' with delta wing), Dassault (with Rafale), Eurofighter and Sukhoi (with the Su-30MK) are also in the hunt for this lucrative contract. Only time will tell. **David Donald**

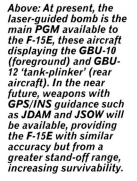

Above: At present, the laser-guided bomb is the main PGM available to the F-15E, these aircraft displaying the GBU-10 (foreground) and GBU-12 'tank-plinker' (rear aircraft). In the near future, weapons with GPS/INS guidance such as JDAM and JSOW will be available, providing the F-15E with similar accuracy but from a greater stand-off range, increasing survivability.

A 3rd Wing F-15 makes a 'dirty' pass over Elmendorf, fighter Eagles clustering on the ramp below. While USAF procurement of this epoch-making fighter may have reached an end, low-rate production continues to satisfy orders from Israel and Saudi Arabia, and licence-production continues in Japan.

F-15E Operators

United States Air Force

Production of the F-15E for the United States Air Force stands at 209 aircraft, ordered in seven batches spanning Fiscal Years 1986 to 1991. Lot I covered eight aircraft (86-0183 to 86-0190), Lot II comprised 42 aircraft (87-0169 to 87-0210), Lot III another 42 aircraft (88-1667 to 88-1708), followed by three batches of 36 aircraft (Lot IV – 89-0471 to 89-0506, Lot V – 90-0227 to 90-0262 and Lot VI – 91-0300 to 91-0335). Finally Lot VII comprised the add-on batch of nine aircraft (91-0600 to 91-0608), of which three were for Gulf War attrition and six paid for by the proceeds of a sale of ex-USAF F-15Cs to Saudi Arabia.

Aircraft generally serve with the units to which they were originally issued. Consequently, the early Dash 220-engined aircraft fly with the 4th Wing at Seymour Johnson and test units, with subsequent diversions made to the 366th Wing at Mountain Home, while the Dash 229-engined aircraft were first delivered to the 3rd Wing in Alaska (from 90-0233 onwards). The last unit to convert was the 48th FW in England, which therefore operates most of the latest production aircraft.

3rd Wing (21st Tactical Fighter Wing)

'AK' Elmendorf AFB, AK
11th Air Force, Pacific Air Forces

90th Fighter Squadron 'Pair o' Dice' (red fin-stripe)

What is now known as the 3rd Wing has been in Alaska since the middle of 1966, when the unit was established at Elmendorf AFB as the 21st Composite Wing. It undertook the air defence of the state under Alaskan Air Command, although this organisation was subsequently downgraded to be the 11th AF of PACAF. F-4 Phantoms and F-15s provided the main mission equipment, although other transport and support types were also flown, including target facilities Martin B-57s and Lockheed T-33s.

In 1990 the unit, by then designated 21st TFW, began to receive the first aircraft of a squadron of F-15Es, to add to the two squadrons of F-15C interceptors already operated. Two F-15Es were delivered to instruct maintenance personnel some time before the main batch of operational aircraft.

These equip the 90th FS, which had previously served under 3rd TFW control at Clark AFB in the Philippines, where it had flown F-4E Phantoms. The squadron officially transferred to the 21st TFW on 17 May 1990, but IOC was not achieved until the spring of 1991. On 26 September 1991, the 21st TFW dropped the 'Tactical' from its designation, but the 21st FW was short-lived as on 19 December it adopted the 3rd Wing designation, thereby preserving one of the USAF's most historic unit numbers. The demise of the Clark-based 3rd TFW had been caused by the agreement by the US to leave the Philippines, which had been dramatically accelerated by the eruption of Mount Pinatubo.

Today the 90th FS has a complement of 20 aircraft operating from a hangar complex at Elmendorf, occasionally taking part in PACAF exercises and venturing south for other USAF exercises. The 3rd Wing has revived its former composite nature by also parenting F-15C/Ds (19th and 54th FS), C-130H and C-12F (517th AS), and TDY E-3 Sentries (962nd ACS).

Above: The 3rd Wing's 'boss-bird' carries no fewer than five colours on the fin-stripe for the wing's constituent squadrons.

Above and above right: The current tail markings for the 90th FS consist of the unit's red tail band with the 'Pair o'Dice' insignia superimposed. The inside of the fin has the 'Big Dipper' constellation and the Pole Star.

Right: The 'Pair o'Dice' insignia was previously worn by F-4G 'Wild Weasels' based in the Philippines.

4th Wing

'SJ' Seymour Johnson AFB, NC
9th Air Force, Air Combat Command

333rd Fighter Squadron 'Lancers' (red fin-stripe)
334th Fighter Squadron 'Eagles' (blue fin-stripe)
335th Fighter Squadron 'Chiefs' (green fin-stripe)
336th Fighter Squadron 'Rocketeers' (yellow fin-stripe)

'Fourth but First' is the wing's motto, and this was particularly apt for the F-15E, as it was the first front-line operator of the type. Most famous for its role in the Korean War, when it was one of the two main Sabre-operating units, the 4th TFW returned from the Far East in 1957, and settled at

Right: The 4th Wing's latest squadron is the 333rd FS. This number was previously assigned to a Davis-Monthan A-10 squadron, while the aircraft came from the Luke-based training squadron.

Above: For many years an F-4E user, the 4th Wing is now the USAF's premier F-15E operator, with four squadrons assigned. The 'boss-bird' shown here now has red added to the fin-band to cater for the new training squadron.

Seymour Johnson, where it has been ever since. The major mission types were North American F-100, Republic F-105 and, from 1967, the McDonnell F-4, all used primarily in the fighter-bomber role. The F-4E served from 1970 until late 1990, by which time the wing had fully re-equipped with the F-15E.

The first F-15E arrived at Seymour Johnson AFB on 29 December 1988. This machine, serial number 87-0178, was named 'Spirit of Goldsboro' in recognition of the nearby city, and carried special markings for the wing commander, including a fin-band of all three squadron colours. The 336th TFS achieved IOC on 1 October 1989, followed by the 335th TFS on 1 October 1990, the latter date brought forward by the demands of the Gulf War. Both squadrons were dispatched to the 4th TFW(P) in the Gulf for Operation Desert Storm. During the campaign, the 334th TFS continued to work-up, achieving IOC on 1 July 1991 to complete the re-equipment of the wing.

As a result in a shift of USAF policy, the 4th TFW took control of the 68th Air Refueling Group which operated KC-10As from Seymour Johnson in June 1991, the parent organisation redesignating as simply

the 4th Wing. In October the squadrons dropped the 'Tactical' from the designation. In the ongoing reshuffle of USAF units, the two KC-10 squadrons are being disbanded and the aircraft reassigned to Air Mobility

Command units at other bases, while the 4th Wing has assumed the type conversion mantle for the F-15E. This function had previously been undertaken by the 550th FS at Luke with the 56th FW. The gradual

transfer of the aircraft (and mission) to Seymour Johnson in the latter part of 1994 followed the activation of the 333rd Fighter Squadron on 1 October, and the 4th should redesignate as a fighter wing.

The three operational squadrons are the 334th FS (left), 335th FS (above) and 336th FS (right).

Right: This four-ship comprises the wing commander's aircraft leading examples from the three operational squadrons.

Above: A flaming spear is the 4th Wing's badge.

4th Tactical Fighter Wing (Provisional)/4404th Composite Wing

'SJ' Al Kharj Air Base, Saudi Arabia
Dhahran Air Base, Saudi Arabia

335th Tactical Fighter Squadron 'Chiefs'
336th Tactical Fighter Squadron 'Rocketeers'

When Operation Desert Shield opened on 6 August 1990, the F-15E was seen as one of the prime weapon systems for rapid deployment. The 336th TFS was the only squadron considered combat-ready, and arrived in-theatre on 12 August. Initially the aircraft were stationed at Thumrait in Oman, but moved to their intended operating location at Al Kharj in Saudi Arabia. Here the 4th TFW(P) was established under the 14th Air Division (Provisional) to control the based tactical aircraft. The 335th TFS completed its work-up in time to be deployed to Al Kharj by the time Desert Storm opened on 17 January 1991, making a total of 48 F-15Es in-theatre. One aircraft (87-0203) was lost in a pre-war training accident on 30 September 1990 with the loss of Major Peter S. Hook and Captain James B. Poulet. Combat claimed two aircraft: 88-1689 on 18 January with the loss of Major Thomas F. Koritz and Major Donnie R. Holland, and 88-1692 on 20 January. The crew of the latter, Colonel David W. Eberly and Major Thomas E.

Right: Green-tails from the 335th TFS wait between missions at Al Kharj. This squadron deployed in December 1990, bringing with it the all-important LANTIRN targeting pods which were then shared with the 336th TFS.

Griffith Jr, were captured by Iraqi forces and held until released on 4 March.

In addition to the two F-15E squadrons, the 4th TFW(P) controlled a single F-15C fighter squadron (53rd TFS/36th TFW from Bitburg) and two Air National Guard F-16 ground attack squadrons (138th TFS/New York ANG from Syracuse and 157th TFS/South Carolina ANG from McEntire ANGB).

Following the end of the war, F-15Es remained in-theatre at Al Kharj for a few weeks, but the 336th TFS returned home shortly after the end of hostilities. The 335th returned a short time later.

Subsequently the 4th TFW/Wing manned detachments to the 4404th Composite Wing established at Dhahran to maintain a strong USAF presence in the Gulf to deter further aggression and to provide muscle behind the various UN sanctions applied post-war to Iraq. The F-15Es were called into action in January 1993, and the detachment was maintained (with occasional aircraft swaps) until mid-1994. The 4404th CW is still in place, and Seymour Johnson is able to dispatch aircraft back to the region with little notice. This eventuality was nearly forced shortly after the F-15Es' return to CONUS when Saddam Hussein moved his tanks provocatively close to the Kuwaiti border, sparking a massive reinforcement of the slowly-dwindling US presence in the Gulf. Although not deployed, 36 F-15Es were held on immediate deployment alert at Seymour Johnson.

Left: With tail marks to honour the outstanding work of the maintenance crews, this 335th F-15E has the inscription 'To Saddam, from the N.J. Posse, Sandusky' scrawled on a GBU-10.

Right: In addition to the three Eagle squadrons, the 4th TFW(P) also had two F-16A attack squadrons manned by Guardsmen.

46th Test Wing (3246th Test Wing)

'ET' ('AD') Eglin AFB, FL
Air Force Development Test Center, Air Force Materiel Command

40th Test Squadron (3247th Test Squadron) (red/white fin-stripe)

On 2 October 1992, the 3246th Test Wing was renumbered as the 46th Test Wing, and its subordinate flying unit renumbered from 3247th to 40th Test Squadron. The 'AD' tailcode worn for many years stood for Armament Division and is more indicative of the unit's role than the 'ET' (Eglin Test)

carried since 30 September 1989. The wing is primarily concerned with the testing and evaluation of aircraft ordnance, and for that reason has operated small numbers of most front-line tactical types throughout their operational careers.

The 3246th conducted some early weapon separation trials during the 1982/83 DRF competition which produced the F-15E, flying an F-15D modified with bomb pylons on the CFTs. The wing was an early recipient of the F-15E, and has had a large and ongoing job clearing for use the huge array of weapons that the aircraft can carry, from B61 nuclear 'shapes' to dumb weapons. Early F-15Es 86-0185 and 86-0188 are both 40th TS stalwarts, often operating with TV cameras in fairings under the wingtips and engine nozzles to record the weapon separation in detail for later analysis. Recent trials have involved clearing the AGM-130 rocket-boosted glide bomb.

The badge of the 46th Test Wing is the same as its predecessor, the 3246th TW, seen below and left on an F-15E.

48th Fighter Wing

'LN' RAF Lakenheath, England
3rd Air Force, United States Air Forces in Europe

492nd Fighter Squadron 'Bowlers' (blue fin-stripe)
494th Fighter Squadron 'Panthers' (red fin-stripe)

Previously in France, the 'Statue of Liberty' wing has been based at RAF Lakenheath since 1960 as a cornerstone of Western European defence. Equipped with F-84s, F-86s, F-100s and F-4s, the 48th TFW adopted the F-111F in 1977, and took the 'Earth Pig' into action against Libya and in a starring role in Desert Storm. Following the Gulf War, the wing began winding down F-111F operations in preparation for the F-15E.

The first aircraft for the wing, marked for the wing commander and with a red/blue fin-stripe, arrived on 21 February 1992. The 492nd FS was the first unit to convert, standing up on F-15Es on 20 April 1992, followed by the 494th on 13 August. The 493rd FS stayed with the F-111F until 15 December, but did not convert to the F-15E, becoming instead an F-15C squadron. Both F-15E squadrons operate the latest version, powered by the F100-PW-229 IPE engine. Regular deployments are made to Aviano to provide night attack cover for the UN ground forces in Bosnia, detached to the resident 31st Fighter Wing, while 48th FW F-15Es also detach to Incirlik for Operation Provide Comfort over northern Iraq. Aircraft from the 492nd FS were involved in a strike against the Serbian airfield at Udbina on 21 November 1994, destroying the runway with LGBs.

Right: Seen on a training mission carrying SUU-20 practice bomb dispensers, this is the 492nd FS commander's aircraft. In 1994 the blue-tails were manning the detachment at Aviano for operations over Bosnia, undertaking two attacks in November against Serb positions.

Below: Lakenheath's other commitment is to Provide Comfort, policing the UN safe haven in northern Iraq. Seen on such a mission, this aircraft has a mix of air-to-air missiles and LGBs.

Left: The suitably numbered 90-0248 was chosen for the wing commander, and was the first F-15E delivered to the 48th FW.

Above: Lakenheath's F-15Es are the only such aircraft to operate from hardened shelters. This aircraft has Mk 82 AIR retarded bombs fitted.

F-15E Operators

56th Fighter Wing (58th Fighter Wing)

'LF' Luke AFB, AZ
19th Air Force, Air Education and Training Command

461st Fighter Squadron 'Deadly Jesters' (black/yellow fin-stripe)
550th Fighter Squadron 'Silver Eagles' (silver/black fin-stripe)
555th Fighter Squadron 'Triple Nickel' (green/white fin-stripe)

On 1 October 1991 the F-15E squadrons of the 405th TTW joined the 58th Fighter Wing to consolidate the training assets at Luke under one parent wing. Training continued much as before, although on 1 April 1994 the wing was renumbered as the 56th Fighter Wing, adopting the number from the deactivating F-16 training unit at MacDill AFB, FL. The 58th number was then assigned to the 542nd CTW at Kirtland AFB, NM, which trains Special Operations crews. On 1 April 1994 the 555th FS was disbanded, and reactivated in Italy as an F-16C squadron with the 31st FW at Aviano. The F-15E training squadron reverted to its previous incarnation as the 550th Fighter Squadron on the same date, operating alongside the 461st FS. The 'Deadly Jesters' themselves deactivated on 4 August 1994, leaving just one F-15E training squadron. It was subsequently deemed to be more efficient from a maintenance standpoint to transfer the training function to the operational F-15E unit at Seymour Johnson AFB. The transfer began in the latter part of 1994 following the activation of the 333rd FS under the 4th Wing, although the 550th FS continued to train crews during the transition period. At the time of writing the final class was expected to graduate in February 1995, and the last F-15E to have left Luke by the end of March.

Above: In its final incarnation, the 550th FS dispensed with the previous complicated fin-band for a simple black stripe with the squadron name. This aircraft carries the 56th FW badge on the intake.

Below: The original 550th FS was renumbered as the 555th to maintain the traditions of one of the USAF's most famous fighter squadrons, the 'Triple Nickel'. The green fin-stripe contained five stars.

Right: 'LF'-coded F-15Es originally wore the badge of the 58th Fighter Wing, shown far right, but in the spring of 1994 adopted the 56th badge. In early 1995 the last F-15E left Luke.

Below: Included in the 58th FW organisation in 1993 were three F-16 squadrons, two of F-15Es, and one ground instruction unit, all of the badges being presented on the 'boss' F-15E. The 56th now boasts seven F-16 units.

Below: Somewhere 'over the rainbow' fly the commanders' aircraft from the 58th FW and 461st FS 'Deadly Jesters'.

57th Wing

'WA' Nellis AFB, NV
Weapons and Tactics Center, Air Combat Command

422nd Test and Evaluation Squadron 'Vampires' (yellow/black fin-stripe)
F-15E Fighter Weapons School 'WSN' (yellow/black fin-stripe)

Although it had a brief existence in the USAF structure from 1948-51 as a P-80 interceptor unit in Alaska, the 57th activated in its present form at Nellis by renumbering from the 4525th Fighter Weapons Wing on 15 October 1969. On 1 April 1977 the unit was redesignated 57th Tactical Training Wing, and has subsequently returned to fighter weapons wing, become a fighter wing and, from 1994, simply a wing, the latter reflecting its wide-ranging tasks.

Two of those tasks are trials and advanced combat instruction, both roles being undertaken for each major tactical type in the Air Combat Command inventory. The trials unit is the 422nd TES, which flies examples of the F-4G, F-15C, F-15E and F-16C/D for OT&E (operational test and evaluation) work. This entails the continual refinement of combat techniques and tactics, including weapon release profiles, manoeuvring and electronic warfare tactics. Part of the 57th Test Group, the 422nd also continually tests and improves software and support equipment, and is responsible for developing, validating and verifying technical orders for the A-10, F-15C, F-15E, F-16, F-111 and F-117. In its work the 422nd TES often requires the assistance of the co-located adversary threat units, which fly F-16s to replicate hostile aircraft and operate captured and replicated ground-based air defence systems. The 422nd TES works closely with other USAF tactical trials agencies such as the AWC and 46th Test Wing, and with others outside the service.

Many of the new tactics and techniques evaluated and developed by the 422nd TES are passed on to the operational force through the work of the F-15E Fighter Weapons School, known for short as the WSN (Weapons School, Night). Separate FWS divisions serve the A-10 (WST), F-15C (WSE) and F-16 (WSF) communities also. Each FWS operates as an advanced 'college', where the state of the art in terms of tactics and weapons employment is taught. The 'students' are experienced crews with considerable operational time under their belts. Only fully competent crews can absorb the kind of advanced combat flying instruction given by the FWS. Upon graduation as qualified weapons instructors, crews return to their operational units, where they pass on their new-found

Right: The 422nd TES badge depicts a cartoon vampire figure, surrounded by four, two and two stars, while the F-15E Weapons School badge (far right) has an eagle flying at night. These badges are worn on the port CFT, with the 57th Wing badge of a bomb hitting a target to starboard.

knowledge at a more acceptable pace to their less experienced squadron-mates.

Aircraft for both the F-15E FWS and 422nd TES operate from one section of the Nellis ramp. Aircraft are marked for one unit or the other, with about half assigned to

each unit, but there is considerable cross-over between the two depending on the requirements. The 57th Wing normally has between 10 and 12 F-15Es on strength, and currently includes early production example 86-0190.

Above: Specially-marked for the 422nd TES, this aircraft carries 10 CBU-87 cluster bombs. Each weapon contains 202 BLU-97 combined effects munitions.

With two Dayglo-painted test rounds for the B61 tactical nuclear weapon, an F-15E heads for the vast Nellis ranges. The main task of the 422nd TES is to develop tactics.

78th Air Base Wing

'RG' Robins AFB, GA
Warner-Robins Air Logistics Center, Air Force Materiel Command

339th Test Squadron

The Warner-Robins ALC handles depot-level maintenance for the USAF's F-15 fleet, also providing a similar function for the C-130 and C-141. Flying is organised by the 78th ABW, with the subordinate 339th TS providing crews for the FCFs (functional check flights) undertaken when aircraft have emerged from maintenance. The Center also generates sufficient engineering evaluation work to warrant the permanent assignment of test aircraft. In addition to two F-15Cs, the unit has acquired a single F-15E (86-0189) for this purpose.

For many years the Warner-Robins ALC has operated the fighter Eagle on engineering test purposes. Recently this single F-15E was also assigned to the unit. The aircraft shows traces of its former use by the 422nd TES, with the legend 'Team Robins' on the nose.

79th Test and Evaluation Group

'OT' Eglin AFB, FL
USAF Air Warfare Center, Air Combat Command

85th Test and Evaluation Squadron (4485th Test and Evaluation Squadron)
(black/white fin-stripe)

At least one F-15E (87-0209) was assigned to the Tactical Air Warfare Center for trials purposes, the flying squadron of this unit then being designated the 4485th TES. The aircraft operated from Seymour Johnson rather than the TAWC's base at Eglin. On 1

June 1992 the TAWC was amalgamated with the Air Defence Weapons Center at Tyndall to become the USAF Air Warfare Center, and the squadron renumbered as the 85th TES. The F-15E is no longer on the strength of this unit.

366th Wing

'MO' Mountain Home AFB, ID
12th Air Force, Air Combat Command

391st FS 'Bold Tigers' (orange/black fin-stripe)

One of the mainstays of the tactical effort in Southeast Asia with F-4s, the 366th TFW 'Gunfighters' returned from the theatre without aircraft in October 1972 to Mountain Home AFB, where it began operating the F-111F. These were swapped for F-111As in 1977, and were operated until retired in the spring of 1992. At this juncture the wing underwent a radical reshaping to become the USAF's rapid intervention unit, with a mix of types forming an 'air force within an air force'.

The first two squadrons to be activated within the wing attended to the attack function, standing up on 13 March 1992. While the 389th FS began operating the F-16C Block 25, the 391st Fighter Squadron received F-15Es. Known as the 'Bold Tigers', the 391st had previously been the F-111A training squadron. Later in September the 390th FS stood up with F-15Cs, while the wing was completed by the 22nd Air Refueling Squadron with KC-135Rs and the 34th Bomb Squadron with B-52Gs (B-1Bs from March 1994). The 391st has 12 Primary Aircraft Authorized, all of which would deploy as part of the main 366th package to meet a sizeable threat. Smaller numbers are assigned to reduced packages for lower-threat scenarios. The ability of the wing to deploy large numbers of aircraft and to begin operations immediately has been tested several times, including an F-15C/F-15E/F-16C deployment to Egypt for the Bright Star exercise.

The wing's motto is 'Audentes Fortuna Juvat' – 'Fortune favours the Bold'.

Above: During their 21-year career with the F-111, the 391st wore a blue fin-stripe, but with the arrival of the F-15E this was changed for more appropriate tiger stripes, in keeping with the squadron's badge shown at top. The wing's rapid intervention role has been widely practised, including participation in Exercise Bright Star.

Left: PGM delivery for the 366th Wing is largely entrusted to the F-15E, more so since the departure of the B-52G from the wing's mixture, the 'BUFF' having previously offered a limited precision capability through the AGM-142 Have Nap. Shown here carrying four GBU-10s, this is the commander's aircraft, resplendent in the badges of the wing's five constituent squadrons (22nd ARS, 34th BS, 389th FS, 390th FS and 391st FS).

405th Tactical Training Wing

'LA' Luke AFB, AZ
832nd Air Division, 12th Air Force, Tactical Air Command

461st Tactical Fighter Training Squadron 'Deadly Jesters'
(yellow/black fin-stripe)
550th Tactical Fighter Training Squadron 'Silver Eagles'
(silver/black fin-stripe)
555th Tactical Fighter Training Squadron 'Triple Nickel'
(green/white fin-stripe)

Until its inactivation in September 1974, the 405th was based at Clark AB as the main Philippines-based USAF unit, concerned primarily with air defence. Numerous deployments were made to Southeast Asia during the Vietnam War. The wing was brought to life again on 29 August 1979 to act as the RTU (replacement training unit) for the F-15A/B Eagle, taking over the role from the 58th TTW at Luke and inheriting the 'LA' tailcode.

Having successfully trained many fighter Eagle pilots, the 405th TTW and its four squadrons were chosen as the main F-15E training unit, the fighter models being progressively phased out as training was switched to the 325th TTW at Tyndall AFB, FL. The first squadron to receive the E model was the 461st TFTS, acquiring its first aircraft on 1 August 1987 to begin conversion from the F-15A/B/D (no C models were ever assigned to the 405th). Next to convert was the 550th TFTS, which began its transition on 12 May 1989. The 555th TFTS was next, but only by the renumbering of the 550th on 14 November 1991 to preserve the famous squadron number (the 555th had been the top-scoring USAF squadron in Vietnam). The 426th TFTS was not intended to convert to Es, and this unit deactivated with fighter Eagles on 29 November 1990.

Right: The 550th was the second F-15E squadron at Luke, and adopted the 461st's fin design, albeit with revised colours.

Back in 1983, the 405th had been joined at Luke by the 58th TTW, an F-16 training unit with the 'LF' ('Luke Falcon') tailcode. By the time of the contraction of the 832nd Air Division (which controlled Luke's activities) into just one wing in 1991, the 405th TTW was down to just the 461st and 555th, which were then absorbed into the much larger F-16 training organisation on 1

Above: The 'LA' tailcode stood for 'Luke, Arizona', and was worn for many years by fighter Eagles.

October 1991. The two squadrons' F-15Es were repainted with the 'LF' tailcode.

Above: Badge of the 405th TTW on an F-15E. The motto was 'Movere et Aggredi' – 'Deploy and attack'.

412th Test Wing (6510th Test Wing)

'ED' Edwards AFB, CA
Air Force Flight Test Center, Air Force Materiel Command

415th Test Squadron (6515th Test Squadron) (blue/white fin-stripe)

Based at the USAF's principal flight test centre, the 412th Test Wing parents all of the flight test activities, in addition to running a test pilot school. Squadrons are organised primarily according to aircraft type, the 415th TS being assigned all variants of F-15 on charge. The alternative name is the F-15 Combined Test Force. F-15E Nos 1 and 2 (86-0183 and 86-0184) were assigned straight to the AFFTC for

Right: This is the badge of the F-15 CTF, worn by crew members of the 415th Test Squadron. The unit flies the F-15A/B/D/E and F-15 S/MTD.

flight trials, and other early aircraft were also used at Edwards, including 86-0190, although this aircraft now serves at Nellis. The current fleet consists of 86-0183, 86-0184 and 87-0180, the latter aircraft having been used to test the General Electric F110-GE-129 engine.

Above: Most Edwards aircraft feature the blue fin-band with a series of white crosses. The AFSC badge shown here has been replaced by the AFMC insignia.

Left: Aircraft 87-0180 was used to test the F110 engine. It now wears the F-15 CTF badge on the fin.

NATO Tigers

NATO's Tiger Association is an organisation comprising squadrons who feature the predator in their badge. Each year one of these squadrons hosts a 'Tiger Meet' for mutual training, the sharing of tactical expertise and socialising. In May 1994 it was the turn of Escadron de Chasse 1/12 at Cambrai-Epinoy.

Above: Arguably the most striking of this year's 'tiger' aircraft was this Tornado ECR of JBG 32, complete with HARM anti-radiation missiles on the fuselage pylons.

Below: Tiger spirit – a Mirage 2000C and Mirage F1C operated by the host EC 1/12 lead a formation of participants, while (inset) a group of No. 74(R) Sqn crew pose in front this suitably-attired F1C.

Above: Participation at Tiger Meet '94 came from Belgium, France, Germany, Italy, the Netherlands, Norway, Portugal, Spain, Turkey and the United Kingdom. Newcomers to the event were the Tornados of JBG 32 and AKG 51, the latter having claimed membership by adopting the former badge of the now defunct AKG 52.

Right: The sole rotary-wing participation came from No. 814 Squadron, Royal Navy, which sent a single Sea King HAS.Mk 5. Here the crew hastily apply some tiger stripes to the aircraft to keep up appearances.

Below: Although the host unit, EC 1/12, is a Mirage 2000 operator, this aircraft is from the Centre d'Expériences Aériennes Militaires, also known as EC 5/330, which sent a 2000B and this 2000C to Tiger Meet '94. Quite apart from the surfeit of tiger stripes, this aircraft is notable for having a false cockpit painted on the underside of the nose for air combat trials.

Left: Norway continues to operate the Northrop F-5 with 336 Skvadron, based at Rygge. The unit sent two aircraft to Cambrai, a single-seat F-5A and this two-seat F-5B. Although the F-5 still has a front-line role, it is increasingly used as a fighter lead-in and EW trainer, particularly for 'Europeanisation' of newly-qualified aircrew returning from advanced training in the United States. The aircraft are being updated under the Tiger-PAWS programme, with new systems including the radar warning receiver which projects from the nose.

Right: The Aéronavale's tiger squadron is Flottille 11F, shore-based at Landivisiau, although the squadron's insignia is a seahorse. The two Super Etendards which attended Tiger Meet '94 both sported tiger-striped drop tanks.

Below: Mirage F1s of the Spanish air force's Escuadrón 142 are Tiger regulars, although the aircraft wear the badge of the parent wing Ala de Caza 14. At Cambrai were examples of the three Mirage variants used by the wing: F1BE, F1CE (illustrated) and F1EE.

Above: Hosts EC 1/12 now fly the Mirage 2000, but borrowed this aircraft which had previously flown with the unit to provide the full Tiger treatment.

Right: Unfortunately not present at Cambrai is this L-29 Delfin of the Czech air force's 1. Letka. This unit previously flew the MiG-29, but these have since been retired from service. Neighbour Slovakia has painted at least one MiG-29UB in tiger marks, but this aircraft was another absentee.

Below: No less than five F-16As from Belgium's 31 Sm/Esc attended the meet, including this one aircraft with tiger tail.

Above: Turkey's 192 Filo put in a weekend-only appearance at Cambrai, but did at least add a tiger badge to the F-16C and F-16D (illustrated) which were sent.

Left: The Groupement Ecole 314 at Tours is the Armée de l'Air's advanced training unit, equipped with Alpha Jets. The unit has four training squadrons (plus a standards squadron), of which one, 2 Escadron d'Instruction 'Henri Jeandet' features a tiger's head as its badge. Standard markings for GE 314 aircraft consist of the group's stork superimposed on a star.

Below: In addition to the Tornados of JBG 32 and AKG 51, another new type/unit combination to be seen at Tiger Meet '94 were the Alpha Jets of the FAP's 301 Esquadra. Recently delivered from the Luftwaffe, the aircraft still wear the same dark camouflage. Esq 301 is at Montijo, where the Alpha Jets were much-needed replacements for the G91R.

Above: One of the RAF's most famous fighter squadrons, No. 74 is now a reserve unit flying the Hawk on advanced training duties at RAF Valley. The unit has more reason than most to maintain its tiger traditions: the badge dates back to World War I when it was equipped with SE.5As and one of the flight leaders was Major Mick Mannock, VC, the top-scoring British pilot of the war.

Above: 53º Stormo at Cameri is one of the last Starfighters, and its F-104S fighters are welcome attendees at Tiger Meets. The tiger badge belongs to 21º Gruppo, which began flying the F-104G in April 1964 when the unit was autonomous. 53º Stormo formed in April 1967 with 21º Gruppo being assigned. The F-104S began to replace the G model during the early 1970s.

Below: JBG 32 marked their Tiger debut with two different schemes, this aircraft featuring tiger tanks (complete with paws), and the name 'The Twins' under the cockpit rail. In addition to the HARM missile capability, the Tornado ECR lacks cannon but has an underfuselage bulge housing a Honeywell/Sondertechnik infra-red linescan.

Above: This tiger-tailed Magister is from the Armée de l'Air's Ecole de l'Air at Salon-de-Provence, also known as the Groupement d'Instruction 312. The unit has three Escadrons d'Instruction en Vol (EIV) for basic training and an Escadron de Controle et Standardisation (ECS) for instructor training, all flying the Magister. GI 312 also parents the two French display teams ('Patrouille de France' and Equipe de Voltige de l'Armée de l'Air) and an initial training flight.

Lockheed F-16
Variant Briefing Part 1

How does an F-16 pilot drive to work? The Vermont ANG provides one answer in the form of this superb runabout, complete with its own power. The 'Green Mountain Boys' of the 134th Fighter Squadron have recently swapped their Block 15 ADF aircraft for fighter-bomber F-16C/Ds.

Highly agile and hard-hitting, Lockheed Fort Worth's F-16 is the West's standard fighter-bomber. It has evolved from a lightweight hot rod into a complex multi-role warplane that is capable of challenging the world's best in hard-fought competitions to secure all-too-rare new fighter contracts.

The Lockheed F-16 Fighting Falcon is the most plentiful fighter in Western air forces. In terms of numbers it is also the best buy. Lockheed Fort Worth, which was General Dynamics and will be Lockheed Martin, (Lockheed acquired General Dynamics' Fort Worth plant on 1 March 1993 when the latter divested itself of aircraft manufacturing and is expected to merge with Martin Marietta to become Lockheed Martin on 31 March 1995), says that if the US Air Force buys a further batch, these spanking new Block 50/52

Falcons will be flown away from the factory for a mere $20 million. The company says, "We'll even throw in a full tank of gas."

The manufacturer's formal offer is to deliver 100 new Fighting Falcons over four years, 1999-2002, at a firm flyaway unit price of $20 million each (in 1994 dollars), a bargain-basement amount $3 million less than the price tag on the final F-16 currently scheduled for delivery in 1997. The builder of the Fighting Falcon says it can offer these deals because it knows the fighter business.

Bizarre confirmation of this comes not from Fort Worth but from St Louis where, on 1 December 1994, McDonnell Douglas put out a press release offering to participate in a customer-sponsored fly-off competition "anytime, anywhere," to demonstrate the superiority of the F-15E Eagle over the F-16ES Fighting Falcon. "This is maybe the most incredible thing I've seen in a half-century of watching aerospace," says Washington analyst Michael P. Curphey. "A short time ago, nobody would have dreamed of comparing the F-16 as a dual-role, fighter/strike aircraft with the F-15E Eagle, which costs almost three times as much. It would have been unthinkable that people like McDonnell Douglas vice president James P. Caldwell would 'lower' themselves by admitting they're threatened by the fighter from Fort Worth."

In fact, the Fort Worth, Texas, production line – where men and women at the wiring harnesses and on the drill presses know their F-16 as the 'Viper' – is itself a high-stakes sym-

Early General Dynamics test-birds include the two YF-16s, one of which is in CCV configuration, and two of the full-scale development machines. The nose shape changed considerably with the adoption of APG-66 radar.

bol in a nation anxious about the deterioration of its industrial base. In 1955, 22 production lines churned out American fighters. In 1995, production facilities for fighters add up to just three, at St Louis, Missouri (F-15, F/A-18), Marietta, Georgia (F-22), and Fort Worth (F-16). None among the trio is secure from shutdown. The plant which manufactured A-10 'Warthogs' as recently as the 1980s is now a credit card company. Calverton Plants VI and VII which produced F-14 Tomcats are soon to become a civic center owned by the town of Riverhead, New York, which has no money or plans for the property. The F-22 factory won't go away (it is also the home of the C-130 Hercules) but the F-22 itself is at risk because of its sticker price in a world where no advanced fighter seems to threaten it.

To offer a good product at a good price, Lockheed has tightened its belt, applied quality-control techniques devised for its other fighter, the F-22, and reduced its own F-16 company supplier base from 2,900, and some to 960, at the very time the number of parts brought in for the F-16 leapt upward from 5.2 million to 10.9 million per month. Two years ago, it took 276 days to build an F-16. Today, it takes 215.

Type comparison

Having fought well in Desert Storm the F-16 has nevertheless been overshadowed by other types. The F-16 makes no claim to the 'low observables' radar-eluding capability of an F-117 Nighthawk (although it iss stealthier than usually acknowledged). The F-16 lacks the reach and brute striking power of an F-111 (although it costs far less to operate and an F-16ES version with improved combat radius is under development), yet it is locked in a head-to-head, mid-1990s competition with the F-15E Eagle – an aircraft of wholly different size, capability and cost with which it would never have been compared in an economically more robust era – fighting for a production contract which the US Air Force repeatedly says it does not want and will not award since it sees this as a threat to the sacrosanct F-22 (although a new majority on Capitol Hill may re-open the supposedly 'closed' issue of building more Falcons and Eagles for American units). Even some foreign sales slipped out of the grasp, notably the Finnish Hornet order.

Except for Sparrow-equipped ADF (air defence fighter) variants plus a few airplanes delivered to Egypt, the F-16 was developed without the capability to shoot down an intruder beyond visual range. F-16 pilots slogged through the 100-day Desert Storm war (flying 13,500 sorties, more than any other aircraft, with a 95.2 per cent mission-capable rate) without racking up a single air-to-air victory, being tasked exclusively with CAS/BAI missions. Over their shoulders, they watched Eagle pilots pick apart Saddam Hussein's air force like meat on the table.

Perhaps it is some compensation that the Fighting Falcon can, and does, a superb job in the air-to-ground role, particularly on short- and medium-duration sorties but, increasingly,

Above: Stripped of much operational equipment, the US Navy's F-16Ns are the highest-performing of the service variants, befitting their role as adversary aircraft.

Below: Belgian, Danish and Norwegian Falcons line up for the camera. NATO's requirement for a Starfighter replacement was essential to the development of the F-16.

Lockheed F-16 Variant Briefing

Above: The most radical departure from the basic design was the F-16XL, featuring a lengthened fuselage and completely new cranked-arrow wing. Despite the impressive range-load performance, the aircraft lost out to the much bigger F-15E.

Right: Israel has made much use of its F-16s, including the raid on an Iraqi nuclear reactor and a 44-nil performance in air combat over the Bekaa Valley. Many IDF/AF F-16s such as this F-16C feature local modifications

on deeper penetrations of enemy territory as well. On an interdiction mission, the F-16 would refuel in flight but, even without refuelling, can fly at medium to high altitude to a combat radius of about 550 miles (885 km) carrying two 310-US gal (1173-litre) wing drop tanks on inboard ordnance stations, 12 Mk 82 500-lb (227-kg) general-purpose bombs on MER (multiple ejector racks) at mid-wing ordnance stations, and a centreline AN/ALQ-131(V) ECM pod. On another typical interdiction sortie, the F-16 would refuel in flight but can fly at medium to high altitude to a combat radius of about 605 miles (973 km) unrefueled with two 310-US gal (1173-litre) wing drop tanks on inboard ordnance stations, a 300-US gal (1136-litre) drop tank on the centerline, and six AGM-65 Maverick air-to-ground missiles on mid-wing ordnance stations. As the F-16 has evolved over the years, its capacity for fighting at night in bad weather, at lower altitude and longer range, with greater precision, has increased. This strike capability is particularly impressive in an aircraft conceived as a 'hot rod.' Once upon a time, the F-16 was meant to be a lightweight fighter and was – in early days at least – viewed primarily as a close-quarters, air superiority fighter.

LWF (Lightweight Fighter)

In part as the result of pleadings by an upstart group of Pentagon officers dubbed the 'fighter Mafia' – men who were concerned that American fighters like the F-4 and F-15 were becoming too large, too complex and too costly – the US Department of Defense approved a Lightweight Fighter (LWF) programme on 6 January 1972 and a request for proposals (RFP) was issued to industry. The RFP embodied a proposal by Pentagon analyst Pierre Sprey for a

so-called F-XX philosophy, with a high thrust-to-weight ratio, a 6.5 g load factor, an optimum gross weight of 20,000 lb (9072 kg), and high manoeuvrability. In March 1972, after reviewing designs from five manufacturers, the Air Staff determined that the Boeing Model 908-909 was its first choice as an LWF, followed by General Dynamics Model 401 and Northrop's Model P-600, a twin-engined Cobra. Vought and Lockheed were far behind.

The Source Selection Authority (SSA) chose the General Dynamics and Northrop fighters ahead of Boeing's. This became the final decision and LWF moved toward the prototype stage. The USAF awarded contracts to General Dynamics and Northrop for two service-test prototypes each of the Model 402 and Model P-600, designated YF-16 and YF-17.

Inextricably linked with the US Air Force decision was the search by NATO (North Atlantic Treaty Organization) memberss for a replacement for the veteran Lockheed F-104 Starfighter. A quartet of 'core' NATO countries had agreed to standardise; among other fighter candidates, they examined the Mirage F1E, the proposed Northrop F-18L land-based version of the Hornet, and the Saab 37E Viggen Eurofighter. In June 1975, General Dynamics' F-16 clinched *le marché du siècle*, as Belgians called the 'deal of the century', with Belgium, Denmark, the Netherlands and Norway

announcing plans to purchase 348 F-16 fighters. At the time, it was not at all clear that the F-16 would also see widespread service in American colors. It was assumed, mistakenly, that the winner of this fighter competition would also be ordered on a grand scale by the US Navy, Canada, Australia, Japan and other nations.

By now, the F-16 was gaining weight. A multi-role capability was wanted, and the idea of a 'no frills' bantam fighter – a misguided concept never really well suited to American or allied needs – was going by the board.

European co-production

The European F-16 programme was shared by a network of co-producers in the four countries. All three final assembly lines – at Fort Worth, SABCA's Gosselies plant, and Fokker's Schipol base – produced aircraft for all four users. Belgium's Fabrique Nationale (FN) handled powerplants for the European aircraft. The Belgian production line opened in February 1978, followed by the Dutch line in April 1978. Primary contracts for the F-16 were placed in 1975 with European industry. Having by now created an F-16 intended to carry an air intercept radar and a wide range of air-to-ground ordnance – no longer an LWF, by any definition – the US Air Force proceeded with full-scale development (FSD) work. Even after eight FSD aircraft were ordered for the USAF, it was

still not clear that Congress would authorise the purchase of any of the fighters for American use.

Even so, American and European co-operation on the F-16 became a remarkable success story. The F-16 programme was complex and programme director Brigadier General James Abrahamson termed it a "management nightmare." On both continents, an intricate MSIP (Multinational Staged Improvement Program) was launched to formalise co-operation in upgrading the aircraft on a planned, gradual basis. The F-16 Operational Test and Evaluation Program was followed at Hill AFB by the six-week MOTE (Multinational Operational Test and Evaluation) programme with nine airframes, including two from Belgium and the Netherlands.

In 1977, the US Air Force announced plans to purchase 738 F-16s. They would have multi-purpose capability but would serve primarily as fighter-bombers. The Air Staff had drummed up support by touting the F-16's air-to-ground prowess, based in part on early stores separation and ordnance trials. The first production aircraft

from Fort Worth flew in August 1978, the first in Europe at Gosselies on 11 December 1978, and delivery of operational aeroplanes began in January 1979, the 388th TFW at Hill AFB, Utah, and the Belgian air force receiving the first machines. The Netherlands accepted its first F-16 in February 1979, and deliveries to Denmark, Norway and Israel began in January 1980.

The F-16 has evolved in a time when advances in radar, electronics, and missiles enable any potential enemy – including less-developed Third World nations – to mount formidable defences. In response, the 'Viper' evolved from a fighter-bomber into a night attack ship, configured to make war at treetop altitude in the nocturnal hours.

By now, the F-16 has become so ubiquitous that it is easy to forget how revolutionary the aircraft looked when it was first seen. With its reliance on a central management computer system and electronic fly-by-wire control surfaces, the F-16 was the world's first fighter to be so inherently unstable that it departs from con-

Lockheed F-16 Variant Briefing

Illustrating just how far the F-16 has come since its lightweight fighter conception, this Edwards test-ship carries an ALQ-131 ECM pod, AIM-120 AMRAAM BVR missiles and an AGM-130 rocket-boosted glide bomb. This powerful 2,000-lb class weapon can be launched from great stand-off distances and 'flown' by the pilot to a precise hit via datalink.

trolled flight if the computers stop working. This instability, however, confers unequalled agility, allowing the control surfaces to be made smaller and the airframe lighter. The F-16 is distinct in appearance, with its air intake or shock inlet located directly below the pilot. The fighter's configuration uses wing/body flare to enhance lift at high angles of attack, the wing itself being straight albeit with leading-edge sweep, and with hinged leading and trailing flaps to increase manoeuvrability.

The F-16 pilot sits on a Douglas-designed, Weber-built ACES II (Advanced Concept Ejection Seat) zero-zero seat canted to recline 30°; his cockpit has HUD and multifunction displays, a sidestick controller instead of a control stick, and a one-piece canopy of blown polycarbonate which, in later versions, is lined with RAM (radar absorbent materials), giving the 'Viper' a far smaller radar signature than might be surmised.

Fixed armament comes in the form of a Martin Marietta (formerly General Electric) M61A1 Vulcan 20-mm cannon with 511 rounds located on the port side of the fuselage at the blend between wing and fuselage. The gun uses PGU-28 cannon rounds which have more mass and are aerodynamically more efficient than the earlier Mk 56 rounds now gradually being replaced throughout the fleet. The F-16 carries up to a maximum of 16,700 lb (7,575 kg) of ordnance, including Mk 20 Rockeye and CBU-87 cluster bombs, Mk 82 and Mk 84 500-lb (227-kg) and 2,000-lb (907-kg) bombs, AGM-65 Maverick missiles, and GBU-10 and GBU-12 laser-guided weapons.

Powerplant choices

The F-16 design evolved around the single 23,840-lb (106.05 kN) thrust Pratt & Whitney F100-PW-200 afterburning turbofan engine used to propel all F-16A and B models and the Westinghouse AN/APG-66 pulse-Doppler radar, also characteristic of F-16A and B models. The ultimate in the A and B production line, the F-16A/B Block 15 OCU (operational capability upgrade) airplanes, are powered by the more powerful F100-PW-220E. F-16A/B aeroplanes were built in Blocks 1, 5, 10, and 15, all powered by the P&W F100. A Multinational

Staged Improvement Program (MSIP) was initiated in February 1980 to expand the F-16's all-weather ground attack capability, and began with wiring and structural improvements to some F-16A/B Block 15s. A new block number was created retroactively with the purchase of 130 F-16A/B Block 20 aircraft by Taiwan in the mid-1990s; these will be built to F-16A/B Block 15 OCU standard with minor differences.

With a centre of gravity located farther back on the aircraft, the second-generation F-16C/D family of Fighting Falcons is nevertheless heavier, resulting in reduced manoeuvrability but greater range. The F-16C/D series employed a different approach to the selection of an engine powerplant. After the initial monopoly enjoyed by P&W, the USAF required engine manufacturers to compete for engine contracts. To prevent one builder of powerplants from growing lax, the concept evolved of a 'common engine bay' to permit the Viper to fly and fight with either of two engine choices. Over time, this was renamed a 'configured' engine bay, which (to use official language) "accommodates either engine using an engine-peculiar installation kit." In fact, the two powerplants are not interchangeable and a fighter wing (with two to four squadrons) employs only one engine type, but a spirited competition has resulted in both P&W and GE supplying engines to F-16 versions by batch, beginning with F-16C/D Block 30/32. The General Electric F110 powers F-16C/D aircraft in Blocks 30, 40, and 50, while the P&W engine (which employs a smaller air intake) is used in F-16C/D Blocks 32, 42, and 52.

Improvements to the F-16C/D include the Westinghouse AN/APG-68 multi-mode radar with better range and resolution and more operating modes. The F-16C/D series has also benefitted from the MSIP effort, which improved the core avionics of Block 25 F-16C/Ds beginning in July 1984 and has been expanded to include installation of various new systems as they become available, going up to Block 50/52. Progressive improvements of the Fighting Falcon have included the introduction of Martin Marietta LANTIRN (low-altitude navigation and targeting infrared for night) pods beginning with Block 40/42, improved performance engines (IPE) GE F110-GE-129 and F100-PW-229 with Block 50/52, and full integration of AGM-88 HARM (high-speed anti-radiation missile) with AN/ASQ-213 HTS (HARM targeting system) in Block 50/52D. The final 144 F-16Cs and 20 F-16Ds funded for the US Air Force, including the final dozen

funded in fiscal year 1994, will be Block 50/52Ds.

None of this air-to-ground sophistication should compel the conclusion that the F-16 can not dogfight. Despite its apparent lack of glamour, the F-16 belongs on any short-list of the world's best fighters, using Baron von Richthofen's definition ("The fighter pilots have to rove in the area allotted to them in any way they like, and when they spot an enemy they attack and shoot him down; anything else is rubbish"). In the air-to-air realm, pilots praise the F-16's manoeuvrability, high-g tolerance, heat-seeking missiles, and gun, especially in the 'coal-burning' F-16A model which is the best dogfighter in the series.

Falcon kills

In American hands, F-16s have scored a half-dozen kills: one MiG-25 'Foxbat-E' in the 'No-Fly Zone' of northern Iraq in December 1992 (the first kill, ever, by the AIM-120A AMRAAM missile), a MiG-23 a month later in the same place with the same missile, and four Bosnian Serb SOKO Super Galebs during a Deny Flight mission over the troubled ex-Yugoslav province. Pakistan's F-16s have shot down at least eight aircraft along the Afghan border. In Israeli hands, the F-16 has claimed at least 44 kills, mostly against MiG-23s.

Perhaps it is an omen of that Brave New World that many of the Falcon's kills have been primitive jets. The Pentagon's dilemma is that it must resist purchase of more F-15 and F-16 fighters in order to protect its stake in the F-22. However, everyone in Washington agrees that the United States can ill afford to lose any one of its three remaining factories which makes any of its three fighters, while many say the F-22 is

not needed in today's combat scenarios.

However, while the F-15 and F-16 can deal effectively with current threats, several potentially hostile nations are on the brink of acquiring fighters which could upset the balance. Russian marketing drives offering advanced versions of the MiG-29 and Su-27 to any nation may prove detrimental to the ability of the United States to maintain air superiority, but not as damaging as the development and possible sales of Mikoyan's much-vaunted 1-42 fighter, reputedly in the same class as the F-22.

Bad enough for Lockheed that it manufactures both the F-16 and F-22, creating a Hobson's choice when deciding how to lobby on Capitol Hill. Any future sale of more F-16s to the US Air Force, deemed an impossibility before the November 1994 elections, but merely an unlikelihood today, would in the words of one company official "come to us only if it were ripped out of the guts of the F-22." But in an even more tantalising dilemma not created by the manufacturer but foisted on Lockheed by the USAF, the manufacturer is competing with itself in a second way: a new F-16 for any customer must compete with hundreds of older-model 'Vipers' already available for refurbishment and upgrade. The US Air Force, not the manufacturer, is pushing the programme to revamp old 'Vipers' and resell them – but every time one is bought, that is potentially a lost sale of a new F-16. It does, on the other hand, also provide more cash for further US Air Force fighter buys.

Transforming the F-16 from a daylight freefall bomber into a 'smart' nocturnal hunter is the LANTIRN system, which adds laser designation for PGM attack, TFR for safe low-level flight and two FLIRs for night flying and target acquisition.

Evidence that the F-16 is still an important, viable and cost-effective weapon system was dished out in dramatic fashion in late 1994, when pilots flying Lockheed/Fort Worth F-16 Fighting Falcons won ordnance competitions in both air-to-ground and air-to-air categories, competing 'close up and personal' with other well-known warplanes. The 'Viper' came out on top in a bombing competition at Moody AFB, Georgia in October 1994 and at the William Tell '94 fighter meet at Tyndall AFB, Florida.

These victories merely underlined the fact that the F-16 cannot be written off. The aircraft

Block 50/52 is the latest standard of F-16, exemplified by this 20th FW pair flying alongside an OA-10. The aircraft in the foreground is equipped with the ASQ-213 system for 'Wild Weasel' defence suppression duties.

has involved over the years to meet new threats and new situations yet has remained affordable for most potential customers. Development continues, notably of the F-16ES and F-16U, the latter a delta-winged proposal for a long-range strike fighter. Despite anything that happens on Capitol Hill, it seems highly unlikely that the F-16 story will end with the Block 50s currently under construction.   **Robert F. Dorr**

Lockheed F-16 Variants

YF-16

The YF-16 was a no-frills service-test prototype. Its wing, reflecting the design chosen by Harry Hillaker's engineering team after considering several planforms, had a leading edge sweep of 40°, an aspect ratio of 3.0, wing loading of 60 lb/sq ft (2.53 kg/m²), and a span of 31 ft (9.45 m), the last-named being the only principal dimension the YF-16 shared with later F-16s. Its fuselage length of 48 ft 5 in (14.75 m) was more than 12 in (30 cm) less than subsequent F-16s and its tailfin was marginally shorter. The YF-16 differed from subsequent F-16s in having no weapons or radar, and thus being lighter with its centre of gravity further forward, affording greater manoeuvrability. Its maximum take-off weight of about 27,000 lb (9798 kg) was less than 75 per cent that of subsequent F-16s. The YF-16 had a trim nose which provided advantages in manoeuvrability and was also, overall, smaller than the nose of later F-16s. The YF-16 had analog flight controls with no computer software. Powerplant was the Pratt & Whitney F100-PW-200 (JTF22A-33) turbofan engine rated at 23,830 lb (106 kN) thrust at full afterburner, found with a handful of exceptions on all F-16A/B aircraft.

A C-5A Galaxy delivered the first YF-16 to Edwards AFB, California on 8 January 1974, resplendent in a red, white and blue paint scheme. During high-speed taxi testing on 20 January 1974, pilot Phil Oestricher encountered a rolling divergent oscillation, fell out of alignment with the runway, and saw no solution but, as he said it, "to fly out of the situation." The first planned flight with Oestricher at the controls was a less abrupt, 90-minute sortie on 2 February 1974. YF-16 No. 1 flew at Mach 1.0 for the first time on 5 February 1974 and at Mach 2.0 on 11 March. Neil Anderson made the maiden flight of the second YF-16 on 9 May 1974.

The No. 2 ship was scheduled to go to the Paris air show in 1975 but, before it could do so, was damaged in a May 1975 mishap when Anderson skidded the aircraft on its belly in the grass beside the Carswell AFB runway. Although only slightly damaged, ship No. 2 eventually ended up in non-flying electronic test duties at Rome Air Development Center, New York. YF-16 No. 1 appeared in Paris and was subsequently converted to become the F-16 CCV (below). The two YF-16s appeared

In line with its intended air superiority role, the YF-16 was equipped with Sparrow pylons on the lower fuselage, demonstrated here by the second machine.

Looking every inch a lightweight hot rod fighter, the first YF-16 takes shape in the Fort Worth workshop. The radical shape provided outstanding agility, performance and visibility for the pilot.

in various paint schemes: best known was the mottled blue experimental camouflage applied to the No. 2 ship. It proved an embarrassment. Intended to submerge the aircraft visually in the sky, it surprisingly made the No. 2 YF-16 easier to spot than the red, white and blue No. 1 aircraft.

The flyoff competition between YF-16 and YF-17 was exhaustive. The two YF-16s racked up 330 missions and 417 flight hours, reaching altitudes above 60,000 ft (18576 m), speeds above Mach 2.0, and 9 *g* manoeuvre forces. The YF-17s flew 268 sorties. During these tests, a special effort was made to put as many pilots behind the controls as possible. The YFs were flown against other USAF fighters, a MiG-17 and a MiG-21, but not against each other. The US Air Force announced on 13 January 1975 that the YF-16 had been chosen for production over the Northrop candidate, a decision which made it likely that the type would also be chosen by NATO nations.

Restored to its original configuration, the No. 1 YF-16 is now displayed at the Hampton Roads History Center, Virginia.

YF-16 serials: 72-01567/01568.

The second YF-16 wore several schemes during its working life, including this all-over grey. It is seen here during ground attack trials, carrying AGM-65 Mavericks on outboard triple-launcher rails and Mk 84s on the inboard pylons.

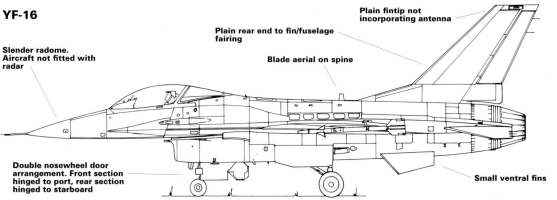

YF-16

Plain fintip not incorporating antenna

Plain rear end to fin/fuselage fairing

Blade aerial on spine

Slender radome. Aircraft not fitted with radar

Double nosewheel door arrangement. Front section hinged to port, rear section hinged to starboard

Small ventral fins

YF-16 CCV

The YF-16 CCV (Control Configured Vehicle) was distinguished by twin vertical canards added beneath its air intake in a splayed, inverted-V configuration. The aircraft was also modified with flight controls to permit use of wing trailing-edge flaperons in combination with the all-moving stabilator. This one-off testbed was modified from the No. 1 YF-16.

Its standard fly-by-wire (FBW) flight controls and relaxed static stability made the YF-16 an ideal candidate to evaluate control of a fighter beyond conventional means, with independent or 'decoupled' flight surfaces. 'Decoupling' means manoeuvring in one plane without movement in another, for example, turning without having to bank. The YF-16 CCV pioneered the capability to point the nose without changing the aircraft's flight path – an early step into the new world of high-angle manoeuvre and decoupled flight, later explored by the F-16 AFTI and the Rockwell X-31. The YF-16 CCV could rise or fall using direct lift, move laterally by direct side force, or yaw, pitch or roll regardless of the direction of flight.

After a trip to Europe which marked the maiden foray overseas for the F-16 type and included the 1975 Paris air show, YF-16 No. 1 returned to Fort Worth to be modified to YF-16 CCV along the lines of a company press release which extolled its 'fishy' appearance. The YF-16 CCV flew on 16 March 1976, piloted by David J. Thigpen. On its 29th CCV flight on 24 June 1976, the ship was seriously damaged in a landing after its powerplant failed on approach. The flight test programme was resumed and lasted until 31 July 1977, when 87 sorties and 125 air hours had been logged. The tests paved the way for even more radical flight tests in the AFTI/F-16 (described separately).

CCV testing was cut short when company pilot Dave Thigpen made a hard landing just short of the planned touchdown point during a mission at Edwards a mere 10 weeks into the planned eight-month programme. The hard landing brought a premature end to the CCV programme but not to experiments with the No. 1 Fighting Falcon. The aircraft was eventually sent to Wright-Patterson AFB, Ohio where it was used in studies of a potential escape module application for the F-16. The fuselage skins were cut all the way around

Above: Easily indentifiable by the large control surfaces under the intake, the CCV was involved in trials into decoupled manoeuvring. The ventral fins deflected through a considerable angle, their position being indicated by the deflection angle marks which are just visible where the leading edge meets the intake body.

Plain fintip, small light on side

Flaperons modified to operate in conjunction with tailplanes

YF-16 CCV

Small ventral fins

Control Configured Vehicle based on first YF-16 airframe

Two large all-moving controllable surfaces mounted under intake to provide direct side forces

the cockpit to show how it could be converted to an ejection capsule similar to those on some F-111s and the B-58 Hustler.

The escape system modification was abandoned and the aircraft was stored for some years. When it was returned to YF-16 configuration for display in Hampton as noted above, removal of evidence of the escape system trials was the biggest challenge to aircraft restorers.

YF-16 CCV serial: 72-01567

FSD F-16A/B

The FSD F-16A/B can be identified by its black radome and black RWR (radar warning receivers) on opposite sides of the fuselage; after the initial production block (described below) both of these items were coloured grey. The FSD F-16 (full-scale development) introduced Westinghouse AN/APG-66 radar, increased fuselage length of 49 ft 6 in (15.09 m) and fin height of 16 ft 8 in (5.08 m). As with all variants, addition of a second seat to the FSD F-16B – the last two of eight ships in the series – changes none of the wing or fuselage dimensions or aircraft weight, and adds no aerodynamic drag, but sacrifices 1,500 lb (580 kg) of fuel and, hence, endurance and range. All variants of the F-16 progress along the

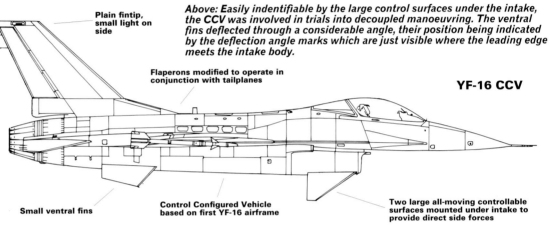

F-16A FSD

Deeper nose radome housing APG-66 radar

Antenna bulge on side of nose

Full-Scale Development aircraft showed different antenna fits. This aircraft (50746) lacks spine blade antenna and under-intake antenna

Redesigned, larger tailplane

Redesigned nosewheel door hinging to starboard

Larger, redesigned ventral fins

*The first **FSD** machine appeared in the same house colours as the two **YF-16s**, but was instantly recognisable by the much fatter radome. This aircraft was subsequently re-engined to become the F-16/101.*

*By the time of the **FSD** aircraft, the F-16 was seen as a true multi-role type. Underlining the fact is the No. 2 **FSD** aircraft, loaded with an **MER** on the inboard pylon and a **TER** on the outboard.*

Left: Fitted with a spin-recovery parachute, the first F-16B FSD is seen during trials with the GBU-8 HOBO EO-guided bomb.

Above: The sixth FSD aircraft was tested with the Hornet's APG-65 radar, necessitating the 'big nose' modification.

assembly line with single- and two-seat examples mingled together.

General Dynamics built eight full-scale development F-16A/B airframes based on a 13 January 1975 US Air Force decision to proceed with this fighter instead of the competing Northrop YF-17. The first FSD F-16A flew at Fort Worth on 8 December 1976 with Neil Anderson at the controls.

The first two-seat FSD F-16B flew on 8 August 1977.

The second FSD F-16A was employed in 1984 by NASA (National Aeronautics and Space Administration) at Langley AFB, Virginia to test a decoupler pylon concept. The third and fifth FSD F-16A aircraft were modified with 'cranked wing' delta configuration, and the third converted to

two-seat configuration to become F-16XL ships.

The first FSD F-16A was retrofitted with General Electric YF101 turbojet to become the F-16/101, beginning a long association with this engine manufacturer which resumed many years later with the F-16C Block 30 variant.

The sixth and final FSD F-16A became

the AFTI (Advanced Fighter Technology Integration) and later the AFTI/CAS (close air support) demonstrator, as described separately. The eighth aircraft became the F-16/79 and later the F-16B-2 demonstrator.

FSD F-16A serials: 75-0745/0750.
FSD F-16B serials: 75-0751/0752.

F-16/79

The F-16/79 was a two-seater converted from the second FSD F-16B (alias F-16B-2) and painted in an attractive scheme with high-gloss light grey over most of the aircraft with the canopy frame, a swatch along the fuselage spine, and the vertical tail in high-gloss medium blue. Its most distinctive feature was the longer, narrower tailpipe associated with its 12,450-lb (55.55-kN) thrust General Electric J79-GE-119 turbojet, the powerplant used on the B-58 Hustler and F-4 Phantom. Since the J79 engine was 18 in (46 cm) longer than the P&W F100-PW-200 on early production F-16A/Bs, the rear fuselage was extended aft of the stabilator pivot point by that amount. A steel shield weighing almost 2,000 lb (907 kg) surrounded most of the length of the new engine to provide protection from heat which was not needed in turbofan-powered ships, making the new aircraft correspondingly heavier than standard F-16As. The F-16/79 also had a redesigned air intake inlet which extends farther forward than the standard shape.

Although the F-16 was never the LWF (lightweight fighter) wanted by some Pentagon mavericks, the very last chance

for a 'no frills' or 'hot rod' version came with President Jimmy Carter's February 1977 arms transfer policy which dictated that US allies receive fighters less advanced than those in US inventory. Carter's attempt to reduce arms proliferation was short-lived but it forced General Dynamics to develop and fly the F-16/79. This was GD's effort to produce a simpler F-16 solely for export. The General Electric powerplant was originally designated J79-GE-17X and was a single-shaft turbojet. As the J79-GE-119, this engine was installed on an FSD F-16B bailed back from the USAF.

The F-16/79 flew on 29 October 1980. It was a deliberately downgraded version of the fighter. As such, it appealed to purchasers temporarily, and only so long as politics stood in the way of sales of the higher-performing F-16A. Many reacted like Venezuela's Lieutenant Colonel Paredes Nino, who found the F-16/79 "didn't fill many of our specific requirements, especially in long-time maintainability and range, just to mention two areas." USAF officers gave briefings on the F-16/79 to 20 air arms, including Austria, Jordan, Malaysia, Nigeria, Singapore, Taiwan and

Thailand.

The F-16/79 was not well received by pilots. Though the J79 had been a superb engine in its day, F-16/79 performance was inferior to F100-powered F-16s.

The F-16/79 was not sold, not because of any fault in the aircraft, but because Carter relaxed his policy in 1980. The election of Ronald Reagan that year told foreign purchasers they no longer need a 'downscale' fighter: they, like the USAF, could have the F-16A/B.

F-16/79 serial: 75-0752

The much extended intake ramp was necessary to smooth the airflow into the J79. Here the aircraft carries an MBB recon pod.

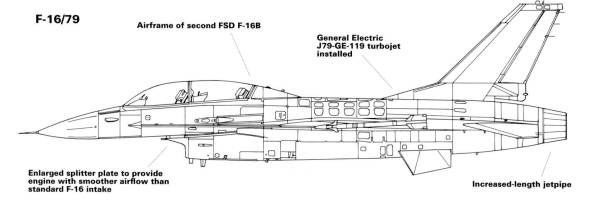

F-16/79

Airframe of second FSD F-16B

General Electric J79-GE-119 turbojet installed

Enlarged splitter plate to provide engine with smoother airflow than standard F-16 intake

Increased-length jetpipe

F-16/101

The F-16/101 was identified by minor changes in air intake and tailpipe and by the red, white and blue paint design it wore first as an FSD F-16, a colour scheme it shared with the first YF-16.

While the F-16 moved toward operational service in the mid-1970s, it appeared that General Electric would be shortchanged even if the F-16/79 was sold overseas. Pratt & Whitney seemed to have clinched the engine market for American F-14s, F-15s and F-16s. The GE YJ101 two-shaft augmented turbojet engine delivering about 15,000 lb (66.72 kN) thrust, had performed well on the Northrop YF-17 and its builder wanted to demonstrate the much-improved DFE (derivative fighter engine) version, eventually known as the F110 and capable of up to 26,500 lb (117.88 kN) thrust, on a single-engined F-16.

The retrofit was made on the first FSD F-16A (75-0745) which flew with the GE engine on 19 December 1980. The engine performed better than the P&W F100 which suffered a plethora of teething problems. A high-frequency oscillation at the engine inlet and an instance of a fuel leak were minor glitches which were easily and quickly remedied. The F-16/101 made 58 test flights and logged 75 air hours before the programme ended in July 1981. The F-16/101 was not adopted and the P&W F100 remained standard for F-16A/Bs, but the way had been paved the GE F110 to arrive on the scene much later, with the F-16C Block 30.

F-16/101 serial: 75-0745

The YJ101 engine was originally designed for the YF-17, but a more powerful version was fitted to the first FSD F-16A as a major stepping stone to the adoption of General Electric power for the Fighting Falcon. The jetpipe was more rounded than that fitted to Pratt-powered F-16s.

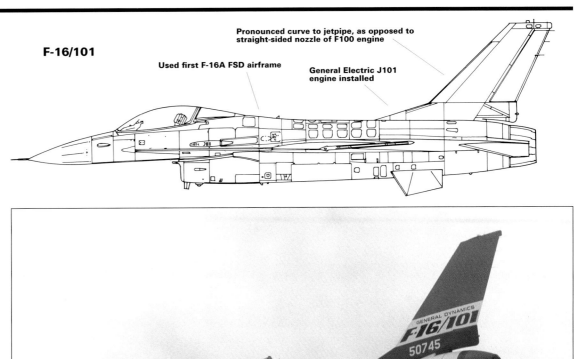

F-16/101

Pronounced curve to jetpipe, as opposed to straight-sided nozzle of F100 engine

Used first F-16A FSD airframe

General Electric J101 engine installed

F-16B-2

The eighth FSD aircraft, an F-16B, was modified to become the F-16/79 in an unsuccessful effort to export a version less advanced than the one in USAF service. This aircraft, later referred to as the F-16B-2 with P&W engine restored and repainted in European One camouflage, became a private-venture testbed for close air support and night/bad weather attack systems including the Falcon Eye head-steered FLIR or Martin Marietta LANTIRN navigation and targeting pods, a digital terrain system (TERPROM – TERrain PROfile Matching), and an automated target hand-off system. This aircraft also flew with systems offered in competition with the LANTIRN eventually chosen for the F-16C/D Night Falcon, namely the GEC-Marconi Atlantic and Martin Marietta Pathfinder. The late Joe Bill Dryden, GD's chief test pilot, said that the F-16B-2 flew with "bits and pieces of every F-16C/D ever made and a lot of pieces that

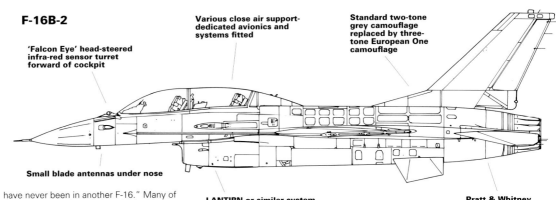

F-16B-2

'Falcon Eye' head-steered infra-red sensor turret forward of cockpit

Various close air support-dedicated avionics and systems fitted

Standard two-tone grey camouflage replaced by three-tone European One camouflage

Small blade antennas under nose

LANTIRN or similar system sometimes fitted to intake positions

Pratt & Whitney F100-PW-220 engine fitted

have never been in another F-16." Many of the systems evaluated aboard this ship were later tested on the AFTI F-16.

F-16B-2 serial: 75-0572

NF-16A AFTI and AFTI/CAS

The AFTI/F-16 (Advanced Fighter Technology Integration) test aircraft (also known as the NF-16A) is recognised by canard flight surfaces protruding in an inverted V from beneath the engine intakes, and a 'hump' or dorsal spine of the kind found on late MiG-21s and – uniquely in the 'Viper' world – on some Israeli F-16Ds. It initially retained the black radome of early 'Vipers' but this has now given way to the standard grey. Over time, the AFTI and later AFTI/CAS aircraft has evolved into a configuration which includes F-16A Block 15 horizontal tail, F-16C Block 25 wing and F-16C Block 40 avionics.

The AFTI/F-16 (originally, the sixth FSD F-16A) was a full-scale development Fighting Falcon "torn apart and put together again," as Lieutenant Colonel Michael P.

Newman describes it, to achieve a 'one of a kind' configuration to apply digital technology advances to high-angle manoeuvre.

The AFTI/F-16 first flew on 10 July 1982. Never assigned a NASA number, the AFTI ship went through 'Phase 1' of NASA flight tests, covering digital flight control systems, at the Dryden facility at Edwards AFB, California July 1982 to July 1983. The aircraft returned to General Dynamics for further modification and came back to

Seen during Phase 2 of its trials, the AFTI aircraft sports a forward-looking infra-red sensor mounted in the wingroot. The swollen spine houses additional avionics.

Left: Under the designation AFTI/CAS, the NF-16A entered Phase 4 trials in mid-1991, equipped with four attack sensors in the wingroots and above the nose. Among the varied trials undertaken by the aircraft have been head-steered sensor work, voice activation of systems and automatic hand-off of targets by data modem, including relay of radar data from satellites for accurate HARM missile launch.

Right: This close-up provides an illustration of the size of the movable ventral fins. These allowed the aircraft to rapidly point the nose off-axis for a missile shot, an area of combat tactics being explored with later high-manoeuvrability trials aircraft such as the NF-16D and X-31.

Dryden in May 1984 for 'Phase 2', auto manoeuvring and attack systems (AMAS), over July 1984 to May 1987. The aircraft returned to General Dynamics for additional modification and came back to Dryden in January 1988 for 'Phase 3', CAS 1 (close air support systems) including voice-actuated arming of systems, over January 1988 to December 1989.

Initially intended for a short-duration programme to test evolving flight principles, including continuation of work performed by the YF-16 CCV, this aircraft also contributed to programmes for automatic target designation and attack (1988), night navigation and map displays (1988-1989), digital datalink and two-aircraft operations (1989), autonomous attack (1989-91) and night attack (1989-92). In 1991, the AFTI F-16 tested an automatic ground collision avoidance system and a pilot-activated, low-level pilot disorientation recovery system.

The aircraft returned to GD yet again for additional modification. By then known as the F-16 AFTI/CAS, it returned once more to Dryden for Phase 4, or CAS 2, tests on 10 July 1991, five months later than scheduled. In this configuration the large destabilising foreplanes were removed, and various attack sensors mounted in wingroot turret fairings and above the nose.

The AFTI/F-16 fired a HARM missile for the first time in a 19 May 1994 as part of the Talon Sword Bravo Program in a demonstration of technology that could be used for the SEAD (suppression of enemy air defences) mission. Purpose of the demonstration was to show that sensor data from satellites, received and correlated by a support aircraft, could allow an attack aircraft to cue weapons against selected emitters. The support plane, a Navy EA-6B Prowler, sent the data to the AFTI/F-16 through an Improved Data Modem (IDM).

NF-16A AFTI/CAS serial: 75-0750

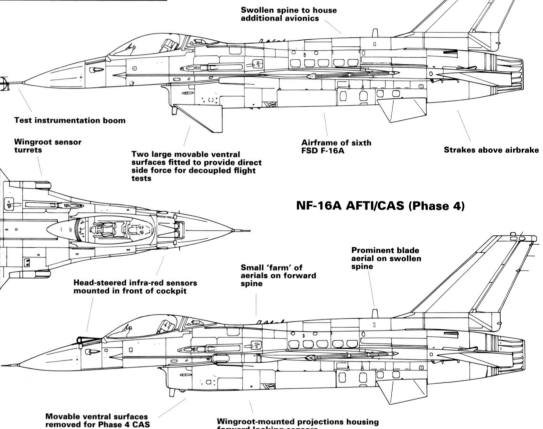

NF-16A AFTI (Phase 2)

Swollen spine to house additional avionics

Test instrumentation boom

Wingroot sensor turrets

Two large movable ventral surfaces fitted to provide direct side force for decoupled flight tests

Airframe of sixth FSD F-16A

Strakes above airbrake

NF-16A AFTI/CAS (Phase 4)

Head-steered infra-red sensors mounted in front of cockpit

Prominent blade aerial on swollen spine

Small 'farm' of aerials on forward spine

Movable ventral surfaces removed for Phase 4 CAS trials

Wingroot-mounted projections housing forward-looking sensors

Left: The spine fitted to AFTI is not as voluminous as the modification applied to some Israeli F-16Ds.

Above: For Phase 4 trials, also known as CAS 2, the NF-16A lost the original ventral fins.

F-16A/B Block 1

The F-16A/B Block 1 is distinguished by its black radome and black RWR cover located below and forward of the pilot, features it shares only with the FSD F-16A/Bs. Powerplant is the Pratt & Whitney F100-PW-200 (JTF22A-33) turbofan engine rated at 23,830 lb (106 kN) thrust at full afterburner.

First flight of a production F-16A Block 1 (78-0001) on 7 August 1978 highlighted the US Air Force's decision to invest heavily in the new General Dynamics fighter for both air-to-air and air-to-ground combat assignments. Long before the maiden flight, the F-16 was selected by Belgium, Denmark, the Netherlands and Norway to replace the Lockheed F-104G Starfighter. Production lines for the four NATO launch countries were established by SABCA at Gosselies and Fokker at Amsterdam. The Belgian Fabrique Nationale (FN) handled powerplants for the European aircraft. The Belgian line opened in February 1978, followed by the Dutch line in April 1978.

The new fighter was named Fighting Falcon at a 21 July 1980 Fort Worth ceremony when the winged predator was painted on an F-16A Block 1. Other names had been pondered, including Mustang II and (the appellation used as a radio callsign for flights in the Fort Worth pattern) Viper. The falcon is the mascot and the name of sports teams at the US Air Force Academy at Colorado Springs. The adjective 'Fighting' was added to head off any hassle with Dassault, manufacturer of the Falcon executive aircraft.

To distinguish one F-16 from another, the US Air Force makes liberal and often illogical use of 'block number' designations, created to identify aircraft models with common features. As conceived in 1942 when the first 'block number' was assigned to a Curtiss P-40E-5-CU Warhawk, the system used letter suffixes to distinguish one aircraft model from another (P-40E to P-40F) and block numbers to mark exceedingly minor changes to an aircraft model (P-40E-5-CU to P-40E-10-CU). Block numbers were assigned on the assembly line in increments of five, so that if Air Force created further, equally minor changes after initial delivery, it could assign the intermittent block numbers to existing aircraft (P-40F-5-CU to P-40F-6-CU). The two-letter abbreviation at the end of a designation rendered in this fashion

Norwegian aircraft differed from the outset by having a brake parachute in a housing at the base of the fin, necessary to aid braking on icy runways.

revealed not just the manufacturer but the builder's location (P-51D-25-NA built by North American in Inglewood; P-51D-25-NT built by North American in Dallas). The block suffix letters applicable to the F-16 are CF, based upon the manufacturer's one-time identity as Convair Fort Worth. Using this system, the first production F-16 Fighting Falcon should have been an F-16A-1-CF. The next minor change should have resulted in an F-16A-5-CF, the next an F-16A-10-CF, and so on. If an aircraft received a very minor in-service modification after leaving the factory, the F-16A-1-CF would be redesignated F-16A-2-CF, the F-16A-5-CF would become F-16A-6-CF, and so on. The next change in model should have resulted in an F-16B-1-CF.

But as used from the start, the system for identifying 'Vipers' has ignored all of these rules. First, a change in model letter suffix (F-16A to F-16B) is used, *inter alia*, to distinguish a single-seat (F-16A) from a two-seat aircraft (F-16B) which is otherwise almost identical, belongs to the same block and moves down the same production line. Thus, the first batch of F-16As and F-16Bs are both Block 1 aircraft. Block numbers have been used to signify both minor changes and major changes in models. Finally, the style used to refer to these aircraft has changed. The result of this alphabet soup is that the former Air Force style (F-16A-1-CF) is not employed on any official documents. The style which has gained fashion, instead, is the one used here (F-16A/B Block 1).

The first aircraft in this block entered service with the 388th Tactical Fighter Wing at Hill AFB, Utah on 6 January 1979 and attained IOC (initial operating capability) on 1 October 1980.

Minor changes in usage of the F-16 abound throughout the F-16 community. One of the F-16 launch customers, Denmark, elected not to invest in the ladder required for the aircraft and chose instead to use an F-100 Super Sabre workstand to enable its pilots to board its aircraft. Belgium and Norway wanted a braking parachute.

Surviving F-16A/B Block 1 aircraft, together with Block 5s, were retrofitted with minor equipment changes and brought to F-16A/B Block 10 standard in 1982-84.

F-16A Block 1 serials: 78-0001/0021 (USAF); 78-0116/0132 (Belgium FA01/17); 78-0174/0176 (Denmark E-174/176); 78-0212/0223 (Netherlands J-212/223); 78-0272/274 (Norway 272/274).

F-16B Block 1 serials: 78-0077/0098 (USAF); 78-0162/0167 (Belgium FB01/06); 78-0204/0205 (Denmark ET-204/205); 78-0259/0264 (Netherlands J-259/264); 78-0301/0302 (Norway 301/302).

Above: Illustrating the 'Sale of the Century', the F-16B Block 1 aircraft for each of the participant nations pose for the camera. The Block 1 was the only service variant to feature a black radome.

Below: During attack trials in 1980, some 388th TFW aircraft wore a 'lizard' camouflage. The 388th TFW was the first operational unit to bring the type into service: today it operates the latest variant.

F-16A/B Block 5

F-16A/B Block 5 aircraft introduced the grey radome and nose RWR cover which became standard. Powerplant is the P&W F100-PW-200.

Beginning with Block 5, Israel, which calls the aircraft Netz (Falcon, or Hawk), was added to the roster of operators comprising the US and the four NATO launch customers. Iran negotiated with the United States to acquire 160 of these aircraft, a figure which rose to 300 during the talks; the deal was stymied by political change but led to pre-production efforts which eased the subsequent Israeli sale. F-16A/B Block 5 aircraft for that country have minor, unspecified modifications which are unique to Israel. Long after entering service, some may have had improvements which include installation of Loral Rapport III ECM (electronic countermeasures) equipment and new chaff/flare dispensers, possibly AN/ALE-40s, otherwise found on the F-16C/D. Some Israeli aircraft may have Elta 2021B radar in place of APG-66.

Surviving F-16A/B Block 5 aircraft, together with Block 1s, were retrofitted with minor equipment changes and brought to F-16A/B Block 10 standard in 1982-84.

F-16A Block 5 serials: 78-0022/0027, 78-0038/0076, and 79-0288 (USAF); 78-0133/0140 (Belgium FA18/25); 78-0177/0188 (Denmark E-177/188); 78-0308/0325 (Israel); 78-0224/0237 (Netherlands J-224/237); 78-0275/0284 (Norway 275/284).

F-16B Block 5 serials: 78-0099/0115 and 79-0410/0419 (USAF); 78-0168/0171

(Belgium FB07/10); 78-0206/0208 (Denmark ET-206/208); 78-0355/0362 (Israel); 78-0265/0266 (Netherlands J-265/266); 78-0303/0304 (Norway 303/304).

Block 5 aircraft differed principally by having the definitive grey dielectric radome. These joined the Block 1 aircraft with the 388th TFW at Hill AFB. Many remained at Hill after assignment to the Air Force Reserve and upgrading to Block 10 standard.

F-16A/B Block 10

An identifying feature of F-16A/B Block 10 aircraft, shared with Block 1s and 5s, is the 'small tail', a horizontal stabiliser which has significantly less area, and extends backward less far, than that on subsequent Fighting Falcons. 'Vipers' in Blocks 1, 5 and 10 can also be distinguished by a blade UHF (ultra-high frequency) antenna located beneath the radome. F-16A/B Block 10 retains the P&W F100-PW-200 turbofan engine. Block 10 aircraft introduced minor internal changes, and all surviving Block 1 and 5 machines were brought to this standard in the early 1980s.

Twenty-four F-16A/B Block 10s modified for CAS and for use by the 138th Fighter Squadron, New York Air National Guard at Syracuse, circa 1990-1993, were unique in being equipped for the 339-lb (154-kg) General Electric GPU-5/A centreline pod, developed as the Pave Claw, which housed the GAU-13/A four-barrelled derivative of the seven-barrelled GAU-8/A cannon used in the A-10A. Following favourable firing trials on a test F-16 in 1985, some 24

'Vipers' were so modified. The gun pod was never satisfactorily integrated with the aircraft, so the 'Boys from Syracuse' deployed to Desert Storm with traditional F-16 weaponry. The unit has since converted to F-16C/D Block 25 aircraft and the 24 gun pod-capable F-16A/B Block 10s are in storage.

Some F-16A/B Block 10 fighters (including many which began life as Blocks 1 and 5) took on new duty as GF-16A teaching aids at the crewchiefs' 'schoolhouse', the 82nd Training Wing, Sheppard AFB, Texas, beginning in 1993. The G prefix refers to a 'ground' (non-flying) instructional airframe.

The US Air Force is embarked on an ambitious Coalition Force Enhancement (CFE) programme under which older F-16s are being sold to generate cash for newer models. The first of 50 F-16A/B fighters provided to Israel from excess US stocks were delivered in August 1994. The first batch consisted of five aircraft, with an additional 30 to have been delivered by the end of 1994 and 15 more awaiting funding in FY1995. Much of the work on these aircraft is being done by Israeli industry rather than Lockheed. Turkey is considering

joining the CFE instead of upgrading its Northrop F-5s. In December 1994, Defense Secretary William Perry said that older Block 10 F-16s would be offered to Argentina, Brazil, Morocco, Spain and the Philippines. Latin American countries were previously mandated 'off limits' to advanced US arms sales and a 1991 F-16 sale to Morocco was approved by Congress but never took place. Spain has decided

In profile the Block 10 F-16 is recognisable thanks to the prominent blade antenna under the intake. The brake chute is a retrofit for Dutch aircraft.

against purchasing F-16 Block 10s through the CFE programme, preferring a buy ex-French and ex-Omani Mirage F1s. Turkey, which manufactures the F-16C/D, is considering participating in the CFE to acquire F-16A/B Block 10s instead of upgrading its Northrop F-5s.

CFE is viewed by the USAF and by some in Congress as a 'trade a plane' idea which

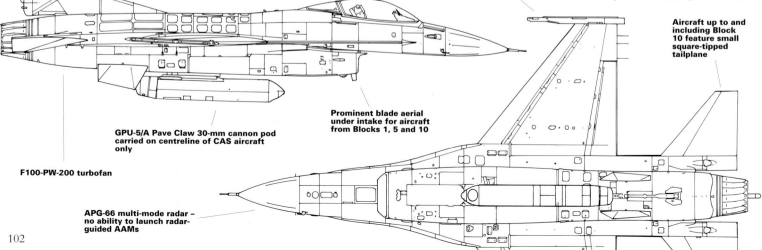

F-16A Block 10 (CAS dedicated)

Wingtip launch rails for AIM-9 Sidewinder AAM

Aircraft up to and including Block 10 feature small square-tipped tailplane

Prominent blade aerial under intake for aircraft from Blocks 1, 5 and 10

GPU-5/A Pave Claw 30-mm cannon pod carried on centreline of CAS aircraft only

F100-PW-200 turbofan

APG-66 multi-mode radar – no ability to launch radar-guided AAMs

will sell older F-16s overseas and produce revenue to purchase more modern versions for the American air arm. The effort resulted from a 'waterfall' of F-16s being retired in large batches. Sufficient income from CFE would enable the USAF to reverse its long-standing policy against purchasing any more F-16s (after fiscal year 1994) and to begin purchasing up to 12 F-16C/D Block 50/52D aircraft annually over 1997-2010.

Closely linked to the CFE programme is the Falcon Up structural rebuild for tiring F-16A/B Block 10 and Block 15 fighters, performed at the Fort Worth factory and aimed at doubling the projected 4,000 hours' flying lifetime of these 'Vipers'. Falcon Up is one of several options which enable new or repeat purchasers to incrementally upgrade their Fighting Falcons. Not every customer is taking advantage of Falcon Up: a used F-16A/B may have 500 hours left before reaching the 4,000 hour limit, enough for five more years of flying without this $600,000 improvement. The Falcon Up structural rebuild, which changes none of the systems in the aircraft, will also become available for later F-16C/D aircraft.

Beginning with the Block 10 series, the US Air Force's misuse of its 'block number' system suffers a further defilement with the addition of a letter suffix within each block. Within Block 10, a changed letter suffix (F-16A/B Block 10A to F-16A/B Block 10B) signifies little more than the sequence in which batches of aircraft were turned out. With F-16A/B Block 15, and much later with F-16C/D Blocks 50/52, these letter suffixes take on greater significance.

F-16A Block 10 serials: 79-0289/0357 (USAF); 78-0141/0145 (Belgium FA26/30); 78-0189/0194 (Denmark E-189/194); 78-0326/0335 (Israel); 78-0238/0242 (Netherlands J-238/242); 78-0285/0289 (Norway 285/289).

F-16B Block 10 serials: 79-0420/0423 (USAF); 78-0209 (Denmark ET-209); 78-0267 (Netherlands J-267); 78-0305 (Norway 305).

F-16A Block 10A serials: 79-0358/0385 (USAF); 78-0146/0152 (Belgium FA31/37); 78-0195/0197 (Denmark E-195/197); 78-0336/0345 (Israel); 78-0243/0249

The Block 10s of the 174th TFW were wired to carry the Pave Claw gun pod for dedicated CAS work. The combination was not a great success: the 174th subsequently converted to the F-16C/D.

(Netherlands J-243/249); 78-0290/0293 (Norway 290/293).

F-16B Block 10A serials: 79-0424/0428 (USAF); 78-0172 (Belgium FB11); 78-0210 (Denmark ET-210); 78-0268 (Netherlands J-268).

F-16A Block 10B serials: 79-0386/0409 and 80-0474/0478 (USAF); 78-0153/0158 (Belgium FA38/43); 78-0198/0199 (Denmark E-198/199); 78-0346/0349 (Israel); 78-0250/0253 (Netherlands J-250/253); 78-0294/0299 (Norway 294-299).

F-16B Block 10B serials: 79-0429/0432 and 80-0623/0624 (USAF); 78-0173 (Belgium FB12); 78-0211 (Denmark ET-211); 78-0269 (Netherlands J-269); 78-0306 (Norway 306).

Above: The Block 10 has largely been retired from USAF service. This aircraft flew with the 419th TFW.

F-16A Block 10C serials: 80-0479/0505 (USAF); 78-0159/0161 (Belgium FA44/46); 80-3538/3540 (Belgium FA47/49); 78-0200/0203 (Denmark E-200/E-203); 78-0350/0354 (Israel); 80-0649/0659 (Israel); 78-0254/0257 (Netherlands J-254/257).

F-16B Block 10C serials: 80-0625/0628 (USAF); 78-0270/0271 (Netherlands J-270/271); 78-0307 (Norway 307).

F-16A Block 10D serials: 80-0506/0540 (USAF); 80-3541/3546 (Belgium FA50/55); 80-0660/0668 (Israel).

F-16B Block 10D serials: 80-0629/0636 (USAF).

LTV Aerospace Model 1600

The LTV Aerospace Model 1600, had it been built, would have emerged as a heavier version of the F-16 Fighting Falcon with tailhook, structural reinforcement and sturdier landing gear for carrier operations.

In the mid-1975s, a proposal was made under which LTV Aerospace would manufacture a tailhook-equipped, carrier-based version of the F-16 Fighting Falcon for the United States Navy, while General Dynamics would produce Air Force versions. The system giving naval aircraft separate designations was by then a decade out of use, otherwise LTV's carrier-based variant might have become the XF10U-1 Fighting Falcon. The LTV Aerospace Model 1600 never actually received a designation, but apparently was a beefed-up F-16A Block 10 with the small tail associated with Block 10 and earlier models. Had the US Navy chosen the F-16 as expected, rather than a development of the competing Northrop YF-17, the LTV Model 1600 would have had exactly the same relationship to the YF-16 as the F/A-18 Hornet enjoys with the YF-17.

Vought carried out design work on several carrier-based Fighting Falcon concepts, all under the general 1600 nomenclature. These included Model 1600 (F404 engine), Model 1601 (improved F100 engine) and Model 1602 (F101 engine). A US Navy Bureau of Aeronautics engineer recalls that, "the issue of major aerodynamic configuration changes to achieve carrier suitability and the absence of a mechanical back-up to the digital FBW flight control are the main issues that came to our attention." The recollection is that

LTV "had a better solution to the mission readiness problem but couldn't really manage carrier suitability." LTV's prospects as an F-16 manufacturer were dashed when the Navy announced on 2 May 1975 that it had selected the YF-17 derivative which became the F/A-18.

It is understood that the LTV proposals never reached the mock-up stage. When the US Navy chose the F/A-18 Hornet instead, LTV filed a lawsuit which was unsuccessful.

An artist's impression shows Model 1600s in Navy colours. Among the reasons the F/A-18 was chosen over the F-16 was the twin-engined safety for overwater operations.

LTV Model 1600 (early proposal)

Proposed launch rail for AIM-9 Sidewinder on side of intake

Wingtip launch rail for AIM-7 Sparrow

Original study based on radarless YF-16

Strengthened and redesigned nosewheel strut with catapult attachment

Arrester hook for carrier operations

F-16A/B Block 15

F-16A/B Block 15 marks the biggest changes in the Fighting Falcon from its entry into production. Identifying feature of F-16A/B Block 15 aircraft and subsequent Fighting Falcons, is the 'big tail', a horizontal stabiliser with significantly more area, extending backward farther, than on earlier versions. The 'big tail' reduces take-off rotation angle and allows flight at higher angles of attack but does not make the aircraft fly better or take more *g*. F-16A/B Block 15s can also be recognised by two dogteeth antennas parallel to each other beneath the radome (for radar warning receivers) and deletion of the blade antenna under the intake.

With F-16A/B Block 15, minor changes to the Westinghouse AN/APG-66 radar provide what one pilot calls 'poor man's track-while-scan' capability. F-16A/B Block 15 introduces the Have Quick UHF secure voice radio system. The cockpit is laid out with a new instrument array and a different altimeter and VVI (vertical velocity indicator). F-16A/B Block 15s were the last to be delivered with monochrome CRTs (cathode ray terminals), although colour has been added as part of upgrading efforts. A variety of IFF (Identification, Friend or Foe) systems are in use with overseas Fighting Falcons in Blocks 1, 5, 10 and 15.

Egypt became the sixth overseas customer for the 'Viper' when it acquired 41 fighters beginning with F-16A/B Block 15B. Pakistan became non-US operator number seven with its acquisition of 40 Fighting Falcons starting at F-16A/B Block 15E. This happened long before the 1985 Pressler amendment (first enforced in 1992), a Congressional ban on US aid inspired by Pakistan's nuclear weapons programme which embargoed shipment of later F-16Cs to that country.

The eighth offshore user abroad was Venezuela, with its purchase of an F-16A Block 15K aircraft which was the first of 24 Venezuelan 'Vipers'. Venezuelan aircraft are equipped with braking parachutes.

In the early 1980s at Eglin AFB, Florida, the US Air Force tested systems and software to improve the Falcon's capability to seek, find and destroy targets using a low-level attack profile. Over time, these trials offered up the LANTIRN system. At least one F-16A Block 15 (80-0550) used to develop weapon systems at Eglin AFB, Florida became a 'one of a kind' test-ship (roughly, the Air Force's equivalent of the company-financed FSD F-16B-2) when it was modified several times to evaluate early LANTIRN prototypes.

Netherlands Block 15 F-16A(R) aircraft carry the Oude Delft Orpheus day/night reconnaissance pod previously employed on F-104s. In Netherlands service, the pod houses TA-8M2 cameras and an IRLS-5 linescanner. The pod weighs 818 lb (400kg) and can be attached in 30 minutes.

Improvements to the basic F-16A/B aircraft result from an MSIP (Multinational Staged Improvement Program) instituted in 1980. Stage I of MSIP involved structural improvements and writing changes incorporated into Block 15 production. Subsequent MSIP improvements apply to the F-16C/D series.

F-16A Block 15 serials: 80-0541/0571 (USAF); 80-3596/3597 (Denmark E-596/597); 78-0258 (Netherlands J-258);

Demonstrating two different radome colours, these Block 15 aircraft serve with the 93rd FS at Homestead AFB. Most Block 15 aircraft have two small antennas under the nose in place of the blade under the intake.

80-3616/3618 (Netherlands J-616/618); 78-0300 (Norway 300);80-3658/3659 (Norway 658/659).

F-16B Block 15 serials: 80-0635/0636 (USAF); 80-3612 (Denmark ET-612); 80-3689 (Norway 689).

F-16A Block 15A serials: 80-0572/0596 (USAF); 80-0639/0641 (Egypt 9301/9303).

F-16B Block 15A serials: 80-0637 (USAF); 80-0644/0647 (Egypt 9201/9204).

F-16A Block 15B serials: 80-0597/0622 (USAF); 80-3547 (Belgium FA56); 80-3598/3602 (Denmark E-598/602); 80-0642/0643 (Egypt 9304/9305); 80-3619/3623 (Netherlands J-619/623); 80-3660/3663 (Norway 660/663).

F-16B Block 15B serials: 80-0638 (USAF); 80-3588 (Belgium FB13); 80-3613 (Denmark ET-613); 80-0648 (Egypt 9205); 80-3649/3650 (Netherlands J-649/650); 80-3690 (Norway 690).

F-16A Block 15C serials: 81-0663/0688 (USAF); 81-0643/0644 (Egypt 9306/9307).

F-16B Block 15C serials: 81-0812 (USAF); 81-0662 (Egypt 9206).

F-16A Block 15D serials: 81-0689/0713 (USAF); 80-3548/3551 (Belgium FA57/60); 80-3603/3606 (Denmark E-603/606);

81-0645/0647 (Egypt 9308/9310); 80-3624/3629 (Netherlands J-624/629); 80-3664/3667 (Norway 664/667).

F-16B Block 15D serials: 81-0813/0814 (USAF); 80-3589/3592 (Belgium FB14/17); 80-3651 (Netherlands J-651); 80-3691 (Norway 691); 81-0931/0932 (Pakistan 601/602).

F-16A Block 15E serials: 81-0714/0738 (USAF); 81-0648/0650 (Egypt 9311/9313); 81-0899/0900 (Pakistan 701/702).

F-16B Block 15E serials: 81-0815/0816 (USAF); 81-0933/0934 (Pakistan 603/604).

F-16A Block 15F serials: 81-0739/0763 (USAF); 80-3552/3556 (Belgium FA61/65).

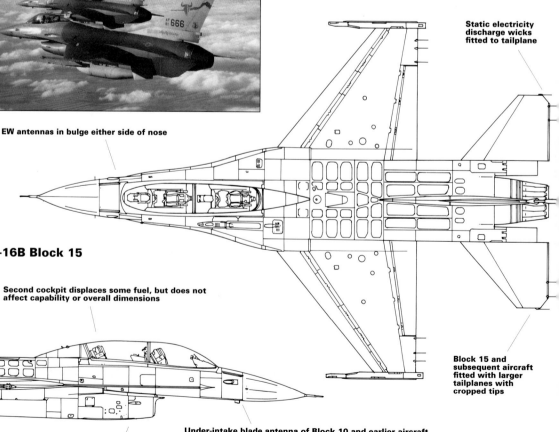

Left: Block 15 aircraft were assigned to ANG air defence units prior to them being upgraded to ADF standard. These are from the 186th FS.

Above: Belgian F-16 Block 15s are unusual in not having the twin antennas under the nose. The aircraft are fitted with brake parachutes.

F-16B Block 15

EW antennas in bulge either side of nose

Second cockpit displaces some fuel, but does not affect capability or overall dimensions

Static electricity discharge wicks fitted to tailplane

Block 15 and subsequent aircraft fitted with larger tailplanes with cropped tips

Navigation light on either side of engine intake

Under-intake blade antenna of Block 10 and earlier aircraft removed, replaced by two small antennas under the nose

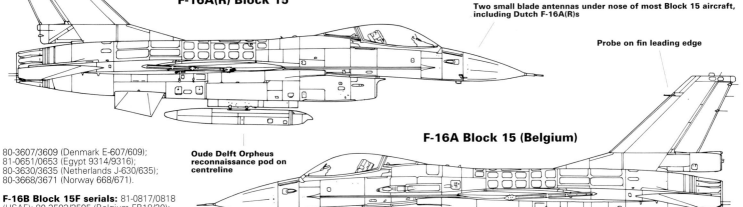

F-16A(R) Block 15

Two small blade antennas under nose of most Block 15 aircraft, including Dutch F-16A(R)s

Probe on fin leading edge

F-16A Block 15 (Belgium)

Oude Delft Orpheus reconnaissance pod on centreline

Blade antennas under nose absent from Belgian aircraft

Extended tail housing for brake parachute

80-3607/3609 (Denmark E-607/609); 81-0651/0653 (Egypt 9314/9316); 80-3630/3635 (Netherlands J-630/635); 80-3668/3671 (Norway 668/671).

F-16B Block 15F serials: 81-0817/0818 (USAF); 80-3593/3595 (Belgium FB18/20); 80-3614 (Denmark ET-614); 80-3652/3653 (Netherlands J-652/653); 80-3692 (Norway 692).

F-16A Block 15G serials: 81-0764/0787 (USAF); 81-0654/0657 (Egypt 9317/9320).

F-16B Block 15G serials: 81-0819/0820 (USAF).

F-16A Block 15H serials: 81-0788/0811 (USAF); 80-3557/3562 (Belgium FA66/FA71); 80-3610/3611 (Denmark E-610/611); 81-0658/0661 (Egypt 9321/9324); 80-3636/3641 (Netherlands J-636/641); 80-3672/3675 (Norway 672/675).

F-16B Block 15H serials: 81-0821/0822 (USAF); 80-3654/3655 (Netherlands J-654/655); 80-3693 (Norway 693).

F-16A Block 15J serials: 82-0900/0924 (USAF); 82-1056/1057 (Egypt 9325/9326).

F-16B Block 15J serials: 82-1026/1028 (USAF).

F-16A Block 15K serials: 82-0925/0944 (USAF); 80-3563/3570 (Belgium FA72/79); 82-1058/1060 (Egypt 9327/9329); 80-3642/3645 (Netherlands J-642/645); 80-3676/3683 (Norway 676/683); 82-1050 (Venezuela 1041).

F-16B Block 15K serials: 82-1029/1033 (USAF); 80-3656/3657 (Netherlands J-656/657); 82-1053/1055 (Venezuela 1715, 2179, 9581).

F-16A Block 15L serials: 82-0945/0965 (USAF); 82-1061/1063 (Egypt 9330/9332); 82-1051/1051 (Venezuela 0051, 6611).

F-16B Block 15L serials: 82-1034/1037 (USAF).

F-16A Block 15M serials: 82-0966/0986 (USAF); 80-3571/3578 (Belgium FA80/87); 82-1064/1065 (Egypt 9333, 9334); 80-3646/3648 (Netherlands J-646/648); 81-0864 (Netherlands J-864); 80-3684/3688 (Norway 684/688); 81-0901/0902 (Pakistan 703/704).

F-16B Block 15M serials: 82-1038/1041 (USAF); 81-0882 (Netherlands J-882); 81-0935/0936 (Pakistan 605/606).

F-16A Block 15N serials: 82-0987/1007 (USAF); 81-0903 (Pakistan 705).

F-16 Block 15N serials: 82-1042 (USAF); 82-1043 (Egypt 9208); 82-1044/1045 (USAF); 81-0937/0938 (Pakistan 607/608).

F-16A Block 15P serials: 82-1008/1025 (USAF); 80-3579/3583 (Belgium FA88/FA92); 81-0865/0869 (Netherlands J-865/869); 81-0904/0906 (Pakistan 706/708).

F-16B Block 15P serials: 82-1046/1049 (USAF); 81-0883 (Egypt 9207).

F-16A Block 15Q serials: 83-1066/1087 (USAF); 81-0907/0911 (Pakistan 709/713).

F-16B Block 15Q serials: 83-1166/1171 (USAF); 80-3615 (Denmark ET-615).

F-16A Block 15R serials: 83-1088/1106 (USAF); 80-3584/3587 (Belgium FA93/96); 81-0870/0879 (Netherlands J-870/879); 81-0912/0915 (Pakistan 714/717).

F-16A Block 15S serials: 83-1107/1117 (USAF); 81-0916/0920 (Pakistan 718/722).

F-16B Block 15S serials: 83-1172/1173 (USAF); 81-0884/0885 (Netherlands J-884/885).

F-16A Block 15T serials: 81-0880/0881 (Netherlands J-880/881); 83-1192/1196 (Netherlands J-192/196); 81-0921/0922 (Pakistan 723/724); 83-1186/1188 (Venezuela 8900, 0678, 3260).

F-16B Block 15T serials: 83-1208/1209 (Netherlands J-208/209); 83-1189/1191 (Venezuela 2337, 7635, 9583).

F-16A Block 15U serials: 83-1197/1206 (Netherlands J-196/206); 81-0923/0926 (Pakistan 725/728); 84-1346/1353 (Venezuela 7268, 9068, 8924, 0094, 6023, 4226, 5422, 6426).

F-16B Block 15U serials: 83-1210/1211 (Netherlands J-210/211); 81-1504 (Pakistan 609).

F-16A Block 15V serials: 84-1354/1357 (Venezuela 4827,9864, 3648, 0220).

F-16B Block 15V serials: 81-1505/1507 (Pakistan 610/612).

F-16A Block 15W serials: 83-1207 (Netherlands J-207); 84-1358/1365 (Netherlands J-358/365).

F-16B Block 15W serials: 84-1368/1369 (J-368/369).

Pakistan's F-16 Block 15s have scored at least eight victories over Soviet and Afghan aircraft crossing the border. This aircraft displays the unique camouflage applied to these aircraft, with a broad central band of dark grey with small patches on the tailplane.

F-16A Block 15X serials: 84-1366/1367 (Netherlands J-366/367); 85-0135/0140 (Netherlands J-135/140).

Known by the designation F-16A(R), or occasionally RF-16, the reconnaissance-dedicated aircraft of the KLu's 306 Squadron are Block 15s wired to carry the Oude Delft Orpheus multi-sensor tactical reconnaissance pod.

F-16A/B Block 15 ADF

The F-16A/B Block 15 ADF (Air Defense Fighter) is readily recognised by four L-shaped blade antennas located just ahead of the canopy and four more on the bottom of the nose, all associated with the Teledyne/E-Systems AN/APX-109 Mk XII AIFF (Advanced Identification, Friend or Foe) system unique to this variant and not approved by the United States for export. A more prominent feature of the ADF found on F-16A examples only is the Bendix/King AN/ARC-200 HF (high frequency) single-sideband radio which is deemed more effective for long-range transmissions required during an intercept fly-out. Because of the addition of the HF radio's antenna on the leading edge of the fin, a pair of hydraulic actuators for rudder operation previously mounted one above the other were moved downward and forward, and placed side-by-side resulting in a distinctive bulge to where the fin meets the base of the aircraft. The misconception is widespread that the bulge itself is an HF antenna, when in fact it is the nerve centre for the rudder. Yet another distinguishing feature of the ADF, although some European Falcons have it, is the ID (identification) light, often misleadingly called a searchlight, mounted on the forward left side of single-seat F-16A/B Block 15 ADFs.

The ADF proposal called for two features

which were not adopted, namely a drag chute and 600-US gal (2271-litre) tanks on stations 4 and 6 in lieu of the 370-US gal (1400-litre) tanks actually carried.

The ADF emerged as a major programme in the late 1980s while the Cold War was still thawing – a modification of existing Block 15 Fighting Falcons for strategic defence of North America against bombers and cruise missiles. ADFs, as they are known, were ordered in October 1986 to replace F-106s, F-4s and F-15s in the interceptor role with Air National Guard squadrons. These aircraft were chosen after the US Air Force considered a version of the Northrop F-20A Tigershark.

The Grimes-built ID light on the nose of the ADF, which lacks a military designation, is canted 70° to the left of forward and 10° up, deemed an annoyance by some pilots because the radar gimbal limit for the AN/APG-66(V)1 is 60°, meaning that the 'Viper' cannot aim both the ID light and its radar at a target simultaneously. Worse, positioning the ID light on the port side makes it necessary to carry out an intercept from the left side of the target rather than, as international rules and custom demand, from the right. ADFs are the only American Falcons with the ID light. Danish Block 10s and 15s and Norwegian Block 15s have the ID light but lack the Americans' separate 'on/off' toggle setting, so that theirs must

be turned on using the taxi light switch.

The Westinghouse AN/APG-66(V)1 radar on the ADF was modified to improve small target detection and provide continuous-wave illumination. The archetypal weapons loadout for an F-16A/B Block 15 ADF Fighting Falcon on a high-altitude, medium/long-range intercept sortie consists of two Raytheon AIM-9M Sidewinder infra-red missiles on weapon stations 1 and 9, which are the wingtip launch rail locations; two Hughes AIM-120A AMRAAM (advanced medium-range air-to-air missiles) on stations 2 and 8 beneath the wing at the outboard location, and two Raytheon AIM-7M Sparrow semi-active radar missiles on inboard stations 3 and 7. The ADF retains the standard M61A1 20-mm Vulcan 'Gatling' cannon with 511 rounds. In addition to the centreline fuel 'bag' containing 300 US gal (1135 litres), sometimes replaced by a 'travel pod' on

Not a true ADF, this Edwards Block 15 nevertheless tested many of the systems. In addition to the AIFF system, the aircraft carries AIM-7 Sparrows for launch tests.

short jaunts, all American F-16s typically carry two 360-US gal (1362-litre) fuel tanks on stations 4 and 6 and have the capability to carry two 610-US gal (2309-litre) fuel tanks, although the latter are not stocked in inventory. Although it does not usually do anything so unrealistic, the ADF can carry AIM-9s or AMRAAMs on stations 1, 2, 3, 7, 8 and 9. The air defence fighter can carry AIM-7 Sparrows only on stations 3 and 7 and only with pylons known as RDRCs or 'radar rails'. The F-16A/B Block 15 ADF is the only American version of the 'Viper' with Sparrow capability. A 'real life' mission load would be influenced by the fact that

Lockheed (General Dynamics) F-16 Block 15 ADF

1 Pitot head
2 Glass-fibre radome
3 Planar radar scanner
4 ILS glideslope antenna
5 Scanner drive unit
6 Radar mounting bulkhead
7 Forward avionics equipment bay
8 Upper IFF antenna array
9 Westinghouse AN/APG-66 digital pulse-Doppler radar equipment module
10 Night identification light
11 Radar warning antenna
12 Cockpit front pressure bulkhead
13 Instrument panel shroud
14 Weapons system fire control electronics
15 Fuselage forebody strake fairing
16 Wide-angle raster-video head-up-display (WARHUD)
17 Sidestick controller, fly-by-wire control system
18 Cockpit pressure floor
19 Frameless cockpit canopy
20 McDonnell Douglas ACES II 'zero-zero' ejection seat
21 Seat harness
22 Canopy fairing
23 Engine throttle lever
24 Port side console panel
25 Cockpit section close-pitched frame structure
26 Rear pressure bulkhead
27 Ejection seat headrest
28 Seat arming safety lever
29 Cockpit pressure sealing frame
30 Canopy hinge point
31 Ejection seat launch rails
32 Rear avionics equipment bay
33 Boundary layer splitter plate
34 Fixed geometry engine air intake
35 Lower IFF antenna array

36 Aft-retracting nosewheel
37 Shock absorber scissor links
38 Retraction strut
39 Nosewheel door
40 Forward position light
41 Intake trunking
42 Cooling air louvres
43 Gun gas suppression muzzle aperture
44 Air system piping
45 Forward fuselage fuel tank, total system capacity 1072.5 US gal (4060 litres)
46 Canopy aft glazing
47 Starboard 370-US gal (1400-litre) external fuel tank
48 Forebody blended wingroot
49 Upper position light and flight refuelling floodlight
50 Fuel tank bay access panel
51 Rotary cannon barrels
52 Forebody frame structure
53 M61A1 Vulcan 20-mm rotary cannon
54 Ammunition feed and link return chutes
55 Ammunition drum, 515-rounds
56 Ammunition drum flexible drive shaft
57 Hydraulic gun drive motor
58 Leading-edge flap control shaft
59 Hydraulic equipment service bay
60 Primary system hydraulic reservoir
61 Leading-edge manoeuvre flap drive motor
62 TACAN antenna
63 No. 2 hydraulic system reservoir
64 Leading-edge flap control shaft
65 Inboard pylon
66 Pylon hardpoint
67 Wing centre stores pylon
68 Missile launch adaptor
69 AIM-7F/M Sparrow III air-to-air missile

70 A/A 37U-36 Aerial Gunnery Target System (AGTS)
71 TDK-39 towed target container
72 Winch housing and airframe adaptor
73 Air-driven turbine housing
74 AIM-9P2/3 Sidewinder air-to-air missile
75 ACMI datalink pod
76 Twin Sidewinder installation
77 AIM-9M Sidewinder air-to-air missiles
78 Missile launch rails
79 Outboard stores pylon
80 Aluminium honeycomb leading-edge flap structure
81 Starboard navigation light
82 Static dischargers
83 Fixed section of trailing edge
84 Multi-spar wing structure
85 Starboard wing integral fuel tank
86 Starboard flaperon
87 Fuel system piping
88 Access panels
89 Centre fuel tank bay
90 Intake ducting
91 Wing attachment main bulkheads
92 Universal air refuelling receptacle (UARSSI)
93 Engine compressor face
94 Pratt & Whitney F100-PW-220E afterburning turbofan engine
95 Jet fuel starter
96 Airframe mounted engine accessory equipment gearbox
97 Gearbox drive shaft
98 Ground pressure refuelling connector
99 Flaperon servo actuator
100 Rear fuselage frame construction
101 Rear integral fuel tank
102 Main engine mounting suspension link
103 UHF antenna
104 Starboard side body fairing

105 Finroot fillet
106 HF tuner
107 Anti-collision light power supply
108 Flight control system hydraulic accumulators
109 Starboard tailplane
110 Tailplane panels interchangeable port and starboard
111 Fin torsion box structure
112 Steel leading-edge strip
113 Dynamic pressure sensor
114 Aluminium honeycomb leading-edge panel
115 VHF antenna
116 Anti-collision light
117 Static dischargers
118 Tail radar warning antennas
119 Aluminium honeycomb rudder construction
120 Rudder servo actuator
121 Radar warning power supply
122 ECM antenna fairing
123 Tail navigation light
124 Variable-area exhaust nozzle
125 Nozzle flaps
126 Split trailing-edge airbrake, upper and lower surfaces
127 Airbrake hydraulic jack
128 Port all-moving tailplane
129 Static dischargers
130 Graphite epoxy tailplane skin panels
131 Corrugated aluminium sub-structure
132 Tailplane pivot mounting

133 Tailplane servo actuator
134 Nozzle sealing fairing
135 Fueldraulic nozzle actuators
136 Afterburner tailpipe
137 Rear fuselage bulkheads
138 Rear engine mounting
139 Aft position light
140 Port side-body fairing
141 Runway arrester hook
142 Ventral fin, port and starboard
143 Port flaperon
144 Flaperon hinges
145 Aluminium honeycomb flaperon construction
146 Static dischargers
147 Fixed trailing edge section

air-to-air versions of the Sparrow are no longer in production in the United States, while AMRAAMs now in inventory with virtually all F-16 users.

Much of the developmental work on the ADF programme was carried out at Edwards AFB, California by an F-16B Block 15F aircraft which carried a special red/yellow 'ADF' fin flash bearing a silhouette of a Sparrow. The first successful guided launch of an AIM-7 Sparrow was made over the Point Mugu range, California in February 1989.

Two hundred and seventy aircraft were to have been modified to this standard (from 'plain' F-16A/B Block 15 status), although the actual number appears to be 241. General Dynamics converted the first, then shipped modification kits for installation by the Ogden Air Logistics Center, Hill AFB, Utah. The Hill ADF aircraft was completed in October 1988. Development continued at Edwards and operational test and evaluation was carried out by the 57th Fighter Weapons Wing at Nellis AFB, Utah. The first operational aircraft was delivered to the 114th Fighter

Training Squadron at Kingsley Field, Klamath Falls, Oregon on 1 March 1989. The 144th Fighter-Interceptor Wing, California ANG, Fresno, achieved IOC in 1989 following receipt of the wing's first aircraft 13 April 1989. In December 1994, 120 ADFs were used by operational Air National Guard squadrons and a further 16 at the Kingsley Field 'schoolhouse'.

With the end of the Cold War and the rise of the perception that bombers and cruise missiles no longer threaten North America, the air defence mission is likely to be phased out in the late 1990s. The General Accounting Office (GAO), which oversees Congressional spending, has strongly urged such a phase-out and about half of the ADF fleet has already been retired (the airframes being 'de-ADF'ed', or stripped of AIFF, HF radio, and some AIM-7 software), but plans for the remainder of the ADF force are unlikely to be announced before mid-1995. Often overlooked, as the Pentagon's Lieutenant Colonel Carl Nuzzo puts it, is that the ADF 'Viper' "has exactly the same bombing capability as other Block 15s." The Puerto Rico Air National Guard,

Not all ADFs are dedicated fighters. Those of the Illinois (illustrated) and Puerto Rico Guard units have a battlefield assignment, and are seen carrying bombs. This aircraft has a Mk 82 bomb and an ALQ-131 ECM pod.

for example, has long been equipped with ADFs while assigned air-to-ground duties. Since ADFs are considered 'low hour' flying machines, they could remain in service and revert to 'mud moving', air-to-ground duty before the turn of the century.

Some 217 F-16A and 24 F-16B fighters

(241 total) were modified to ADF standard based on US Air National Guard records.

A reliable source indicates that one F-16A Block 10D aircraft (80-0525) was modified to ADF standard, but the manufacturer and the USAF claim no record of it.

148 Port AIM-9M Sidewinder air-to-air missile
149 Missile launch rail
150 Wingtip launch rail fitting
151 Port navigation light
152 Port outer pylon/ missile rail
153 AIM-120 Advanced Medium Range Air-to-Air Missile (AMRAAM)
154 Port AIM-7 Sparrow air-to-air missile
155 Pylon missile adaptor
156 Port centre pylon
157 Centre pylon hardpoint
158 Multi-spar wing structure
159 Leading-edge flap rotary actuators
160 Port wing integral fuel tank
161 Inboard pylon hardpoint
162 Wingroot attachment fishplates
163 Landing/taxiing lamp
164 Main undercarriage shock absorber strut
165 Mainwheel leg strut
166 Articulated retraction/drag link
167 Mainwheel door
168 Port mainwheel forward retracting
169 Port external fuel tank
170 Centreline 300-US gal (1136-litre) external fuel tank
171 AN/ALQ-184(V)2 (short) ECM pod
172 AN/ALQ-131 (shallow) ECM pod

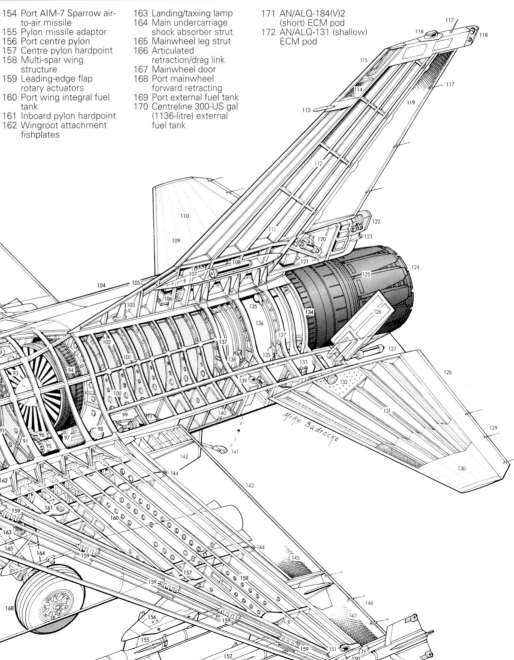

Armament

Despite being optimised for the air defence role, the ADF retains the Block 15's air-to-ground capability. The Puerto Rican aircraft can undertake either the air defence mission (as illustrated here) or ground attack, for which a variety of bombs and cluster munitions can be carried.

Radar-guided AAMs

The ADF is the only USAF F-16 version compatible with the AIM-7 Sparrow, which is carried only on stations 3 and 7 (centre wing pylons). Up to six AIM-120 AMRAAMs can be carried on any of the six wing missile positions.

ADF force

At its peak the F-16 ADF equipped a defensive chain of units around the periphery of the continental United States, serving with ANG units in California, Florida, Michigan, Minnesota, Montana, New Jersey, New York, North Dakota, Texas and Vermont, in addition to the tactical units in Illinois and Puerto Rico, and a dedicated ADF training squadron in Oregon. These augmented two NORAD-dedicated F-15 units (in Massachusetts and Oregon). With no identifiable threat to the United States from either bombers or cruise missiles, the ADF force is now without a mission, resulting in the gradual retirement of the fleet and re-equipment of ADF units with surplus F-16C/Ds.

Radar

The ADF has the APG-66(V)1 radar fitted, modified to feature a continuous illumination mode for guiding Sparrow missiles. Standard air-to-air modes are look up, look down, search and track, track while scan, automatic tracking and air combat search.

F-16A Block 15 ADF serials: 80-0541, 80-0543/549, 80-0552/0555, 80-0562/0563, 80-0565/0567, 80-0569/0572, 80-0575/0576, 80-0580/0583, 80-0585, 80-0589/0594, 80-0596, 80-0598, 80-0601, 80-0604/0605, 80-0607/0608, 80-0610/0611, 80-0614/0616, 80-0618/0622, 81-0665/0666, 81-0668/0669, 81-0672/0675, 81-0680/0682, 81-0684/0685, 81-0689/0691, 81-0693/0708, 81-0710/0716, 81-0718/0723, 81-0725/0729, 81-0731/0744, 81-0746, 81-0748/0749, 81-0751-0765, 81-0767/0774, 81-0776/0787, 81-0789, 81-0791, 81-0793, 81-0795, 81-0799, 81-0801, 81-0803, 81-0805, 81-0807, 81-0809, 81-0811, 82-0901, 82-0903, 82-0905, 82-0907, 82-0910, 82-0913, 82-0915, 82-0917, 82-0919, 82-0921, 82-0923, 82-0926, 82-0929/0930, 82-0932, 82-0934/0935, 82-0937, 82-0942, 82-0945, 82-0950, 82-0953, 82-0955/0956, 82-0960/0961, 82-0963, 82-0966/0967, 82-0969, 82-0972/0974, 82-0978/0979, 82-0981, 82-0983/0986, 82-0990, 82-0992, 82-0995, 82-1008, 82-1010, 82-1012, 82-1014, 82-1016, 82-1019, 82-1021, 82-1023.

F-16B Block 15 ADF serials: 80-0636/0637, 81-0812, 81-0817/0819, 82-1026/1028, 82-1030/1036, 82-1039/1042, 82-1044, 82-1046, 82-1048/1049.

Thirty F-16A and two F-16B fighters were earmarked for conversion to ADF standard (raising the overall total to 273) but may have been only partially converted, or not converted at all. These F-16A Block 15 ADF candidates were 80-0542, 80-0550, 80-0558/0561, 80-0568, 80-0587/0588, 80-0602/0603, 80-0612/0613, 81-0686, 81-0709, 81-0717, 81-0775, 81-0797, 82-0916, 82-0947, 82-0951, 82-0987, 82-0989, 82-1000/1003, and 82-1005/1006.

F-16B Block 15 ADF candidates were 81-0814 and 81-0820.

From most angles the large bulge on the fin/fuselage fairing is the most obvious distinguishing feature of the Block 15 ADF. This houses the relocated rudder actuators.

Lockheed F-16A Block 15 ADF Air Defense Fighter

The total of 241 ADF conversions from Block 15 aircraft was greater than the number required to equip the Air National Guard squadrons tasked with a NORAD air defence mission, the remainder being delivered to two regular battlefield-assigned units, the 168th FS/Illinois ANG and the 198th FS/Puerto Rico ANG. Both of these units differ from the NORAD-dedicated squadrons by wearing TAC-style two-letter tailcodes ('IL' and 'PR') in line with their general tactical tasking.

Communications
In addition to the standard suite, the ADF has an ARC-200 HF/SSB radio for long-range work when on long overwater intercepts.

Infra-red AAMs
The standard IR AAM is the AIM-9M Sidewinder, carried on the wingtip and outer wing attachments. A twin 'Winder arrangement can be carried on the underwing pylon, and the older AIM-9P is another weapon option.

ADF features
ADF aircraft have three principal features. The first is the port-side ID light for the aerial illumination of aerial targets for identification. The second is the fin bulge, caused by the relocation of the rudder actuators to make way for HF communications, while the third is the AIFF (advanced identification, friend or foe) equipment, for which two antenna arrays are provided (one forward of the canopy and one below the intake). The latter were retrospectively applied to ADFs after initial conversion, and have not yet been cleared for export.

Markings
With a few exceptions, all USAF F-16s feature this two-tone grey camouflage which has been carefully designed to be enhanced by the aircraft's natural blending and shape, while being effective against most backgrounds. The 'Bucaneros' of the PR ANG have added their special touches, including different colours for the forward portion of the fin-stripe to denote the different flights within the squadron.

The F-16B ADF (left) sports the distinctive AIFF blade antenna array, also seen in the close-up of an F-16A (above), but does not have the fin bulge.

F-16A/B Block 15 OCU

F-16A/B Block 15 OCU (Operational Capability Upgrade) aircraft introduced structural beefing, minor changes and the enlarged HUD found on F-16C/Ds. The programme updates radar and software, fire control and stores management computers, and adds a data transfer unit, combined radar-barometric altimeter, and provision for AN/ALQ-131 jamming pods. The OCU effort includes provision for installation of a ring laser INS (inertial navigation system) and for upgrade from Pratt & Whitney F100-PW-200 to the more reliable, 26,660-lb (118.32-kN) thrust F100-PW-220E.

OCU is a US Air Force/NATO co-operative programme to modernise F-16A/B fighters to employ next-generation BVR (beyond visual range) air-to-air and air-to-surface weapons. F-16A/Bs manufactured since 1988 have been built to F-16A/B Block 15 OCU standard (beginning with Block 15Y), while earlier aircraft have been retroactively brought up to OCU status. OCU makes them comparable in most respects to F-16C/D models, with features employed by the latter which include ring laser INS, AN/ALR-69 RWR (radar warning receiver), -220 engine, and AIM-9P-4 Sidewinder infrared missile capability.

F-16A/B Block 15 OCUs were delivered as add-ons for Belgium (44), Denmark (12), the Netherlands (51) and Norway (two), as well as aeroplanes for Indonesia (12) and Pakistan (11). In the late 1980s and early 1990s, after overseas purchasers had invested in other models including later models, Singapore (eight), Thailand (18) and Portugal (20) joined the roster of F-16A/B Block 15 OCU operators. Portugal is the only user to employ the port-side, Grimes-built ID light and ADF-style HF.

F-16A Block 15Y OCU serials:
86-0073/0077 (Belgium FA97/101); 87-0046/0047 (Belgium FA102/103); 85-0141/0146 (Netherlands J-141/146); 86-0054 (Netherlands J-054).

Although designated Block 15 OCU, the aircraft for Portugal are in near-ADF configuration, with ID light and fin bulge. The AIFF is not fitted, however.

The Block 15 OCU has accounted for many export sales, including the 36 aircraft ordered by Thailand.

F-16B Block 15Y OCU serials:
86-0197/0199 (Denmark ET-197/199); 87-0022 (Denmark ET-022); 86-0064 (Netherlands J-064).

F-16B Block 15Z OCU serial: 87-0401 (Singapore 70401).

F-16A Block 15AA OCU serials:
87-0048/0054 (Belgium FA104/110); 87-0004/0007 (Denmark E-004/007); 86-0055/0061 (Netherlands J-055/061); 87-0397/0398 (Singapore 70397/70398); 86-0378 (Thailand 60378).

F-16B Block 15AA OCU serials:
87-0001 (Belgium FB21); 86-0065 (Netherlands J-065); 87-0402/0403 (Singapore 70402/70403); 86-0379/0381 (Thailand 60379/60381).

F-16A Block 15AB OCU serials:
87-0399/0400 (Singapore 70399/70400); 87-0702/0708 (Thailand 70702/70708). F-16B Block 15AB OCU serials: 87-0404 (Singapore 70404); 87-0709 (Thailand 70709).

F-16A Block 15AC OCU serials:
87-0055/0056 (Belgium FA111/112); 88-0038/0042 (Belgium FA113/117); 87-0008 (Denmark E-008); 88-0016/0018 (Denmark E-016/018); 86-0062/0063 (Netherlands J-062/063); 87-0508/0512 (Netherlands J-508/512).

F-16B Block 15AC OCU serials:
88-0048 (Belgium FB22); 87-0066 (Netherlands J-066).

F-16B Block 15AD OCU serials:
87-0711/0712 (Norway 711/712).

F-16A Block 15AE OCU serials:
88-0043/0047 (Belgium FA118/122); 89-0001 (Belgium FA123); 87-0513/0516 (Netherlands J-513/516); 87-0710 (Netherlands J-710); 88-0001/0002 (Netherlands J-001/002).

F-16B Block 15AE OCU serials:
88-0049 (Belgium FB23); 89-0012 (Belgium FB24); 87-0721/0722 (Indonesia S-1601/1602); 87-0067/0068 (Netherlands J-067/068).

F-16A Block 15AF OCU serials:
87-0713/0714 (Indonesia S-1605/1606).

F-16B Block 15AF OCU serials:
87-0723/0724 (Indonesia S-1603/1604).

F-16A Block 15AG OCU serials:
89-0002/0009 (Belgium FA124/131); 87-0715/0720 (Indonesia S-1607/1612); 88-0003/0010 (Netherlands J-0031/010).

F-16A Block 15AJ OCU serials:
89-0010/0011 (Belgium FA132/133); 89-0025/0027 (Belgium FA134/136); 88-0011/0012 (Netherlands J-011/012); 89-0013/0018 (Netherlands J-013/018); 91-0062/0067 (Thailand 10062/10067).

F-16A Block 15AL OCU serials:
89-0019/0021 (Netherlands J-019/021).

F-16A Block 15AM OCU serials:
90-0942/0947 (Pakistan 729/734).

F-16B Block 15AM OCU serials:
90-0948/0952 (Pakistan 613/617).

F-16A Block 15AQ OCU serials:
92-0404-0408 (Pakistan 735/739).

F-16B Block 15AQ OCU serial:
92-0452 (Pakistan 618).

F-16A Block 15AR OCU serials:
92-0409/0410 (Pakistan 740/741).

F-16B Block 15AR OCU serials:
92-0453/0455 (Pakistan 619/621).

F-16B Block 15AS OCU serials:
92-0456/0457 (Pakistan 622/623).

Singapore's aircraft are Block 15 OCUs, now serving with No. 140 Sqn. Prior to delivery they wore USAF-style markings while operating from Luke in the type conversion role.

F-16A Block 15AT OCU serials:
93-0465/0467 (Portugal 6101/6103).

F-16B Block 15AT OCU serials:
93-0482/0484 (Portugal 6118/6120).

F-16B Block 15AU OCU serials:
92-0458/0463 (Pakistan 624/629).

F-16A Block 15AV OCU serials:
92-0411/0413 (Pakistan 742/744); 93-0468/0477 (Portugal 6104/6113).

F-16A Block 15AW OCU serials:
92-0414/0418 (Pakistan 745/749); 93-0478/0481 (Portugal 6114/6117).

F-16A Block 15AX OCU serials:
92-0419/0423 (Pakistan 750/754).

F-16B Block 15AX OCU serials:
90-7032/7035 (Thailand 07032/07035).

F-16A Block 15AY OCU serials:
92-0424/0428 (Pakistan 755/759); 90-7020/7023 (Thailand (07020/07023).

F-16A Block 15AZ OCU serials:
92-0429/0436 (Pakistan 760/767); 90-7024/7031 (Thailand 07024/07031).

F-16B Block 15AZ OCU serials:
90-7036/7037 (Thailand 07036/07037).

F-16A Block 15BA OCU serials:
92-0437/0445 (Pakistan 768/776).

F-16A Block 15BB OCU serials:
92-0446/0451 (Pakistan 777/782).

Left: All four NATO countries received follow-on Block 15 OCU batches, although Norway only took a pair of two-seaters. The Netherlands led the way with 52 aircraft delivered from 1988.

Above: Pakistan's second order consisted of 54 F-16As and 17 F-16Bs, all to Block 15 OCU standard. The completed aircraft were embargoed by the US government, and stored at Davis-Monthan.

F-16A/B Block 15 MLU (Mid-Life Update)

F-16A/B Block 15 MLU aircraft are to be refurbished with a cockpit similar to that of the F-16C/D Block 50/52 fighter. They will be equipped with AN/APG-66(V2A) fire-control radar, GPS (global positioning system) navigation system, and other features including a wide-angle HUD, night vision goggle compatibility, a modular mission computer replacing the existing three, and a digital terrain system. As with all Fighting Falcon upgrade efforts, this one will produce somewhat different aircraft for different users, since the customer is afforded flexibility with ECP (engineering change proposals) which are roughly equivalent to an 'option' on a new car: most recipients of this upgrade will be offered helmet-mounted display and Hazeltine AN/APX-111 IFF interrogator/transponder (to be acquired at minimum by Netherlands and Norway both of which requested, but were denied, the AIFF system employed on the American F-16A/B Block 15 ADF).

The MLU programme to bring earlier Fighting Falcons up to a standard approximating that of the F-16C/D Block 50/52 is intended primarily for early F-16C/D models but will also involve a significant number of European F-16A/B Block 15 aircraft. The multinational MLU agreement was signed on 3 May 1991 and is the subject of a US government contract with General Dynamics (now Lockheed Fort Worth) dated 15 June 1991. MLU was originally to encompass 533 aircraft of the United States (130), Belgium (110),

Denmark (63), Netherlands (172) and Norway (58) beginning 1 October 1995. The US Air Force withdrew from the MLU effort in 1992 but ordered 223 modular computer retrofit kits from the programme to equip its F-16C/D aircraft. The European MLU pact was renegotiated on 28 January 1993 to change the totals: Belgium (48, plus 24

options), Denmark (61), Netherlands (156) and Norway (56). Lockheed Fort Worth was awarded a contract for 301 MLU kits for the 'gang of four' NATO countries on 17 August 1993 and is to begin delivery of kits on 1 October 1996 for completion by 30 September 1999.

Four Fighting Falcons were delivered to

Fort Worth in September 1992 to serve as the prototypes for conversion under the MLU programme. These were one aircraft each from Denmark (F-16B 78-0204/ET-204) and Netherlands (F-16B 80-3650/J-650), Norway (F-16A 78-0299/299), and one American aircraft.

Dutch, Danish and Norwegian aircraft are stripped down at Fort Worth in preparation for becoming the first MLU machines.

F-16A/B Block 20

F-16A/B Block 20 Fighting Falcons are being built for Taiwan. Development of the F-16 series leaped several years ago from Block 15 to Block 25 (the latter being the first F-16C/D series) and the term Block 20 was created retroactively. Although the term applies technically only to the 120 F-16As and 30 F-16Bs being built for Taiwan, Lockheed Fort Worth uses the term interchangeably with MLU and may eventually refer to all MLU aeroplanes as Block 20s. Taiwan's aircraft will have minor differences, however. Although Taiwan will receive the improved Westinghouse AN/APG-66(V)2 radar also to be fitted on MLU aircraft, it will employ different IFF and will have other minor differences. Taiwan chose the Raytheon AN/ALQ-183 electronic countermeasures pod in preference to the Westinghouse AN/ALQ-131 in a decision announced in May 1994.

F-16A Block 20 aircraft have been assigned manufacturer's numbers TA-1/120; F-16B Block 20 aircraft are TB-1/30. USAF serials have not yet been announced.

Unbuilt F-16A/B Variants

More than 100 distinct variants of the F-16A/B design have existed on the drawing board or in planning stages since the aircraft was designed. Some of these have been little more than an idea whose time had not arrived, such as a beefed-up F-16A/B powered by a PW1130 derivative of the F100 engine which was proposed but on which no serious design work was done.

In addition, General Dynamics/Lockheed Fort Worth has examined hundreds of options for the F-16A/B series which might

not require creating a new variant: for example, while the M61A1 cannon remains standard, the manufacturer has studied 30-mm Oerlikon, 30-mm DEFA, 27-mm Mauser, and 25-mm Martin Marietta GAU-12 guns as possible alternative armament. Real-life F-16A/Bs have flown with, or been considered for, a wide range of ordnance items which they do not employ operationally including the Norwegian Penguin Mk 3 anti-shipping missile (employed in Norway but tested and not adopted by the USAF), the Anglo-German

ASRAAM (Advanced Short-Range Air-to-Air Missile), the French MATRA Magic II air-to-air missile and the British Aerospace Sabre air-to-ground missile. Several F-16 airframes have been tested with the Martin Marietta ATARS (advanced tactical air reconnaissance) system which the USAF elected not to purchase; most work on a proposed reconnaissance RF-16, including work with a General Dynamics pod, was done with an F-16 Block 30 aircraft (described separately).

An SFW F-16A/B (Swept-Forward Wing) variant was designed under contract to the Defense Advanced Research Projects Agency (DARPA) in the 1970s and

appeared to be based upon the F-16A/B Block 10 basic airframe. Forward-swept wings would have proffered good low-speed handling characteristics and low drag but would have been difficult to manufacture; at this stage, SFW research with the Grumman X-29 had not yet taken place, although the concept had been studied repeatedly, by Heinkel in Germany and others. The SFW F-16A/B was eventually discarded by DARPA which went on to fund a portion of the research carried out by two X-29 test vehicles.

A STOVL E7 (Short Takeoff and Vertical Landing) variant of the F-16A/B was offered by General Dynamics to the US Navy at a time when thought was being given to building smaller, more versatile aircraft-carriers with STOVL or VTOL aircraft on board. The STOVL E7 aircraft was powered by a 28,000-lb (1246.35-kN) afterburning thrust General Electric F110 turbofan and would have had a modified delta wing mated to a much-modified F-16A/B fuselage with redesigned tailpipe and braking parachute. Air from the engine fan would have been collected in a plenum chamber and used to provide vertical lift or to boost forward speed when in the horizontal mode. The E7 would have had two forward-located thrust sources and an aft-mounted vectoring nozzle. The catastrophic failure of the US Navy's Rockwell XV-12A and continuing emphasis on conventional warplanes doomed the STOVL E7 before further development could take place.

The Agile Falcon would have been an enlarged F-16 with its wing increased in area by about 25 per cent, from the current 300 sq ft (27.9 m²) to 375 sq ft (34.8 m²). Notionally, the aircraft could be an F-16A/B or F-16C/D. The big wing of Agile Falcon would have brought wing loading down by about 20 per cent. This proposed derivative was intended to complement, or offer a low-cost alternative to, the USAF's ATF (Advanced Tactical Fighter), which became the F-22. Studies of several Agile Falcon configurations were undertaken, including versions with the Pratt & Whitney YF119 and General Electric YF120 engines.

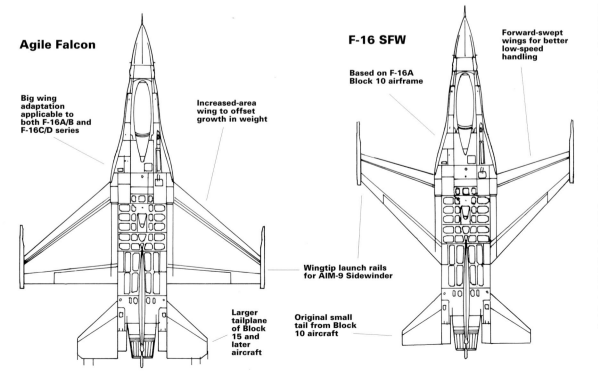

Agile Falcon

Big wing adaptation applicable to both F-16A/B and F-16C/D series

Increased-area wing to offset growth in weight

Larger tailplane of Block 15 and later aircraft

F-16 SFW

Forward-swept wings for better low-speed handling

Based on F-16A Block 10 airframe

Wingtip launch rails for AIM-9 Sidewinder

Original small tail from Block 10 aircraft

Red Stars over Germany (Part 2)

Bases and Regiments

Between 1945 and 1994 the Soviet Union (and its successor, the Commonwealth of Independent States) maintained massive armed forces in East Germany, facing the combined armies and air forces of NATO. The ground forces of the Western Group of Forces had their own organic tactical air force, the 16th Air Army, which included some of Russia's elite fighter, fighter-bomber, reconnaissance and bomber regiments, equipped with the latest aircraft types and manned by the best aircrew. Here we present the first guide to the major airfields used by the Western Group of Forces, with details of their histories and of the units which occupied them.

Most of the airfields used by the 16th Air Army had been built during the 1920s and early 1930s, during the clandestine expansion of Hitler's Luftwaffe. Some were used by German aircraft firms as test airfields, and even as factories, and were thus large and well-equipped. Far from the front lines for most of the war, many of the airfields housed training units and then, as the military situation deteriorated, home defence and night-fighter squadrons. Most became the targets of attacks by Russian and Allied bombers and fighter-bombers,

Above: Pilots of the 20th GvAPIB leave their briefing room, whose fold-out briefing boards sit below a large scale plan of the Gross Dölln aerodrome.

and some were taken over by advancing Frontal Aviation close support units as Zhukov's tanks 'steamrollered' on towards Berlin. At the end of the war, they were the ideal choice for the aviation units of the Russian occupation forces. Occasionally having magnificent hard runways and usually with massive, superbly equipped hangars, the airfields were well served by Hitler's network of autobahns and railways. A little bomb damage repair, and the removal of Nazi Eagles and Swastikas, was often all that was necessary to prepare an airfield for its new role in the front line of the new conflict, the Cold War. While new runways were often laid by the Russians, conforming to a standard pattern, airfield infrastructure and many buildings frequently remained in use unchanged. Even in 1994, examination of some of the hangars and buildings showed clear signs of their previous occupants, with 'Nicht Rauchen' ('No Smoking') notices on hangar walls, applied in the heavy gothic script favoured by the Nazi Luftwaffe. When such faded notices appeared beside typically Soviet slogans exhorting the engineers to fulfil their socialist obligations to the motherland, the effect was somewhat bizarre.

While NATO air forces' strengths in Europe declined steadily after 1957, the strength of the 16th Air Army remained broadly constant, leading to a widening

Left: This young MiG-29 pilot of the 787th IAP at Eberswalde wears lightweight summer flying clothing. Only the best of Russia's pilots were posted to the 16th Air Army, where the average length of tour was five years.

disparity in strength. From the early 1960s, the Western Group of Forces was split into two Corps, Northern and Southern, with some nine direct-reporting bomber, reconnaissance and transport regiments. The Northern Tactical Air Corps controlled a three-regiment fighter division headquartered at Pütnitz, and a three-regiment fighter-bomber division headquartered at Lärz. In the Southern Tactical Air Corps there were two three-regiment fighter divisions at Zerbst and Merseburg, with a fighter-bomber division at Grossenhain. By 1991 these basic divisional headquarters were still in place, (each still controlling three regiments) and although the Werneuchen bomber division had long disappeared, there had been a

massive influx of attack helicopters, and two full regiments of Su-25s.

For many years, airfields used by the Soviets were known simply by their old Luftwaffe names (which were sometimes changed by their new owners) or by newly invented names allocated by Allied intelligence officers on the basis of a nearby village name. 'Translations' of the best-known names are given below. The exception is Kobitz, which never existed at all, and was merely a mis-spelling of the real name in a Russo-German semi-official book about the 16th Air Army.

NATO NAME	SOVIET NAME
Altenburg	Nöbitz
Damgarten	Pütnitz
Demmin	Tütow
Dresden	Hellerau
Falkenburg	Alt Lönnewitz
Finow	Eberswalde
Juterbog	Altes Lager
Kobitz	Nöbitz
Mirow	Lärz
Parchim	Damm
Stendal	Borstel
Templin	Gross Dölln
Weimar	Nohra

There are a number of airfields in East Germany which have been used by the Soviets, but which are not described below, and which have not appeared in the orders of battle printed in the first part of this article because they fell into disuse before

Left: This Su-17M-4 'Fitter-K' of the 20th GvAPIB in its shelter at Gross Dölln is surrounded by some of the stores which it could carry. Fuel tanks and B8M rocket pods are under the wings, while 250-kg bombs hang from the shelter sides. The Su-17 is a snug fit in the shelter.

the reunification of the two Germanies. These include Altengrabow (also HQ of a 'Scud' missile brigade), Benkendorf and Retzow, all used as helicopter training grounds.

The aerodromes at Bork, Brandenburg, Dessau, Dresden-Klotzsche, Erfurt-Bindersleben, Furstenwalde, Klein Koris, Luckau, Prenzlau, Schonefeld (which became East Germany's premier international airport), and Schönwalde were all reserve or active airfields abandoned or transferred to other uses before the final withdrawal.

Airfields at Gross Mohrdorf, Haina, Juterbog 2 (the original Juterbog Damm), Mockau, Mortitz, Schlotheim and Schonhauserdam were all FOLs for aircraft (PVO fighters, or Frontal Aviation bombers or fighter-bombers) which were normally based outside East Germany. Facilities at such bases varied enormously.

Unfortunately, it was never possible to get a regular or uniform flow of information about the 16th Air Army or the units which constituted it, contemporary or historic,

although the 16th Air Army did have its own museum at the Zossen Headquarters. Nor were there local East German spotters, since demonstrating an interest in the Soviet forces could have easily been misconstrued, and would have led to certain imprisonment. Thus, this coverage of the airfields from which the units of the 16th Air Army operated is by necessity somewhat sketchy and incomplete.

The entries below describe the histories of those airfields which still remained in Russian use at the beginning of 1991, with historical details of the based units, where known. These entries each include a brief run-down of the codes allocated to the aircraft on strength with the based regiments and squadrons (but not with HQ liaison flights) before withdrawal. MiG-29 'Fulcrum-A' codes suffixed with a small 'v' (e.g. 09^V) indicate early series aircraft with ventral fins and without overwing chaff/flare dispensers. The entries are presented in alphabetical order (by official name). Although this represents the most complete account of the Soviet air forces'

presence in East Germany yet published, we are continuing to compile information for future publication. Any additions, ammendments, photographs or details of airframe serials and/or construction numbers should be sent to the author at the editorial address. **Jon Lake.**

Glossary

APIB	Aviatsionnaya Polk Istrebeitelei-Bombardirovchikov) (Aviation Regiment Fighter-Bomber)
IAP	Istrebeitelnyi Aviatsionnaya Polk (Fighter Aviation Regiment)
OERVE	Otdelnyi Eletronika Radiorazvedka Vertoletnyi Eskadriliya (Independent Electronic (and) Radio Reconnaissance Squadron)
ORAP	Otdelnyi Razvedyvatelnyi Aviatsionnaya Polk (Independent Reconnaissance Aviation Regiment)
OSAP	Otdelnyi Smechannyi Aviatsionnaya Polk (Independent Transport Aviation Regiment)
OShAP	Otdelnyi Shturmovoi Aviatsionnaya Polk (Independent *Shturmovik* Aviation Regiment)
OVE	Otdelnyi Vertoletnyi Eskadriliya (Independent Helicopter Squadronn)
OVP	Otdelnyi Vertoletnyi Polk (Independent Helicopter Regiment)

'Black Men' (as Russian ground crew were inevitably known) cycle back to dispersal alongside their charge as it is towed to its HAS. One hangs onto the tailplane, getting a free ride. Each aircraft would have its own crew, responsible for routine servicing, led by an officer.

Allstedt

Located in the south-western corner of Saxe Anhalt, about 35 miles (56 km) west of Leipzig, just south-east of the town of Allstedt and close to the village of Ladgrafroda, Allstedt airfield lay closer to the border with West Germany than any other airfield permanently used by Soviet fast jets, with a single hard runway (roughly 08/26). Haina, a forward deployment base for various types was closer still. Just east of Eisenach, Haina lay well within 20 miles (32 km) of the border. A tactical reconnaissance airfield in Soviet use, Allstedt housed MiG-15s and MiG-17s until about 1976, and then MiG-21Rs for many years, before its based regiment converted to the Su-17 in 1987 or 1988. Some have suggested that the Su-17s actually replaced a mix of MiG-21s and Yak-28s. Precise details of unit changes and conversion dates remain unknown. Orders of battle prepared by the prestigious *Soldat und Technik, Osterreich Militar Zeitschrift* and Netherlands air force magazine during the 1980s do not mention Allstedt at all, and in the period between 1965 and 1967 it is believed that the airfield was inactive, probably taking over the reconnaissance role from nearby Borstel after helicopter activities there became too intensive for both fixed- and rotary-wing operations to continue. Because they were the first

Soviet aircraft to leave Germany, in April 1991, little is known about the Su-17s of the 294th RAP. Probably including both red-coded Su-17M-3 'Fitter-Hs' and black-coded Su-17M-4s, the Allstedt-based aircraft carried the massive KKR-1TA/2-54 day/night reconnaissance pod as primary sensor. The triple-digit black codes (beginning with the number 6) worn by the Su-17M-4s may have indicated assignment to a test or trials unit. Some aircraft reportedly had a white flash or cheat line along the fuselage sides. The 294th RAP was smaller than usual, with a reported strength of 25 Su-17M-3s and five two-seat Su-17UM-3s. Some Allstedt-based Su-17s may have been transferred to Gross Dölln, perhaps replacing the last 20th APIB Su-17M-3s. Allstedt also housed the Mi-24s and Mi-8s of the 225th OVP, the lead regiment of the 1st Guards Tank Army, headquartered in Dresden. The helicopters were mostly red-coded. The regiment's primary attack helicopter was the Mi-24D 'Hind-D', although conversion to the later Mi-24V 'Hind-E' had commenced, and was well underway when the regiment returned to the USSR.

This Mi-24D 'Hind-D' was one of those assigned to the 225th OVP at Allstedt, which became the first army aviation unit to withdraw from East Germany when it left in April 1991, shortly after the departure of the co-located Su-17s.

294 Otdelnyi Razvedyvatielnyi Aviatsionnaya Polk

Aircraft: Su-17M-4
Known codes: Black 601, 604, 607, 608, 610, 612, 615, 619, 623

Aircraft: Su-17M-3
Known codes: Red 23, 30, 47

Aircraft: Su-17UM-3
Known codes: Red 99

225 Otdelnyi Vertoletnyi Polk

Aircraft: Mi-24D
Known codes: Red 05, 10, 48, 50, yellow 68

Aircraft: Mi-24V
Known codes: Red 01, 18, 22, 27, 28, 31, 32, 34, 38, 40, 41, 44, 46, 49, 50, 53, 54, 55, 57, 58

Altes Lager

Known as Juterbog on NATO maps and low flying charts, with another airfield appearing as Juterbog 2, the airfields at Juterbog can trace their history back to before the earliest days of Hitler's Luftwaffe. At the end of World War I, Juterbog housed an independent home defence balloon group and an observer school. During World War II, the two airfields seem to have been known as Juterbog-Damm and Juterbog-Altes Lager, with Juterbog-Damm being the first and most important. Juterbog-Damm saw the establishment of the second of the Luftwaffe's covert fighter units, 'Fliegergruppe Damm' in 1935, this becoming II./JG 132 'Richthofen'. The airfield was also the home of the second Luftwaffe bomber school, and later became the first airfield in Germany to receive the Messerschmitt Bf 109. Later in the war, a variety of units were based at Juterbog-Damm for day/night defence of the Reich.

Altes Lager, by contrast, appears less often in histories of the Luftwaffe, and it housed the ferry command headquarters when it formed in 1942. By early 1945, Altes Lager housed JG 4, which was tasked with the escort of the bomber and *jabo* aircraft that were vainly trying to halt the Soviet advance on Berlin. Altes Lager ended the war by participating in one of its most

The helicopters of the 486th OVP, like this Mi-24V 'Hind-E', wore white regimental codes. The 486th OVP was the second of two full-strength attack/assault helicopter regiments assigned to the 8th Guards Infantry Army headquartered at Weimar Nohra. This Mi-24V carries a pair of 20-round 80-mm rocket pods under its stub wings, these having largely replaced the older 57-mm rockets in recent years. The red star under the belly was common on Soviet tactical helicopters.

The gate guard at Altes Lager (inevitably and incorrectly known as Juterbog), mounted on a plinth painted in the air forces' sunburst colours, was a redundant MiG-23ML 'Flogger-G', coded Blue 70. Its wings were fully swept and it carried an improbable array of ordnance. There were actually two Juterbog airfields used by the Russians, Altes Lager (a fighter base) and Juterbog-Damm (known as Juterbog 2 on NATO maps) which housed a fighter-bomber regiment before it was closed and became a FOL for Russia-based aircraft.

bizarre missions. The 'Leonidas' Staffel launched the last two suicide missions of the war, using Messerschmitt Bf 109s, Focke Wulf Fw 190s and Ju 88s with bombs actually bolted onto the airframes. On 16 April, 17 aircraft were launched against the Oder bridges, one crashing on take-off and 16 failing to return. On 20 April, the Führer's birthday, 20 aircraft were launched. Two were downed by flak, one disappeared, and 17 attacked with negligible results. With these last futile gestures, the Luftwaffe at Altes Lager ended its struggle against the advancing allies.

Located only 30 miles (48 km) south-south-west of the Berlin suburbs, in the State of Brandenburg, Altes Lager lay just west of the garrison town of Juterbog, south of the Berlin-Frankfurt air corridor, with a single hard runway orientated roughly 10/28 (010° to 280°).

Some sources have listed Altes Lager as having been a bomber base. This confusion may have arisen because of the proximity of the dedicated FOL at Juterbog 2, which had earlier been a fighter-bomber base in its own right, or because Su-24 'Fencers' did make at least two brief deployments to Altes Lager itself, one in 1987 and the other a few years earlier. In 1965 the main airfield at Altes Lager housed a fighter regiment with 36 MiG-21s (variant unknown), six

MiG-17Fs, four Yak-12s and four MiG-15UTIs, and reported to the fighter division headquartered at Zerbst. Juterbog 2 then housed a fighter-bomber regiment with 46 MiG-17Fs and the usual base flight with four MiG-15UTIs and four Yak-12s. By 1967 Altes Lager had a mixed all-weather fighter regiment with 20 MiG-21PF 'Fishbed-Ds' and 30 Yak-27 'Firebars', while Juterbog 2's fighter-bomber regiment (reporting to the fighter-bomber division at Grossenhain) had added MiG-21PFs to its MiG-17s, with a total of 46 aircraft on strength. Both base flights had disappeared by 1967. On a map published in a prominent Dutch military magazine during 1986, Altes Lager was merely shown as housing 48 MiG-23s, which was probably accurate insofar as it went, although it remains uncertain when 'Floggers' replaced 'Fishbeds'.

The final Soviet fixed-wing type based at Altes Lager was the MiG-23MLD 'Flogger-K', the latest and most capable version of the MiG-23 fighter. Lightened and fitted with improved avionics, including improved radar and a new IRST, the MiG-23MLD also incorporated aerodynamic refinements which improved high-Alpha capability. There have been reports that the Altes Lager-based aircraft were equipped to carry the all-aspect R-73 AA-11 'Archer' and new-generation R27 AA-10 'Alamo' AAMs, but this seems unlikely. The regiment as a whole (or at least on *eskadrilya*) may have had a secondary ground attack role, since 'Flogger-Ks' at Altes Lager were occasionally sighted with UV-16-57 rocket pods, each containing 16 57-mm rocket projectiles.

Official sources suggested that 26 of these aircraft, together with six two-seat MiG-23UBs and a single An-2, were on charge, although at least 31 were noted, with eight two-seaters and an An-2. Numbers had reduced to the official total by the time the regiment departed. The 833rd IAP may have been due to convert to the

MiG-29, but the withdrawal of Soviet forces from Germany made this impossible. Alternatively, it may have been felt desirable to retain one regiment of MiG-23s (which enjoyed a longer range than the MiG-29), perhaps pending the later introduction of the Sukhoi Su-27, which re-equipped MiG-23 regiments in Poland. The MiG-23MLDs of the 833rd wore red codes, outlined in white. The regiment left Germany early, on 13 May 1992, having been scheduled for departure during the second half of 1992. Its designation was given as Orenburg, a massive base which served as a MiG-23/MiG-27 storage and maintenance unit, where it almost certainly disbanded. Some sources suggest that the regiment actually flew to Totskoye, where they say it disbanded, but this seems less likely.

Altes Lager also housed the 486th OVP, the second of the two attack helicopter regiments assigned to the 8th Guards Infantry Army, headquartered at nearby Weimar-Nohra. The regiment was among the first army aviation units to leave, returning to Russia even before the MiG-23s, on 1 August 1991.

833 Istrebeitelnyi Aviotsionnaya Polk

Aircraft: MiG-23MLD
Known codes: Red 01, 02, 03, 04, 05, 06, 07, 09, 11, 12, 14, 15, (first *eskadrilya*?) Red 20, 21, 22, 24, 25, 26, 27, 28, 29, 30, 31, 33 (second *eskadrilya*?) Red 40, 41, 42, 44, 47, 48, 50, 51, 52 (third *eskadrilya*?)

Aircraft: MiG-23UB
Known codes: Red 90, 91, 92, 93, 95, 96, 97, 98

486 Otdelnyi Vertoletnyi Polk

Aircraft: Mi-24V
Known codes: White 01, 03, 04, 05, 07, 09, 11, 12, 14, 15, 16, 17

Aircraft: Mi-24RKR 'Hind-G'
Known codes: White 41

Aircraft: Mi-24K 'Hind-G2'
Known codes: White 35, 37, 40

Most of the 833rd IAP's MiG-23MLD 'Flogger-Ks' were fully modernised, with massive, upward-firing chaff/flare dispensers scabbed onto the upper surfaces of the centre fuselage. The MiG-23MLD had a longer range than the later MiG-29, and it may have been intended to keep a single 'Flogger' regiment operational in Germany until it could be replaced by an Su-27 'Flanker' unit.

Alt Lönnewitz

Known as Falkenberg to NATO, Alt Lönnewitz is another ex-Luftwaffe airfield. Located in the south of Brandenburg, 35 miles (56 km) north-east of Dresden, Alt Lönnewitz airfield lay due south of the town of Falkenburg and was bordered on its southern perimeter by the main road from Torgau to Bad Liebenwerda.

A DLV (the German aerosport organisation) airfield during the 1930s, Alt Lönnewitz became a Luftwaffe primary flying training school, a role it undertook until July 1944. The airfield was used as the assembly plant for the Arado Ar 234B and Ar 234C, the first pre-production 'Blitz' flying from here on 8 June 1944. During late 1944 the airfield housed I/EKG 1, with a mix of Me 262s and Arado Ar 234s, serving as a jet OTU for the pilots of KG 76, the first 'Blitz' unit. Between February and April 1945 the airfield housed 14./KG 55, an anti-railway unit equipped with Heinkel He 111s, these being replaced by the Me 262s of 3., 9. and 11./JG 7.

Alt Lönnewitz had a hard runway added during Luftwaffe tenure, and in Russian times this was extended west and east, effectively doubling its length. A parallel taxiway was added north of the runway, with two huge operating ramps. Four shelter areas were eventually constructed, three clustered around the western end of the runway, and the other north of the eastern runway threshold. Along with the new construction, Luftwaffe hangars and other buildings remained in regular use.

Post-war home to the 31st Guards 'Nilopolskyi' Fighter Aviation Regiment, Alt Lönnewitz was a long-term fighter base, initially reporting to the fighter division at Merseburg. In 1965 the regiment's strength included 12 MiG-21s, 24 MiG-17Fs and four MiG-17PFs, together with the obligatory four Yak-12s and four MiG-15UTIs for training and liaison. By 1967 the base had lost these dedicated transport and training aircraft, relying instead on the HQ flight at

Above: This is one of the handful of MiG-29UBs allocated to the 31st GvIAP landing at Alt Lönnewitz. Presentation of the Guards badge is typical. Two MiG-29UBs were joined by two or three more from departing regiments and were augmented by a fleet of some four MiG-23UBs, whose importance shrank as the new MiG-29UBs arrived. Although Soviet bases in the former East Germany were generously endowed with hardened aircraft shelters, routine operations were carried out from a conventional flight line, to and from which aircraft were towed before and after the day's flying.

Right: The stylised Guards badge was carried by aircraft belonging to all Guards regiments or eskadrilyas. The Guards title was an honour awarded for outstanding service in war, and the 16th Air Army had more than its fair share of such elite units. The badge itself consisted of a red star, surrounded by a gold laurel crown, surmounted by a red banner bearing the word 'Gvardia' in Cyrillic script. A shield at the bottom of the laurel wreath bore the letters SSSR. Such badges were applied with varying degrees of elaboration. This one decorated an Alt Lönnewitz-based MiG-29.

Right: Unusual among Alt Lönnewitz-based MiG-29s in lacking a Guards badge, Red 21 was unique in being the only early series production 'Fulcrum-A' (with distinctive ventral fins and without chaff/flare launchers) assigned to the 31st GvIAP. The two-tone radome is interesting, the darker colour marking the extent of the bin-like twist cassegrain radar antenna under the radome. Some of Falkenburg's shelters may have been too small to accommodate a MiG-29, and some 31st GvIAP 'Fulcrums' were housed in the open.

Below: A 'Fulcrum-C' of the 31st GvIAP lands at Alt Lönnewitz, with hardened aircraft shelters and a Luftwaffe wartime hangar visible in the background. Alt Lönnewitz's position made it the linchpin in the defence of the southern industrial cities, including Leipzig and Dresden, while also guarding the southern approaches to Berlin. In wartime its aircraft would have provided battlefield air defence for the 1st Guards Tank Army.

Right: About 18 of the 'Fulcrum-Cs' based at Alt Lönnewitz were capable of carrying underwing fuel tanks. Such tanks were not stressed for combat and were used for ferry flying only. The rarity with which such tanks were used can be gauged by the fact that this aircraft carries tanks with the correct code numbers on them, an eventuality that would be unlikely if the tanks were interchangeable between aircraft and used often. About 20 of the regiment's aircraft wore Guards badges, although these were restricted to the port side only.

Merseburg, and had a mix of 40 MiG-21PFs and MiG-17PFs. The base was shown as housing 48 MiG-23s on a map published in a prominent Dutch military magazine in 1986, while *Soldat und Technik* described the base as housing a fighter regiment which reported to a fighter division at Merseburg. Local reports suggest that four Yak-28Ps were based at Alt Lönnewitz until 1988, alongside the regiment's MiG-23s.

Alt Lönnewitz became the seventh Soviet MiG-29 base in Germany during March 1989, when it traded its ageing red-coded MiG-23M 'Flogger-Bs' for MiG-29s. Conversion to the new type was accompanied by a reduction in aircraft numbers, with the normal complement of 15 aircraft per squadron reducing to 12 aircraft per squadron. It may at one time have been the intention to slowly build regiments back up to their old strengths, as sufficient MiG-29s became available.

A widespread conversion from the basic 'Fulcrum-A' to the newer 'Fulcrum-C' began shortly before German reunification. The two types often served side by side, sometimes even within the same *eskadrilya*. Apart from a small increase in

fuel capacity and (according to some reports) an improved defensive avionics suite, there was little difference between the two versions, and because both could be operated side-by-side the conversion process was leisurely.

By the time the based 31st GvIAP departed from Germany on 8 June 1993, its 'Fulcrum-As' had been almost entirely supplanted by 'Fulcrum-Cs', with only five of the early variants on strength. One of the latter was one of the very early series aircraft, with ventral fins and no overwing chaff/flare dispensers. There have been suggestions that the early-series MiG-29s were sometimes retained for high-altitude air defence and interception. The 32 single-seat MiG-29s were augmented by four two-seat MiG-29UBs and four MiG-23UBs. Regimental aircraft wore red codes with white outlines (usually repeated in white on

the tailfin), and virtually all carried a large Guards badge on the forward fuselage. There were persistent rumours that some of the shelters at Alt Lönnewitz were too small to accommodate a MiG-29, and it was certainly common to see aircraft parked outside, heavily wrapped in tarpaulins. The 31st GvIAP finally left Alt Lönnewitz on 8 June 1993, bound for Zernograd, just ahead of its scheduled departure in the 'second half of 1993'. Alt Lönnewitz was reportedly once earmarked as the future home for the two squadrons of ex-East German MiG-29s inherited by the Luftwaffe, which had to move from their base at Preschen, on the Polish border. The cost of refurbishing Alt Lönnewitz was felt to be too high, and the former East German air force Su-22 base at Laage was selected in its stead.

31 'Nilopolskyi' Gvardeiskaya Istrebeitelnyi Aviotsionnaya Polk

Aircraft: MiG-29 'Fulcrum-A'
Known codes: Red 01, 12, 21ᵛ, 22, 23, 35

Aircraft: MiG-29 'Fulcrum-C'
Known codes: Red 02, 03, 04, 06, 07, 08, 10, 11, 20, 24, 25, 27, 28, 29, 30, 31, 32, 33, 34, 35, 36, 37, 38, 40, 45, 46, (54?)

Aircraft: MiG-29UB
Known codes: Red 70, 71, Blue 75, 76

Aircraft: MiG-23UB
Known codes: Red 60, 63, 64, Blue 61

Borstel

Otherwise known as Stendal, the airfield at Borstel was built by the Luftwaffe, and its Luftwaffe Paratroop Training School, established in January 1936, served the *Fallschirmjager* (paratroop) depot in the nearby garrison town of Stendal, just to the south, flying Ju 52s and He 111 glider tugs. A simple grass field was quite sufficient for such operations, but in Soviet hands the aerodrome was destined for a major expansion, with a new hard runway (08/26).

Located in the northern part of Saxe Anhalt, Borstel was about 35 miles (56 km) from the West German border, just north of the Buckeburg-Berlin corridor. Its location made it an ideal reconnaissance base, and in 1965 it housed a mixed reconnaissance

This well-shrouded Mi-24D 'Hind-D' wears a badge on the nose consisting of the arms of the town of Stendal superimposed on a ribbon incorporating the Russian tricolour and the sunburst flag of the Soviet air forces. Red codes identify it as belonging to the 440th OVP. Stendal was an extremely busy helicopter base, with two full front-line attack/assault helicopter regiments.

regiment with 11 Il-28s, 14 MiG-17s and 12 Mi-1 helicopters, with the ubiquitous base flight of four MiG-15UTIs and four Yak-12s. Stendal also housed a target-towing unit with 10 Il-28s, including three two-seaters. By 1967 the reconnaissance regiment had almost completed conversion to the Yak-27R 'Mangrove' (36 of which were on strength), while the target-towing unit had reduced its holding of Il-28Us to two aircraft, with eight Il-28 target tugs. There have been reports of MiG-19s operating from Borstel. At an unknown date, Stendal switched to the helicopter role, forcing the reconnaissance unit to move to Allstedt. One of two Mil Mi-24 'Hind-A' regiments deployed to Germany for evaluation in 1973 was based at Borstel, the other going to Damm. Several Borstel-based helicopters wore a unit badge, in the shape of the Stendal city crest and Russian flag.

During the late 1980s and early 1990s, Borstel was perhaps the most important army aviation base in East Germany, housing both full attack helicopter regiments assigned to the elite Third Guards 'Udarniya' Shock Army, which would have spearheaded any Warsaw Pact advance. The 178th OVP, the lead helicopter regiment, was equipped entirely with Mi-24V 'Hind-Es' and Mi-24P 'Hind-Fs', while the 440th retained a large number of older Mi-24D 'Hind-Ds' alongside its Mi-24Vs and transport and support helicopters. Both units returned to Russia in July 1992.

178 Otdelnyi Vertoletnyi Polk

Aircraft: Mi-24V
Known codes: White 25, 29, 30, 31, 32, 33, 34, 35, 37, 38, 40, 41, 42, 43, 45, 49

Aircraft: Mi-24P
Known codes: White 01, 02, 06, 09, 10, 12, 14, 17, 20, 26, 27, 28

440 Otdelnyi Vertoletnyi Polk

Aircraft: Mi-24D
Known codes: Red 01, 02, 03, 04, 05, 06, 07, 08, 18, 19, 20, 21, 46, 47, 48, 49, 50, 52, 53, 69, 70

Aircraft: Mi-24V
Known codes: Red 24, 25, 26, 27, 28, 29, 30, 31, 73, 74

Aircraft: Mi-24RKR 'Hind-G'
Known codes: Red 40, 41, 64, 65

Aircraft: Mi-24K 'Hind-G2'
Known codes: Red 19, 42, 43, 62, 63

Aircraft: Mi-8TB
Known codes: Red 36, 60

Aircraft: Mi-8 (sub-variant unknown)
Known codes: Red 32, 33, 34, 35, 55, 56

Aircraft: Mi-8MT
Known codes: Red 09, 11, 38, 39

Aircraft: Mi-8MTV
Known codes: Red 10, 12, 15, 17

Aircraft: Mi-9
Known codes: Red 22, 61

Another Borstel resident was this Mi-8MTV. The two regiments at Stendal reported to the 3rd Guards Shock Army, headquartered at nearby Magdeburg. The primary or 'lead' regiment was the 178th OVP, which used white codes and had the standard 'lead regiment' structure of two eskadrilyas with a mix of Mi-24Vs and Mi-24Ps, and a third transport eskadrilya with 'Hips'. The 440th OVP, which used red codes, followed the standard structure for 'second regiments', with three identical eskadrilyas, each of which had flights of Mi-24s, transport/assault Mi-8s, and specialist Mi-24RKRs, Mi-24Ks and Mi-9s or Mi-8VZPUs.

Brand

Like the other bases used by the Russians as bomber airfields, Brand was located in the eastern part of the GDR, some 35 miles (56 km) from the Polish border and 25 miles (40 km) south-south-east of the Berlin suburbs. Unusual in having two parallel east-west runways, Brand was served by its own railway line, ideal for moving bombs (including nuclear weapons) from their nearby storage areas.

Operating a total of 62 aircraft in 1965, with 44 Il-28s, eight Yak-28s and the usual bomber base flight of six Il-28Us and four Yak-12s, Brand housed one of the three bomber regiments reporting to the bomber division at Werneuchen. By 1967, 36 Yak-28s were augmented by 20 Il-28s and the base flight had disappeared. By 1969 the bomber regiment at Brand had disappeared, and the base had become home to a fighter regiment reporting to the division headquartered at Grossenhain, replacing the regiment at Juterbog 2, which closed. The exact status of Brand between 1970 and 1982 is uncertain, although it may have housed Su-7s or Su-17s operating in the fighter-bomber role. During 1982 Brand received the first of two Su-24 'Fencer' bomber regiments reporting to the newly formed 128th Bomber Aviation Division at Grossenhain. The Brand-based Su-24 unit was the 727th Bomber Aviation Regiment, which was withdrawn to Kanatovo in the Ukraine during early 1989, as part of a political move to reduce the offensive posture of the 16th Air Army. In the Ukraine, the 727th BAP joined its former colleagues from Grossenhain, the 7th BAP, as part of the Odessa-based 5th Air Army's newly-formed 32nd BAD. During their stay at Brand, the regiment's 'Fencer-Bs' and 'Fencer-Cs' wore white codes, but the colour of the outlines remains unknown. There are persistent reports that some of the Brand-based Su-24s had camouflaged upper surfaces. Replacing the Su-24s were the MiG-27K 'Flogger-J2s' of the 911th IBAP (and not the 116th IBAP, as has been reported elsewhere), which moved to Brand from a base in Russia during early 1989. Their stay in Germany was to be a short one, however, the regiment departing Brand for Finsterwalde on 1 July 1992

Brand and Finsterwalde were the only bases in East Germany operating the MiG-27K 'Flogger-J2', the advanced Kaira-equipped version of this versatile fighter-bomber and strike aircraft. This aircraft has scabbed-on panels of armour on the cockpit sides, which was a common, though not universal, MiG-27K modification. Brand's MiG-27Ks served with the 911th APIB and wore red codes outlined in white, while Finsterwalde's 559th APIB used blue codes.

before flying on to an unknown base in Byelorussia on 7 July. The MiG-27K marked a major improvement even over the MiG-27D and MiG-27M 'Flogger-J' with a *kaira* weapons system which incorporated a FLIR and a collimated TV/laser designator. The Brand-based 'Floggers' wore red codes, thinly outlined in white. Official sources indicated a regimental strength of 27 MiG-27s and eight MiG-23UBs, together with a single An-2. Spotters' reports would indicate that a slightly higher number of MiG-27s and MiG-23UBs were on charge prior to departure. Brand was reportedly nominated as a forward operating base for IA-PVO interceptor units, and regularly hosted deployments. These included a regiment of Su-15 'Flagons' during the mid-1970s, and an Su-27 'Flanker' regiment during 1991.

Like many bases, Brand enjoyed the use of its own An-2 'Colt' communications and liaison aircraft. These rugged and dependable biplanes remained active with the 16th Air Army until the end, and the type remains in service with the Russian and former Soviet air forces. This An-2 is seen at Nöbitz delivering spares for a MiG-27 that had become unserviceable after a weekend air show. This was a typical task, although the type may also have had a more active special forces support role.

911 Aviotsionnaya Polk Istrebeitelei-Bombardirovchikov

Aircraft: MiG-27K
Known codes: Red 01, 02, 03, 04, 05, 06, 07, 08, 09, 11, 12, 15, 16, 18, 19, 21, 23, 24, 25, 27, 28, 29, 30, 31, 32, 33, 34

Aircraft: MiG-23UB
Known codes: Red 88, 89, 90, 91, 92, 94, 96, 97, 98

Like MiG-29 bases, airfields housing MiG-27s placed heavy reliance on MiG-23UBs for training and support tasks. A typical 30-aircraft MiG-27 regiment included 10 MiG-23UBs, for example. This MiG-23UB was from the 911th APIB at Brand.

Brandis

Fifteen miles (24 km) east of Leipzig, in the north-west corner of Saxony, Brandis airfield lay between the villages of Brandis, Leulitz and Polenz. A pre-war training airfield, with blind-flying and navigation training units, Brandis gained a combat role during the latter part of World War II, when it housed several *Nachtjagdfliegergruppen*, and, most spectacularly, the Stab, I and II Gruppen of JG 400, the Luftwaffe's first Me 163 Komet rocket fighter unit. In April 1945 Me 262 jet fighters of JG 7 were operating from Brandis.

Used on a rather *ad hoc* basis by the Soviets, eventually with its own transport/helicopter squadron, Brandis was not, during the 1950s, a very important airfield, although this was to change. By 1965 two *eskadrilyas* of the 239th GvOVP were operating from Brandis with 45 Mi-4s and 10 Mi-6s, with the number of Mi-4s rising to 50 by 1967. The Mi-4s and Mi-6s are believed to have moved back to Furstenwalde before taking up residence at Oranienburg. Su-25s arrived at Brandis in October 1985, with the 357th OShAP, reportedly necessitating the provision of a longer runway and a network of hard taxiways on an airfield which had previously been used only by helicopters and light transports and, many years before, by piston-engined combat aircraft. Although the Su-25 can operate from grass, or from PSP, or from semi-prepared dirt strips, regular operations from grass would soon have eroded the airfield surface to an unacceptable degree, while the transport aircraft which might have resupplied the Su-25s with weapons and spares in time of war did need a hard taxiway. Dispersal pans

The significance of the bright blue disc on which the code of this Brandis-based Su-25 was carried remains unknown. It may have been a device for marking out the aircraft of a squadron commander, or may have been a common decoration in the unit to which the aircraft previously belonged.

were added to the western taxiway, while revetments appeared at the southern end of the airfield, and in the north-eastern corner.

Reporting directly to the 16th Air Army headquarters, operational control would have passed to a tank army in time of war, and the aircraft would almost certainly have forward-deployed to a variety of urban and rural FOLs. Well equipped for dispersed site operations, the Su-25 could carry servicing equipment, fuel bunds, pumps, covers and the miscellany of airfield gear in specially designed underwing pods. It is believed that a similar underwing pod was designed for the carriage of ground crew, but this was not deployed operationally, presumably to the great relief of the regiment's crew chiefs. The 357th OShAP had formed at Pruzhany in Byelorussia in October 1984, deploying to Brandis one year later. Pilots from the regiment fought in Afghanistan, deploying to the 368th OShAP and other Su-25 units in-theatre for up to one year.

Official sources suggest that the regiment should have had 35 single-seaters on charge, with two twin-stickers and five L-39s, but only 32 were ever noted by Western observers, with the correct number of L-39s and Su-25UBs. All aircraft had red codes, outlined in white. The L-39s departed in March 1992, flying to Ryazhsk and Demmin, with the last 22 Su-25s leaving for Buturlinovka and disbandment on 28 April 1992. Four Su-25s transferred to Demmin, along with the two Su-25UBs and a pair of L-39s. The 357th OShAP at Brandis never had the later, re-engined Su-25BM on charge. Augmenting the Su-25s at Brandis was a large number of army aviation helicopters.

The 485th OVP reportedly formed at Merseburg in May 1989, initially as single *eskadrilya* with 18 helicopters, from a core provided by a unit which had seen extensive service in Afghanistan, operating from Bagram, Kabul, and Shinand. The strength of the regiment built up rapidly, with 40 helicopters on charge by April 1990 and about 60 by April 1991. The regiment maintained a large detachment at Brandis until the withdrawal from Merseburg in August 1991, when the entire regiment moved in beside its former detachment. The 485th OVP finally departed from

Brandis in three groups on 25, 27 and 29 May, bound for a base near Murmansk and transiting via Kolobrzeg and Kaliningrad. Stonethrowing by local youths led to a tightening of security around the helicopter dispersals at Brandis, and on one occasion a Western aircraft spotter was 'warned off' by shots fired in the air.

357 Otdelnyi Shturmovoi Aviatsionnaya Polk

Aircraft: Sukhoi Su-25
Known codes: Red 01, 02, 03, 04, 05, 06, 07, 08, 09, 11, 14, 15, 16, 18, 20, 21, 22, 23, 24, 25, 26, 27, 28, 29, 30, 31, 32, 33, 34, 35, 36, 37, 38, 39, 40

Aircraft: Su-25UB
Known codes: Red 71, 72

Aircraft: Aero L-39C
Known codes: Red 63, 64, 65, 66, 80, 82

Above: The gate at Brandis was guarded by a convincing replica of an Il-2 Shturmovik, an appropriate contribution by the incoming 357th OShAP, operators of the Il-2's modern equivalent, the Su-25 'Frogfoot'. Regiments placed great emphasis on memorials and gate guards. Such monuments always had a Stalinist/Modernist feel to them, however, and were unmistakably Soviet.

Below: This Su-25 is on final approach. The introduction of the Su-25 led to a major upgrading of the airfields at Brandis and Tütow, which had previously operated helicopters. Brandis had a hard runway which was extended, and a network of taxiways was added. The Su-25 could have operated from grass, but not without serious erosion.

A 357th OShAP Su-25 emerges from a complex of revetments carrying underwing fuel tanks and the ubiquitous 20-round B8M 80-mm rocket pods. Brandis did not have hardened aircraft shelters, the Su-25s instead operating from primitive revetments with great banked-earth walls. In time of war Brandis would have been abandoned, and the Su-25s would have moved forward, operating from fields or strips of road or track.

Cochstedt

About 20 miles (32 km) south-south-west of Magdeburg, Cochstedt lay within 30 miles (48 km) of the West German border, between the villages of Cochstedt in the north and Schadeleben in the south. With one runway (orientated 08/26), the Soviets used Cochstedt as a helicopter base.

Cochstedt's geographical proximity to the West German border made it the natural operating location for the 292nd OERVE, a small unit which had the dual roles of airborne jamming and Elint. The unit left for Russia in June 1992.

292 Otdelnyi Eletronika Radiorazvedka Vertoletnyi Eskadrilya

Aircraft: Mi-8T
Known codes: Red 01

Aircraft: Mi-8PPA
Known codes: Red 04, 05, 06, 07 08, 09

Aircraft: Mi-8SMV
Known codes: Red 15, 16, 17, 18, 19, 20

Aircraft: Mi-9
Known codes: Red 21, 22

Left: Two Mi-8PPA jamming platforms head a line of four Mi-8SMVs at Cochstedt. In wartime the SMVs presumably would have been engaged in finding targets for the PPAs to jam. There were only six of these dedicated Elint platforms in East Germany, and they left in June 1992. All Cochstedt-based helicopters wore plain, dull red codes, without outlines. These are the best and most clearly detailed photos of the 'Hip-J' ever published.

Photographs of Cochstedt's Mi-8SMV 'Hip-Js' are extremely rare, although they were a common sight to West German border guards as they patrolled the border, listening to NATO communications traffic, locating and classifying all manner of electro-magnetic emissions. The aircraft's distinctive box-like antenna fairings are clearly visible on the cabin sides, together with the narrow vertical 'handles' whose purpose remains unknown.

Damm

Located in the south of Mecklemburg, about 20 miles (32 km) south-west of Schwerin, Damm airfield lay about 40 miles (64 km) from the West German border, just west of the town of Parchim, with the village of Damm further away to the west. Bordered by the road from Parchim to Damm to the north, and by a railway line in the south, Damm started life as a Luftwaffe satellite airfield for Neustadt. From mid-1943 the airfield, then known as Parchim, housed various components of NJG 5 for the night defence of Berlin, and a number of day fighter units, including, at one stage, a *Staffel* of the Me 262-equipped JG 7. From February 1945 Parchim housed Erprobungsgruppe 25 (later JGr. 10), a three-*Staffel* test unit whose task was the testing of heavy anti-bomber weapons. Parchim was the base of I/JG 1, the first unit to convert to the Heinkel He 162.

In Soviet hands, Damm had a single hard runway running 07/25 and was for many years a major fighter-bomber and fast jet base. In 1965 it housed one of the three fighter-bomber regiments of the fighter-bomber division at Lärz, with 36 MiG-17Fs, six MiG-17PFs, four MiG-15UTIs and four Yak-12s. It also had a target-towing unit, with eight Il-28s, two Il-28Us and two

Red codes, outlined in white, identify this Mi-8MTV as belonging to the lead regiment assigned to the 2nd Guards Tank Army, the Damm-based 172nd OVP. The aircraft sits on a pad of pierced steel planking, commonly used to provide dispersals on the grass areas of army aviation airfields.

Lisunov Li-2s. By 1967, the Su-7 had largely replaced the MiG-17, although a handful of MiG-17Fs remained active, while the target-towing flight remained unchanged. The MiG-15UTIs and Yak-12s had been withdrawn. Damm reportedly housed a MiG-25 reconnaissance regiment until about 1984, when it was handed over to army aviation for their use as a helicopter base. There were also conflicting reports of a mixed regiment with *eskadrilyas* of MiG-21s, MiG-23s and MiG-25s. It is believed that the Damm-based Il-28 target tugs, which disappeared from the order of battle in 1969, ended their days as a constituent part of the divisional HQ at Pütnitz, to which they transferred to support the Baltic firing ranges. They may have been replaced by MiG-21s, with reports of red-coded MiG-21s still present in September 1990, these aircraft having Dayglo fuselage stripes. Helicopter operations were, however, already very well established, and the airfield had been home to one of the two Mil Mi-24 'Hind-A' regiments deployed to Germany in 1973 for evaluation. By 1990 Damm was an established helicopter base, and was one of the two biggest Soviet rotary-wing airfields in Germany, with two full helicopter regiments, one of which had

a detachment at Rechlin-Larz. Damm was emptied in October 1992, both regiments going to an airfield near Kaliningrad.

172 Otdelnyi Vertoletnyi Polk

Aircraft: Mi-24V
Known codes: Red 05, 06, 07, 08, 14, 15, 16, 17, 18, 19, 20, 21, 22, 23, 24, 25, 26, 27, 28, 29, 30, 39, 40, 41, 42

Aircraft: Mi-24P
Known codes: Red 01, 02, 03, 04, 09, 10, 12, 31, 32, 33, 34, 35

Aircraft: Mi-8TB
Known codes: Red 60, 61, 62, 63, 64, 65, 66, 67, 68, 69, 70, 72, 73

Aircraft: Mi-8MT
Known codes: Red 51, 52, 53, 54, 56, 57, 58, 59

439 Otdelnyi Vertoletnyi Polk (see also Lärz)

Aircraft: Mi-24V
Known codes: Yellow 01, 02, 03, 04, 05, 06, 07, 08, 09, 10, 11, 12, 14, 15, 16, 17

Aircraft: Mi-24RKR 'Hind-G'
Known codes: Yellow 18, 19, 20, 21

Aircraft: Mi-24K 'Hind-G2'
Known codes: Yellow 22, 23, 24, 25, 46, 47

Aircraft: Mi-8TB
Known codes: Yellow 26, 28, 29, 30, 32, 34, 35, 37, 38, 40, 46, 49

Aircraft: Mi-8MT
Known codes: Yellow 27, 31, 33, 39, 41

This Mi-9 of the 439th OVP is unusual in that it carries the army aviation badge on its nose. The small (sealed) clamshell doors and central 'cut-out' are clearly visible.

Yellow 08, an Mi-24V 'Hind-E' of the 439th OVP, takes off from Damm laden with auxiliary fuel tanks and underwing rocket pods, watched by its crew chief. Blue intake filters were an eskadrilya marking, perhaps applied to the commander's aircraft.

Eberswalde

Located just to the east of the E28 motorway which runs north-east from Berlin to Szczecin in Poland, Eberswalde airfield was located south of the road running from the motorway to the towns of Finow and Eberswalde, which today run almost seamlessly together, with Finow in the west merging into Eberswalde to the east.

Used by the Luftwaffe as Finow, the airfield housed a number of night-fighter units tasked with the defence of Berlin. In Luftwaffe hands Finow had two hard runways (06/24 and 10/28), but in Russian hands the south-east/north-west runway was relegated to the status of taxiway,

Eberswalde-based MiG-29 'Fulcrum-Cs' taxi out for their final departure to Ros, in Byelorussia. Only half of the Eberswalde-based MiG-29s (the later production aircraft) had provision for external fuel tanks, and most of these were clustered within the second eskadrilya.

This poor-quality black and white photo shows one of the MiG-25PD 'Foxbat-Es' used by the 787th IAP before it converted to the MiG-29 in 1989. The MiG-25s were red- (or occasionally blue-) coded, and were tasked with intercepting the USAF's high-flying Mach 3+ Lockheed SR-71s operating from RAF Mildenhall in Suffolk, England.

while the east-west runway was extended west to effectively double in length. It is believed that a semi-prepared grass-covered runway lay south of the main runway. A uniquely Soviet feature was the addition of two massive swinging gates, which could be locked across the runway to prevent 'unauthorised flights' (defections).

Early Soviet use of the airfield remains unknown, although Eberswalde eventually became a bomber base, with 44 Il-28s and eight Yak-28s on charge by 1965, with a base flight of six Il-28Us and four Yak-12s. The regiment reported to the three-regiment division headquartered at Werneuchen, whose Werneuchen- and

Brand-based regiments switched to other roles during 1968. By this time the Eberswalde regiment had only 36 Yak-28s, which served at the base until 1970. Eberswalde was briefly home to the helicopter regiment assigned to the 20th

Guards Infantry Army (headquartered at Eberswalde).

Eberswalde took over a fighter role in 1970, when its last resident, the 787th IAP, moved in. The base was then refurbished and hardened, with some 60 HASs being built, some of them on the site of former Luftwaffe aircraft shelters. Responsible for the air defence of Berlin, the 787th IAP is believed to have formed part of the Western Group of Forces since the war. Formed at Tula, near Moscow, on 22 July 1941, the 787th flew air defence missions with the Polikarpov I-16, the MiG-1, the Hawker Hurricane and the Yak-1M, scoring 36 confirmed kills against German aircraft. One early pilot became a Hero of the Soviet Union by downing three enemy aircraft during the battle of Moscow, two of them by ramming. The unit moved to Neuruppin in 1951, where it re-equipped first with the

Below: One of the 787th IAP's MiG-29s taxis back along a rain-soaked Eberswalde runway. A former bomber airfield, Eberswalde was well provided with HASs and hangars, and its proximity to Berlin made it a popular posting for junior officers. Because it was the eighth and last MiG-29 regiment in East Germany to form, the 787th IAP received factory fresh 'Fulcrum-Cs' and never operated the baseline 'Fulcrum-A'.

This is an unusual overhead view of an Eberswalde-based MiG-29UB. The MiG-29UB was based on the airframe of the basic MiG-29, and thus lacked the swollen spine of the 'Fulcrum-C'. Fuel capacity was reduced by the provision of the second cockpit. Like the MiG-23UB, the MiG-29 trainer lacks radar and so cannot be considered a fully-operational aircraft. By contrast, the Su-27UB does have radar, and lacks only some of the single-seat 'Flanker's prodigious internal fuel capacity.

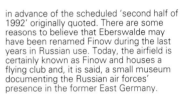

MiG-15 and then with the MiG-17, moving to Gross Dölln for conversion to the MiG-19 in 1956, and staying there until 1970.

The 787th IAP's association with Eberswalde began in 1970, when it moved from Gross Dölln and converted to the MiG-21PFM (and later the MiG-21SM). MiG-23M 'Flogger-Bs' were received during 1975 or 1976. In late 1981 one *eskadrilya* re-equipped with the MiG-25PD 'Foxbat-E' and was tasked with intercepting the high-flying Mach 3+ Lockheed SR-71s operating from Det. 4 of the 9th SRW at RAF Mildenhall. Some sources suggest that the remaining two *eskadrilyas* converted to the MiG-25PD during 1982 and 1983, giving an eventual total of 40 (mainly red-coded) MiG-25s, while others suggest that the regiment

was never fully 'Foxbat'-equipped, instead retaining two *eskadrilyas* of MiG-23M 'Flogger-Bs'. A detachment of MiG-25s was reportedly maintained at Wittstock, perhaps with another at one of the southern fighter airfields. On a map published in a prominent Dutch military magazine in the mid-1980s,

Eberswalde was still shown as housing 48 MiG-23s, despite the base's proximity to Berlin and Western air attachés. The withdrawal of the SR-71 from Mildenhall in 1989 led to the re-equipment of the 787th IAP with factory-fresh, white-coded MiG-29 'Fulcrum-Cs' from November 1989. The regiment's white codes were usually thinly outlined in black. Even after the withdrawal of the MiG-25, at least three 'Foxbats' remained at Eberswalde. One was dumped near the eastern end of the runway and became a children's plaything, while the others served as instructional airframes. The appearance of a MiG-25 on the Rangsdorf dump wearing a three-digit blue code may have marked the final appearance of a 787th IAP MiG-25.

Conversion to the 'Fulcrum' made the 787th IAP the eighth and last MiG-29 unit in Germany. Official sources listed 35 MiG-29s on strength, but only 28 have been noted by Western observers, together with two MiG-29UBs and six MiG-23UBs. The regiment left for Ros, in Byelorussia, on 11 May 1992,

in advance of the scheduled 'second half of 1992' originally quoted. There are some reasons to believe that Eberswalde may have been renamed Finow during the last years in Russian use. Today, the airfield is certainly known as Finow and houses a flying club and, it is said, a small museum documenting the Russian air forces' presence in the former East Germany.

787 Istrebeitelnyi Aviotsionnaya Polk

Aircraft: MiG-29 'Fulcrum-C'
Known codes: 01, 02, 03, 04, 05, 06, 07, 08, 09, 10, 68, 69, 70, 71, 73, 74, 75, 76, 77, 78, 79, 80, 82, 83, 84, 85, 87, 89

Aircraft: MiG-29UB
Known codes: White 11, 33, 72

Aircraft: MiG-23UB
Known codes: Red 20, 22, 52, 65, Blue 62

Like all of the MiG-29 and MiG-27 bases in East Germany, Eberswalde had its own fleet of about five MiG-23UBs for training, liaison and support duties. These wore a variety of code colours, and did not fit into the numerical sequences used by the front-line eskadrilyas of the 787th IAP.

Below: White 79 was among the more colourful of the Eberswalde-based MiG-29s, with an unusual camouflage pattern giving a scalloped dark fuselage spine. It was also adorned with the logo of the Mikoyan OKB and carried an excellence award on the nose. These two embellishments were applied to several other second eskadrilya aircraft.

Finsterwalde

Like other airfields used by the Russians as bomber and fighter-bomber bases, Finsterwalde is located in the eastern part of the former GDR, quite close to the Polish border in the state of Brandenburg. About 20 miles (32 km) east of Alt Lönnewitz and 30 miles (48 km) north of Dresden, Finsterwalde airfield lay immediately south of the town of Finsterwalde.

The airfield was one of the earliest used by the Luftwaffe, with some of the earliest Ju 52, Ju 86 and Do 17/Do 23 units. Later mainly housing Defence of the Reich units, but with some transport and ground attack squadrons, Finsterwalde was also used by some unusual formations, including the B-17Gs of KG 200. Finsterwalde ended the war as a long-range transport base, with Ju 290s and Ju 352s of I/KG 200 and Transportstaffel 5 responsible for the evacuation of leading Nazis at the end of the war, undertaking mysterious flights to unusual destinations, including a Ju 290A-6 flight to Barcelona on 26 April 1945.

A square-shaped grass airfield, with seven hangars ranged along the southern edge when in Luftwaffe use, Finsterwalde retained most of its Luftwaffe buildings, but was dramatically extended both east and west to allow the construction of a massive

On departure from Finsterwalde, a MiG-27K passes a pair of MiG-23UBs being readied for flight. Both are still attached to the truck-mounted APU parked between them, which extends its power cables towards the aircraft on swinging gantries.

new hard runway (running roughly 09/27) and a parallel southern taxiway. Three shelter areas were later constructed, with a total of more than 30 HASs.

Under Soviet ownership Finsterwalde soon became an Il-28 bomber base, and probably lost its aircraft as part of the same high-profile reductions that led to the withdrawal of the Il-28 from Oranienburg. It housed a fighter-bomber regiment during the 1960s, reporting to the fighter-bomber division at Grossenhain. In 1965 the

regiment had 18 MiG-17Fs and 24 Su-7s, together with four MiG-15UTIs and four Yak-12s. MiG-17s finally gave way to MiG-27s at Finsterwalde in 1976, when the 559th APIB became the first 16th Air Army unit to re-equip with the new 'Flogger-D' variant. There have been reports that MiG-23BNs were briefly used before the MiG-27, and that these aircraft were then modified and delivered directly to Caslav for service with the Czechoslovak air force. This cannot be confirmed.

The baseline MiG-27 proved to be an improvement over the MiG-17 or Su-7, but it lacked the sophisticated avionics of later sub-types. The type nevertheless remained in service at Finsterwalde long after other MiG-27 regiments had received the later MiG-27D/M 'Flogger-J', and it was not until the early 1980s that the 559th APIB re-equipped with MiG-27K 'Flogger-J2s'. This represented a significant increase in capability even by comparison with the MiG-27Ds and MiG-27Ms at Nöbitz and Lärz.

The regiment's MiG-27Ks wore pale blue codes, thinly outlined in white, until they withdrew to Morozovsk on 22 March 1993, in advance of the specified 'second half of 1993'. Some sources suggest that the destination of the 559th APIB was Bobruysk in Byelorussia, but this is not confirmed.

'Floggers' in the mist. Laden with three external fuel tanks, the MiG-27Ks of the 559th APIB taxi out from their shelter areas. The oval shape of the 'window' in the nose of the MiG-27K is apparent, together with the broad rectangular window below and behind it. MiG-27s tend to adopt a tail-down attitude on the ground, particularly when carrying tanks.

559 Aviotsionnaya Polk Istrebeitelei-Bombardirovchikov

Aircraft: MiG-27K
Known codes: Blue 01, 02, 03, 04, 05, 06, 07, 08, 09, 10, 11, 12, 21, 22, 23, 24, 25, 26, 27, 28, 29, 30, 31, 41, 42, 43, 44, 45, 46, 47, 48, 49, 50

Aircraft: MiG-23UB
Known codes: Blue 90, 91, 92, 93, 94, 95, 96, 97, 99

The MiG-27Ks of the 559th APIB carried their regimental codes in an unusual bright but fairly pale blue, and outlined them in white. This MiG-27K carries underwing B8M rocket pods, a favourite MiG-27 weapon in the 16th Air Army, although the aircraft was compatible with a wide range of guided missiles and munitions.

Gross Dölln

Labelled Templin on NATO maps, the airfield at Gross Dölln lies 35 miles (56 km) north of Berlin, 35 miles (56 km) west of the Polish border and about 7 miles (11 km) south of the town of Templin. Like other fighter-bomber and bomber bases in East Germany, Templin is well clear of the air corridors to Berlin, and lies well east of the imaginary line that would split East Germany into eastern and western halves. NATO charts show an auxiliary runway (01/19) leading away to the south from the western threshold of the main runway (09/27). Templin was for many years an important forward deployment base for bomber aircraft permanently stationed at airfields within the USSR, as well as being an important fighter and fighter-bomber airfield in its own right. In 1979, Gross Dölln hosted a 20-aircraft evaluation unit for the Su-24 'Fencer', which stayed until the spring of 1981. It is believed that this deployment allowed Western air attachés and intelligence agents to obtain the first pictures of Russia's new bomber. Tupolev Tu-16 'Badgers' and Tu-22 'Blinders' were among the regular visitors to Gross Dölln until the early 1990s, when the bomber ramp was given over to the helicopters of the 487th OVP, which arrived from Prenzlau, before moving on to Werneuchen.

Gross Dölln housed an air defence regiment (the 787th IAP, later at Finow) between 1956 and 1970, providing for the air defence of Berlin and reporting to the fighter division headquartered at Pütnitz. By 1965 the regiment was equipped with 18 MiG-17PFs and 24 MiG-21s, the latter having reportedly replaced MiG-19s. It also had a base flight with four MiG-15UTIs and four Yak-12s, which had gone by 1967.

From 1954 Gross Dölln hosted a fighter-bomber unit, the 20th APIB, initially

*The badge of the second **eskadrilya** of the 20th **APIB** was a polar bear's head in front of an up-ended bomb, flanked by the words 'Komsomol Zapolyami' and presented in a blue pentagon.*

*The badge of the first **eskadrilya** was not widely applied, and consisted of a bat superimposed on a storm cloud, and two red flashes of lightning. The design was similar to one seen on Su-17s serving in Afghanistan.*

equipped with MiG-15s. This unit had been formed in 1939, flying Polikarpov I-153s in Finland, where it had fought with some distinction, with two of its pilots becoming Heroes of the Soviet Union. Captain Alexei Poshnikov gained his award for his 28 kills and single ramming attack (*taran*) while Lieutenant Stepanovich gained his for three such attacks. Moving to Leningrad, the 20th APIB moved on to Warsaw and to Frankfurt am der Oder, flying the MiG-3 and the Lavochkin La-5 and, reportedly, the MiG-9 'Fargo', Russia's first purpose-built front-line jet fighter. It spent brief periods at Pütnitz and Damm after the war, flying Yak-9s and Yak-3s, and perhaps Bell P-39 Airacobras and P-63 Kingcobras. The unit converted to the MiG-15 at Alakourtii in Karelia in 1951, and moved to Gross Dölln in 1954. MiG-17s were received in 1955, and these were replaced by Su-7s in 1962 (or 1964 according to some sources). The unit may have moved to Damm during the period between 1956 and 1970, when Templin housed a fighter regiment. There are some suggestions that MiG-17s were received again during 1973, but this cannot be confirmed or explained. 1976 (or 1977) saw the issue of the Su-17M, making the 20th APIB the first front-line operator of the new type, with the Su-17M3 'Fitter-H' following in 1981. 1981 also marked the retirement of the Su-7U and its replacement by two-seat swing-wing Su-17s. This allowed an Su-7U to be erected as a gate guard at Gross Dölln. Despite the long connection between Gross Dölln and the 'Fitter', Western orders of battle published in the mid-1980s usually managed to describe the airfield as being a MiG-27 base.

Conversion to the Su-17M-4 began in 1987. It has been suggested that conversion was completed by the absorption of Su-17M-4s from the retreating units at Allstedt and Neuruppin. The unit's

*Right: This second **eskadrilya** 'Fitter' wears a simplified version of the squadron badge, with the bomb and wording removed, the bear's head presented in profile and a gold-edged blue arrowhead.*

Below: Yellow 20 undergoes routine maintenance outside shelter No. 19, and is wearing the 2nd Eskadrilya badge seen beside this caption. Interestingly, the aircraft's code letters do not have the usual red outline.

Above: A handful of Gross Dölln Su-17M-4s wore plain bright red codes, without outlines, while others had new codes on fresh patches of paint. These may have been aircraft inherited from Neuruppin or Allstedt.

Even the Su-17UM-3s at Gross Dölln received individual markings. This aircraft, assigned to the second eskadrilya, carried an unusual griffon badge on the port side of the nose.

aircraft wore yellow codes, thinly outlined in red. The fighter-bomber units were among the largest in Germany, and official sources estimated the strength of the 20th APIB at 40 aircraft. Western observers noted at least 34 Su-17M-4s and seven Su-17UM-3s during the period between the fall of the Berlin Wall and the final departure.

The commander of the 20th APIB was among the officers more open to new ideas, and during the period between the wall's collapse and the departure of his regiment a number of the unit's aircraft received special markings. Several Su-17M-4s and Su-17UM-3s carried individual markings, with a griffon, a rhinoceros, a

The short-lived initial badge of the third eskadrilya featured a diving eagle (with the number 3 superimposed) and a blue and white pennant.

whale and a top hat all being noted soon after the Berlin Wall came down. A gaudy sharkmouth was applied to at least one aircraft during this period. More formalised unit markings began to make an appearance during the run-up to departure, but never became 'fleet-wide'. The first *eskadrilya* used a stylised bat (previously seen on Su-17s in Afghanistan), while the second opted for the head of a polar bear, in a blue chevron or pentagon. This insignia was borrowed from the Zapolyarnii Komsomol (the Communist youth organisation of a town near Murmansk) which had paid for 12 of the unit's aircraft in 1942, and which had retained some links with the second *eskadrilya*. The third *eskadrilya* (a Guards squadron) used a diving eagle, in blue on a yellow shield, with a blue and white pennant, and later a double-headed Romanov eagle in red, white and blue on a quartered shield. All third *eskadrilya* Su-17s also wore a Guards badge on the nose.

Gross Dölln also opened its gates for a number of dragster races along its runway, some of which involved car versus MiG-29 runs along the runway. These latter meetings were promoted under the unlikely title (in English!) of 'Kick the MiG'. The regiment even used flying suit patches, and its pilots sold photographic prints at open days. The 'Fitters' left Gross Dölln on 5 April 1994, reportedly bound for Taganrog. Here the regiment disbanded, but it is not known whether its aircraft were scrapped or turned over to the AV-MF. The 20th APIB reformed, however, some of its pilots forming the nucleus of a new Su-24

Below: Many of Gross Dölln's Su-17M-4s bore obvious signs of having been recoded, with their new codes applied over hastily daubed rectangles of green paint. The winged insignia (actually a winged archer) on the nose of this aircraft is the Sukhoi OKB badge.

'Fencer' unit at Kamenka near Penza. At one time there were reports that Gross Dölln might re-open as the home of the Luftwaffe's WTD.61, but this idea came to nothing.

20 Aviotsionnaya Polk Istrebeitelei-Bombardirovchikov

First *eskadrilya*:
Aircraft: Su-17M-4
Known codes: Yellow 01, 02, 03, 04, 05, 06, 07, 08, 09, 10, 11, 12, 15

Second *eskadrilya*:
Aircraft: Su-17M-4
Known codes: Yellow 17, 20, 22, 23, 24, 25, 26, 27, 28, 29, 30

The third eskadrilya went to town with this Su-17UM-3, 'Tiger 3', perhaps angling for an invitation to the NATO Tiger Meet. The third eskadrilya was a Guards unit, and its aircraft all wore Guards badges on each side of the nose, in addition to their individual markings.

Third *eskadrilya*:
Aircraft: Su-17M-4
Known codes: Yellow 04, 40, 41, 42, 43, 44, 45, 46, 47, 48, 49

Aircraft: Su-17UM-3
Known codes: Yellow 81, 82, 83, 84, 87, 88, 89

The redesigned badge of the third eskadrilya featured a double-headed Romanov eagle wrapped in the Russian tricolour.

Grossenhain

Grossenhain airfield is located about 20 miles (32 km) north-east of the centre of Dresden, north-west of the town of Grossenhain and north of the road which runs to Folbern. Like several other former bomber bases the airfield is served by its own railway line. Grossenhain was one of the Luftwaffe's first airfields. A reconnaissance squadron (Aufklärungstaffel 1./324) was formed during 1934, and Fliegerstaffel Grossenhain was activated in 1935 as a bomber unit. During the war, Grossenhain hosted a number of fighter, bomber, *Zerstörer* and *Schlacht* units.

By 1965 Grossenhain accommodated a fighter-bomber regiment with 36 MiG-17Fs and 12 Su-7s. The four MiG-15UTIs and four Yak-12s of the base flight had vanished by 1967. Continuing to operate MiG-17 and Su-7 fighter-bombers during the 1960s and 1970s, Grossenhain returned to the bomber role in the early 1980s. The 128th Bomber Aviation Division (which had previously overseen Il-28 bomber operations in Germany) was re-established at Grossenhain during 1981, to control soon-to-form Su-24 bomber units at Grossenhain and Brand, and replacing the fighter-bomber division headquarters that had controlled the Grossenhain, Juterbog 2 and Finsterwalde regiments. Although administratively reporting to the 16th Air Army HQ at Zossen-Wunsdorf, the 'Fencer' units came under the operational control of the 4th Air Army, along with Su-24 regiments in Poland and the Ukraine. The tension-reducing lowering of the Western Group of Forces' offensive posture led to the withdrawal of the Su-24 from Germany, and the 7th Bomber Aviation Regiment withdrew to Stary Konstantinov in the Ukraine in 1989, where it, together with the 727th BAP from Brand, formed part of the new 32nd BAD and reported to the Odessa-based 5th Air Army. During their stay at Grossenhain the Su-24s (a mix of 'Fencer-Bs' and 'Fencer-Cs') wore white codes. Reports that some of the aircraft had camouflaged upper surfaces cannot be confirmed.

The 'Fencers' were replaced by the red-coded MiG-27Ms and MiG-27Ds of the 296th IBAP, which moved in from Nöbitz. The vacated headquarters of the 128th Bomber Aviation Division became the HQ of the 105th Fighter Bomber Aviation Division, controlling the MiG-27 regiments at Brand and Finsterwalde, as well as the Grossenhain 'Floggers'. Grossenhain finally closed to flying on 22 March 1993, when the last of its 'Floggers' departed for storage or scrapping at Orenburg. This comfortably beat the Russian's timetabled withdrawal date of 'the second half of 1993'.

Above and right: The Grossenhain gate was guarded by a pair of dramatically mounted aircraft, an Su-7 'Fitter-A' and a MiG-17F 'Fresco-C', both of which had served with based ground attack units during the 1960s and 1970s.

Below: A MiG-27M of the 296th APIB taxis in after a sortie, still dragging its cruciform braking parachute. Service designations for the various MiG-27 sub-types differ – somewhat confusingly – from those allocated by the design bureau.

296 Aviotsionnaya Polk Istrebeitelei-Bombardirovchikov

Aircraft: MiG-27D
Known codes: Red 17, 25, 26, 29, 32, 33

Aircraft: MiG-27M

Known codes: Red 01, 02, 03, 04, 05, 06, 07, 08, 09, 10, 11, 12, 14, 15, 16, 18, 19, 20, 21, 22, 23, 24, 28, 30

Aircraft: MiG-23UB
Known codes: Red 60, 61, 62, 63, 64, 66, 68, 69, Blue 74

Armed with an underwing B8M rocket pod and a single tiny bomb on the side of the rear fuselage, this 296th APIB aircraft is a MiG-27D 'Flogger-J'. The MiG-27D and the MiG-27M are virtually identical, and share the 'Flogger-J' epithet. The MiG-27M was newly built, while the MiG-27D was produced by conversion of 'Flogger-D' airframes.

Hassleben

Located in central Thuringia, Hassleben is a grass airfield lying about 5 miles (8 km) north of Erfurt and just over 20 miles (32 km) north-west of Nohra.

The headquarters squadron of the 8th Guards Infantry Army was the 298th OVE, which was based at Hassleben until August 1992, when it returned to Russia, passing its Mi-2s to the 41st OVE at Werneuchen. Unusually, the squadron had a pair of 'Hook-Bs' instead of the usual 'Hook-B' and 'Hook-C' combination.

298 Otdelnyi Vertoletnyi Eskadrilya

Aircraft: Mi-2T
Known codes: Red 01, 04, 05, 06, 16, 17, 18, 20

Aircraft: Mi-6VKP
Known codes: Orange 05, Red 50

Aircraft: Mi-8T
Known codes: Red 21, 22, 23

Aircraft: Mi-24RKR 'Hind-G'
Known codes: Red 10, 11

Aircraft: Mi-24K
Known codes: Red 12, 14

After the withdrawal from Hassleben, several of the 298th OVE's Mi-2Ts were passed on to the 41st OVE at Werneuchen, which became the only airfield accommodating the 'Hoplite' and where this photo was taken.

Hellerau

Lying in Klotzsche, one of the northern suburbs of Dresden, Hellerau is within a few miles of the emergency highway strip at Ottendorf. References to an airfield named Dresden-Klotzsche are understood to refer to a nearby aerodrome which has since been built over. Both Klotzsche and Hellerau are believed to have been used by the Luftwaffe and the Russians.

In Russian hands Hellerau latterly housed the 6th OVE, the HQ squadron for the army

aviation units which reported to the Dresden-based First Guards Tank Army. This small unit was equipped with the usual mix of command post, reconnaissance and jamming helicopters, and used yellow codes. During 1991 and 1992 the unit seems to have borrowed about three Mi-8MTVs from the 172nd OVP at Damm, these aircraft retaining their red codes during their stay at Hellerau. The unit returned to an unknown destination in Russia on 20 August 1992.

A pair of Mi-8PPA 'Hip-K' jammers is seen at Dresden-Hellerau. Airborne communications jamming would have played a major part in any Russian battle plan, and the Mi-8PPA was therefore an important and relatively common type in East Germany. It served in twos or fours with several of the headquarters squadrons attached to the various armies, and in larger numbers with the specialist Elint/EW squadron at Cochstedt.

6 Otdelnyi Vertoletnyi Eskadrilya

Aircraft: Mi-6VKP 'Hook-B'
Known codes: Yellow 09

Aircraft: Mi-22 'Hook-C'
Known codes: Yellow 07

Aircraft: Mi-8T
Known codes: Yellow 11, 19, 23

Aircraft: Mi-8TB
Known codes: Yellow 20

Aircraft: Mi-8PPA
Known codes: Yellow 21, 22

Aircraft: Mi-24RKR 'Hind-G'
Known codes: Yellow 15, 16

Aircraft: Mi-24K 'Hind-G2'
Known codes: Yellow 17, 18

Some of the 6th OVE's helicopters were extremely well weathered. This Mi-24RKR, for example, has almost lost the dark green of its disruptive camouflage. Despite its scruffy appearance, this example is fully equipped and has the wingtip 'claws' often omitted from these aircraft.

Köthen

Lying about midway between Zerbst in the north and Merseburg in the south, Köthen lay some 15 miles (24 km) north-west of Wolfen and its nearby motorway strip, marked on NATO charts as the Thurland highway strip. In German hands Köthen became the home of a Junkers factory in 1938, and then housed a number of Luftwaffe operational, training and test units. The *Freya* radar on the island of Wangenrooge was owned and operated by a detachment from Köthen when it was used to alert the defences of the first RAF raid on Wilhelmshaven, in which half of the attackers were shot down, largely as a result of this early warning.

A relatively modest grass airfield in German use, the base was extended west by its new masters and a hard runway (08/26) was laid, with a parallel southern taxiway. When the base was later hardened, more than 45 HASs were built.

The airfield was among the first in East Germany to house jet fighters and, by virtue of its position, these were frequently encountered by NATO and Western aircraft transiting to Berlin via the southernmost of the three corridors. By 1965 Köthen housed a fighter regiment equipped with 28 MiG-21s and 14 MiG-17Fs, with the usual base flight of four Yak-12s and four MiG-15UTIs. From 1966 Köthen reportedly housed 30 Yak-28P 'Firebar' all-weather fighters, and by 1967 these had been joined by 16 MiG-21PF 'Fishbed-Ds'. The base flight had been withdrawn.

The MiG-21PF was replaced by later MiG-21 versions during the 1970s, but by the mid-1980s the 'Fishbed' had itself been replaced by the MiG-23M 'Flogger-B'. The final MiG-21 sub-type in use at Köthen was almost certainly the MiG-21bis 'Fishbed-L'.

Red-coded MiG-23MLD 'Flogger-Ks' were replaced by MiG-29s in early 1988, probably soon after Merseburg had replaced its MiG-23Ms. This had the effect of making Köthen home to the fifth MiG-29 regiment in East Germany, joining Wittstock, Pütnitz, Zerbst and Merseburg. By 1991 conversion to the 'Fulcrum-C' was well underway, and few 'Fulcrum-As' remained by the time the regiment left for Russia.

Köthen was the closest fighter base to the West German border, and this gave the airfield a particular importance, its aircraft standing 24-hour alert against the possibility of incursions. There have also been suggestions that the regiment had an important strike-escort role, perhaps explaining the relatively early and relatively swift conversion to the longer-legged 'Fulcrum-C'.

Despite its proximity to the inner German border, Köthen did not attract many Western photographers, and details of the colour schemes worn by its aircraft remain sketchy. Red codes were outlined in white, and a very small Guards badge usually appeared behind the 'point' of the intake, ahead of the cockpit. There were tantalising reports that at least one Köthen-based MiG-29, a 'Fulcrum-C' coded Red 11, was painted in desert sand camouflage, while there are also reports that the Köthen-based unit (perhaps alone among 16th Air Army Regiments) actually used the unlucky '13' code, which was usually scrupulously avoided.

This MiG-23UB lacks many of the antennas fitted to most current 'Flogger-Cs' and was used by the 73rd GvIAP for training and liaison duties. The MiG-23UB was well-suited to fulfil such a role, being cheap to operate, available in huge numbers, and enjoying a high degree of cockpit commonality with the MiG-29. The Köthen-based regiment was unusually large, with an estimated 35 MiG-29s and 10 MiG-23UBs when the Berlin Wall was finally torn down. MiG-23UBs assigned to the MiG-29 regiments seldom used the standard regimental code colours, instead retaining whatever colours they had worn with their previous units.

Above: One of Köthen's rather camera-shy 'Fulcrum-Cs' is caught on final approach to its base. The aircraft shows signs of having been recently recoded, with the number '51' still visible on the dielectric fin cap. The small size and unusual location of the Guards badge made Köthen's MiG-29s unique in Germany, although some Hungary-based Soviet 'Fulcrum-Cs' used a similar-sized badge in the same location. The bright red regimental codes were thickly outlined in white. There have been reports that one Köthen-based MiG-29 wore an overall desert camouflage.

There remains some confusion as to the true identity of the Köthen-based regiment, which has been quoted as the 73rd GvIAP and as the 85th GvIAP, an identity usually associated with the MiG-29 regiment at Merseburg. Since both regiments were Guards units, the use of Guards badges cannot confirm which unit was which. In an order of battle published in a Russo-German semi-official book about the Western Group of Forces, Merseburg was not mentioned at all, and Köthen was described as the home of the 85th GvIAP.

An 85th IAP now serves as part of the Ukrainian air force's 5th Air Army headquartered at Lvov. The regiment is based at Starokonstantinov and reports to the 130th IAD at Mirgorod. Its connection, if any, with the 85th GvIAP, formerly at Merseburg or Köthen, remains uncertain. The Köthen-based MiG-29s left Germany during May 1991, transiting to Anyosovo Gorodishe via Zerbst. There are persistent reports of a major change-over of aircraft, with newer Köthen 'Fulcrum-Cs' being retained in Germany while older 'Fulcrum-As' (especially from Zerbst and Nöbitz) were sent back to the USSR but, in retrospect, this seems unlikely to have happened to any great extent. Supporters of this theory point to the presence of red-coded 'Fulcrum-Cs' at Nöbitz and Zerbst, although such aircraft had been seen at both bases before the Köthen regiment departed. There are persistent reports that Köthen acted as a deployment base for a variety of aircraft types, most recently including Ilyushin (Beriev) A-50 'Mainstays'.

73 Gvardeiskaya Istrebeitelnyi Aviotsionnaya Polk

Aircraft: MiG-29 'Fulcrum-A'
Known codes: Red 21, 22, 23, 24, 28, 29, 30, 43, 44, 45, 46, 47, 48, 54

An atmospheric view of Köthen on the morning of 23 February 1991 reveals examples of all three of the aircraft types used by the based regiment, sitting outside shelters swathed in tarpaulins. Nearest are a 'Fulcrum-A' and a MiG-23UB, with a 'Fulcrum-C' in the background. It has been suggested that there were insufficient shelters at Köthen to accommodate all the based aircraft.

Aircraft: MiG-29 'Fulcrum-C'
Known codes: Red 01, 02, 03, 04, 05, 06, 07, 08, 09, 10, 11, 12, 13, 14, 20, 40, 41, 42,

Aircraft: MiG-29UB
Known codes: Red 70, 91

Aircraft: MiG-23UB
Known codes: Blue 89, 90, Red 93

Lärz

During World War II, Rechlin-Lärz was little more than a satellite of the major test airfield at Rechlin, some 4 miles (6 km) north. Its vital role as the 'German Farnborough' was accomplished without hard runways, and it is believed that Lärz was also a grass airfield. In Soviet times a hard runway (08/26) was provided with a cross runway (15/33), which fell into disuse. Lärz was the most westerly of the airfields used by the Russians as fighter-bomber and bomber bases, located halfway between the West German and Polish borders, in the southern part of Mecklemburg. The airfield was north of the village of Lärz, bounded to the north by the road running between the villages of Vietzen and Kotzow.

Under Soviet ownership, Lärz, sometimes known as Mirow, or as Rechlin-Lärz, became the long-term home of the fighter-bomber division controlling the fighter-bomber regiments at Lärz, Neuruppin and Damm (later replaced by Gross Dölln). Lärz's own regiment was equipped with 24 MiG-17Fs, six MiG-17PFs and an unknown number of Su-7s by 1965, together with four Yak-12s and four MiG-15UTIs for liaison and training. As a

Air combat manoeuvring training was an everyday occurence, even on the fighter-bomber units. Here one of the 19th GvAPIB's MiG-27Ds jettisons its single brake chute as it taxis in after an air combat training sortie, with a captive R-60 (AA-8 'Aphid') acquisition round below the starboard wing glove.

This pair of 19th Guards APIB MiG-27Ds, each carrying a single B8M rocket pod, returns to Lärz after a training sortie. The B8M pod contains 20 80-mm rockets, and has largely replaced the older UV-32-57 pod on fast jet types. Soviet tactical aircraft in Germany usually flew long, flat, fast approaches, and routinely used brake parachutes to reduce the ground roll.

divisional headquarters it also had four MiG-17Fs forming an HQ flight. By 1967 the Su-7 was the sole aircraft type on charge with the based regiment, although a handful of MiG-17Fs remained with the HQ flight, along with four more Su-7s. Sukhoi Su-7 'Fitter-As' gave way to more modern MiG-27 'Flogger-Ds' in 1978, although a handful may have survived until 1980 or 1981. Some Western orders of battle continued to describe Lärz as an Su-7 base until well into the 1980s. Between 1984 and 1987 these were returned to Russia in groups of four for conversion to MiG-27D 'Flogger-J'. The MiG-27s wore yellow codes, thinly outlined in red, although a handful of aircraft had yellow codes outlined in white. Most also wore Guards badges on the engine intakes, and a handful of aircraft were observed wearing a unit badge consisting of a Soviet star and the outline of the GDR. By 1991 the regiment had 31 MiG-27Ds on strength, with seven MiG-23UBs and a single An-2 serving the co-located headquarters of the 105th ADIB, which controlled the fighter-bomber regiments at Lärz, Gross-Dölln and Neuruppin. On 23 March 1993 the 19th GvIAP departed for Orenburg, a major MiG-

23/MiG-27 storage and maintenance unit, where it disbanded. The 16th Air Arrmy had met its target date of the 'second half of 1993' for the departure from Lärz.

Most of the 19th GvAPIB's aircrew converted to the MiG-29 and to the fighter role, and many returned to Germany to join the Pütnitz and Wittstock regiments, where they built up experience on the MiG-29, before returning to a reborn 19th GvIAP which had reformed at Millerovo near Rostock with MiG-29s. Like other Soviet bases in Germany, Lärz was often visited by Russia-based aircraft, reportedly including two Tu-160s during January 1992. A detachment from the 439th OVP at Damm operated from Lärz until August 1992, when the helicopters returned to their home base prior to its evacuation in October 1992.

19 Gvardeiskaya Aviotsionnaya Polk Istrebeitelei-Bombardirovchikov

First *eskadrilya*:
Aircraft: MiG-27D
Known codes: Yellow 01, 02, 03, 04, 05, 06, 07, 08, 09, 10, 11

Second *eskadrilya*:
Aircraft: MiG-27D
Known codes: Yellow 21, 22, 23, 24, 25, 26, 27, 28, 29, 30, 31

Third *eskadrilya*:
Aircraft: MiG-27D
Known codes: Yellow 42, 43, 44, 45, 46, 47, 48, 49, 50, 51

Aircraft: MiG-23UB
Known codes: Yellow 90, 91, 92, 93, 94, 95, 97

439 Otdelnyi Vertoletnyi Polk – detachment

Aircraft: Mi-24V
Known codes: Yellow 50, 51, 52, 53, 54, 55, 56, 57

Aircraft: Mi-24RKR 'Hind-G'
Known codes: Yellow 58

Aircraft: Mi-24K 'Hind-G2'
Known codes: Yellow 59, 72

Aircraft: Mi-8TB
Known codes: Yellow 62, 63, 65, 66, 68, 71

Aircraft: Mi-9
Known codes: Yellow 69, 70

Armed with four UV-16-57 rocket pods, a Lärz-based Mi-8 hovers above the runway. Behind it are some of the other helicopters maintained at Lärz by the 439th OVP.

Mahlwinkel

About 20 miles (32 km) north-west of Magdeburg, in the middle of the Berlin-Buckeburg corridor, Mahlwinkel airfield lay about 3 miles (5 km) south of Tangerhutte, with the hard runway running east-west (09/27) from Cobel to just short of the village of Mahlwinkel. Mahlwinkel has been a major helicopter base since about 1968, when it housed the single helicopter unit allocated to the 3rd Guards Shock Army at Magdeburg. This followed a period during which the airfield was used only sporadically, with reports that MiG-15s were once based there. By the late 1980s, Mahlwinkel had transferred to the control of the 20th Guards Infantry Army headquartered at Eberswalde, and housed the lead regiment assigned to this formation, with another regiment at Prenzlau (later moving to Gross Dölln, and later still to Werneuchen) and a headquarters squadron (the 296th OVE) also at Mahlwinkel. The departure of the regiments at Borstel allowed the 337th OVP to re-equip, trading its older Mi-24Ds and Mi-8TBs for newer and more capable Mi-24Vs and Mi-8MTVs. The regiment remained at Mahlwinkel until its departure in May 1994, although the HQ squadron left much earlier, dispersing some of its aircraft to other units and taking some aircraft back to Russia during 1991, leaving only two Mi-6 sub-types, which were almost certainly attached to the 337th OVP for the remainder of their stay.

337 Otdelnyi Vertoletnyi Polk

Aircraft: Mi-24V
Known codes: Yellow 05, 06, 07, 08, 18, 19, 20, 21, 22, 23, 24, 25, 34, 35, 36, 37, 38, 39, 40, 41

Aircraft: Mi-24P
Known codes: Yellow 01, 02, 03, 04, 09, 10, 11, 12, 14, 16, 17, 26, 27, 28, 29, 30, 31, 32, 33

Aircraft: Mi-8TB
Known codes: Yellow 41, 43, 46, 47, 48, 49, 50

Aircraft: Mi-8MT
Known codes: Yellow 53, 54, 61, 63

Above: As the lead regiment assigned to the 8th Guards Infantry Army, the 337th OVP operated a mix of Mi-24Vs and Mi-24Ps in its first two eskadrilyas, with Mi-8s, Mi-8MTs and Mi-8MTVs in the third eskadrilya. This aircraft is a 30-mm cannon-armed Mi-24P 'Hind-F', and wears the pale, plain yellow codes associated with this regiment. Because these codes were not outlined, they were often difficult to read.

Aircraft: Mi-8MTV
Known codes: Yellow 51, 52, 55, 56, 57, 58, 59, 60

296 Otdelnyi Vertoletnyi Eskadrilya

Aircraft: Mi-6VKP 'Hook-B'
Known codes: Red 01, 02

Aircraft: Mi-8PPA
Known codes: Red 03, 05

Aircraft: Mi-9

Known codes: Yellow 22

Aircraft: Mi-24RKR 'Hind-G'
Known codes: Red 09

Aircraft: Mi-24K 'Hind-G2'
Known codes: Red 11, 12

Above: Among the aircraft used by the 337th OVP at Mahlwinkel was this sharkmouthed Mi-8MT, Yellow 53. The aircraft also has a Russian flag painted on its door, together with a representation of the air forces' sunburst flag. The Mi-8 is actually an extremely effective attack helicopter, capable of carrying up to six 32-round 57-mm rocket pods, although its primary role is assault transport.

The Mi-6VKP 'Hook-B' usually partnered the Mi-22 (Mi-6BUS) in the command post role, with mixed pairs attached to most HQ squadrons and second regiments. Mahlwinkel's 296th OVE had a pair of Mi-6VKPs, with no 'Hook-C' on strength. The Mi-6VKP can be distinguished from other Mi-6 variants by the tubular antenna below the tailboom, the array of blade aerials around the rear part of the tail boom, and an external heat exchanger pod and cylindrical fairing on the starboard side.

Merseburg

Located less than 20 miles (32 km) west of Leipzig, on the western outskirts of the Halle-Neustadt/Merseburg-Salle conurbation, Merseburg was one of the most southerly fighter bases used by the Russians in East Germany. It had a single runway running roughly east-west.

An early Luftwaffe bomber base, from 1935 Merseburg housed the Fliegergruppe Merseburg with Ju 52s and Do 11s, this becoming I/KG 153 and converting to Ju 86s and Do 17Es. Junkers built a factory here in 1938. On the outbreak of war Merseburg housed the *Stab* of JG 3, controlling *Gruppen* at Zerbst, Döberitz and Guterfeld. During the war the airfield continued to be active, with a mix of units and types.

When overrun by the US Army in 1945, Merseburg was littered with unused Mistel composites, each consisting of a manned Fw 190 and a crude Ju 88 unmanned flying bomb. The Mistels had been concentrated at Merseburg for Operation Eisenhammer, intended as a knock-out blow against the Soviet armament industry. The airfield was part of the territory from which US forces later withdrew, to be left as part of the Soviet zone of Germany.

Merseburg's excellent facilities and relative lack of damage made it a natural choice as a Soviet Frontal Aviation base, and it accommodated a succession of fighter types, quickly also becoming the home of the 6th Guard 'Donnyetskaya' Red Banner Fighter Division, controlling the fighter regiments at Alt Lönnewitz, Merseburg and Nöbitz. When Nöbitz went over to the reconnaissance and ground attack roles, the division briefly became a two-regiment organisation. The airfield was provided with a hard runway (08/26) and was later hardened, with more than 50 HASs. By 1965 Merseburg had a Divisional HQ flight with two MiG-17Fs and two MiG-17PFs, while the based regiment operated 32 MiG-17Fs and 12 MiG-21s, together with four Yak-12s and four ubiquitous MiG-15UTIs. The latter aircraft had disappeared by 1967, although Yak-12s remained active with the divisional headquarters (alongside a flight of MiG-17s and another of MiG-21PFs). The regiment itself operated MiG-21F-13s and MiG-17Fs.

MiG-21s were the mainstay by 1969, although a handful of elderly MiG-17s remained active at Merseburg, perhaps even into the 1970s. Successive versions of MiG-21s were eventually replaced by MiG-23M 'Flogger-Bs'. These MiG-23Ms themselves gave way to MiG-29s during 1988, making Merseburg the fourth (or possibly the third) MiG-29 regiment of the 16th Air Army.

The 'Fulcrums' of the 73rd Guards Sevastapolskyi Fighter Aviation Regiment at Merseburg wore blue codes, thinly outlined in white, and had large Guards badges below the cockpit. At least one aircraft had a large badge below the port side of the cockpit, depicting a running or leaping big cat (a tiger or leopard).

Official sources suggested that the regiment had as many as 40 MiG-29s on

Above: The Merseburg-based MiG-29s wore blue regimental codes, outlined in white. This was unusual in East Germany, although some sources suggest that the first two MiG-29 regiments in Germany were similarly coded. All wore a large Guards badge below the windscreen on the port side. This aircraft also displays an excellence award. These awards consisted of a stylised contrailing aircraft superimposed on a pentagon, and denoted an aircraft in excellent technical condition. As such they were a reward for the aircraft's ground crew, which would inevitably be led by an officer.

charge, but only about 20 of these seem to have been photographed. Conversion to the 'Fulcrum-C' had begun by 1991, but only three of the 18 confirmed single-seaters were these advanced versions. There has been frequent speculation that blue-coded MiG-29s at Wittstock and Pütnitz were from Merseburg, but this cannot be confirmed. Such evidence that there is does not support such a contention, however, since blue-coded MiG-29s were present at both Wittstock and Pütnitz well before the 73rd GvIAP departed from Merseburg. Photos of Wittstock's Blue 26 (taken three months before Merseburg's Blue 26 departed) show an aircraft with a rather different camouflage pattern, with no trace of an overpainted Guards badge, Mikoyan bureau badge or outstanding aircraft badge, all of which appeared on the Merseburg original. There remains some confusion as to the identity of the Merseburg-based regiment, which has been quoted as the 73rd GvIAP

and as the 85th GvIAP. Whatever its designation, the regiment left Merseburg in July 1991, transiting via Alt Lönnewitz.

As well as the MiGs of the 85 GvIAP, Merseburg was home to a large number of helicopters. It was previously thought that these served with a detachment of the regiment based at Brandis, but the latest information would seem to suggest that Merseburg was, until mid-1991, the regiment's home, and that Brandis was, until that time, the detachment.

The helicopter unit was the 485th OVP, the second assault helicopter regiment assigned to the 1st Guards Tank Army at Dresden, augmenting the Allstedt-based 225th OVP. As such it operated Mi-9s, Mi-8VZPUs, Mi-24RKRs and Mi-24Ks, in addition to its Mi-24s and Mi-8/Mi-8MTVs.

The unit had a long and distinguished history, although the 485th OVP designation was a new one. Under a different identity, the regiment had been engaged in the long

Taken from an enormous distance, this slightly soft photograph is the only one which shows the massive badge applied to at least one of the Merseburg-based MiG-29s. Very few starboard-side views of Merseburg-based 'Fulcrums' have been seen, and this is believed to be the first published. The badge is extremely similar to a leopard insignia seen more recently on some Ukrainian air force MiG-29s.

and difficult struggle in Afghanistan, its aircrew winning many decorations, and the unit could trace its history back even further. The helicopters wore yellow and orange codes, often outlined in red. Many of the aircraft had orange intake filters or intake lips, like the helicopters serving at Werneuchen. They moved *en masse* to join

Only a handful of Merseburg's MiG-29s were 'Fulcrum-Cs', and all wore the same colour scheme as the older 'Fulcrum-As'. Conversion to the 'Fulcrum-C' was not accorded a high priority, and thus tended to be undertaken slowly, with regiments and even individual eskadrilyas frequently operating both variants side-by-side. Apart from its slight increase in internal fuel capacity and marginal improvements to the defensive avionics suite, the 'Fulcrum-C' offered little improvement over the original variant. Some Germany-based 'Fulcrum-Cs' were capable of carrying underwing fuel tanks, and all would have eventually been upgraded to MiG-29S standards, with enhanced avionics, flight control system improvements and AAM-AE compatibility.

Above: The Mi-24K served in small numbers with each of the five army headquarters squadrons, and with the headquarters unit at Sperenburg. Three pairs also served with the five 'second' regiments assigned to each of the numbered armies. The type was used primarily for fire correction duties. This 485th OVP aircraft wears the unit's typical deep yellow codes, outlined in red.

the Brandis detachment in mid-1991, when Merseburg closed. When the unit finally left Brandis, in May 1992, several helicopters from other units tagged along.

85 Gvardeiskaya Istrebeitelnyi Aviotsionnaya Polk

Aircraft: MiG-29 'Fulcrum-A'
Known codes: Blue 01, 02, 03, 04, 05, 06, 07, 08, 09, 10, 14, 22, 23, 24, 25, 26, 27, 29, 30, 33, 34

Merseburg's helicopter regiment seems to have adopted the colour orange with particular enthusiasm, using it even for insignia like excellence awards, as seen on the nose of this first eskadrilya Mi-24V 'Hind-E'.

Aircraft: MiG-29 'Fulcrum-C'
Known codes: Blue 31, 37, 38, 39, 40

Aircraft: MiG-29UB
Known codes: Blue 71, 76

Aircraft: MiG-23UB
Known codes: Blue 71

485 Otdelnyi Vertoletnyi Polk

Aircraft: Mi-8TB
Known codes: Yellow 40, 41, 43, 44, 45, 46, 72, 74, 75, 77, 80, Orange 42, 48, 71, 73, 76, 79

Aircraft: Mi-8MT
Known codes: Yellow 11, 12, 14, 15, 16, 18, 19, Orange 17,

Aircraft: Mi-8VKP
Known codes: Yellow 55

Aircraft: Mi-9
Known codes: Yellow 25, 26, 87, Orange 56, 85

Aircraft: Mi-24V 'Hind-E'
Known codes: Orange 01, 02, 04, 06, 07, 08, 31, 32, 33, 34, 35, 36, 37, 38, 61, 62, 63, 64, 65, 67, Yellow 03, 05, 66, 68

Aircraft: Mi-24RKR
Known codes: Orange 23, 24, 52, 54, 83, 84

Small clamshell doors and distinctive antennas below the tailboom and rear cabin mark this aircraft as being one of the six Mi-9s assigned to the 485th OVP. Like most of the regiment's other helicopters, it carries deep yellow code numbers, outlined in red.

Aircraft: Mi-24K 'Hind-G2'
Known codes: Orange 21, 22, 51, 53, 81, 82

Neuruppin

Located about 30 miles (48 km) north-west of Berlin, Neuruppin airfield lay to the north of Neuruppin itself, south of the village of Storbeck. It was built to the same pattern as Finsterwalde and Merseburg, with airfield buildings and a domestic/technical site south of the grass airfield. In Soviet hands the aerodrome was upgraded and extended in the same way as Merseburg, with a new runway (10/28) parallel taxiway and HASs. Its single runway ran roughly east-west. One of the more unusual features of Neuruppin was that the runway was lined with old oil drums, filled with diesel, and in foggy conditions these could be ignited to give a crude form of 'FIDO', burning off the fog to allow aircraft to land.

A pillar of the expansion of the Luftwaffe, Neuruppin housed one of its earliest flying units. This was known as the Deutsche Verksrofliegerschule (German commercial pilot's school) until 1935, when it was officially activated as Fliegerschule Neuruppin. During the war Neuruppin housed a variety of units, flying a number of types in different roles, but was perhaps most active as a night-fighter base. During March and April 1945, Nachtschlachtgruppe 30 used Neuruppin as its base for attacks on bridges over the Oder, a futile attempt to halt the Soviet advance on Berlin.

Between 1951 and 1956 the 787th IAP operated its MiG-15s and MiG-17s from Neuruppin, moving first to Gross Dölln and then, in 1970, to Finow. Since then, Neuruppin has operated mainly in the fighter-bomber role, hosting the 730th APIB. By 1965 the regiment had a strength of 36 MiG-17Fs and six MiG-17PFs, with four MiG-15UTIs and four Yak-12s. Conversion to the Su-7 had begun by 1967, although MiG-17s remained in large numbers. The MiG-15UTIs and Yak-12s had disappeared, however. Reports of Il-28 bombers and MiG-21s operating from Neuruppin (except on detachment) are believed to be erroneous, although the base was a popular deployment base, housing various Frontal Aviation and IA-PVO units for brief periods, including Su-15s during the late 1970s.

Su-7 'Fitter-As' later gave way to swing-wing 'Fitters' of various sub-types, with

Seen at Neuruppin, this Mi-8K was one of the aircraft assigned to the 9th OVE at Neuruppin. The squadron moved to Oranienburg on the closure of Neuruppin in April 1991 but did not finally withdraw from Germany until August 1993. The Mi-8K remains something of a mystery ship, and the purpose of the fairing which projects from the cut-out in the clamshell doors remains unknown.

Above: The Su-17M-7s of the 730th APIB wore red codes, outlined in white. The aircraft were assigned to the defence suppression role, and were often seen carrying Kh-58 (AS-11 'Kilter') ASMs or pods of unguided rockets. The regiment transited to Russia via Gross Dölln, where about a dozen single-seaters, and perhaps as many as six two-seaters, were left behind for use by the 20th APIB.

Su-17M-4 'Fitter-Ks' arriving by 1986. These aircraft wore red codes, outlined in white, and about 32 were on charge, together with about eight Su-17UM-3s. The 730th APIB left Neuruppin on 26 April 1991 for an unknown destination and future. Some reports suggest that a single *eskadrilya* remained at Gross Dölln, replacing the third *eskadrilya* of the 20th APIB (or the second, according to some analysts) which had not (according to these reports) completed conversion to the Su-17M-4. This seems unlikely. Several Neuruppin-based Mi-8s wore the army aviation badge, with a blue and yellow sunburst and small red hammer and sickle, star, torch and the letters 'AA' superimposed in red, with a black wolf.

Co-located alongside the 'Fitters' of the 730th APIB were the helicopters of the 9th OVE, headquarters squadron for the Magdeburg-headquartered 3rd Shock Army. The unit transferred to Oranienburg on the closure of Neuruppin in April 1991, and remained there until August 1993, when it returned to Russia.

730 Aviotsionnaya Polk Istrebeitelei-Bombardirovchikov

Aircraft: Su-17M-4
Known codes: Red 01, 02, 03, 04, 06, 07,

This Su-17M-4 has a triangle of blue paint filling in the space within its intake warning. This marked it out as the aircraft assigned to the commander of the first eskadrilya. It is seen taxiing out from Neuruppin for the final departure, on a typically overcast and grey East German April morning. Cranes have already started dismantling equipment.

11, 12, 14, 15, 16, 19, 20, 21, 25, 26, 28, 29, 31, 40, 41, 43, 44, 45, 46, 47, 48, 49, 50, 51, 55

Aircraft: Su-17M-3
Known codes: Red 90, 91, 92, 93, 94, 95, 97, Orange 99

9 Otdelnyi Vertoletnyi Eskadrilya

Aircraft: Mi-6VKP 'Hook-B'
Known codes: Red 02

Aircraft: Mi-22 'Hook-C'
Known codes: Red 01

Aircraft: Mi-8T
Known codes: Red 32, 38

Aircraft: Mi-8TB
Known codes:

Aircraft: Mi-8PPA
Known codes: Red 16, 17, 18, 19

Aircraft: Mi-9
Known codes: Red 15

Aircraft: Mi-24RKR
Known codes: Red 40, 41

Aircraft: Mi-24K 'Hind-G2'
Known codes: Red 42, 43

Nöbitz

The most southerly fast jet base used by the Russians in East Germany, Nöbitz is located in the easternmost part of Thuringia, some 40 miles (64 km) north of the Czech border and about 15 miles (24 km) north-west of Karl-Marx-Stadt. About two miles south-west of the town of Altenburg, Nöbitz airfield was bounded by the villages of Bocka, Kraschwitz, Nöbitz and Zschernichen, and was concealed in thick woodland on two sides.

As Altenburg, the airfield was first used during World War I and was then recommissioned in 1936. The early home of III/KG 153, the airfield housed the unit's Ju 52s, which were soon replaced by Ju 86s and then by Do 17Es, which flew combat sorties from Altenburg during the 1938 Sudeten crisis. During World War II Altenburg was occupied by a succession of bomber, training and night-fighter units, including KG 3 'Blitz' and KG 51 'Edelweiss'. Under Russian control the airfield was much improved and significantly upgraded, with the existing runway (04/22) extended north-east to almost triple its original length.

By 1965 Nöbitz was one of three reconnaissance bases of the 16th Air Army, with a mix of 50 MiG-17Fs and single-seat MiG-15s, and with four MiG-15UTIs and four Yak-12s. By 1967 the number of MiG-17s had risen to 50, with six MiG-15UTIs and four Yak-12s. Seven MiG-21Us were on charge, presumably pending the introduction of the MiG-21R, and the regiment had also gained 12 high-flying Yak-27 'Mangroves'. By 1969 the regiment had entirely re-equipped with the MiG-21R 'Fishbed-H'. The history of Nöbitz in Soviet hands from then until the mid-1970s remains clouded in secrecy. The base gate guard was a MiG-21SMT 'Fishbed-K', but this may have been a regimental plaything brought to Nöbitz by the incoming 968th IAP, and may have never been based at the airfield itself. The MiG-21SMT was, in any

case, perhaps the rarest of the operational MiG-21 variants, and was rather short-lived.

Some Western orders of battle published during the mid-1980s described Altenburg as a MiG-21 fighter base. This may have reflected an earlier 'truth', or may have been a confused reference to the airfield's use of the MiG-21R.

The time at which Altenburg transferred to the fighter-bomber role remains

uncertain, but Su-7 'Fitter-As' reportedly gave way to MiG-27 'Flogger-Ds' between late 1976 and mid-1977, making the 296th APIB the second 16th Air Army MiG-27 unit. Some sources maintain that Nöbitz never housed MiG-27s, and that the base housed Su-24s before MiG-29s arrived. This seems most unlikely, although it may be that the Su-24 regiment that temporarily depolyed to Altes Lager first operated briefly from

This MiG-23UB 'Flogger-C' trainer carries its two-digit regimental code in yellow, outlined in blue, like the regiment's early-version MiG-29s. Unlike the MiG-29s, there is no repetition of the code on the tailfin, however. The shortage of MiG-29UBs made two-seat MiG-23UBs a very necessary part of each MiG-29 regiment in Germany. The aircraft were used for liaison, weather reconnaissance and instrument training duties, and for keeping senior officers in current flying practice.

Above: By the time they departed from Nöbitz, many of the early series MiG-29s of the 968th IAP were beginning to show their age. Several had large areas of fresh paint, giving them a somewhat patchwork appearance. The aircraft each carried a unit badge below the windscreen on the port side. This consisted of a swept red star, with hammer and sickle superimposed, with a blue wing sweeping aft from it. A similar badge, with the wing in white, had been carried by Yak-7s, Yak-1Ms and Yak-9s assigned to the Third Independent Air Corps during the Great Patriotic War.

Below: This is one of two MiG-29UBs assigned to the 968th IAP at Nöbitz. Both aircraft wore the same 'swept star' badge and blue-outlined yellow codes as the regiment's early-version 'Fulcrum-As'. One of the two aircraft moved on to Wittstock, where it retained its badge and blue/yellow codes for many months, before the badge was overpainted and the code was reapplied as a dark blue outline only. Like most Soviet-built two-seat trainer versions of operational fighters, the MiG-29UB lacks radar, and has a retractable periscope to enhance the instructor's view on the ground or on approach.

Nöbitz, perhaps as an operational test to prove that the base was capable of handling such deployments. A later, temporary bomber deployment reportedly occurred for two weeks during 1990, when six Tu-22M-3 'Backfire-Cs' operated from the base. Between 1982 and 1985 the original MiG-27 'Flogger-Ds' were replaced by a mix of new-build MiG-27M 'Flogger-Js' and rebuilt aircraft to the same standard which were designated MiG-27D. The basic MiG-27s were flown back to Russia for conversion in groups of four, with a four-month interval between groups. The MiG-27D and MiG-27M are externally identical, and share the 'Flogger-J' reporting name. The MiG-27D has an RSBN-6S navigation system, however, while the MiG-27M has RSBN. Both versions have the uprated Tumanskii R-29B-300 engine and the Pelenga weapons system, giving compatibility with a range of laser-guided PGMs.

Nöbitz remained a fighter-bomber base until 1989, when the based 296th APIB and its MiG-27s moved to Grossenhain to replace a departing regiment of Su-24s. An existing regiment of MiG-29s, then based in Russia, moved in to fill the void, this being the 968th IAP which came under the operational control of the 6th GvIAD at Merseburg. By the time Western spotters and photographers reached Nöbitz, after the fall of the Berlin Wall, the base housed early 'Fulcrum-As' and 'Fulcrum-Cs'. The early series 'Fulcrum-As' of the 968th IAP wore orange/yellow codes thinly outlined in blue (repeated in yellow, without outlines, on the tailfins), while the unit's 'Fulcrum-Cs' wore red codes, outlined in white. This has led to frequent speculation that the red-coded aircraft were actually from Köthen, and replaced other early 'Fulcrum-As' when Köthen's 85th GvIAP departed in the spring of 1991. This cannot be confirmed, and seems unlikely in view of the lack of any trace of Guards badges on the 'Fulcrum-Cs'.

The 'Fulcrum-As' of the 968th IAP were unusual in wearing a distinctive unit badge (a winged swept star, with hammer and sickle superimposed) on the port forward fuselage. This insignia has also been carried by Yak-1Ms, Yak-7s and Yak-9s during the Great Patriotic War, and has been described as being the badge of the 3rd Independent Air Corps. Official sources suggested that

The 968th IAP's 14 early-model MiG-29s were augmented by a similar number of 'Fulcrum-Cs'. These aircraft wore red codes, outlined in white, as were applied to the aircraft at Köthen, Zerbst and Alt Lönnewitz. There are reasons to believe that the regiment had two large eskadrilyas instead of three small ones, perhaps with the trainers clustered in an understrength third eskadrilya.

the 968th IAP had 30 MiG-29s on charge, with a handful of two-seat trainers and MiG-23UBs.

The 968th IAP returned to the USSR on 8 April 1992, its aircraft transiting via Alt Lönnewitz due to Poland's refusal to allow overflights. The departure met the scheduled target of the second half of 1992.

968 Istrebeitelnyi Aviotsionnaya Polk

Aircraft: MiG-29 'Fulcrum-A'
Known codes: Yellow 07^V, 15^V, 16^V, 34^V, 41^V, 42^V, 43^V, 46^V, 49^V, 50^V, 52^V, 57^V, 58^V, 59^V

Aircraft: MiG-29 'Fulcrum-C'
Known codes: Red 01, 03, 05, 06, 09, 21, 22, 25, 26, 35, 36, 38, 39

Aircraft: MiG-29UB
Known codes: Yellow 64, 65

Aircraft: MiG-23UB
Known codes: Red 91, Orange 96, Yellow 97

Nohra

A grass airfield, Nohra lies 2 miles (3 km) west of the town of Nohra, less than 1 mile (1.6 km) north of the motorway running from Eisenach, via Erfurt, Jena and Gera to Chemnitz (formerly Karl-Marx-Stadt). A pre-war DLV airfield, Nohra was used by a number of Luftwaffe training units before and during World War II.

By 1965 Nohra (also known as Weimar-Nohra) was the home of the single helicopter regiment nominally assigned to the 8th Guards Infantry Army, whose headquarters was co-located at Nohra. The expansion of army aviation led to the 8th Guards Infantry Army gaining two more helicopter units, at Altes Lager and Hassleben, but the lead unit, the 336th OVP, remained at Nohra.

While some other army aviation regiments retained the semi-obsolescent Mi-24D, Nohra's 336th OVP was equipped with a mix of Mi-24V 'Hind-Es' and Mi-24P 'Hind-Fs', with a support eskadrilya of Mi-8TB 'Hip-Cs'. The regiment left for Russia in August 1992.

336 Otdelnyi Vertoletnyi Polk

Aircraft: Mi-24V
Known codes: Yellow 01, 02, 03, 04, 06, 08, 10, 15, 16, 17, 19, 22, 23, 24, 25, 26, 29, 30, 31, 32, Orange 05, 09, 11, 21, 24, 27, 33, 34, 35, 37, 39, 41

Aircraft: Mi-24P
Known codes: Yellow 20, 28, Orange 12, 14, 18, 36, 38, 40

Aircraft: Mi-8TB
Known codes: Yellow 50, 54, 56, 58, 60, 70, 72, 74, 76, 80, 84, 88, 90, 92, Orange 52, 62, 66, 68, 78, 82, 86

Right: Swathed in tarpaulins, one of the 336th OVP's Mi-24Vs sits amid the Nohra wildflowers. In time of war the helicopters would have moved forward with the army they were supporting, and would have operated from well-camouflaged and heavily defended urban or woodland sites.

Below: Orange- and yellow-coded Mi-24Vs of the 336th OVP sit dispersed at Weimar-Nohra, most of them well-shrouded by tarpaulins. The 336th was the lead helicopter unit assigned to the 8th Guards 'Order of Lenin' infantry army.

Oranienburg

Lying just north of the Berlin ring road, about 10 miles (16 km) north of Berlin's Tegel airport, Oranienburg's north-south runway lay less than 1 mile (1.6 km) from the outskirts of Oranienburg town.

Heinkel Werke GmbH established a factory in 1936, this becoming primarily responsible for manufacture of the Heinkel He 177 and licence-construction of the Ju 88. The base was also used by front-line and second-line Luftwaffe units, and by other aircraft companies for testing. The Arado Ar 234 V19 and V20, for example, were tested at Oranienburg.

For some years Oranienburg was a tactical bomber base, housing at least one regiment of Ilyushin Il-28 'Beagles', which may have been tasked with nuclear strike duties. A plethora of revetments and dispersals east of the runway (04/22) are believed to date from this period. In 1956 Oranienburg's Ilyushin Il-28s were withdrawn, amid a fanfare of publicity, in a highly visible reduction of the 16th Air Army's offensive posture, foreshadowing the later withdrawal of Su-24s from Grossenhain and Brand. The withdrawal of the Il-28 left Oranienburg empty, but its ramps were soon filled again, this time by the 45 Lisunov Li-2 'Cabs' and, from December 1962, a growing number of An-12 'Cubs' of the theatre transport squadron (designation unknown). By 1967 the unit had some 30 An-12s, 10 An-8s and a handful of Li-2s, and gradually re-equipped until it operated An-12s, An-24s and An-26s, with 20 An-8s. The base also housed three Il-20s (Red 20, 21 and 22) and a single Il-22. The An-12s, -24s and -26s transferred to Sperenburg when the An-8s withdrew in 1978, leaving Sperenburg as the sole fixed-wing transport airfield.

Oranienburg had started to switch to its present helicopter transport role in 1977, when the 239th GvOVP moved in from Furstenwalde. The regiment then comprised two *eskadrilya* of Mi-4, and two *eskadrilya* with a mix of Mi-6s and Mi-8s. From 1977 the Mi-4s were withdrawn, and replaced by more Mi-6s and Mi-8s and Mi-8MTVs.

The 239th 'Belgorodskii' GvOVP has a long and proud history, which began with its formation at Borovskoye on 11 June 1938. Subsequently, the unit, then a bomber/transport regiment equipped with TB-3s, fought in Finland, Romania and Moldova before Hitler's invasion of the USSR. The regiment fought in the defence of Moscow and, with Li-2s, in the Stalingrad operations. Operations in the Kuban and at Kursk followed, producing six Heroes of the Soviet Union and winning the regiment its Guards honour title. The regiment received its first helicopters in 1952, while stationed at Kaunas, Lithuania, when Mi-4s were received. By 1954 the regiment had settled in Germany, at Furstenwalde, where An-2s

Above: This Mi-17 carries unusual streamlined stores (probably mine dispensers) under its outriggers, with a single UV-16-57 rocket pod under the starboard outer station. The scabbed-on cockpit armour was typical of the regiment's Mi-8MTVs. The aircraft also has an IR jammer and chaff/flare launchers below the tailboom.

Right: One of Oranienburg's few Mi-8T 'Hip-Cs' wears an unusual overall matt dark green camouflage achieved by overpainting the original sand and stone camouflage. The aircraft carries a pair of UV-16-57 57-mm rocket pods under its outriggers.

were added to the complement of Li-2s, Po-2s and Mi-4s. The regiment saw active service during the 1956 uprising in Hungary. Mi-6s and Mi-8s were introduced in 1968, in time for participation in the crushing of the Prague Spring – the Soviet invasion of Czechoslovakia.

Like Gross Dölln, Oranienburg remained an important forward deployment base for bomber aircraft usually based within the USSR. This led to regular detachments of Tu-16 'Badgers' and Tu-22 'Blinders' for operational training, to use the nearby ranges, and sometimes just to react to NATO actions which were seen as provocative. A massive Tu-16 deployment was made in 1986, for example, in the wake of the US bombing raids against Libya, which were seen by the Russians as being

provocative and counter-productive. There have been reports that a target-towing detachment of Il-28s served at Oranienburg for many years (perhaps until as late as 1988).

239 'Belgorodsky' Gvardeiskaya Otdelnyi Vertoletnyi Polk

Aircraft: Mi-6A
Known codes: Red 01, 02, 54, 55, 56, 57, 58, 59, 60, 61, 62, 63, 64, 70, 71, 72, 73, 74, 75, 76, 78, 79, 80, 81, 82, 83

Aircraft: Mi-8
Known codes: Red 16

Aircraft: Mi-8MT
Known codes: Red 07, 08, 09, 29, 32, 34, 35, 36, 40, 42, 43, 48

Aircraft: Mi-8MTV
Known codes: Red 03, 04, 05, 06, 10, 11, 12, 14, 15, 16, 17, 18, 19, 20, 21, 30, 31, 33, 37, 38, 39, 41, 44, 45, 47

The 239th Guards OVP was best known as the operator of the transport-tasked Mi-6 'Hooks' assigned to the Western Group of Forces. A handful of command post Mi-6s served with other units, but Oranienburg, with its fleet of more than 26 Mi-6s, was the home of the 'Hook' in Germany.

Pütnitz

The northernmost airfield used by the Russians in East Germany, Pütnitz (inevitably marked as Damgarten on NATO charts) lay less than 20 miles (32 km) north-east of Rostock, to the east of the Recknitz estuary, and north-west of Damgarten. Built during or just before the war, details of the Luftwaffe use of Pütnitz remain sketchy, although it is known that Heinkel He 162 fuselages were constructed here, and that a detachment of NJG 5 operated from the airfield, operating with the first of nine railway-mounted radar stations – 'Sumatra One'.

Although Pütnitz had a hard runway during World War II, the Soviet occupancy saw the addition of a new, longer runway (07/25) closer to the airfield buildings on the north side, with a parallel northern taxiway. Hardened aircraft shelters were built later.

The 773rd IAP (also referred to by some sources as the 733rd IAP) moved to Pütnitz in 1953, and remained there until its final departure on 11 April 1994. Raised at Murmansk in 1942 and based mainly in the Far East during the Great Patriotic War, the regiment nevertheless produced 15 Heroes of the Soviet Union and flew a succession of fighters and light bombers, including the Lavochkin LaGG-3, the Hawker Hurricane, the Curtiss P-40 Kittyhawk, the Ilyushin Il-2, the Petyaklov Pe-2 and the Douglas Boston. By the time it arrived at Pütnitz, the unit was flying MiG-15s in the air superiority role, and replaced these with MiG-17PFs during the early 1960s. By 1965 the regiment had 12 Yak-25 'Flashlight-As', 16 MiG-17s and four MiG-17PFs, with a

training/liaison flight of four Yak-12s and four MiG-15UTIs. In 1967 MiG-17Fs, PFs and PFUs augmented the regiment's first MiG-21F-13 'Fishbed-Cs', and while the Yak-25s and the training and liaison flight had disappeared, the Division HQ operated two MiG-17s and four MiG-21s. The MiG-17PFU 'Fresco-E' was, like the MiG-17PF 'Fresco-D', a radar-equipped night-fighter, but while the MiG-17PF was cannon-armed, the PFU forsook gun armament for a load of four K-9 (AA-1 'Anab') beam-riding air-to-air missiles. The regiment eventually converted to the MiG-21SMs later in the decade. Conversion to the MiG-23M occurred in about 1974, before the switch was made to MiG-23MLD 'Flogger-Ks', which reportedly wore red codes, although an aircraft on the dump (perhaps a 'Flogger-B') still retained blue codes. The 'Flogger-Ks' were short lived, since the 773rd IAP converted to the MiG-29 in 1987, becoming the 16th Air Army's second MiG-29 unit.

Some reports suggest that all of the MiG-29s delivered to Pütnitz and Wittstock initially wore blue codes, and that these were reapplied in white some time later, with some aircraft escaping the repaint as the system of coloured regimental codes fell into disuse. By 1989, all Pütnitz-based MiG-29 single-seaters had white codes with very thin blue outlines. Two-seaters, as was usual, carried a wide mix of code styles and colours. Unit markings were not carried, although by May 1993 two aircraft had been decorated with huge leaping tiger badges below their cockpits on the starboard side only. These were a 'Fulcrum-A', White 23, and a MiG-29UB, White 74.

Officially estimated to have a strength of 35 MiG-29s, with six MiG-23UBs, a single

An-2 and 15 Su-25 target tugs, by 1990 the 773rd IAP actually had 30 single-seat MiG-29s, four MiG-29UBs and four MiG-23UBs, and no permanently attached Su-25s. By 1994 the basic MiG-29 had been largely replaced by the more capable 'Fulcrum-C', although eight of the earlier version remained on charge, including three from the earliest series.

One early series MiG-29 based at Pütnitz during 1992 (White 24) was seen with its ventral fins removed, and with overwing chaff/flare dispensers retrofitted. This was the only early series MiG-29 known to have lost its distinctive ventral fins, and to have received the chaff/flare dispensers, though the modification was quite obviously not a difficult one.

One *eskadrilya*, together with an *eskadrilya* from Wittstock, departed early, flying out on 27 March 1994. The rest of the regiment departed for Andreapol on 11 April 1994. Some of the pilots of the 773rd IAP, together with some from the 33rd IAP at Wittstock, were posted to Zernograd, where a PVO MiG-23 unit was transitioning to the MiG-29, and transferred to Frontal Aviation control. Others went to a MiG-29 regiment at Primorsko-Akhtarsk.

As well as hosting the 773rd IAP, Pütnitz was the home of the 16th Guards 'Svirskaya' Red Banner Fighter Aviation Division, which controlled the MiG-29 regiments at Wittstock and Eberswalde. Pütnitz always had an important secondary role of supporting deployments by aircraft using the firing ranges over the Baltic, for which (at one time) it almost certainly had its own dedicated target-towing squadron. At least four of the Ilyushin Il-28s used by this unit remained on the Pütnitz dump for some time after the fall of the Berlin Wall, but they were eventually removed (almost certainly to Rangsdorf) for scrapping. In later years, detachments of dedicated target tugs were deployed to Pütnitz on an as-required basis, these including frequent deployments of yellow-coded Su-25s, one of the last being made in August 1990. A SAR detachment equipped with Mi-8s is believed to have been present until early 1994.

Bombers and maritime reconnaissance as well as fighters deployed to Damgarten, including Tu-16 'Badgers' and, it is believed, Tu-22M 'Backfires'. There have even been reports of a deployment by Tu-160 'Blackjacks'. Such deployments were not always without incident: an Il-38 was

reported to have crashed on approach to Pütnitz during the late 1970s, for example. Such deployments have not only been for training, some having been mounted in response to NATO military actions or deteriorations in the political climate, as when a massive Tu-16 deployment followed the 1986 bombing raids against Libya. A-50 'Mainstays' were also regular visitors to

Left and below: The significance of this gaudy leaping tiger motif, which appeared on the port side of the noses of an early, ventral-finned MiG-29 and on that of a MiG-29UB, remains unknown. It was, however, applied some time before the final withdrawal and perhaps even before the collapse of the Berlin Wall. It may be coincidence that a similar 'leaping cat' insignia was also applied to at least one Merseburg-based MiG-29.

Pütnitz, at one time deploying every Wednesday. The last 'Mainstay' at Pütnitz was seen in January 1994.

773 Istrebeitelnyi Aviotsionnaya Polk

Aircraft: MiG-29 'Fulcrum-A'
Known codes: White 20, 21, 22, 23^V, 24^V, 25^V, 26^V, 32, 34

Aircraft: MiG-29 'Fulcrum-C'
Known codes: White 01, 02, 04, 05, 06, 07, 08, 09, 10, 11, 12, 41, 42, 44, 45, 49, 51, 52, 53, 54,

Aircraft: MiG-29UB
Known codes: Blue 66, White 74, 80

Aircraft: MiG-23UB
Known codes: Yellow 50, White 60, 90, Blue 96

Above: Armed with a single IR missile acquisition round (perhaps for an R-60 AA-8 'Aphid'), an early-series MiG-29 lands at Pütnitz, deploying its drab-coloured braking parachute behind it to reduce ground roll and brake wear.

Right: Single examples of the 'Fulcrum-A' and 'Fulcrum-C' (seen here) were painted in this unusual two-tone green camouflage scheme. One of the regiment's three eskadrilyas had a ground attack role.

Below: A 'Fulcrum-C' on final approach to Pütnitz. The aircraft shows signs of having been recoded, with a repainted intake and '72' painted on the fin cap.

Rangsdorf

Rangsdorf enjoyed an excellent position, just south of the town of Rangsdorf, which itself lay on the intersection of the southern part of the Berlin ring road and the railway running south to Dresden.

A DLV airfield during the 1930s, Rangsdorf became the home of the Bucker Flugzeugbau in 1935, when the company moved from Johannisthal. With its solid light aviation background Rangsdorf became home to the Reichschule für Motorflugsport and the Aero Club von Deutschland. The Luftwaffe aerobatic squadron, with 12 Bucker Jungmeisters, was another pre-war resident. During the war Rangsdorf was home to the Luftverkhrsgruppe der Reichsregierung, the government transport unit with Fw 200s, Ju 90s and Ju 290s and the Ju 352.

An important maintenance unit and engineering base for the Western Group of Forces, Rangsdorf latterly had its own flight of helicopters. When it became clear that the Soviet forces were pulling out of East Germany, there was a massive effort to remove or sell anything of value before the final handover of Soviet bases to the new German government. Accordingly, airfield dumps and ranges were cleared of their derelict airframes, which were gathered at Rangsdorf for scrapping, along with gate guards and airframes considered too old to be taken back to Russia.

Thus, Rangsdorf's scrapping compound filled up with MiG-15s and MiG-17s rescued from the firing ranges. MiG-23s and MiG-25s – and even Il-28s and Yak-28s – arrived from airfield dumps all over East Germany.

Above: A pair of recently arrived Mi-8s awaits their turn for scrapping. The nearest aircraft, which has non-standard antennas below the tailboom, has already started to be dismantled.

Left: An untidy pile of airframes lies behind the severed nose of an Mi-8, every panel of its extensively glazed cockpit broken. The heap includes the nose of a Yak-28 'Brewer-E' and a pair of MiG-27 forward fuselages, together with at least one MiG-17.

Below: The nose of a MiG-23 lies on its side, beside the nose of an Il-14 which has somehow retained its co-pilot's seat. Beyond these sad relics are a line of MiG-17s, all of them crudely painted green to serve as range targets, but bearing clear traces of their original silver finish and colourful three-digit regiment codes.

Sperenberg

Located less than 20 miles (32 km) south of Berlin, and only 10 miles (16 km) from the Western Group of Forces and 16th Air Army headquarters at Zossen, Sperenburg airfield lay about 2 miles (3.2 km) west of Sperenburg town.

The airfield opened in 1963, on the site of a former gunnery range, replacing Schönefeld as a Soviet transport base when it became Berlin's airport. It had a single hard runway (orientated 09/27) and purpose-built hardstandings. Home to a light transport regiment tasked primarily with flights within East Germany, by 1965 Sperenburg hosted 12 Li-2 'Cabs', five An-2s, four Il-14 'Crates' and 20 Mi-4 'Hound' helicopters. By 1967 the regiment had gained six more Il-14s and three An-24 'Cokes'. With the 1970 withdrawal of the An-12/An-8/Li-2-equipped theatre transport regiment from Oranienburg, Sperenburg took over from Oranienburg as the most important transport base in East Germany, and the based 226th OSAP became the *de facto* theatre transport regiment.

By 1991, the 226th OSAP included two An-24Vs, six An-26s, 17 An-12s, 13 Mi-8Ps and Mi-8Ss, a single Mi-8TL, three Mi-8TBs and a pair of Mi-9s. The C-in-C's personal Tu-134A-3 also came under the auspices of the 226th OSAP.

More helicopters were based at Sperenburg with the 113th OVE, whose complement included 10 Mi-8MTV 'Hip-Hs', two Mi-24RKR 'Hind-Gs', an Mi-22 'Hook-C', an Mi-6VKP 'Hook-B' and a single Mi-8K. These departed during May and July 1994, bound for Vorotinsk and, in the case of the Mi-6VKP and Mi-8K, Kubinka. The Mi-22 had transferred to Oranienburg during 1993.

Sperenburg also housed the 390th ORAE, an independant reconnaissance squadron operating a mix of types. These included at least two yellow-coded An-26RTR 'Curl-Bs', two red-coded Il-20 'Coot-As' and a single Il-22 'Coot-B' in Aeroflot colours. Some sources suggest that only the Il-20s and Il-22s belonged to the 390th, which, it was suggested, was merely a detachment of a squadron based at Levashovo. The An-26RTRs and An-12BK were said to belong to the 226th OSAP. In August 1991, an Elint-configured Il-76 was reported at Sperenburg, supported by a pair of Il-78s.

As well as housing its own transport, reconnaissance and helicopter regiments, Sperenburg always served as the hub for all transport, mail and cargo flights from Russia, and handled a steady flow of Aeroflot and VTA (Voyenno Transportnaya Aviatsiya – military transport aviation) airliners and transport aircraft, and latterly regularly welcomed An-12s, An-26s and

Above: Sperenburg's gate guard was a dramatically-mounted, red-coded MiG-21, although the base was never a fighter airfield.

Right: Sperenburg's fleet of transport An-26s and An-24s was augmented by a pair of An-26RTRs. Bedecked with an array of blade and wire antennas, the An-26RTRs were Elint aircraft and may have been operated on behalf of the 390th ORAE, although they wore codes within the 226th OSAP's range.

An-72s from neighbouring Soviet air armies based in Poland, Czechoslovakia and Hungary. Sperenburg has reportedly been earmarked as the proposed sight of Berlin's new international airport. The 226th OSAP did not depart *en masse*, but instead steadily shed aircraft as its transport role diminished. Nine helicopters had left by the middle of 1993, together with six An-12s. In March and April 1994, six An-26s, six Mi-8s, an An-24 and an An-12 departed. The rest of

the based aircraft left in August and September, the last to go being an An-12 on 6 September. Destination for most of the aircraft was Kubinka, with three An-12s and the Tu-134A-3 going to Rostov, and one An-12 to Severnii, an An-24 and an An-26 to Kaluga, another An-24 and another An-26 to Ivanovo, and two An-26s to Krasnodar. The final movement by a Russian aircraft occurred on 6 September when the last An-22 departed.

Below: The 390th ORAE's detachment at Sperenburg operated a single Aeroflot-marked Il-22 'Coot-B' and a pair of Il-20 'Coot-As', one of which is seen here on finals. It is possible that some of the Elint- and EW-configured aircraft nominally assigned to the 226th OSAP were actually operated under the same command.

Above: The single An-12BK operated by the 226th OSAP was externally distinguishable by its extended ECM tailcone. This was a feature normally associated with the version known to NATO as 'Cub-C', although this version also had a variety of belly-mounted antennas and fairings.

Left: By 1994, this Mi-8MTV 'Hip-H' of the 113th OVE, and several of its companions, wore a Russian flag on each engine intake, reflecting the end of the old USSR and its short-lived successor, the Commonwealth of Independent States. During 1993 and 1994 the old Russian tricolour started appearing in many forms on aircraft, vehicles and buildings, although the ubiquitous red star remained.

226 Otdelnyi Smechannyi Aviatsionnaya Polk

Aircraft: An-2
Known codes: Red 01, 04, Black 05

Aircraft: An-12BP
Known codes: Red 83, 86 - 99

Aircraft: An-12 'Cub-B'
Known codes: Red 84

Aircraft: An-12BK 'Cub-B/C'
Known codes: Red 85

Aircraft: An-24RV
Known codes: Red 24

Aircraft: An-24B
Known codes: Red100, 101

Aircraft: An-26
Known codes: Red 02, 07, 08, 10, 15, 16, Yellow 12,14 (An-26L)

Aircraft: An-26RTR
Known codes: 06, 11

Aircraft: Mi-8P and Mi-8PS
Known codes: Yellow 01, 34, 35, 39, 40, 54

Aircraft: Mi-8T
Known codes: Yellow 36, 38, 41, 56, 57, 58, 59

Aircraft: Mi-8TB
Known codes: Yellow 32, 33, 37

Aircraft: Mi-8TL
Known codes: Yellow 55

Aircraft: Mi-9
Known codes: Yellow 60, 61

Aircraft: Tu-134A3
Known codes: Red 25

390 Otdelnyi Razvedyvatielnyi Aviatsionnaya Eskadrilya

Aircraft: Il-20
Known codes: Red 20, 21

Aircraft: Il-22
Registration: SSSR-75913

113 Otdelnyi Vertoletnyi Eskadrilya

Aircraft: Mi-6VKP 'Hook-B'
Known codes: Red 53

Aircraft: Mi-22 'Hook-C'
Known codes: Red 51

Aircraft: Mi-8MTV
Known codes: Yellow 11, 12, 15, 16, 17, 18, 20, 22, 24, 36

Aircraft: Mi-8K
Known codes: Yellow 81

Aircraft: Mi-24RKR
Known codes: Yellow 41, 44, 45

Left: The 'salon' version of the Mi-8 'Hip' was used by the 226th OSAP in its Mi-8PS form. These aircraft had deep rectangular cabin windows and airline-type seats, but retained camouflaged paint and tactical codes. They were used primarily for VIP transport durties. This particular example has a Doppler box below the tailboom.

Tütow

The northernmost base used by the Russians in East Germany, with the exception of Damgarten, Tütow was marked on NATO charts as Demmin. Itself only about 15 miles (39 km) from the coast, Tütow lay 15 miles (39 km) south-west of Griefswald, and about 7 miles (11 km) east of Demmin, north of the road between Demmin and Tütow. The single runway, reportedly laid in the late 1980s specifically to allow the operation of Su-25s, ran roughly north-south (17/35), linking what had been, in Luftwaffe days, two separate grass airfields. Soviet construction also included no fewer than 39 revetments.

An Arado factory was built at Tütow before the war, and the base also hosted a number of Luftwaffe units. The first of these was Fliegergruppe Tütow operating Do 11Ds, ostensibly as civilian freighters. Later in the war, the presence of the Arado factory (then producing Fw 190 components and assembling Fw 190s) necessitated the establishment of an industrial defence fighter unit. Heavy/long-range transport operations came to Tütow in late 1944 with the arrival of the Grossraum Transportgruppe, with its 23 Ju 352As. 15./TG 4 transferred to Tütow during March 1945, but flew very few missions due to fuel shortages. Among the last Luftwaffe missions flown from Tütow was an airlift of naval infantry to Berlin to bolster the defences of the Reich's Chancellory. A single Ju 352 flew into Gatow, in the early hours of 26 April, deplaning the infantry and picking up wounded before returning home. Tütow was finally evacuated on 1 May 1945, with 15./TG 4 fleeing westwards.

For many years a helicopter base with Mi-4 'Hounds' and Mi-8 'Hips', Demmin gained fixed-wing aircraft in December 1988, when the 368th OShAP moved in from Chortkov in the Ukraine, having moved there from Kalinov, becoming the second Su-25 unit in Germany. Originally formed at Zjovtnevoye (or Kalinov according to some sources) in September 1986, the 368th

The Su-25BM is externally distinguishable from the earlier version because it lacks an intake at the base of the fin, and instead has ram air intakes on the top of each engine nacelle. From each jet pipe protrudes a hollow pipe.

Above: A handful of Su-25s at Tütow had coloured intake lips, perhaps signifying that these were the aircraft allocated to eskadrilya commanders. The 12 Su-25BMs on charge seem to have been divided between the first and second eskadrilyas.

OShAP had enjoyed an active early life, deploying to Tjiirttsjik (sometimes transliterated as Chirchik) in Uzbekistan in October 1986 and then splitting into its component eskadrilyas for deployment in Afghanistan, one going to Kandahar and the other two to Bagram, with occasional deployments to Shindand and Kunduz. The regiment's tour of duty lasted until November 1987, and one pilot, Konstantin Pavlukov, became a Hero of the Soviet Union for his heroism, although he killed himself with a grenade before his tour was complete. Strategically located across the inner German border from the perfect tank country of the North German Plain, the 368th OShAP had an estimated strength of 34 Su-25s, with five Su-25UB two-seaters and a flight of seven Aero L-39Cs for training, forward air control and hack duties, although the total number of aircraft of all types had fallen to 35 by the time the regiment left Tütow. All wore red codes, with white outlines. The 368th OShAP came under the direct control of the 16th Air Army headquarters, and would probably have been assigned directly to a tank army

in time of war. The unit left Demmin on 15 June 1993, stopping overnight at Templin before flying on to its new home at Buddyenovsk. The 16th Air Army had bettered its promise to vacate Tütow during the second half of 1993.

Local residents probably breathed a sigh of relief, remembering the 12 April 1990 incident in which an Su-25 accidentally loosed off a pair of 57-mm rockets, one exploding on the airfield at Tütow and the other writing off five grain silos in Demmin.

368 Otdelnyi Shturmovoi Aviatsionnaya Polk

Aircraft: Su-25
Known codes: Red 01, 03, 05, 10, 12, 21, 22, 23, 25, 26, 27, 28, 29, 30, 31, 33, 35, 36, 37, 38

Aircraft: Su-25BM
Known codes: Red 02, 04, 06, 07, 08, 09, 11, 14, 15, 16, 17, 18

Most single-seat Su-25s carry a version of this cartoon rook on their port intake, reflecting the type's common nickname. Two-seaters tend to carry the bear insignia of the Ulan Ude factory which produced them.

Aircraft: Su-25UB
Known codes: Red 50, 70, 71, 72, 73

Aircraft: Aero L-39C
Known codes: Red 62 – 67, 84

Welzow

Sometimes known as Neu Welzow or Spremberg, the air base which latterly housed the Su-24s of the 11th 'Vitebski' RAP was surrounded by the fiercest signs to appear around any Soviet base in former East Germany, warning the unauthorised to keep away in several languages, including English. Once the shadowy 'Fencer-Fs' had departed in early 1991, however, security at the base became extremely slack, and it was one of the few airfields to host official visits by journalists, while other photographers took advantage of the broken-down perimeter fences to penetrate to the flight lines, shelter areas and taxiways. Located in the easternmost part of the former GDR, about 15 miles (24 km) east of Finsterwalde and 35 miles (56 km) north-east of Dresden, Welzow was unusual in having two parallel NNE-SSW (04/22) runways. Just west of the town of Welzow, the airfield was surrounded by railways on three sides, perhaps denoting an earlier assignment to nuclear strike.

Welzow was one of the airfields used by the Luftwaffe (including IV/NJG 2), although details of such use remain little-known. In Luftwaffe hands it was a simple grass airfield, similar in pattern to Finsterwalde or Merseburg, but post-war was extended dramatically to the south-west, cutting into what had been forest. This allowed the laying of the twin runways referred to earlier. The 11th RAP moved to Welzow in 1951, having previously operated the Il-28 in the Baltic States (lastly at Jekabpils and Krustpils in Latvia). Originally formed at Goroshino near Torzhok, Kalinin, on 19 July 1942, the 11th RAP gained the honour title 'Vitebskii' on 11 June 1944, and the Order of the Red Banner on 10 August. The regiment flew a succession of reconnaissance aircraft and by 1965 had 28 Il-28s, three Il-14 'Crates' and three Mi-1 'Hares' on charge, with four Yak-12s and four Il-28Us forming a training and liaison flight. By 1967 the regiment had expanded, with 35 Il-28s, four Il-28Us, 12 Yak-27R 'Mangroves' and a mix of Il-14s, Mi-1s and Yak-12s. The first Yak-28s entered service in 1968, just in time for active participation in the invasion of Czechoslovakia. By 1969 these had replaced the Yak-27s, although Il-28s were still in use. A further honour was the award of a Red Banner by the Komsomol (Communist Youth Organisation)

in 1970, a small representation of which has since been painted on one of the regiment's aircraft. Two eskadrilyas each with 12 Su-24MRs replaced Yak-28R and Yak-28I 'Brewer-Ds' and 'Brewer-Cs' during 1986. The Yak-28Is had almost certainly been converted for the recce role, and one (White 22) flew out to Werneuchen to serve as an instructional airframe. The Yak-28s left in February and April, with the first and second eskadrilyas beginning Su-24 operations in February and July respectively. A single eskadrilya of Su-24MPs (Modifikatsii Pastanovchik-Pamech) escort jammers replacing the last Yak-28PP 'Brewer-Es' after these departed in July 1986. All wore plain white codes.

The Su-24MPs were withdrawn to Chortkov in the Ukraine in two groups on 5 and 7 June 1991, joining the 118th Independent Aviation Regiment of the L'vov-headquartered 14th Air Army. On 21 May 1991, one eskadrilya of the 931st RAP at Werneuchen had moved to Welzow with its 13 MiG-25s. These stayed until 6 July 1992, when they moved to an airfield near Novosibirsk. When the two types operated from the flight line together it was interesting that while the Su-24s used the system of underground fuel pipes leading directly, the MiG-25s had to be refuelled by bowser, possibly indicating that the 'Foxbats' used some sort of specialised

high flashpoint fuel like the SR-71's JP-7. The two types flew among the longest training sorties regularly undertaken by the 16th Air Army. While MiG-27 and MiG-29 missions seldom lasted for more than half an hour, the Su-24s often flew one-hour missions, and the MiG-25s were usually airborne for an hour and a quarter or more. The Su-24MRs finally left Welzow on 8 June 1993, bound for Marinovka.

11 Otdelnyi Razvedyvatielnyi Aviatsionnaya Polk

First eskadrilya:
Aircraft: Su-24MR
Known codes: White 01, 02, 03, 04, 05, 06, 07, 08, 09, 10, 11, 12

Second eskadrilya:
Aircraft: Su-24MR
Known codes: 20, 21, 22, 23, 24, 25, 26, 27, 28, 29, 30, 31

Third eskadrilya:
Aircraft: Su-24MP
Known codes: White 40, 41, 42, 44, 45, 46, 47, 48

Above: The third eskadrilya *of the 11th* ORAP *was equipped with the Su-24MP 'Fencer-F'. This variant is believed to be a dedicated escort jammer and a replacement for the Yak-28PP 'Brewer-E'. The Welzow-based Su-24MPs usually carried a single centreline pod, similar in shape and size to the Sphil-2M recce pod carried by some of the reconnaissance Su-24MRs at Welzow. Some sources suggest that the Su-24MP could carry Kh-58 (AS-11 'Kilter') ASMs for defence suppression.*

Below: A well-worn Su-24MR carries only a Sphil-2M laser reconnaissance pod to back up its internal sensors (SLAR, TV, IR and optical). Although the Sphil-2M and the smaller, slab-sided Tangazh Elint pod were notionally interchangeable, at Welzow particular aircraft seemed to be roled to carry one or the other, and none were seen or photographed carrying both types of pod.

Werneuchen

Werneuchen is located on the north-eastern edge of the Berlin control zone, under 10 miles (16 km) from the Berlin ring road. Just east of the town of Werneuchen, the airfield lies south of the road and railway line running from Berlin to Bad Freienwalde and Wriezen. The single east-west runway had an eastern threshold close to the village of Hirschfelde.

In Luftwaffe hands Werneuchen played a decisive role in the development of night-fighter equipment and tactics. It housed the Erprobungsstelle Werneuchen, which developed and tested radar, aircraft and weapons, while the January 1944 activation of NJGr. 10 established another operational test unit with three full *Staffel* of Bf 109s and Fw 190s, Bf 110s and Ju 88s, and with Hs 129s equipping the third *Staffel*. This later took over the Bf 110s and Ju 88s from the second *Staffel*, which re-equipped with He 219s and Ta 154s. Other activities at Werneuchen included flight tests of the Ar 234 V12 and Do 335 V16.

Built to the same pattern as Finsterwalde, Merseburg and Neuruppin, Werneuchen was extended eastwards by the Russians, who laid a 2500-m (8,202-ft) hard runway, and later added dispersals and hardened aircraft shelters. In Soviet hands Werneuchen was a bomber base for many years, and was also home to a bomber division controlling regiments at Werneuchen, Brand and Finow. By 1965 the Werneuchen regiment had 44 Il-28s, 14 Yak-28s, six Il-28Us and four Yak-12s on charge, with some reports of a handful of Yak-28P 'Firebars' as well. Two years later only Yak-28s were in use (numbering about 36), with Il-28Us, Yak-28s and Il-12s serving with the divisional HQ flight. The base continued to support bomber deployments even after its resident squadron disbanded. Local reports suggest that there was a major deployment by Tu-22s during 1986 or 1987.

Werneuchen re-roled as a reconnaissance base during 1969 with Yak-27R 'Mangroves', which were probably joined by reconnaissance versions of the Yak-28 in the early 1980s. MiG-25s replaced the Yaks during the early 1980s. These may have been the aircraft previously based at Damm, which may have brought their own unit designation with them, or which may have adopted the unit identity used by the Yaks. Whatever the case, the MiG-25 regiment at Werneuchen was the 931st RAP. There is some confusion as to what MiG-25R variants were used by the unit, but these

are believed to have included the MiG-25RB, the MiG-25RBT and the MiG-25RBV, the MiG-25RBK, the MiG-25RBS and similar MiG-25RBF and the MiG-25RBSz.

The MiG-25RB 'Foxbat-B' was the basic dual-role reconnaissance/bomber, with optical cameras in the nose, an SRS-4A Elint system, and a Peleng automatic bombing system with four underwing and two underfuselage hardpoints each capable of carrying a 500-kg (1,102-lb) bomb. The MiG-25RBV was a similar aircraft, with SRS-9 Elint equipment, while the MiG-25RBT had Tangazh Elint equipment. The MiG-25RBK was a dedicated Elint aircraft, with its cameras removed and replaced by a Kub SLAR, with a pair of small flush antennas on the sides of the nose and an extended nosecone. The MiG-25RBS and RBF had much larger flush antennas further back on the nose, serving a Sablia SLAR. The MiG-25RBF was produced by conversion of MiG-25RBK airframes. The MiG-25RBSz served a similar role, but had a new Szar SLAR behind RBK-type forward-located flush antennas with the same extended nosecone and and with four flush square antennas roughly over the old camera ports.

The last Yak-28PP 'Brewer-Es' were withdrawn in 1989, replaced by MiG-25BMs. It is unclear as to whether the 931st RAP had two or three constituent *eskadrilyas*. It seems likely that there were two reconnaissance squadrons, with a single squadron of the 'Wild Weasel' MiG-25BM 'Foxbat-Fs'. These aircraft were armed with up to four Kh-58 (AS-11 'Kilter') AAMs underwing, and were painted to represent MiG-25PD 'Foxbat-E' fighters, with their noses painted dark grey to simulate radomes. In fact, the MiG-25BM was based on the MiG-25R airframe, and had many flush antennas on the sides of the nose, serving the aerials of the emitter detector/locator system.

One *eskadrilya* of the 931st RAP left Werneuchen for Schuschin in Byelorussia during 1990, leaving 14 aircraft (all recce and trainer versions) at Werneuchen. This departure may have been of the first reconnaissance squadron, or of the MiG-25BM squadron. The remaining *eskadrilya*

Below: Laden with a massive centreline fuel tank, one of the 931st ORAP MiG-25RBSzs is started up prior to a training sortie from Welzow. The rump of the unit moved to Welzow in May 1991, when the rest of the regiment returned to the USSR. This was the only camouflaged MiG-25 assigned to the Soviet forces in East Germany.

Above: Werneuchen's gate was guarded by two symbols of a bygone era, a bust of Lenin and an ancient Yak-28I bomber.

Below: The MiG-25s of the 931st ORAP were the last DDR-based 'Foxbats', outlasting Eberswalde's MiG-25PDs by five years.

Left: The 487th OVP decorated its helicopters with blue codes. The unit moved to Gross Dölln on the closure of Prenzlau, and then moved into Werneuchen in late 1991. This Mi-24V has orange intake filters, a common decoration on the regiment's helicopters.

Twin braking parachutes are common on heavyweight Soviet tactical aircraft since they provide extra area without risking damage by being scraped along the runway. Here a MiG-25RU of the 931st ORAP taxis in at Welzow, brake chutes bobbing behind it.

left Werneuchen on 21 May 1991, moving on to Welzow. The 931st RAP reportedly operated sporadic detachments at Haina (and perhaps at other bases), but such detachments had finished by 1991. Werneuchen's recce MiG-25s wore red codes, outlined in white, while the MiG-25BMs wore orange codes. The last MiG-25s left Welzow on 6 July 1992, bound for an airfield near Novosibirsk.

Werneuchen has been a helicopter base on a number of occasions, housing the 20th

This Mil Mi-2T was one of those originally allocated to the 41st OVE at Werneuchen, although the unit later gained more Mi-2Ts when the 8th OVE left Hassleben. All the Mi-2 'Hoplites' were withdrawn during April 1992, four months before the rest of the 41st OVE's complement.

Guards Infantry Army's helicopter regiment during the mid-1960s, until it moved to Eberswalde.

The tiny headquarters squadron attached to the Second Guards Tank Army, the 41st OVE, remained at Werneuchen. Eventually all Mi-2s based in East Germany were gathered at Werneuchen, but these returned to Russia during April 1992, with the regiments other helicopters following in early August 1992.

The transfer of Werneuchen's MiG-25s to Russia and to Welzow left room for another helicopter unit to transfer in for a brief period. This was the 487th OVP, one of the regiments assigned to the 20th Guards Infantry Army and a long-term resident of Prenzlau before transferring to Gross Dölln. The regiment moved to Werneuchen in late 1991 after the departure of the MiG-25s, and eventually returned to Russia in August 1993.

931 Otdelnyi Razvedyvatielnyi Aviatsionnaya Polk

Aircraft: MiG-25RU
Known codes: Red 01, 02, 65

Aircraft: MiG-25RB, RBT, RBV
Known codes: Red 53, 57, 61

Aircraft: MiG-25RBK
Known codes: Red 55

Aircraft: MiG-25RBS/RBF
Known codes: Red 50, 51, 52

Aircraft: MiG-25RBSz
Known codes: 38, 58, 59, 60, 62

Aircraft: MiG-25BM
Known codes: Orange 76

487 Otdelnyi Vertoletnyi Polk

Aircraft: Mi-24V
Known codes: Blue 01, 02, 03, 04, 05, 06, 07, 08, 24, 25, 26, 27, 28, 29, 30, 31, 46

Aircraft: Mi-24RKR 'Hind-G'
Known codes: Blue 20, 21, 40, 41

Aircraft: Mi-24K 'Hind-G2'
Known codes: Blue 18, 19, 42, 43

Aircraft: Mi-8MT
Known codes: Blue 10, 17, 32, 37, 39

Aircraft: Mi-8MTV
Known codes: Blue 09, 11, 12, 14, 15, 16, 33, 34, 35, 36, 38

Aircraft: Mi-9
Known codes: Blue 22, 23, 44, 45

41 Otdelnyi Vertoletnyi Eskadrilya

Aircraft: Mi-2T
Known codes: Yellow 05, 28, 47, 57 (plus one uncoded)

Aircraft: Mi-6VKP 'Hook-B'
Known codes: Yellow 25

Aircraft: Mi-22 'Hook-C'
Known codes: Yellow 23

Aircraft: Mi-8T
Known codes: Yellow 21, 24, 26

Aircraft: Mi-24RKR 'Hind-G'
Known codes: Yellow 14, 15

Aicraft: Mi-24K 'Hind-G2'
Known codes: Yellow 16, 17

Like most of the headquarters squadrons, the 41st OVE had a pair of 'Hooks' on charge. This aircraft was the squadron's Mi-22 'Hook-C' (also known as the Mi-6BUS). The distinguishing feature of this sub-variant was the large blade antenna above the rear fuselage.

Wittstock

Located in the northernmost part of Brandenburg, Wittstock lay about 15 miles (24 km) south-west of Lärz, north-north-east of the town of Wittstock and just north of the road to Berlinchen. It had a single east-west runway.

Known as Wittstock-Dosse in Luftwaffe use, the airfield was the long-time home of Fallschirmschule 1. It later accommodated a variety of other units, including transport and night-fighter squadrons.

A long-time fighter base in Soviet hands, the airfield was extended east by the Russians, covering the old adjacent parachute jumping field. A hard runway (08/26) was added, with a parallel northern taxiway, and HASs followed. Wittstock was one of three regiments controlled by the Pütnitz fighter division. By 1965 the based regiment operated 28 MiG-19S 'Farmer-Cs' and 14 MiG-19P 'Farmer-Cs' and MiG-19PM 'Farmer-Ds'. A base flight operated four MiG-15UTIs and four Yak-12s. Two years later the 'Farmer-Ds' and the base flight had disappeared. MiG-21s augmented and then replaced MiG-19s before themselves being replaced by MiG-23Ms. During the 1980s Wittstock reportedly hosted a detachment of MiG-25s from Eberswalde, but the size and status of this detachment (permanent, rotational or occasional) remains uncertain. The 33rd IAP became the first MiG-29 regiment in Germany in 1986, when 'Fulcrum-As' replaced blue-coded MiG-23M 'Flogger-Bs'. It was probably only the fourth MiG-29 regiment in the whole of Frontal Aviation, following the 866th IAP at Ros, Byelorussia, the 234th GvIAP at Kubinka, and the 176th IAP at Mikhail Tshakaya in Georgia.

The Wittstock MiG-29s were occasionally seen carrying B8M rocket pods (each containing 20 80-mm rockets) and there have been reports that they even used underwing gun pods, practising air-to-ground gunnery on the Wittstock and Baruth ranges. It seems likely that at least one *eskadrilya* had a ground attack committment. 1988/89 reports that the Wittstock regiment had re-equipped with the 'Fulcrum-C' proved ill-founded, only one such aircraft being on charge during the 1991-1994 period. This particular aircraft, White 39, was unique in being painted off-white overall, except for its tailfins, radomes and anti-dazzle panel. Wittstock may,

Above: One of only two MiG-29 'Fulcrum-Cs' assigned to the 33rd IAP lands at its Wittstock home base. Wittstock hosted the 'Fulcrum-C' operational evaluation, leading to erroneous reports that its based unit had converted to the later variant.

however, have hosted an early 'Fulcrum-C' evaluation unit, and White 39 may have been left behind by that unit. Alternatively, the single 'Fulcrum-C' might have been a 'command spare', or a loan from the regiment at Pütnitz.

White codes predominated at Wittstock, usually with a very thin blue outline, although one aircraft had a very thin red outline to its codes, and five others wore blue codes thinly outlined in white. The latter were said to have been refugees from Merseburg, but this seems unlikely. A more likely explanation is that all of the Wittstock aircraft originally had blue codes, and that they escaped a general repainting of codes before the system of coloured regimental codes fell into disuse.

There have been suggestions that the Pütnitz-based regiment had a heavy training commitment, perhaps functioning as an adversary-type unit or as a regular host for courses broadly equivalent to NATO's TLP, and reportedly borrowing aircraft from other regiments to meet this requirement. This

woul help to explain the frequent deployments by Soviet fighters from other bases in East Germany, and by East German MiG-21s and MiG-23s. The blue-coded MiG-29s may have been left-overs from such a training deployment.

One *eskadrilya* departed early, flying to Damgarten on 17 March 1994 to join a squadron from the 773rd IAP which flew to Andreapol with it on 22 March. Poor weather led to three aircraft being written off in landing accidents and a ground collision as they arrived back in Russia.

Shortly before their withdrawal, some of the 33rd IAP's remaining MiG-29s received a regimental badge on their port tailfins, this consisting of a white, blue and red Imperial Russian roundel on which were superimposed a bison, what appeared to be a stylised shark (or dolphin) and a MiG-29. Two more aircraft were noted earlier with huge angular lightning flashes painted in grey on the foremost part of the LERX. Wittstock's MiG-29s flew the nest on 7 April 1994, flying to Pütnitz. The 33rd IAP

This badge was applied to the port tailfins of a few 33rd IAP MiG-29s before they departed. The bison is associated with Byelorussia, where the unit originally formed.

Below: White 37 wore a lightning flash insignia on its LERXes, with the regiment badge on its fin. Runway barriers were intended to prevent defections.

Above: The shortage of two-seat MiG-29UBs meant that as regiments departed, their two-seaters were often reallocated. Wittstock picked up MiG-29UBs from Nöbitz and Zerbst (seen here). These retained their codes.

Above: White 30 was unusual (perhaps even unique) among Wittstock-based MiG-29s in having its codes thinly outlined in red, instead of the usual blue.

and the 773rd IAP left Pütnitz together, on 11 April, although two Wittstock aircraft that 'went tech' (White 08 and 09) actually left the following day, becoming the last Soviet tactical aircraft to leave East Germany. Like the 773rd IAP, the destination of the 33rd IAP was Andreapol, where the unit disbanded, although some of its aircraft and pilots went on to Žernograd, where a PVO MiG-23 regiment re-equipped with MiG-29s and reformed as a Frontal Aviation unit.

33 Istrebeitelnyi Aviotsionnaya Polk

Aircraft: MiG-29 'Fulcrum-A'
Known codes: White 01, 02, 03, 05, 06, 07, 08, 09, 10, 11, 12, 20, 22, 23, 29, 30, 31, 33, 34, 36, 37, Blue 21, 24, 26, 27, 28

Aircraft: MiG-29 'Fulcrum-C'
Known codes: White 38, 39

Aircraft: MiG-29UB
Known codes: White 55, 71, 72, Outline 64, Red 91

Aircraft: MiG-23UB
Known codes: Outline 66, 68, 69

This well-worn 'Fulcrum-A' was one of about five Wittstock aircraft with blue codes. It was not an ex-Merseburg aircraft.

Zerbst

Located 40 miles (64 km) north-north-east of Leipzig and 20 miles (32 km) south-west of Magdeburg, Zerbst lay within the Frankfurt-Berlin corridor, 20 miles (32 km) north of Köthen. North-east of the town of Zerbst, the airfield lay to the north of the road from Zerbst to Dobritz, and had one south-west to north-east runway (07/25).

A pre-war Luftwaffe fighter airfield with early model Bf 109s, Zerbst later accommodated a fighter training school. Wartime duties included the Defence of the Reich, and highlights included the brief tenancy by 1.Staffel of NAGr.1, with recce-tasked Me 262s during March-April 1944, and a detachment by the similarly equipped *Geschwaderstab* of KG(J) 54.

The Russian take-over brought with it expansion to the north-east, and laying of the hard runway already described. Headquarters of a fighter division controlling the regiments at Zerbst, Köthen and Altes Lager, Zerbst's based regiment had 44 MiG-19s on charge, with an unknown number of MiG-21s and, according to some reports, Su-9 'Fishpots'. The base also accommodated a training and liaison flight with four MiG-15UTIs and four Yak-12s. By 1967 this flight had gone, but the division HQ operated 16 MiG-21PFs and a pair of MiG-17Fs, while the based regiment had 20 MiG-21PFs and 30 Yak-27 'Firebars'.

There have been reports that the Zerbst-based regiment converted from the MiG-21 to the MiG-23, with one *eskadrilya* later gaining MiG-25s. The presence of MiG-25s, except on temporary deployments, cannot be confirmed, however. Certainly blue-coded MiG-23M 'Flogger-Bs' were replaced by MiG-29s during late 1987 or early 1988, probably just before the regiment at Merseburg re-equipped, making the 35th IAP the third MiG-29 unit in the 16th Air Army. 'Broken', stencilled red codes were worn by Zerbst's MiG-29s, these being very thinly outlined in white. By 1991, re-equipment with the later 'Fulcrum-C' was well underway although the process was never completed, and one *eskadrilya*, with 12 aircraft, retained early 'Fulcrum-As' (of 14 early series MiG-29s known to have been in use at Zerbst) up until the final departure, which also included 16 'Fulcrum-Cs'. All of these were from the earliest production series, with ventral fins and no overwing chaff/flare dispensers. By the time they departed, on 10 June 1992, a number of Zerbst-based MiG-29s carried a squadron badge below the cockpit. The 126th GvIAD used at least one An-2, and perhaps some Mi-8s for liaison and support duties.

Above: Early MiG-29s, with ventral fins, park on the Zerbst flight line with bowsers and truck-mounted APUs in attendance. Each aircraft is parked in front of a primitive steel jet blast deflector.

35 Istrebeitelnyi Aviotsionnaya Polk

Aircraft: MiG-29 'Fulcrum-A'
Known codes: Red 09^V, 10^V, 11^V, 12^V, 20^V, 21^V, 22^V, 23^V, 24^V, 25^V, 26^V, 27^V, 28, 29

Aircraft: MiG-29 'Fulcrum-C'
Known codes: 01, 02, 03, 04, 05, 06, 07, 08, 34, 40, 41, 42, 43, 44, 45, 46, 47, 49

Aircraft: MiG-29UB
Known codes: Red 60, 70, 91

Aircraft: MiG-23UB
Known codes: Red 64, 90, 91, 92, 93, 94, 96, 97

Above: This 'Fulcrum-C' wears a small badge below the cockpit. The repainted intake perhaps indicates that it once wore a Guards badge and was an ex-Köthen aircraft.

Below: Laden with a centreline fuel tank, a well-weathered early MiG-29 taxis out prior to its final departure from Zerbst. Some WGF 'Fulcrum-Cs' could carry underwing tanks.

National Aeronautics and Space Administration

In the minds of many, NASA is most closely associated with the United States' space programme and high-profile, ongoing projects such as the Space Shuttle and Hubble telescope. A new era in co-operation with the Russians is also beginning, as the Administration prepares for the first Shuttle-'Mir' space station docking. There is another side to NASA's activities, however, that is perhaps more important and is certainly far more widespread. NASA operates a varied fleet of aircraft devoted to a myriad of research and training tasks. From this pool of aeronautical expertise it provides invaluable research and development assistance to the US military and government, as well as to many commercial firms. Indeed, NASA's history and organisation is intertwined with the US Department of Defense, and in its own right it operates an 'air force' that is among the world's largest.

Langley Field, Virginia, was the birthplace of the National Advisory Committee for Aeronautics (NACA), created by an act of the United States' Congress in 1915. With Europe embroiled in war, NACA's task was to oversee aeronautical research in both military and civilian fields. The first type to be operated by the organisation was a (borrowed) Curtiss JN-4, but, at that time, restricted funding never allowed NACA to amass a sizable fleet of aircraft. Until the late 1930s the pace of progress at Langley was leisurely. The advent of World War II forced NACA initially to remedy the shortcomings of America's existing warplanes (such as the Brewster XF2A-1 Buffalo) and, ultimately, prompted advances such as the renowned 'NACA cowl', greatly improved wing sections with laminar-flow airfoils and high-lift devices. By way of example, NACA was instrumental in transforming the North American XP-51 Mustang from a stolid design into one of the greatest fighters of all time.

High-speed research became increasingly important as NACA began investigating swept wing and supersonic designs, and at its wartime peak the organisation employed 6,804 men and women. In 1940 a new facility at Moffett Field, California, was established and this was quickly followed by the Flight Propulsion Research Laboratory at Cleveland, Ohio. Later on, in 1944/45, Wallops Island, a barren stretch of the Virginia Eastern Shore Peninsula, was activated for highly secret rocket trials, while facilities at Langley were further enlarged.

The X-planes

After World War II NACA become closely involved with the (increasingly) high-speed research of the X-planes. Starting with the Douglas D-558 Skyrocket (a US Navy-led project), tests were moved to the dry lake bed at Muroc, California in 1946. The first supersonic flight by a NACA aircraft, the Bell X-1, was made on 10 March 1948 by Herbert Hoover, nearly five months after Chuck Yeager's historic flight. Prior to this the X-1 had been in USAAF hands. In 1950 Muroc Field officially became Edwards AFB, in honour of Captain Glenn W. Edwards, who was killed on 5 June 1948 in the crash of the Northrop YB-49 flying wing, near Muroc.

One way in which NACA research demonstrably helped US industry was the publication of the Area Rule, by Dr Richard Whitcomb, in September 1952. Aided by important preliminary work undertaken by R. T. Jones, Whitcomb had determined the correct proportions of wing and fuselage cross-section to ensure the minimum of transsonic drag for any aircraft design. NACA released the findings, still marked SECRET, to US manufacturers. This immediately allowed Convair to rectify serious problems with the YF-102, and Chance Vought their F-8U. Whitcomb's Area Rule was also soon applied to Lockheed's F-104 and Grumman's F9F-9 (later F11F-1 Tiger).

From NACA to NASA

NACA conducted swept-wing flight tests with the Bell X-5, unsuccessful Mach 2 tests with the Douglas X-3 Stiletto, delta-wing research with the Convair XF-92A and tail-less configuration flights with the Northrop X-4 Bantam. In June 1952 a NACA committee decided that the agency should initiate research of high-altitude and exo-atmospheric flight at speeds ranging from Mach 4 to Mach 10. In September 1955 North American Aviation was awarded the contract to build the X-15 (Project 1226), NACA's hypersonic, exo-atmospheric research craft. In July 1958 NACA became NASA – the National Aeronautics and Space Administration – and a new chapter in the organisation's history opened with the first (unpowered) flight on 8 June 1959 at the hands of Scott Crossfield. Among the earliest NASA pilots of the X-15 was Neil Armstrong. While the USAF and US Navy funded the project, NASA had technical control of the X-15. Two B-52s were converted to NB-52A and NB-52B standard to carry the X-15 for its air launches, and these hard-working Stratofortresses later became an important part of many other NASA projects into the 1980s.

Military test duties

While the X-15 programme and other X-plane research was ongoing, NACA/NASA was also involved with the military in solving problems of service aircraft. Quite apart from experimental prototypes, the team at Edwards located a serious weakness in the wing of the F-89 Scorpion that had led to six inflight failures. Extensive tests were undertaken with the B-47, as its wing design gave new insights into aeroelasticity, and its effect on structural loads and other large aircraft studies involved a KC-135. The agency regularly received prototypes of new service aircraft to speed up USAF development.

During the 1960s NASA became involved in VTOL and STOL research along with the USAF and US Army, but the space programme was becoming increasingly important, particularly the Apollo programme. Pioneering research was also undertaken in the fields of supercritical wing design and fly-by-wire controls, the former with a modified General Dynamics F-111, the latter with a modified Vought F-8. The flight control system of the F-16 was first flown in NASA's F-8. During the 1970s NASA's Earth resources monitoring became increasingly important. Two unique Martin WB-57Fs flew alongside a pair of U-2s (released from USAF service in 1971) on high-altitude survey missions. In 1981 NASA took delivery of a TR-1, designated ER-2 in civilian service, joining a P-3 Orion and C-130 Hercules in the remote sensing programme.

Space Shuttle and NASP

NASA regained a manned space mission with the first launch of the Space Shuttle OV-102 'Columbia', in April 1982. As the Shuttle matured attention moved on, in 1986, to the X-30 National Aero Space Plane (NASP), a reusable spacecraft much heralded as the vehicle that would 'shrink travel times from Washington DC to Tokyo to two hours'. NASP was a single-stage to orbit, twin-fin lifting body, powered by a mix of scramjets and solid rocket boosters, which would land and take-off conventionally with a load of passengers. After massive expenditure by both government and industry, NASP was cancelled in May 1993 with little to show for its enormous budget. Some observers have suggested that much of this money found its way to far more concrete military 'black' programmes. Today, NASA has launched the search for a slightly less ambitious Space Shuttle successor.

NASA's attention is also firmly focused on its straightforward aviation activities, although some of the technologies currently under investigation are just as impressive as those of any space programme. A wide range of high-performance military types share the NASA ramps with a collection of prototypes and more mundane, but no less important aircraft. Further details of current trials programmes can be found in the following entries.

This veteran Cessna U-3A was originally 57-5921. It was acquired for slipstream studies, but now serves as a 'hack' with NASA Langley.

One of NASA's most widely seen aircraft is the sole Gulfstream II on charge. This is the agency's flagship, flying top officials to meetings around the country, and occasionally overseas. The callsign is, unsuprisingly, 'NASA One'.

Langley operates a number of light aircraft, including this Piper PA-28RT-201 Arrow. The aircraft is instrumented to record flow, including the effect of wake vortices.

Langley's most potent aircraft is this F-16A, supported by an F-16B for spares. The aircraft has a multi-role function, having replaced the Convair F-106. Interestingly, this aircraft was buit as a Block 15 F-16A, yet features the lengthened dorsal fin fairing of an F-16C.

This Boeing 737 Transport Systems Research Vehicle has undertaken extensive trials from Langley aimed at increasing airliner safety. It is being replaced by a Boeing 757.

Flying from NASA Dryden, the two Rockwell/DASA X-31s are operated by a joint test team incorporating NASA, USAF, US Navy, Rockwell, DASA and the German Defence Ministry.

Left: Known as HARV, this Hornet is operated from Dryden on missions to explore angles of attack up to 70°. Controllability is enhanced by a three-paddle thrust vectoring system integrated with the flight control system.

The Dryden Flight Research Center is located at the north end of the main Edwards AFB complex, sharing the many hard and lakebed runways with the Air Force Flight Test Center. This group of Dryden aircraft, led by the F/A-18 HARV, includes the X-29, F-104, SR-71 and NB-52B, the latter displayed with the Pegasus orbital booster. The Shuttle-carrying 747 is from the Johnson Space Center, but is a regular sight at Dryden where one is usually based. Dryden has 14 F/A-18s on charge, most used for chase duties in which they have replaced F-104s.

Office of Aeronautics

Langley Research Center

Langley Field, near Hampton, Virginia, is one of the oldest continuously active military airfields in the United States, gaining its current name in 1916 in honour of Professor Samuel Pierpoint Langley, one of America's earliest aviation pioneers. NACA was established at this airfield in 1917, when building work began on its first experimental laboratory. Then, the facility was named the Langley Memorial Aeronautical Laboratory. This name changed in 1948 to the Langley Aeronautical Laboratory, and again, in 1958, to its current name. The Langley Research Center covers some 788 acres (319 hectares), with an additional 3,200 acres (1295 hectares) set aside as a drop zone for aerodynamic models. Flying operations are conducted, in the main, from the co-located USAF base which allocates NASA 'space' for 20 aircraft. The staff at Langley (close to 3,000) are primarily concerned with research and development in the fields of aerodynamics, materials and flight systems. One of the Center's key assets is the National Transonic Facility, a high-speed cryogenic wind tunnel that allows detailed fluid dynamics research on airframes and airfoils. Approximately 60 per cent of the lab's work is devoted to future aircraft development, while the remainder of its efforts are devoted to the space programme. Langley scientists were heavily involved in developing structure, aerodynamics and thermal protection for the Space Shuttle and Viking Mars orbiter/landers.

The first NACA-owned aircraft was a Boeing PW-9 pursuit fighter, delivered in January 1927, while many types were operated on temporary assignment from the US Army or Navy. The story of Langley is largely one of pure research, and at various stages in its history aircraft and operations have been moved to other sites to allow the R&D effort at Langley to grow into the (limited) space available. Over 40 wind tunnels are now installed at the facility, including Mach 6 tunnels of varying size, a Mach 17 nitrogen tunnel and a Mach 20 helium tunnel. Other installations include a vertical spin tunnel, arc-heated scramjet tunnel, high-Reynolds number helium tunnel, and a high-temperature tunnel. An extensive range of structures, materials and acoustic test facilities (fatigue and fracture, spacecraft dynamics, impact dynamics, non-destructive testing, composite materials, thermal structures and high-intensity noise laboratories) plus flight systems and advanced simulation equipment is also available.

As of early 1995, 15 active aircraft were allocated to NASA operations from Langley. In addition, NASA's flagship 'NASA 1'– a Gulfstream III – is flown from Langley although nominally based at NASA headquarters in Washington, DC. Several aircraft have performed unusual duties in support of ongoing spaceflight missions. In 1989 a Cessna 402B began the Shuttle Exhaust Particle Experiment (SEPEX), flying through the exhaust plume of the orbiter after its launch to determine if it influenced local climatic/environmental conditions. In 1985 and 1989 it was joined by Langley's T-34C, which has also been involved in laminar-flow, wing glove experiments. Other, smaller, aircraft on the books include a Piper PA-28RT, now engaged in pressure belt measurements and stagnation sensor evaluation, and a Bell 204B (in service since 1964, currently involved in high angle of attack model drops of the X-31). A 10-seat Beech 65-B80 Queen Air, Cessna U-3A and Bell OH-58A all serve in a mission-support capacity. A more unusual support type in use is a Northrop F-5F (converted from an F-5E), which arrived at Langley in 1989. Other ex-USAF aircraft in service include an F-16A and an OV-10A (wake vortex studies). Types currently in storage include a Cessna 172K (entered service in 1975) and Gates Learjet 28 (entered service in 1984). Mention should also be made of NASA 816, the last active Convair F-106, which undertook electrical storm research and leading-edge vortex flap test flying until its retirement in 1990.

Langley's largest type is its Boeing 737, the first production 737, which is in use as the Transport Systems Research Vehicle (TSRV). It has spent 17 years with NASA and over that time has test flown many innovations that are now increasingly commonplace in the commercial air transport world. Experimental microwave landing systems (MLS), glass cockpits, wind shear detection equipment and global positioning system (GPS) navigation were all pioneered in the TSRV. In addition, new technology such as helmet-mounted displays and ground-to-air datalinks are still under development.

Dryden Flight Research Center

Located at Edwards Air Force Base, home to the USAF's own Air Force Flight Test Center and Test Pilot's School, the Dryden Flight Research Center is NASA's primary flight research facility.

Dryden can trace its origins back to 1946 and the NACA-Army Air Corps X-1 programme. The original X-planes which pioneered flight at and beyond the speed of sound operated from Edwards, as did the Douglas D-558 Skyrocket (the first aircraft to exceed Mach 2) and the X-15, which extended manned flight to speeds in excess of 4,500 mph (7242 km/h) and to altitudes of over 350,000 ft (106680 m). Using thrusters for pitch, roll and yaw control, the X-15 had a major role in developing systems for the space programme. Between 1968 and 1975, the M2-F2, M2-F3, HL-10 and X-24 lifting bodies were flown in a programme which contributed materially to the present Space Shuttle.

Dryden projects during the 1970s and 1980s included the Digital Fly By Wire F-8, the Highly Integrated Digital Electronic Control F-15, and a number of aerodynamic/flight control projects. These resulted in the operation of an F-8 with a Supercritical Wing, an F-111 with a Mission Adaptive Wing (whose camber and sweep could be varied in flight), and the purpose-built AD-1 with an oblique or slewed wing which could be skewed by up to 60° in flight, so that one wing was swept back and the other swept forward. Two X-29 forward-swept wing research aircraft conducted a 302-flight research programme from Dryden between 1984 and 1991. Most visibly, the Space Shuttle prototype was air-launched from the NASA 747 Shuttle Carrier Aircraft for glide recoveries to the lakebeds and the Edwards main runway. Early Shuttle missions were all planned to return to Dryden, until braking and nosewheel steering systems were cleared for landings at the Kennedy Space Center itself.

Dryden had an FY1994 budget of $108 million, $65 million spent of it on research and development and the rest on construction, support and salaries. The facility was named on 26 March 1975 after Dr Hugh L. Dryden, NACA's Director of Aeronautical Research from 1946-1949 (when he became NACA Director) and Deputy Administrator of NASA until his death on 2 December 1965. Its location on the northwest edge of the 44-sq mile (114-km²) Rogers Dry Lake, and its proximity to the 22-sq mile (60-km²) Rosamond Dry Lake give it an unparalleled resource for the testing of aircraft and systems requiring long runways, and for emergency landings by (often temperamental) research aircraft. The 20,000 sq miles (52000 km²) of restricted air space over the high desert (known as the R-2508 Complex and forming part of NASA's Western Aeronautical Test Range, together with some restricted airspace off the Californian coast) are also a great boon for research and test flying, giving an average of 345 days of excellent flying weather every year and minimising problems of the impact of noise on major population centres.

Other facilities available at Dryden include an integrated test facility, a high-temperature and loads calibration laboratory, a flow visualisation facility, a flight systems laboratory and comprehensive data analysis and transmission facilities linking Dryden to the Crows Landing facility near Ames and the Western Aeronautical Range.

Dryden operates a diverse fleet of test and trials aircraft. The most important current programmes include the Advanced Fighter Technology Integration (AFTI) F-16, a joint NASA/USAF project evaluating digital flight controls, voice activation of systems and controls and advanced close air support systems on a heavily modified F-16. An F-16XL is being used to explore the characteristics of a swept laminar flow wing at supersonic speeds, which may have great applications in increasing wing efficiency in the next generation of airliners. The Advanced Control Technology for Integrated Vehicles (ACTIVE) F-15 has active canard foreplanes and multi-axis thrust vectoring.

The F/A-18 High Angle of Attack Research Vehicle (HARV) is similarly equipped with a multi-axis thrust vectoring system, and is modified with comprehensive airflow measuring systems. It backs up the work carried out by the two X-31s which are engaged in a separate programme which aims to demonstrate the usefulness of thrust vectoring and advanced flight controls for close-in air combat manoeuvring at high angles of attack. Another of the F/A-18s on charge is the Systems Research Aircraft, which acts as a testbed for new-generation control actuators, fibre optics and flush-mounted air data sensors.

Acquired primarily to provide a research vehicle for the X-30 NASP, NASA operates this single-seat SR-71A alongside an SR-71B. Dryden's other SR-71A (832) returned to Palmdale in late 1994 to be the first reactivated for operational service with the US Air Force.

Several aircraft are stored at NASA Dryden, including the two prototypes of the Northrop/McDonnell Douglas YF-23. These aircraft were assigned to NASA for non-flying tests of aircraft employing state-of-the-art construction techniques.

The second Grumman X-29A is still on charge with NASA at Edwards, currently 'resting' between programmes.

Both examples of the F-16XL are at Dryden for research into laminar flow at supersonic speeds, principally to aid future airliner design.

This F-15B arrived at Dryden in 1993 as a general-purpose testbed. The attachment is the Flight Test Fixture, used to mount various experiments.

Built in 1962, this Convair 990 is going strong at Dryden on Shuttle landing gear research. It previously served at Ames.

The HIDEC (Highly Integrated Digital Electronic Control) F-15 is fitted with 'smart' internal systems (including a self-repairing flight control system which compensates in flight for a damaged control surface) to enhance safety and increase performance.

The 'High and Mighty One' – NASA's longest-serving aircraft is this NB-52B (52-0008), which has launched everything from the X-15 to Shuttle booster rockets. Recently it has been used as the launch platform for the Orbital Sciences Pegasus booster.

Flying from Ames, this C-141A is a flying observatory, mounting a large telescope among other sensors. The aircraft is known as the 'Kuiper'.

With nose and belly laden with sensors, the Ames NC-130B flies earth survey missions. Occasionally, this entails testing satellite sensors prior to them being sent into space.

NASA Ames has a pair of Lockheed ER-2s for earth resources survey. This aircraft is a similar TR-1 borrowed by NASA during the late 1980s, and subsequently returned to USAF use. The ER-2s fly high-altitude missions, often in concert with the Ames DC-8 flying at lower level.

Among the older types in use are two Lockheed SR-71s on loan from the USAF (NASA 832 was returned in December 1994), together with four D-21 drones, a B-52 (currently testing the F-111 escape capsule parachute system) and a modified Convair CV 990 tasked with testing Space Shuttle landing gear assemblies. The B-52 is the oldest example still flying, and was the aircraft used in the X-15, Lifting Body and Himat trials. It has also been used to verify the operation of the parachute recovery system on the Space Shuttle rocket boosters, and the Shuttle's brake chute.

Dryden also continues to support the Space Shuttle programme by serving as a primary and backup landing site, and tests and validates some orbiter systems. After missions, Shuttles are usually serviced at Dryden before being flown (atop the 747) back to the Kennedy Space Center.

Ames Research Center

NACA operations were moved to California, from Langley, in 1940 when construction began at Moffett Field, near San Francisco, in February. The facility was named the Ames Aeronautical Laboratory in April, in honour of Dr Joseph S. Ames, NACA's chairman from 1927 to 1939. Ames was heavily involved in advancing fundamental aerodynamic theory and, by the 1950s, the space race. By the 1960s Ames had become the centre of NASA's V/STOL research and in 1969 work on the Space Sciences Research Laboratory was started. The Flight Simulator for Advanced Aircraft (intended for new widebody transports and SSTs) opened in 1970 and the subsequent Vertical Motion Simulator saw Ames equipped with the best flight simulators in the world. During 1981 the Flight Research Center at Dryden was merged with that at Ames, with the two new installations now referred to as Ames-Moffet and Ames-Dryden. Ames-Moffett possess the world's largest wind tunnel complex, much of it devoted to the Space Shuttle, while its many airborne laboratories support the Airborne Sciences and Applications Program.

Chief among these is the 'Gerald P. Kuiper' flying observatory, a much modified C-141A StarLifter (or Lockheed L 300-50A). Converted on the production line to house a 36-in (91.5-cm) infra-red telescope, the aircraft became operational in 1974. The value of the C-141 lies in its ability to carry its large telescope, or other sensors, to an altitude of 45,000 ft (13716 m), free from man-made light 'pollution' and clear of atmospheric distortion and water vapour. A Gates Learjet 24A, also delivered in 1974, is fitted with a smaller 12-in (30-cm) infra-red telescope, and work is underway on a replacement for the C-141. This will be a converted Boeing 747SP – the SOFIA (Stratospheric Observatory For Infra-red Astronomy) programme – and engineering work on the aircraft is currently underway in conjunction with the German Ministry of Science.

Other high-flying types at Ames include a pair of Lockheed ER-2s, which replaced earlier U-2Cs, in the Earth Resources Aircraft Project. They are used for high-level geological, vegetation or mapping surveys and for atmospheric research. A much-modified NC-130B is also part of the Earth Survey Program and is operated by the Science & Applications Division at Ames. Ames has had a long association with the McDonnell Douglas AV-8 Harrier programme and a YAV-8B is still in use, with several other AV-8s in storage. A sizable number of helicopters, ranging from a Bell AH-1S to several varied Sikorsky UH-60s, are in use for rotor blade development and noise suppression tests. Flying in support of these experiments is a Lockheed YO-3A, an ultra-quiet turboprop built originally for Vietnam-era surveillance missions. Other support aircraft for Ames' flight operations include a Beech 200 Super King Air, Douglas DC-8-72 and Northrop T-38.

Lewis Research Center

In 1941 NACA set up its Aircraft Engine Research Laboratory (later the Flight Propulsion Research Laboratory), in Cleveland, Ohio. Staff moved from Langley to the new facility, adjacent to Cleveland Municipal Airport (now Cleveland Hopkins Airport), and extensive test chambers for propeller and jet engines were installed by the end of World War II. Lewis, named for George W. Lewis, NACA's Director of Research from 1924 to 1947, became a fully-fledged Research Center with the creation of NASA in 1958. Today, Lewis comprises more than 140 buildings, including 24 major facilities, spread over 350 acres (142 hectares), 20 miles (32 km) south-west of Cleveland. Additional facilities are located at Plum Brook Station, near Sandusky, Ohio.

Lewis is NASA's (and one of the world's) leading centre of research into aero propulsion, space power and communications, electric propulsion, microgravity, fluid physics, combustion and materials. It has several large sub-, super- and hypersonic wind tunnels, icing tunnels, a drop tower, engine test cells, engine component labs, rocket labs and test facilities, zero-gravity and cryogenic laboratories.

Its small aviation component consists largely of support aircraft such as a Gulfstream I freighter and a DHC-6 Twin Otter. However, several other types are flown on dedicated test duties. One Twin Otter is in use as an icing trials aircraft, fully instrumented and equipped with a stereographic camera system. Lewis acquired a Rockwell OV-10A for its Propfan Test Assessment Program, as the Bronco was ideal for achieving differing relative propeller rotational directions by substituting various engine/propeller acoustical characteristics. A Learjet 24 is used to fly low-gravity trajectories, and is also fitted with a nadir-looking optical-glass port for other remote sensing applications. A T-34B fitted with a video/audio-recording system in its rear cockpit and two 70-mm Hasselblad infra-red and standard cameras mounted in the fuselage (for views below the aircraft) can fly in support of other missions.

Office of Aeronautics (Code R)

Langley Research Center, Hampton, Va.

REG/SERIAL	TYPE
N1NA	Gulfstream 3
N501NA	American Aviation AA.1 Yankee
N502NA	Schweizer SGS-1-36 Sprite
N503NA	Cessna 402B
N505NA	Cessna U-3A
N506NA	Beech Queen Air 80
N510NA	Beech T-34C Mentor
N511NA	Northrop T-38A
N512NA	Grumman OV-1 Mohawk
N515NA	Boeing 737-130 TSRV
N516NA	General Dynamics F-16A
N519NA	Piper PA.28RT-201 Arrow
N524NA	Rockwell OV-10A Bronco
N530NA	Bell 204B
N535NA	Bell UH-1H
N557NA	Boeing 757-200
N566NA	Gates Learjet 25 Longhorn (stored)
81-0816	General Dynamics F-16B (spares)

Dryden Flight Research Center, Edwards AFB

N719NA	AV-8A Harrier
N803NA	Eirl Pik 20E
N808NA	PA-30 Twin Comanche 160
N810NA	Convair 990
N812NA	Lockheed F-104N Starfighter
N821NA	Northrop T-38A Talon
N824NA	Lockheed TF-104G stored
N825NA	Lockheed TF-104G stored
N826NA	Lockheed F-104G stored
831 (64-17956)	Lockheed SR-71B
832 (64-17971)	Lockheed SR-71A
835 (71-0287)	McDonnell Douglas F-15A HIDEC
836 (74-0141)	McDonnell Douglas F-15B
840 (160780)	McDonnell Douglas F/A-18 HARV
843 (161214)	McDonnell Douglas F/A-18A
844 (64-17980)	Lockheed SR-71A
845 (160781)	McDonnell Douglas F/A-18B SRA
846 (161355)	McDonnell Douglas F/A-18A
847 (161520)	McDonnell Douglas F/A-18A
848 (75-0747)	General Dynamics F-16XL No. 2
849 (75-0749)	General Dynamics F-16XL No. 1
850 (161703)	McDonnell Douglas F/A-18A
851 (161705)	McDonnell Douglas F/A-18A
852 (161217)	McDonnell Douglas F/A-18A
52-0008	Boeing NB-52B
62-3715	Northrop AT-38 (spares)
62-3746	Northrop AT-38 (spares)
64-17967	Lockheed SR-71A
82-0049	Grumman X-29
87-0800	Northrop YF-23A
87-0801	Northrop YF-23A
160775	McDonnell Douglas F/A-18A
160777	McDonnell Douglas F/A-18A
160778	McDonnell Douglas F/A-18A
160782	McDonnell Douglas F/A-18A
160785	McDonnell Douglas F/A-18A
161251	McDonnell Douglas F/A-18A iron bird
164584	Rockwell X-31A
164585	Rockwell X-31A

Ames Research Center, Moffett Field

N701NA	Beech King Air 200
N703NA	Bell XV-15A
N704NA	McDonnell Douglas YAV-8B
N705NA	Gates Learjet 24A
N706NA	Lockheed ER-2
N707NA	Lockheed NC-130B
N709NA	Lockheed ER-2
N714NA	Lockheed C-141 StarLifter
N715NA	C-8A QSRA (DHC-5 Buffalo)
N717NA	Douglas DC-8-72
N718NA	Lockheed YO-3A
N722NA	Northrop T-38A
N733NA	Bell UH-1H
N734NA	Bell UH-1H
N736NA	Bell AH-1S
N748NA	Sikorsky UH-60A
N749NA	Sikorsky UH-60A
N750NA	Sikorsky JUH-60A
158966	McDonnell Douglas AV-8A (spares)
159239	McDonnell Douglas AV-8A (spares)
159381	McDonnell Douglas TAV-8A (spares)
161496	Lockheed C-130Q (spares)
61-0870	Northrop T-38A (spares)

Lewis Research Center, Cleveland

N5NA	Gulfstream 1 (cargo door)
N508NA	DHC-6 Twin Otter 100
N607NA	DHC-6 Twin Otter
N614NA	Beech T-34B Mentor
N616NA	Gates Learjet 25
N635NA	Cessna O-2
N636NA	Rockwell YOV-10A
N637NA	Rockwell YOV-10A (spares)

Originally developed as an ultra-quiet surveillance platform, the Lockheed YO-3A is now used by NASA to measure rotor noise of helicopters in flight.

NASA's Douglas DC-8-72 overflies the Ames Research Center, Moffett Field, with NC-130B, ER-2, C-141 'Kuiper' visible on the ramp and the large wind tunnels in the background. The DC-8 is outfitted as a medium-altitude air sampling platform.

Forerunner to the Bell/Boeing V-22 Osprey, the Bell XV-15 is in the NASA inventory at the Ames Research Center, flying occasionally on tilt-rotor experiments.

The Bell NAH-1S Cobra is used for limited visibility tests, and has been tested with advanced infra-red and laser-based vision systems.

Ames is the home of most V/STOL and rotary-wing research, and operates a pair of Harriers, including this YAV-8B. V/STOL work centres around providing data for future V/STOL design, including the difficult transition from vertical to horizontal flight.

Assigned to NASA Lewis, this Beech T-34B Mentor is used for general test purposes, mounting a variety of sensors to record other test aircraft.

Two DHC-6 Twin Otters are at Lewis to investigate icing conditions and their effect on flight control. The physics of clouds and their formation is another area of research.

On account of its configuration and wide speed range, the OV-10A Bronco is valued by NASA for its wide-ranging test applications. This example is assigned to Lewis, along with another aircraft for spares.

Office of Space Flight

Lyndon B. Johnson Space Center

In May 1961 President Kennedy laid down the challenge to put a man on the moon before the end of the decade. NASA's Space Task Force, at Langley, quickly began the search for a new space centre. The new facility had be be accessible by water, close to an existing USAF base and a civil airport, and have a ready support infrastructure and enough room (about 2½ sq miles/6.5 km²) to build on. The site chosen was near Houston, Texas, on the shore of Clear Lake and close to Ellington AFB. The Manned Spacecraft Center officially opened in September 1963, its first seven trainee astronauts arriving in July 1962. The cenre was renamed after the late President Lyndon Baines Johnson (a Texan) in February 1973.

The Johnson Space Center (JSC) is today the cornerstone of of the United States' manned space programme, responsible for the selection and training of all astronauts. In the Space Shuttle era these fall into three categories: pilots, mission specialists and payload specialists. JSC is also concerned with design and development of spacecraft, the ongoing (proposed) space station programme and much associated medical and scientific work. It is primarily for the benefit of its astronaut corps (today standing at about 100 individuals) that JSC maintains its sizable fleet of aircraft.

The largest type in use is a converted KC-135, the 'Weightless Wonder IV', now in the process of being replaced by a newer aircraft. Flying with a padded interior and high-intensity lighting, the KC-135 is used to simulate weightless conditions by flying a parabolic trajectory after a 50° climb at 350 kt (646 km/h, 402 mph). Periods of microgravity can thus be created for up to 30 seconds and, over a normal sortie, over 50 such profiles can be flown. As a result, the aircraft has gained the telling sobriquet of the 'V,omit Comet'.

Potential Shuttle pilots who survive this experience progress to the four Shuttle Training Aircraft (STAs), which are modified Gulfstream IIs. The first STA flew in 1975, and a fifth Gulfstream (formerly in use as an engine testbed) is currently undergoing conversion to this standard. The STAs are fitted with two large retractable sideforce controls (or vanes) under the wing centresection to simulate the lateral accelerations experienced in the Shuttle. The forces exercised by these vanes are controlled by an onboard computer. Inside, the STA's cockpit is divided in two, with a simulated Shuttle cockpit to port and standard controls to starboard. The great advantage of the STA is that, unlike the Shuttle, it can make a powered approach and landing, although onboard systems alert the crew that they have landed when still 50 ft (15.25 m) in the air, as that is the height above ground of the Shuttle's flight deck.

Associated with the Shuttle programme is the JSC's fleet of Northrop T-38s. These provide refresher training for Orbiter pilots and crew, in addition to high-speed liaison duties (with underfuselage baggage pods) when required. Other important duties flown by the Talons were the Shuttle Approach and Landing Tests (ALTs) when the T-38s acted as safety chase planes for the Shuttle, in the early stages of the programme. The T-38s have also been fitted with extended airbrakes, which provide handling qualities similar to the Shuttle's. The USAF has donated six (weapons-capable) AT-38s to NASA, which are in storage at El Paso for future spares support. JSC's active T-38As are now being upgraded to T-38N standard through the addition of new cockpit avionics and associated MFDs, and a revised nose radome.

The last flying Martin B-57, a WB-57F, still exists at the US Air Force's Vandenburg AFB, California. While KSC sees regular Shuttle launches (and arrivals on the 747), the only aircraft based there are a VIP transport Gulfstream I and several Bell UH-1s (currently in storage) for air ambulance and range security duties.

flies from JSC on behalf of NASA and the Department of Energy on high-altitude sampling missions. A second aircraft has now been retired.

The two converted Boeing 747s that serve as SCAs (Shuttle Carrier Aircraft) are administered by JSC and one aircraft, NASA 911, is nominally based at El Paso airport. NASA 905 (SCA No. 1) spends most of its time at Edwards AFB. Either SCA is capable of carrying the 100-ton orbiter which is raised onto the back of the 747 by 100-ft (30.5-m) MDDs (Mate-Demate Devices) located only at Edwards and Kennedy, although a smaller air-transportable version (the Stiff Legged Derrick) is available for contingency use.

John F. Kennedy Space Center

The Kennedy Space Center (KSC) lies to the north and west of Cape Canaveral, Florida. The site covers an area some 34 miles (54 km) long and at places is 10 miles wide (16 km). It is NASA's prime site for the test, checkout and launch of spacecraft. A similar but less-used facility

George C. Marshall Space Center

Marshall Space Center is co-located with the US Army's Redstone Arsenal at Huntsville, Alabama. Marshall is an important design and manufacturing centre for NASA spacecraft components such as the Shuttle's engines, rocket boosters and external fuel tank. The need to transport such outsize items meant that Marshall was responsible for operating one of NASA's most unusual types, the

Aerospacelines Guppy. Two of these impressive Boeing Stratocruiser conversions, the Model 377PG 'Pregnant Guppy' and the Model 377SG 'Super Guppy', were leased during the 1960s and 1970s. In 1979 NASA acquired its own YC-97J Super Guppy which was retired to MASDC in July 1991. Today, only a Gulfstream I and Beech 200 fly as personnel transports from Marshall.

John C. Stennis Space Center

The Stennis Space Center (so named in 1974 and formerly the Mississippi Test Facility) was set up in 1961, at Bay St Louis, Mississippi and is today

the test site for the Space Shuttle's Rocketdyne main engines. A single NASA Learjet 23 is flown from SSC (National Space Technology Laboratory).

Office of Space Flight (Code M)

REG/SERIAL	TYPE
Lyndon B.Johnson Space Center, Ellington ANGB	
N2NA	Gulfstream I
N901NA	Northrop T-38A
N902NA	Northrop T-38A
N904NA	Northrop T-38A
N905NA	Boeing 747-123 SCA No. 1
N906NA	Northrop T-38A
N907NA	Northrop T-38A
N908NA	Northrop T-38A
N910NA	Northrop T-38A
N911NA	Boeing 747-146SR SCA No. 2
N912NA	Northrop T-38A
N913NA	Northrop T-38A
N914NA	Northrop T-38A
N915NA	Northrop T-38A
N916NA	Northrop T-38A
N917NA	Northrop T-38A
N918NA	Northrop T-38A
N919NA	Northrop T-38A
N920NA	Northrop T-38A
N921NA	Northrop T-38A
N923NA	Northrop T-38N
N924NA	Northrop T-38A
928 (63-13298)	General Dynamics WB-57F
N930NA	KC-135A 'Weightless Wonder IV'
N931NA	KC-135A
935 (N60CC)	Citation II MSTA (leased)
N944NA	Gulfstream 2 STA
N945NA	Gulfstream 2 STA
N946NA	Gulfstream 2 STA
N947NA	Gulfstream 2 STA
N948NA	Gulfstream 2
N955NA	Northrop T-38A
N956NA	Northrop T-38A
N959NA	Northrop T-38A
N960NA	Northrop T-38A
N961NA	Northrop T-38A
N962NA	Northrop T-38A
N963NA	Northrop T-38A
N964NA	Northrop T-38A
N965NA	Northrop AT-38B
61-0870	Northrop AT-38B (spares)
61-0907	Northrop AT-38B (spares)
64-13267	Northrop AT-38B (spares)
65-10450	Northrop AT-38B (spares)
68-8133	Northrop AT-38B (spares)
John F. Kennedy Space Center, Cape Canaveral	
N4NA	Gulfstream I
N417NA	Bell UH-1M
N418NA	Bell UH-1M
N419NA	Bell UH-1H
N420NA	Bell UH-1H
N734NA	Bell UH-1H
George C. Marshall Space Center, Huntsville	
N3NA	Gulfstream I
N9NA	Beech King Air 200
John C. Stennis Space Center, Mississippi	
N933NA	Gates Learjet 23

Above: NASA's best-known aircraft are the two Boeing 747s converted to SCA (Shuttle Carrier Aircraft) configuration, used to transport Orbiters to the launch site at Kennedy Space Center. An aerodynamic fairing is mounted to the back of the Shuttle for its journey.

Providing the means to acclimatise astronauts and space-bound equipment to weightlessness (more correctly microgravity) is this Ellington-based KC-135A.

High over White Sands, New Mexico, one of JSC's Gulfstream II STA aircraft mimics a Space Shuttle. Not only does the nosewheel stay retracted till the last minute, but the flight control system imitates the nose-down pitch of the Shuttle.

Left: Today the STA aircraft have unique controllable fairings which imitate precisely the handling of the Shuttle during the approach phase.

Right: The four Shuttle Training Aircraft all have an unusual split cockpit. The left-hand position has Shuttle-style controls while the right-hand seat retains the traditional Gulfstream II instruments. Both positions have small HUDs which give landing cues for the Shuttle pilot.

Office of Space Science

The US Army's Jet Propulsion Laboratory was transferred to NACA's jurisdiction in 1958, just two months before NASA was established. The JPL is situated in Pasadena, California, 20 miles (32 km) north-east of Los Angeles. It is still a government-owned facility, but staffed and managed for NASA by the Californis Institute of Technology (CALTECH). Much, although not all, of the site is owned by NASA, which funds operations through its own budget. The Jet Propulsion Laboratory designs and tests complete (unmanned) spacecraft, including engines, and is closely involved in deep space scientific missions, tracking and data analysis. The Laboratory also operates the Deep Space Network, a tracking and data collection system which is part of its core function to support present and future exploration missions in our solar system and beyond.

A facility associated with the JPL is the Deep Space Communications Complex at Goldstone, California, on a 40,000-acre (16188-hectare) site leased from the US Army. The Jet Propulsion Laboratory's aviation activities are confined to a Single Beech 200 Super King Air, which replaced a Beech Queen Air in 1982, for transport duties. Several helicopters have been operated by the JPL since the 1960s, but none is in use today. Similarly, an NC-135 was leased from the USAF in 1973 for atmospheric impact tests.

Office of Space Science (Code S)

REG/SERIAL	TYPE
Jet Propulsion Laboratory , Pasadena, California	
N7NA	Beech King Air 200

Mission to Planet Earth

Established in 1945, the Wallops Flight Facility was founded to conduct advanced aeronautical research using rocket-propelled vehicles. It now supports NASA, DoD, government and commercial organisations, providing a range of services.

Located at Wallops Island on Virginia's east coast, and administered by the Goddard Space Flight Center at Greenbelt, Maryland, Wallops has historically been – and remains – primarily a launch site for rockets, although its airfield has three long runways, and supports an intensive flight research and range support flying programme. One runway can be dammed and flooded with water for ingestion/aquaplaning trials. The Microwave Landing System was developed at Wallops, and work continues on the development of a new high-speed turn-off ramp, designed to allow aircraft at busy airports to clear the runway more quickly after landing. The aircraft fleet provides the scientific community with a variety of well-instrumented, reliable, low-cost and versatile tools for the development of instrumentation or the gathering of Earth sciences data.

The NASA mission is to manage and implement suborbital sounding rocket and balloon programmes to support Small Expendable Launch Vehicle Services and Earth sciences studies, to operate the Wallops Test Range, and to provide aircraft support. Wallops is responsible for NASA rocket activity at White Sands Missile Range in New Mexico and at Poker Flat Research Range in Alaska. Wallops is able to design, develop, manufacture and test its own equipment, and provides low-cost, quick-response flight opportunities for space and earth sciences research. It also manages NASA's Suborbital Sounding Rocket Project.

The facility makes extensive use of high-altitude and long-duration balloons, both at Wallops itself and at Fort Sumner, New Mexico and the National Scientific Balloon Facility at Palestine, Texas. Wallops has extensive tracking, data acquisition, communications and control equipment and is able to stage and support mobile launch range activities worldwide.

Wallops supports a number of other agencies operating in the area, including the US Navy, US Coast Guard, National Oceanic and Atmospheric Administration, Fish and Wildlife Service and the National Park Service.

Mission to Planet Earth (Code Y)

REG/SERIAL	TYPE
Goddard Center, Wallops Flight Facility	
N8NA	Beech King Air 200
N415NA	Bell UH-1H
N425NA	North American T-39E Sabreliner
N426NA	Lockheed P-3B Orion
N429NA	Lockheed L.188C Electra
N431NA	North American T-39D Sabreliner
153429	Lockheed P-3B Orion (spares)
161494	Lockheed C-130Q (spares)

Left: 'NASA 8' is a King Air 200 employed on transport tasks by NASA Goddard.

Right: A single Bell UH-1H serves with NASA Goddard, used for a variety of test and transport purposes, including the recovery of rocket-launched items. It operates from this mobile platform.

The Goddard Center has two T-39 Sabreliners assigned for a variety of test purposes. Behind this T-39E is the unit's latest Orion, seen prior to receiving a NASA paint scheme. A second P-3 is held for spares.

Both the Electra (illustrated) and Orion at Wallops are available for a wide range of experiments, their cabins being easily reconfigured to meet new requirements. Overwater programmes are a speciality.

The most numerous NASA type is the Northrop T-38A, used for general training, chase and fast transport purposes. Most are assigned to the Johnson Space Center at Ellington.

Illustrating the new logo being slowly adopted by the NASA fleet, this Talon is in T-38N configuration. The modification substitutes a modern 'glass' cockpit.

A view across Kennedy Space Center at Cape Canaveral shows the apron (with two STAs and the 'Vomit Comet' KC-135A), the Shuttle Landing Facility and the Vertical Assembly Building in the background. KSC is the favoured Shuttle landing site, with Edwards and White Sands being primary diversion sites.

Remarkably this elderly Martin WB-57F Canberra remains in use at Ellington with the JSC. The aircraft is configured for the collection of air samples to investigate tiny particles of space objects (such as meteors) in the upper atmosphere. Weather missions are also flown.

Although NASA's most important space flight centre, Cape Canaveral has few aircraft. This Bell UH-1H is assigned for general transport, test and security duties.

Two staff transports are operated by the Marshall Space Center at Huntsville, one being this Gulfstream I and the other a King Air 200.

The Stennis Space Center is primarily concerned with the manufacture of the Space Shuttle's engines and other components, but does operate this single Learjet 23. In addition to its transport function, the aircraft is fitted with a vertical survey camera

Another NASA transport is this Beech King Air 200, operated by the Jet Propulsion Laboratory at Pasadena. Note the aircraft is fitted with a ventral baggage pannier.

INDEX

INDEX

Picture acknowledgments

Front cover: Randy Jolly. **4:** Matthias Becker, Paul Jackson (two). **5:** Matthias Becker, E.A. Sloot. **6:** Filippini Massimo, Robin Polderman. **7:** A.B. Ward, Andrew H. Cline. **8:** Gert Kromhout, Jon Lake. **9:** Bob Archer, Robin Polderman. **10:** E.A. Sloot, Gert Kromhout, Robert Sant. **11:** Robert Sant, Rockwell. **12:** Dylan Eklund. **13:** Randy Jolly, Nathan Leong, Rockwell. **14:** Nathan Leong, Rockwell. **15:** Ted Carlson/Fotodynamics (three), Nathan Leong. **16:** Robert F. Dorr, Tom Kaminski. **17:** Robert B. Greby, Andrew H. Cline. **18:** Piaggio (two). **19:** Piaggio (three), David Donald. **20-21:** Piaggio. **22-23:** Randy Jolly. **24:** Westland. **25:** David Donald, Gerry Turner, Westland, Photolink. **27:** Westland, Westland via Neil Dundridge (two). **30:** Agusta, Westland (two). **32:** Westland (two), Jeremy Flack/API. **33:** Westland (two), Jeremy Flack/API. **34-37:** Luigino Caliaro. **38-39:** via Randy Jolly. **40:** Rick Llinares/Flightline. **41:** McDonnell Douglas, US Air Force. **42-45:** McDonnell Douglas. **46:** David Draycott/Airshots, David Donald. **47:** Randy Jolly. **48:** James Benson. **49:** Randy Jolly, Bob Archer. **50:** Randy Jolly, McDonnell Douglas. **51:** via Randy Jolly. **52:** Randy Jolly (two). **53:** Ted Carlson/Fotodynamics. **54:** Randy Jolly, Ted Carlson/Fotodynamics. **55:** Rick Llinares/Flightline, Randy Jolly. **56:** Randy Jolly, via Randy Jolly. **57:** Randy Jolly, via Randy Jolly. **58:** via Randy Jolly. **59:** Randy Jolly (two). **60:** McDonnell Douglas. **61:** Randy Jolly (two). **62:** James Benson, Robert F. Dorr. **69:** Randy Jolly (four), David Donald (two), David Draycott/Airshots, James Benson, A.B. Ward. **70:** US Air Force. **71:** Randy Jolly (two), US Air Force. **72:** Randy Jolly. **73:** McDonnell Douglas, Alessandro Bon. **74:** Randy Jolly, James Benson. **75:** Randy Jolly. **76:** James Benson, McDonnell Douglas, Randy Jolly, Alec Fushi. **77:** Randy Jolly, Rankin-Lowe, Randy Jolly. **78:** Randy Jolly (four), McDonnell Douglas. **79:** David Donald, David Draycott/Airshots, Jeremy Flack/API, via Randy Jolly. **80:** Gary Bihary, Jeff Rankin-Lowe, Randy Jolly (three), Graham Robson. **81:** David Donald (two), McDonnell Douglas, Bob Archer, Don Spering/AIR. **82:** James Benson, Tieme Festner, Marcus Fülber, Randy Jolly. **83:** David Donald (two), Robert F. Dorr, Ted Carlson/Fotodynamics, Steven D. Eisner. **85:** E.A. Sloot, Gert Kromhout, Randy Jolly. **85-86:** Gert Kromhout. **87:** Gert Kromhout (two), Hendrik J. van Broekhuizen, E. de Kruyff. **88:** Gert Kromhout (three). **89:** E. de Kruyff (two), Gert Kromhout. **90:** James Benson, Gert Kromhout, Lockheed Fort Worth. **91:** Robert L. Lawson, Ian Black. **92:** NASA. **93:** Ted Carlson/Fotodynamics, Ian Black. **94:** Lockheed Fort Worth. **95:** Randy Jolly, James Benson. **96-97:**
Lockheed Fort Worth. **98:** US Air Force, Lockheed Fort Worth (two). **99:** Lockheed Fort Worth, Joe Cupido. **100:** Lockheed Fort Worth (three), Joe Cupido. **101:** Lockheed Fort Worth. **102:** Lockheed Fort Worth, Gert Kromhout. **103:** Lockheed Fort Worth (two), James Benson. **104:** Peter J. Cooper, Tim Senior, Joe Cupido. **105:** Peter R. Foster, M. Brouwer. **106:** Lockheed Fort Worth. **107:** Lockheed Fort Worth. **108:** Bryan Ward. **109:** Mike Reyno, Randy Jolly. **110:** Lockheed Fort Worth, Jim Rotramel, Alan Key, B. Fischer. **111:** Lockheed Fort Worth. **112:** Martin Herbert, Hans Nijhuis, Hugo Mambour. **113:** Dave Bowers, M. Scharenborg/R. Tiering (Panoravia Air Press). **114:** René van Woezik (two), Lutz Freundt. **115:** Hans Nijhuis, Chris Lofting, Richard Simon, Gert Tricht. **116:** Dave Bowers, Hugo Mambour, G.A. Boymans. **117:** Robert Hewson, Tieme Festner, René van Woezik. **118:** René van Woezik (two), J. de Vries via Gert Kromhout, Martin Baumann. **119:** Rob de Bie, René van Woezik, Marc Brouyere, Marcus Fülber. **120:** via Hugo Mambour, Marcus Fülber, Jon Lake. **121:** Hendrik J. van Broekhuizen, Tieme Festner, Jan Jørgensen. **122:** Jan Jørgensen (two), Dave Bowers. **123:** Marcus Fülber, Dave Bowers, Hugo Mambour, Tieme Festner (two). **124:** Hans Nijhuis (two), Tieme Festner, René van Woezik. **125:** Chris Lofting, Hans Nijhuis, Hendrik J. van Broekhuizen. **126:** M. Scharenborg/R. Tiering (Panoravia Air Press), Lindsay Peacock, Peter R. Foster. **127:** M. Scharenborg/R. Tiering (Panoravia Air Press) (two), Rob de Bie. **128:** Martin Baumann, René van Woezik, Chris Lofting. **129:** Jan Jørgensen, Dave Bowers, Marc Brouyere. **130:** H.A. Gravemaker, Gert Hartman, Anno van Rijn. **131:** Tieme Festner (two), René van Woezik. **132:** Eric Stijger, Mart Jan Gerards, Chris Lofting. **133:** Chris Lofting, Martin Baumann (two). **134:** Berry Vissers, Chris Pocock. **135:** Mart Jan Gerards, Chris Lofting, P. van Weenen. **136:** Hans Nijhuis, Marc Brouyere. **137:** Frank Rozendaal, Hans Nijhuis, Marc Brouyere. **138:** Hugo Mambour, Chris Lofting (two). **139:** Chris Lofting (two), M. Scharenborg/R. Tiering (Panoravia Air Press). **140:** Werner Greppmeier, Chris Lofting, Lutz Freundt. **141:** Jan Jørgensen, Hans Nijhuis, Werner Greppmeier. **142:** Frank Rozendaal, René van Woezik. **143:** Lutz Freundt, Frank Rozendaal, Tieme Festner. **144:** René van Woezik, Hendrik J. van Broekhuizen, M. Scharenborg/R. Tiering (Panoravia Air Press), Marc Brouyere. **145:** Stefan Petersen, Marcus Fülber, Richard Simon. **146:** Dave Bowers, Jan Jørgensen. **147:** G.A. Boymans, Tieme Festner, Frank Rozendaal. **149:** Bob Burns, NASA via Bob Burns (six), NASA via Joe Cupido. **150:** NASA via Bob Burns (seven), Ted Carlson/Fotodynamics, NASA (two), NASA via Joe Cupido. **153:** NASA via Bob Burns (five), NASA (two), NASA via Arthur Pearcy. **155:** NASA, NASA via Bob Burns (two), NASA via Arthur Pearcy, Joe Cupido. **156:** Bob Burns (three), NASA via Bob Burns. **157:** NASA via Bob Burns (three), Graham Robson, Bob Burns (two), NASA via Arthur Pearcy, Ted Carlson/Fotodynamics.